NBER Macroeconomics Annual 2019

NBER Macroeconomics Annual 2019

Edited by
Martin Eichenbaum, Erik Hurst, and Jonathan A. Parker

The University of Chicago Press
Chicago and London

NBER Macroeconomics Annual 2019, Number 34

Published annually by The University of Chicago Press.
www.journals.uchicago.edu/MA/

Subscriptions: Individual subscription rates are $90 print + electronic and $45 e-only ($15 for students). Institutional print + electronic and e-only rates are tiered according to an institution's type and research output: $145 to $305 (print + electronic), $126–$265 (e-only). For additional information, including back-issue sales, classroom use, rates for single copies, and prices for institutional full-run access, please visit www.journals.uchicago.edu /MA/. Free or deeply discounted access is available in most developing nations through the Chicago Emerging Nations Initiative (www.journals.uchicago.edu/ceni/).

Please direct subscription inquiries to Subscription Fulfillment, 1427 E. 60th Street, Chicago, IL 60637-2902. Telephone: (773) 753-3347 or toll free in the United States and Canada (877) 705-1878. Fax: (773) 753-0811 or toll-free (877) 705-1879. E-mail: subscriptions @press.uchicago.edu.

Standing orders: To place a standing order for this book series, please address your request to The University of Chicago Press, Chicago Distribution Center, Attn. Standing Orders/Customer Service, 11030 S. Langley Avenue, Chicago, IL 60628. Telephone toll free in the U.S. and Canada: 1-800-621-2736; or 1-773-702-7000. Fax toll free in the U.S. and Canada: 1-800-621-8476; or 1-773-702-7212.

Single-copy orders: In the U.S., Canada, and the rest of the world, order from your local bookseller or direct from The University of Chicago Press, Chicago Distribution Center, 11030 S. Langley Avenue, Chicago, IL 60628. Telephone toll free in the U.S. and Canada: 1-800-621-2736; or 1-773-702-7000. Fax toll free in the U.S. and Canada: 1-800-621-8476; or 1-773-702-7212. In the U.K. and Europe, order from your local bookseller or direct from The University of Chicago Press, c/o John Wiley Ltd. Distribution Center, 1 Oldlands Way, Bognor Regis, West Sussex PO22 9SA, UK. Telephone 01243 779777 or Fax 01243 820250. E-mail: cs-books@wiley.co.uk.

The University of Chicago Press offers bulk discounts on individual titles to Corporate, Premium and Gift accounts. For information, please write to Sales Department—Special Sales, The University of Chicago Press, 1427 E. 60th Street, Chicago, IL 60637 USA or telephone 1-773-702-7723.

This book was printed and bound in the United States of America.

ISSN: 0889-3365
E-ISSN: 1537-2642
ISBN-13: 978-0-226-70789-1 (pb.:alk.paper)
ISBN-13: 978-0-226-70792-1 (e-book)

Relation of the Directors to the Work and Publications of the NBER

1. The object of the NBER is to ascertain and present to the economics profession, and to the public more generally, important economic facts and their interpretation in a scientific manner without policy recommendations. The Board of Directors is charged with the responsibility of ensuring that the work of the NBER is carried on in strict conformity with this object.

2. The President shall establish an internal review process to ensure that book manuscripts proposed for publication DO NOT contain policy recommendations. This shall apply both to the proceedings of conferences and to manuscripts by a single author or by one or more coauthors but shall not apply to authors of comments at NBER conferences who are not NBER affiliates.

3. No book manuscript reporting research shall be published by the NBER until the President has sent to each member of the Board a notice that a manuscript is recommended for publication and that in the President's opinion it is suitable for publication in accordance with the above principles of the NBER. Such notification will include a table of contents and an abstract or summary of the manuscript's content, a list of contributors if applicable, and a response form for use by Directors who desire a copy of the manuscript for review. Each manuscript shall contain a summary drawing attention to the nature and treatment of the problem studied and the main conclusions reached.

4. No volume shall be published until forty-five days have elapsed from the above notification of intention to publish it. During this period a copy shall be sent to any Director requesting it, and if any Director objects to publication on the grounds that the manuscript contains policy recommendations, the objection will be presented to the author(s) or editor(s). In case of dispute, all members of the Board shall be notified,

and the President shall appoint an ad hoc committee of the Board to decide the matter; thirty days additional shall be granted for this purpose.

5. The President shall present annually to the Board a report describing the internal manuscript review process, any objections made by Directors before publication or by anyone after publication, any disputes about such matters, and how they were handled.

6. Publications of the NBER issued for informational purposes concerning the work of the Bureau, or issued to inform the public of the activities at the Bureau, including but not limited to the NBER Digest and Reporter, shall be consistent with the object stated in paragraph 1. They shall contain a specific disclaimer noting that they have not passed through the review procedures required in this resolution. The Executive Committee of the Board is charged with the review of all such publications from time to time.

7. NBER working papers and manuscripts distributed on the Bureau's web site are not deemed to be publications for the purpose of this resolution, but they shall be consistent with the object stated in paragraph 1. Working papers shall contain a specific disclaimer noting that they have not passed through the review procedures required in this resolution. The NBER's web site shall contain a similar disclaimer. The President shall establish an internal review process to ensure that the working papers and the web site do not contain policy recommendations, and shall report annually to the Board on this process and any concerns raised in connection with it.

8. Unless otherwise determined by the Board or exempted by the terms of paragraphs 6 and 7, a copy of this resolution shall be printed in each NBER publication as described in paragraph 2 above.

Contents

Editorial

Martin Eichenbaum, *Northwestern University and NBER*
Erik Hurst, *University of Chicago and NBER*
Jonathan A. Parker, *MIT and NBER*

The NBER's thirty-fourth Annual Conference on Macroeconomics brought together leading scholars to present, discuss, and debate six research papers on central issues in contemporary macroeconomics. In addition, James Stock, former chief economist and director of research at the International Monetary Fund, delivered a thought-provoking after-dinner talk on the economics of climate change. Video recordings of the presentations of the papers and the after-dinner talk are all accessible on the web page of the NBER Annual Conference on Macroeconomics (https://www.nber.org/macroannualconference2019/macroannual2019.html). These videos, which make the content of the conference more widely accessible, are a useful complement to this volume.

This conference volume contains edited versions of the six papers presented at the conference, each followed by two written comments by leading scholars and a summary discussion of the debates that followed each paper. The volume also contains a paper, "Climate Change, Climate Policy, and Economic Growth," by James Stock, based on his dinner talk. The paper provides an extremely useful introduction to the topic of climate change and climate change policy for macroeconomists. The paper makes four key points. First, simple time-series regression models confirm that essentially all the warming over the past 140 years is due to human activity. Second, policy has a crucial role to play if we are to succeed in decarbonizing the economy. Third, current policies will not succeed in decarbonizing the economy in time to prevent severe damage from climate change. Fourth, the politics, as opposed to the economics, of Pigouvian carbon pricing do not work. This suggests the importance of considering other policies, especially those that drive low-carbon technical innovation.

There was no discussant for the paper because of its origin as a dinner talk. We are grateful to James Stock for taking the time to write up his comments on this vitally important topic.

During the last two decades in the United States, production has become more concentrated, with a smaller set of firms producing a larger fraction of aggregate output. During that same time, firm profits have increased, labor share of output has fallen, and firm investment has decreased. Is increased concentration the efficient response to changing consumer behavior or technology? Or is increasing concentration the inefficient result of increased barriers to firm entry?

These questions are explored in the paper "From Good to Bad Concentration? US Industries over the Past 30 Years," by Matias Covarrubias, Germán Gutiérrez, and Thomas Philippon. Covarrubias et al. draw on insights from the industrial organization literature and provide a simple framework to highlight that increasing concentration is a market outcome and can be the equilibrium result of either less market competition or more market competition.

Using a variety of aggregate data sources, the authors find that during the 1990s, increased aggregate concentration was correlated with rising productivity, falling prices, and higher investment. These findings are consistent with models where increased concentration is driven by increases in the returns to scale in firm production and/or increases in the elasticity of substitution across consumption goods. The authors conclude that the increased concentration in the United States during the 1990s reflected "good" concentration. However, during the 2000s, increased aggregate concentration was correlated with falling productivity growth, rising prices, and falling investment. These findings are consistent with increasing barriers to firm entry during the 2000s. The authors conclude that much of the increased concentration during the 2000s reflects an increase in "bad" concentration.

In the last part of their paper, the authors use cross-industry variation to shed further light on the causes of increased concentration during the 2000s. The authors conclude that the aggregate results may be too coarse to accurately reflect the underlying causes of increased concentration. By exploiting cross-industry variation, the authors conclude that multiple forces are responsible for the increased concentration observed in the United States during the 2000s. Although increased barriers to entry are part of the story—particularly in some industries—changes in firm technology and consumer demand patterns are also an important part of the story.

Both of the discussants applaud the authors for their careful data work and for laying out a simple framework to discuss the potential causes of increased concentration. Both also agree that the cross-industry results are more interesting in that they highlight that multiple factors are likely changing simultaneously within the US economy during the 2000s.

Real wages among lower income groups in the United States have grown very little since the late 1960s. Even strikingly, there has been a reduction in life expectancy among white men born in the 1960s relative to the previous generation. Such declines are not supposed to happen in a healthy growing economy. Margherita Borella, Mariacristina De Nardi, and Fang Yang study this decline in well-being in "The Lost Ones: The Opportunities and Outcomes of White, Non-College-Educated Americans Born in the 1960s." The paper develops a structural life cycle model to quantify the economic outcomes of less educated Americans born in the 1960s.

The paper begins by confirming and documenting a number of important facts about less educated white Americans, largely using the Panel Study of Income Dynamics. Real wages declined between these generations for less educated women (who started from a lower starting point), and postretirement, out-of-pocket medical expenses rose dramatically. Expected life spans declined for both men and women.

The paper analyzes these changes by estimating a rich structural model of life cycle consumption and saving on those born in the 1960 cohort. Taking the estimated preference parameters as given, the authors ask how this generation would have behaved and fared if instead they had faced the wages, medical costs, and health/longevity of those born in the 1940s. The results are striking.

The decline in wages that men born in the 1960s faced lowered their labor supply, whereas that of women increased slightly; the decrease in life expectancy reduced their saving, but the increase in out-of-pocket medical expenses increased by more. Thus, together, consumption falls significantly. The welfare decline is large, ranging from an equivalent of 7% to 13% of lifetime income depending on gender and marital status.

The discussants raised a number of important issues, including whether actual inflation was lower than measured inflation. To the extent this was the case real wages for less educated white men have not fallen. Of course, such mismeasurement of inflation does not alter the declines in life spans. Another issue that was discussed was how to measure the welfare costs of lower life spans.

The financial crisis of 2007–8 and the ensuing recession led central banks around the world to lower short-term interest rates to values near their (rough) lower bound of zero. The Federal Reserve kept its policy rate at that level until the end of December 2015. As a result, the Fed could not use short-term interest rates to combat the recession or fight incipient deflationary pressures. In their paper, "On the Empirical (Ir)Relevance of the Zero Lower Bound Constraint," Davide Debortoli, Jordi Galí, and Luca Gambetti investigate whether this constraint affected the performance of the US economy. They do so by assessing the extent to which the constraint affected the volatility of US macro aggregates and the response of those aggregates to various shocks. They find very little evidence that the constraint materially affected the economy.

This finding is very surprising from the perspective of standard macroeconomic models like the New Keynesian (NK) model. One's first reaction is that this finding is a power issue. But the paper's evidence is persuasive that power is not the issue. From the perspective of the NK model, one should be able to detect substantial effects on macro aggregates when the zero lower bound binds, even in sample sizes as small as those available to the authors.

How can we explain this important finding? According to the authors, the answer is that policy makers developed new tools that were effective in making the zero lower bound constraint not constraining. The prime examples are forward guidance and "unconventional" purchases of long-term assets. The paper's findings are clearly very important, especially in a world where, going forward, short-term policy interests are likely to hit the zero lower bound much more frequently.

The first discussant examined factors, other than the effectiveness of the new tools developed by monetary policy makers, that could explain the authors' main results. He also investigated whether the authors' findings are consistent with other more direct evidence regarding the effectiveness of nonstandard policies. The second discussant raised important methodological questions about statistical inference in sign-restricted structural vector autoregressions, one of the methods used in the paper.

Many researchers and members of the commentariat have announced the death of the Phillips curve. This view is based on the apparent weak statistical relationship between inflation and various measures of unused economic capacity. The latter include unemployment and estimates of the output gap. Such claims, if true, would pose an important challenge to the way macroeconomists think about fluctuations in economic activity and the paradigm within which central banks conduct policy.

In their paper "Optimal Inflation and the Identification of the Phillips Curve," Michael McLeay and Silvana Tenreyro challenge the validity of these claims. Their argument is as follows. Suppose that policy makers seek to minimize welfare subject to a structural Phillips curve. In that world, policy makers will raise inflation when output is below its full potential. Therefore, the better policy makers are at their job, the harder it will be to see a positive relationship between inflation and output. Simple correlations between inflation and output are completely uninformative about the presence of a structural Phillips curve or its slope.

The authors explore the problem of identifying the slope of the Phillips curve under various assumptions about the ability of policy makers to commit to a policy rule, the nature of the shocks to the economy, and the availability of data from different parts of an economy subject to different shocks. The first part of their analysis is conducted within the confines of a simple NK model. To assess the robustness of their results, they also investigate the problem using a full-scale dynamic stochastic general equilibrium model. Finally, the authors consider practical attempts to overcome the problem of identifying the slope of the Phillips curve. One particularly promising approach is the use of cross-sectional regional variation in unemployment.

In sum, the paper makes a very important contribution to a topic that is extremely relevant to the academic literature and ongoing policy debates.

Both discussants spoke enthusiastically about the paper, framing the analysis in terms of the classic problem of identifying a demand or a supply curve from market data. Like those curves, the Phillips curve is a structural relationship, not a reduced-form relationship. This simple but fundamental point is often neglected in popular discussions of the Phillips curve. Both discussants examined the theoretical underpinning of the structural Phillips curve and the practical difficulties of identifying that curve. In addition, one discussant contrasted the reduced-form relationship between inflation and unemployment with the relationship between wage growth and inflation, analyzing the latter in detail.

There has been a large rise in US income inequality over the last four decades. In their paper "Trading Up and the Skill Premium," Nir Jaimovich, Sergio Rebelo, Arlene Wong, and Miao Ben Zhang highlight a relatively unexplored mechanism that could be contributing to the rising skill premium. Their mechanism stems from two assumptions. First, households "trade up" to higher-quality products as they become richer. Second, higher-quality products are more skill intensive. Together, the assumptions imply that as an economy grows, the demand for skills will endogenously grow, providing an additional force generating upward pressure on the skill premium.

Jaimovich et al. begin their paper by providing empirical support for the two assumptions at the heart of their mechanism. First, using data from the Nielsen Homescan database and the Consumer Expenditure Survey, the paper documents that richer households do, in fact, purchase higher-quality goods. Second, using data from Yelp matched with microdata from the Occupational Employment Statistics, the paper shows that higher-quality goods are produced with a higher share of skilled workers. Both discussants emphasized that this empirical work is an important contribution to the literature.

The paper provides a simple model of trading up. The goal of the model is to quantitatively explore the extent of skill-biased technological change that is needed to generate the observed increase in the skill premium in the United States over the last 40 years. In their model, the endogenous skill upgrading results in a larger change in the skill premium with lower amounts of skill-biased technological change. According to their calibrated model, the extent of skill-biased technological change that is needed to match the data is only 1.1% per year as opposed to 5.5% per year in a model without skill upgrading. Although the mechanism is novel and should stimulate further research, both discussants stressed that the authors' model is too simple to provide a definitive quantitative assessment of the importance of skill upgrading as an explanation for the rising skill premium.

Our final paper takes up the important topic of economic growth in China. China has undergone a 30-year economic growth miracle despite economic and political institutions that look nothing like those that appear to be required for prosperity in most of the rest of the world. A fascinating paper by Chong-en Bai, Chang-Tai Hsieh, and Zheng Song, "Special Deals with Chinese Characteristics," argues that the lack of formal institutional, legal, and jurisprudential constraints on politicians creates growth because it has been combined with high-powered incentives.

The paper proposes a theory in which local politicians compete against other localities to maximize local economic growth. The lack of formal and regulatory constraints on politicians means that local officials are free to favor certain industries and to promote particular businesses by handing out "special deals." In many countries, this lack of oversight leads to economic stagnation. But in China, local officials have high-powered incentives instead of formal legal oversight. Politicians' careers benefit from growth, as their locality grows in importance and as their success increases their stature with the central Chinese authorities. They also benefit financially, as they often invest in the businesses in their locality that they are backing. When things go badly, the penalties for local officials can include criminal charges.

The paper brings a range of evidence to support its case. Most novel, in an almost ethnographic approach, the authors describe the workdays of local officials as akin to those of venture capitalists in a Western economy—visiting company headquarters, evaluating business strategies, pulling together financing, and so forth. The authors further elucidate their ideas in a model and show a number of facts about the Chinese economy that are consistent with their interpretation.

The discussants raise a number of concerns with this theory of Chinese growth and argue that the sources of rapid growth in China remain mysterious. They question whether the incentives are really high powered, and how they are maintained. Further, local politicians often erect barriers to intra-China trade, which would seem to work against strong economic growth.

As in previous years, the editors posted and distributed a call for proposals in the spring and summer prior to the conference, and some of the papers in this volume were selected from proposals submitted in response to this call. Other papers are commissioned on central and topical areas in macroeconomics. Both are done in consultation with the advisory board, which we thank for its input and support of both the conference and the published volume.

The authors and the editors would like to take this opportunity to thank Jim Poterba and the National Bureau of Economic Research for their continued support for the *NBER Macroeconomics Annual* and the associated conference. We would also like to thank the NBER conference staff, particularly Rob Shannon for his continued excellent organization and support. We would also like to thank the NBER public relations staff and Charlie Radin in particular for overseeing the high-quality multimedia content. Financial assistance from the National Science Foundation is gratefully acknowledged. We also thank the rapporteurs, Nathan Zorzi and Riccardo Bianchi Vimercati, who provided excellent assistance in the preparation of the summaries of the general discussions. And last but far from least, we are grateful to Helena Fitz-Patrick for her invaluable assistance in editing and publishing the volume.

Endnote

For acknowledgments, sources of research support, and disclosure of the authors' material financial relationships, if any, please see https://www.nber.org/chapters/c14232.ack.

Abstracts

1 From Good to Bad Concentration? US Industries over the Past 30 Years
Matias Covarrubias, Germán Gutiérrez, and Thomas Philippon

We study the evolution of profits, investment, and market shares in US industries over the past 40 years. During the 1990s, and at low levels of initial concentration, we find evidence of efficient concentration driven by tougher price competition, intangible investment, and increasing productivity of leaders. After 2000, however, the evidence suggests inefficient concentration, decreasing competition, and increasing barriers to entry as leaders become more entrenched and concentration is associated with lower investment, higher prices, and lower productivity growth.

2 The Lost Ones: The Opportunities and Outcomes of White, Non-College-Educated Americans Born in the 1960s
Margherita Borella, Mariacristina De Nardi, and Fang Yang

White, non-college-educated Americans born in the 1960s face shorter life expectancies, higher medical expenses, and lower wages per unit of human capital compared with those born in the 1940s; men's wages declined more than women's. After documenting these changes, we use a life-cycle model of couples and singles to evaluate their effects. The drop in wages depressed the labor supply of men and increased that of women, especially in married couples. Their shorter life expectancy reduced their retirement savings, but the increase in out-of-pocket medical expenses increased savings by more. Welfare losses, measured as a onetime asset compensation, are 12.5%, 8%, and 7.2% of the present discounted value of earnings for single men, couples, and single women, respectively. Lower wages explain 47%–58% of these losses, shorter life expectancies 25%–34%, and higher medical expenses account for the rest.

3   On the Empirical (Ir)Relevance of the Zero Lower Bound Constraint
Davide Debortoli, Jordi Galí, and Luca Gambetti

We evaluate the hypothesis that the zero lower bound (ZLB) constraint was, in practice, irrelevant during the recent ZLB episode experienced by the US economy (the 2009Q1–2015Q4 period). We focus on two dimensions of economic performance that were ex ante likely to have been affected by a binding ZLB: (i) the volatility of macro variables and (ii) the economy's response to shocks. Using a variety of empirical methods, we find little evidence against the irrelevance hypothesis, with our estimates suggesting that the responses of output, inflation, and the long-term interest rate were hardly affected by the binding ZLB constraint. We show how a shadow interest rate rule (which we take as a proxy for forward guidance) can reconcile our empirical findings with the predictions of a simple New Keynesian model with a ZLB constraint.

4   Optimal Inflation and the Identification of the Phillips Curve
Michael McLeay and Silvana Tenreyro

Several academics and practitioners have pointed out that inflation follows a seemingly exogenous statistical process, unrelated to the output gap, leading some to argue that the Phillips curve has weakened or disappeared. In this paper, we explain why this seemingly exogenous process arises, or, in other words, why it is difficult to empirically identify a Phillips curve, a key building block of the policy framework used by central banks. We show why this result need not imply that the Phillips curve does not hold—on the contrary, our conceptual framework is built under the assumption that the Phillips curve always holds. The reason is simple: if monetary policy is set with the goal of minimizing welfare losses (measured as the sum of deviations of inflation from its target and output from its potential), subject to a Phillips curve, a central bank will seek to increase inflation when output is below potential. This targeting rule will impart a negative correlation between inflation and the output gap, blurring the identification of the (positively sloped) Phillips curve. We discuss different strategies to circumvent the identification problem and present evidence of a robust Phillips curve in US data.

5   Trading Up and the Skill Premium
Nir Jaimovich, Sergio Rebelo, Arlene Wong, and Miao Ben Zhang

We study the impact on the skill premium of increases in the quality of goods consumed by households ("trading up"). Our empirical work shows that high-quality goods are more intensive in skilled labor than low-quality goods and that household spending on high-quality goods rises with income. We propose a model consistent with these facts. This model accounts for the past rise in the skill premium with more plausible rates of skill-biased technical change than those required by the canonical model. It also implies that an expansion of the skilled labor force reduces the skill premium by much less than in the canonical model.

6   Special Deals with Chinese Characteristics
Chong-en Bai, Chang-Tai Hsieh, and Zheng Song

Chinese local governments wield their enormous political power and administrative capacity to provide "special deals" for favored private firms. We argue that China's extraordinary economic growth comes from these special deals. Local political leaders do so because they derive personal benefits, either political or monetary, from providing special deals. Competition between local governments limits the predatory effects of special deals.

1

From Good to Bad Concentration?
US Industries over the Past 30 Years

Matias Covarrubias, *New York University*
Germán Gutiérrez, *New York University*
Thomas Philippon, *New York University, CEPR, and NBER*

We analyze the evolution of concentration in US industries over the past 40 years. Figure 1 summarizes the four stylized facts that motivate our work. Concentration and profits have increased, while the labor share and investment have decreased (fig. 1*a*–1*d*, respectively).[1] This is true across most US industries as shown by Autor et al. (2017a; labor shares), Gutiérrez and Philippon (2016; investment and profits), and Grullon, Larkin, and Michaely (2019; concentration and profits). Although these stylized facts are well established, we are still far from consensus on what is causing them and what they tell us about the health of the US economy. The most prominent explanations can be organized in two groups:

- **Good concentration:** The observed trends may be explained by good sources of concentration, such as increases in the elasticity of substitution (henceforth σ) or technological change leading to increasing returns to scale and intangible capital deepening (henceforth γ). Autor et al. (2017a, 180) argue for σ, noting that concentration reflects "a winner take most feature" explained by the fact that consumers have become more sensitive to price and quality due to greater product market competition. Haskel and Westlake (2017) argue for γ, emphasizing how scalability and synergies of intangible capital can lead to increasing returns to scale. Under σ and γ, concentration is good news: more productive firms expand yet competition remains stable or increases.

- **Bad concentration:** Alternatively, the trends may reflect bad sources of concentration, which we summarize as rising barriers to competition (henceforth κ).[2] Furman (2015, 12), for example, shows that "the distribution of returns to capital has grown increasingly skewed and the high returns increasingly persistent" and argues that it "potentially reflects the rising influence of economic rents and barriers to competition."[3]

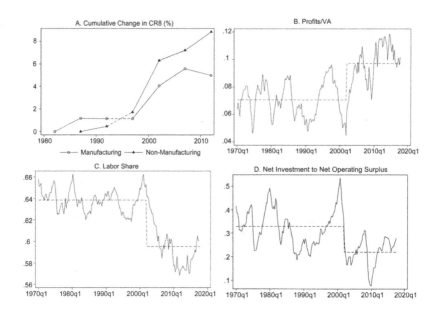

Fig. 1. Evolution of US concentration, profits, labor shares, and investment. (*a*) Cumulative change in eight-firm concentration ratio (CR8; in %), based on the cumulated sales-weighted average change in CR8. Data from the US Economic Census based on Standard Industrial Classification-4 codes before 1992 and North American Industry Classification System-6 codes after 1997. When multiple tax groups are reported, only taxable firms are included. CR8 equals the market share (by sales) of the eight largest firms in each industry. We include only those industries that are consistently defined over each 5-year period. Change from 1992 to 1997 imputed from Autor et al. (2017b). (*b*) Profits/value added (VA), (*c*) labor share, and (*d*) net investment to net operating surplus, based on quarterly data for the nonfinancial corporate sector from the Financial Accounts of the US, via Federal Reserve Economic Data. Profit rate defined as the ratio of after-tax corporate profits with inventory valuation adjustment and capital consumption adjustment to VA (series W328RC1A027NBEA and NCBGVAA027S, respectively). Labor share defined as the ratio of compensation of employees (NCBCEPQ027S) to gross VA (NCBGVAQ027S). Net investment to net operating surplus defined as the ratio of net investment (gross fixed capital formation minus consumption of fixed capital, series NCBGFCA027N minus NCBCFCA027N) to net operating surplus (series NCBOSNQ027S). Dotted lines show the average of the corresponding series before and after 2002.

According to κ, concentration is bad news: it increases economic rents and decreases innovation.

The goal of this paper is to differentiate between these explanations at the aggregate and industry level. Before discussing our approach and results, however, it is important to clarify three points. First, these hypotheses are not mutually exclusive. Leaders can become more efficient and more entrenched at the same time—which can explain their growth but also the rise of barriers to entry (Crouzet and Eberly 2018). Indeed, a combination of these explanations is often heard in the discussion of internet giants Google, Amazon, Facebook, or Apple.

Second, intangibles can play a role in all theories. They may increase the elasticity of substitution (e.g., through online price comparison), increase returns to scale (e.g., organizational capital), and also create barriers to entry (e.g., through patents and/or the compilation of Big Data).

Third, these specific patterns are unique to the US. Figure 2a shows that profits margins have increased in the US, but they have remained stable or decreased in Europe, Japan, and South Korea. Figure 2b shows that concentration has increased in the US but it has remained roughly stable in Europe and Asia.[4] Last, figure 2c shows that the labor share has

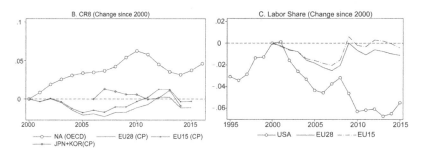

Fig. 2. Profits, concentration, and labor shares across advanced economies. (*a*) Gross Operating Surplus over Production (GOS/PROD) for nonagriculture business sector excluding real estate, from Organization for Economic Co-operation and Development and Structural Analysis (OECD STAN) database. (*b*) Change in eight-firm concentration ratio (CR8; since 2000) for nonagriculture business sector excluding real estate, based on Compustat but adjusted for coverage using OECD STAN. CR8 for Japan and Korea (JPN + KOR) reported only since 2006 because Compustat coverage increases rapidly beforehand. (*c*) Change in labor share (since 2000) for market economy from EU capital (K), labor (L), energy (E), materials (M), and service (S; KLEMS). See appendix E (available online) for details. EU28 = current European Union member states; EU15 = original European Union member states; NA = North America; CP = Compustat.

declined in the US, but it has remained stable in Europe since 2000.[5] Assuming that all advanced economies use similar technologies, the uniqueness of US trends suggests that technology alone cannot explain the trends.

Approach. We begin by using a sequence of simple models to clarify the theories of good and bad concentration. We derive a broad set of predictions regarding the joint evolution of competition, concentration, productivity, prices, and investment under each theory. We then evaluate these predictions empirically, first at the aggregate level, then at the industry level. Although some of these predictions have been studied by the literature, we contribute new facts/results for each of them. We also clarify several measurement issues and, perhaps more important, we show how the combination of all the facts helps us differentiate good and bad concentration.

Aggregate results. Table 1 summarizes our aggregate results. It contrasts the theoretical prediction of theories of good and bad concentration against the observed evolution of each measure.[6] Predictions in the right column are consistent with the data after 2000. Predictions in the middle column are not.

According to theories of good concentration, the growth of large firms is an efficient response to technological change. Under σ, competition increases as consumers become more price elastic. More productive firms expand to capture a larger share of the market, while less productive firms either shrink or exit. Economic activity reallocates toward more productive firms, increasing industry-level productivity and decreasing prices. Under γ, technological change leads to increasing returns to scale.

Table 1
Summary of Test Measures and Predictions

		Theories	
	Data	"Good"	"Bad"
(i) Exit rate	−	+ (σ)	−
(ii) Corr(ΔCR, ΔTFP)	+ to −	+	−
Corr(ΔCR, ΔP)	− to +	−	+
(iii) Aggregate investment rate	−	+	−
Leader investment rate	−	+	−
(iv) Leader turnover	−	+ (σ)/− (γ)	−

Note: CR = concentration ratio; TFP = total factor productivity.

Large firms again respond by expanding, which increases concentration and productivity while decreasing prices. The productivity gap between small and large firms grows.

If the economy experiences good concentration, we should observe: (i) concentration driven in part by exit; (ii) concentration associated with higher productivity and lower prices; and (iii) stable or increasing investment rates relative to Tobin's Q—particularly for leaders. If the increase is driven by σ, we should also find higher volatility of market shares as demand responds more strongly to cost shocks. If the increase is driven by γ, however, the prediction could flip: volatility of market shares could fall as leaders' comparative advantages become (potentially) more persistent (e.g., Aghion et al. 2019).

We already know that σ and γ are important for certain industries during certain periods. For instance, they describe well the evolution of the retail industry from 1990 to 2005 (Basu et al. 2003; Blanchard 2003). The rise of superstores and e-commerce led to more price competition, higher concentration, higher productivity, and the exit of inefficient retailers (Hortacsu and Syverson 2015). The question is whether these theories explain the evolution of the economy as a whole over the past 30 years. We test these predictions in the data and find some support for them during the 1990s. During this period, concentration is correlated with rising productivity, falling prices, and high investment, particularly in intangibles. Since 2000, however, these predictions are rejected by the data. The correlation between concentration and productivity growth has become negative, while the correlation between concentration and price growth has become positive; exit rates have remained stable; investment relative to Q has fallen; and market shares have become more persistent. Estimates of returns to scale based on the methodology of Basu, Fernald, and Kimball (2006) have remained stable, as have other estimates in the recent literature (Ho and Ruzic 2018; Diez, Fan, and Villegas-Sanchez 2019). All these predictions are consistent with the κ theory.

Barriers to competition therefore emerge as the most relevant explanation over the past 15 years. It correctly predicts the evolution of profits, entry, exit, turnover, prices, productivity, and investment in most industries.

Industry results. Aggregate trends are interesting, but the dynamics of individual industries are more informative: σ and γ cannot explain the broad trends but they probably matter for some industries. To obtain a systematic classification of industry-level changes, we perform a principal components analysis (PCA) on a wide range of measures related to competition. We find that the first principal component, PC1, captures the σ and γ theories of good concentration while the second principal component, PC2, captures theories of bad concentration. This distinction is quite stark and allows us to show which industries have experienced good versus bad concentration and compare the importance of each theory over time.

Durable computer manufacturing exhibits the highest loading on PC1. It exhibits high intangible capital intensity but remains relatively competitive, likely as a result of intense foreign competition. By contrast, telecommunications, banking, and airlines are predominantly explained by κ, consistent with the results of Gutiérrez and Philippon (2018). They exhibit high concentration, high profits, and low productivity growth. Interestingly, some industries, such as nondurable chemical manufacturing and information (data), load heavily on both PC1 and PC2. These industries hold large amounts of intangible assets but also exhibit high barriers to entry. They are good examples of intangible assets giving rise to barriers to entry, as emphasized by Crouzet and Eberly (2018). In fact, Crouzet and Eberly (2018) argue that the health-care sector, which includes nondurable chemical manufacturing, is one where market power derived from intangible assets is largest.

Looking at the evolution of loadings over time further emphasizes the transition from good to bad concentration. The average PC1 score (reflecting good concentration) was substantially higher than PC2 in 1997 and increased faster from 1997 to 2002. But PC2 caught up afterward and, by 2012, explained a larger portion of industry dynamics. Our results therefore indicate that the US economy has transitioned from good to bad concentration over the past 30 years.

Related literature. Our paper contributes to a growing literature studying trends in competition and concentration in the US economy. The literature began by (separately) documenting the stylized facts. Haltiwanger, Jarmin, and Miranda (2011, 2) find that "job creation and destruction both exhibit a downward trend over the past few decades." Decker et al. (2015) argue that, whereas in the 1980s and 1990s declining dynamism was observed in selected sectors (notably retail), the decline was observed across all sectors in the 2000s, including the traditionally high-growth information technology (IT) sector. CEA (2016) and Grullon et al. (2019) document the broad increases in profits and concentration; Elsby, Hobijn, and Sahin (2013) and Karabarbounis and Neiman (2014) document the decline in the labor share; and IMF (2014), Hall (2015), and Fernald et al. (2017) discuss the decline in investment in the context of weak overall growth. Akcigit and Ates (2019) review some of the literature.

Over time, the literature began to connect these facts and propose theories of "good" and "bad" concentration (we use "good" and "bad" for didactic purposes). The most prominent explanations of good concentration include Autor et al. (2017a) and Van Reenen (2018, 1), who argue that rising concentration and declining labor shares are explained by an increase in σ, which results in "winner take most/all" competition, and Alexander and Eberly (2018) and Crouzet and Eberly (2018), who link the rise in concentration and the decline in investment to intangible capital. Bessen (2017) links IT use to industry concentration. Ganapati (2018) links concentration to increasing labor productivity and stable prices. Aghion et al. (2019) and Ridder (2019) develop models where information and communication technologies increase returns to scale, leading to higher concentration and lower labor shares.

Moving to bad concentration, Grullon et al. (2019) show that firms in concentrating industries exhibit higher profits, positive abnormal stock returns, and more profitable merger and acquisition deals. Barkai (2017) documents a rise in economic profits and links it to concentration and labor shares. De Loecker, Eeckhout, and Unger (2019) argue that markups have increased. Gutiérrez and Philippon (2016) link the weakness of investment to rising concentration and market power, while Lee, Shin, and Stulz (2016) find that capital stopped flowing to high Q industries in the late 1990s. Eggertsson, Robbins, and Wold (2018) introduce time-varying market power to a standard neoclassical model to explain several of our stylized facts. Gutiérrez and Philippon (2018), Jones, Gutiérrez, and Philippon (2019), and Gutiérrez and Philippon (2019) argue that domestic competition has declined in many US industries because of increasing entry costs, lax antitrust enforcement, and lobbying.

We would like to note that this debate between good and bad concentration has a direct precedent in the industrial organization literature of the 1970s and 1980s. By then, the discussion was centered on how to interpret the positive correlation between profits and concentration at the industry level, first documented by Bain (1951). While this fact was commonly rationalized as evidence of market power ("bad concentration"), Demsetz (1973) argued that the observed pattern was instead explained by differences in productivity ("good concentration"). This seminal contribution spawned a series of empirical papers evaluating these two hypotheses, reviewed in Schmalensee (1987).

Finally, our paper is also related to the effect of foreign competition, particularly from China (see Bernard et al. 2012 for a review). Bernard, Jensen, and Schott (2006) show that capital-intensive plants and industries are more likely to survive and grow in the wake of import competition. Bloom, Draca, and Van Reenen (2016) argue that Chinese import competition leads to increased technical change within firms and a reallocation of employment toward more technologically advanced firms. Frésard and Valta (2015) find that tariff reductions lead to declines in investment in markets with competition in strategic substitutes and low costs of entry. Within industry, they find that investment declines primarily at financially constrained firms. The decline in investment is negligible for financially stable firms and firms in markets featuring competition in strategic complements. Hombert and Matray (2015) show that research and development (R&D)–intensive firms were better able to cope with Chinese competition than low-R&D firms. They explain this result based on product differentiation, using the Hoberg and Phillips (2017) product similarity index. Autor, Dorn, and Hanson (2013), Pierce and Schott (2016), Autor, Dorn, and Hanson (2016), and Feenstra, Ma, and Xu (2017) study the effects of Chinese import exposure on US manufacturing employment. Feenstra and Weinstein (2017) estimate the impact of globalization on markups, and conclude that markups decreased in industries affected by foreign competition. Some of these papers find a reduction in investment for the "average" firm, which is consistent with our results and highlights the importance of considering industry leaders and laggards separately.

The remainder of this paper is organized as follows. Section I derives theoretical predictions. Section II discusses measurement issues related to common empirical proxies of competition. Section III tests aggregate predictions related to business dynamism, productivity, prices, investment, and returns to scale. Section IV replicates the exercise at the industry level, using PCA. Section V concludes.

I.   Theory

We use a few simple models to derive testable predictions for the various hypotheses. The timing of the models follows the classic model of Hopenhayn (1992): (i) there is a sunk entry cost κ; (ii) firms draw their productivities a (and/or idiosyncratic demand shocks); and (iii) they either produce with a fixed operating cost ϕ or they exit early.

A. Good Concentration, Bad Concentration

Let us start with the simple case where there is no heterogeneity. Consider, then, an industry with N identical firms with productivity $a_i = A$ for all $i \in [0, N]$, and industry demand Y. Suppose the game among the N firms leads to a markup μ over marginal cost. In other words, firms set the price

$$p = \frac{1 + \mu}{A}$$

and firm i's profits are

$$\pi_i = \left(p - \frac{1}{A}\right)y_i - \phi = \frac{\mu}{1 + \mu}py_i - \phi.$$

In a symmetric equilibrium with identical firms, all firms produce

$$y_i = \frac{Y}{N} \quad \text{for all } i \in [0, N].$$

So profits are

$$\pi = \frac{\mu}{1 + \mu}\frac{pY}{N} - \phi.$$

Under free entry, we have

$$\frac{E[\pi]}{r + \delta} \leq \kappa,$$

where r is the discount rate, δ is the (exogenous) exit rate, and κ is the sunk entry cost. The free entry condition is then

$$N \geq \frac{\mu}{1 + \mu}\frac{pY}{(r + \delta)\kappa + \phi}.$$

A simple case is when industry demand is unit elastic (Cobb-Douglas). In that case $Y(p) = \bar{Y}/p$ and we have $N \geq (\mu/(1 + \mu))(\bar{Y}/((r + \delta)\kappa + \phi))$. We then have the following proposition.

Proposition 1. In response to shocks to ex post markups μ, concentration is positively related to competition. In response to shocks to κ, concentration is negatively related to competition.

This proposition summarizes the fundamental issue with using concentration as a proxy for competition. Concentration is endogenous and can signal either increasing or decreasing degrees of competition. In other words, when looking at concentration measures, it is crucial to take a stand on why concentration is changing, in particular to see whether it is driven by shrinking margins or by higher barriers to entry.

Corollary 1. Concentration is a valid measure of market power only when concentration is driven by barriers to entry or by mergers.

Note that it is straightforward to extend the analysis to the case where μ depends on the number of firms. We can write $\mu/(1 + \mu) = \bar{l}N^{-\theta}$, where $\bar{l}$ is the baseline Lerner index and θ is the elasticity of the markup to concentration. In a standard constant elasticity of substitution (CES) monopolistic competition model, for instance, we have $\theta = 0$ and $\bar{l} = 1/\sigma$. We can then write the free entry condition as $N^{1+\theta} \geq (\bar{l}Y/((r + \delta)\kappa + \phi))$, which shows that our propositions are valid when markups vary with concentration.

B.   Selection and Ex Post Profits

Consider now the case of heterogenous marginal costs. Heterogeneity creates a selection effect and we need to distinguish between the number of firms that enter ($\hat{N}$) and the number of firms that actually produce (N). Formally, consider the following industry entry game:

• Each entrant pays κ for the right to produce one variety $i \in [0, \hat{N}]$.

• After entry, each firm draws productivity a_i and decides whether to produce with fixed operating cost ϕ and markup μ_i.

Let $N \leq \hat{N}$ be the number of active producers. We reorder the varieties so that $i \in [0, N]$ are active while $i \in (N, \hat{N}]$ exit early. The demand system is given by the CES aggregator

$$Y^{\frac{\sigma-1}{\sigma}} = \int_0^N y_i^{\frac{\sigma-1}{\sigma}} di,$$

where $\sigma > 1$ is the elasticity of substitution between different firms in the industry. This demand structure implies that there exists an industry price index $P^{1-\sigma} \equiv \int_0^N p_i^{1-\sigma} di$ such that the demand for variety i is

$$y_i = Y \left(\frac{p_i}{P}\right)^{-\sigma}.$$

The firm sets a price $p_i = (1 + \mu_i)/a_i$ and the profits of firm i are now given by $\pi_i = (\mu_i/(1 + \mu_i)^\sigma)a_i^{\sigma-1}P^\sigma Y - \phi$. If we assume monopolistic competition, the optimal markup $\mu^m = 1/(\sigma - 1)$ maximizes $\mu_i/(1 + \mu_i)^\sigma$. But we do not need to consider only this case. We could assume limit pricing at some markup $\mu < 1/(\sigma - 1)$, strategic interactions among firms, and so on. For now we simply keep μ as a parameter.

Firms with productivity $a_i < a^*$ do not produce, so the active producers are $N = (1 - F(a^*))\hat{N}$, where $\hat{N}$ is the number of firms that pay the entry cost. Similarly, the density of producers' productivity is $dF^*(a) = -dF(a)/(1 - F(a^*))$. Because all the firms draw from the same distribution of productivity, we have

$$P = \frac{1 + \mu}{A^* N^{\frac{1}{\sigma-1}}},$$

where average productivity is

$$A^* \equiv \left(\int a^{\sigma-1} dF^*(a) \right)^{\frac{1}{\sigma-1}}. \tag{1}$$

Equilibrium profits are then

$$\pi(a_i; a^*, PY, N) = \frac{\mu}{1 + \mu} \left(\frac{a_i}{A^*} \right)^{\sigma-1} \frac{PY}{N} - \phi.$$

There is a cutoff a^* such that only firms above the cutoff are active producers

$$\pi(a^*; a^*, PY, N) = 0.$$

The productivity cutoff a^* solves $(\mu/(1 + \mu))(a^*)^{\sigma-1}(PY/N) = \phi(A^*)^{\sigma-1}$. For simplicity we consider again the log-industry demand case, so PY is exogenous and equal to $\bar{Y}$. Using the definition of A^* in equation (1), and $N = (1 - F(a^*))\hat{N}$ and $dF^*(a) = dF(a)/(1 - F(a^*))$, we find that

$$\frac{\mu}{1 + \mu} \bar{Y} = \phi \hat{N} \int_{a > a^*} \left(\frac{a}{a^*} \right)^{\sigma-1} dF(a).$$

The right-hand side is increasing in σ and decreasing in a^*, so we have the standard selection effect.

Lemma 1. The cutoff a^* increases with the demand elasticity σ.

From the free entry condition we have

$$(r + \delta)\kappa = (1 - F(a^*)) \times E[\pi|a > a^*].$$

Because $1 - F(a^*)$ decreases with σ, it follows that $E[\pi|a > a^*]$ must increase with σ for a given κ.

Proposition 2. For a given free entry condition, an increase in σ leads to higher rate of failed entry (early exits) and higher profits for remaining firms (selection effect). An increase in κ, on the other hand, leads to lower entry, lower exit, and higher profits.

This proposition allows us to distinguish the σ hypothesis from the κ hypothesis.

C.   Increasing Returns

Now suppose that firms can choose between two technologies after entry: low fixed cost and low productivity (A_L, ϕ_L) or high fixed cost and high productivity (A_H, ϕ_H). Let us ignore idiosyncratic productivity differences for now. Profits are then

$$\pi(a, \phi) = \frac{\mu}{1 + \mu} \left(\frac{a}{A}\right)^{\sigma-1} \frac{PY}{N} - \phi.$$

The choice of technology clearly depends on the size of the market and the elasticity of demand.

Lemma 2. Firms are more likely to switch to the high returns to scale technology when σ is high.

Assume that the parameters are such that the firms decide to switch to $a_i = A_H$ for all i. Equilibrium profits are then $\pi = (\mu/(1 + \mu))(PY/N) - \phi_H$. Free entry then requires $\pi = (r + \delta)\kappa$

$$N = \frac{\mu}{1 + \mu} \frac{PY}{\phi_H + (r + \delta)\kappa}.$$

Concentration increases when firms switch to the high returns to scale technology. The behavior of equilibrium profits depends on the selection effect. Without idiosyncratic risk, profits are simply pinned down by free entry. If we take into account idiosyncratic risk, then equilibrium profits increase when firms switch to the high returns to scale technology because the selection effect intensifies.

Proposition 3. A switch to increasing returns technology is more likely when demand is more elastic. A higher degree of increasing returns to scale leads to more concentration, higher profits, and higher productivity for the remaining firms.

This proposition connects σ and γ, as often discussed in the literature. Note that we can measure the degree of returns to scale γ as the ratio of average cost $(\phi/y) + (1/A)$ to marginal cost $1/A$:

$$\gamma - 1 \equiv \frac{\phi A}{y} = \frac{\phi}{\phi + (r + \delta)\kappa\, N^{\frac{1}{\sigma-1}}} \frac{\mu}{},$$

which is increasing with ϕ because N is decreasing in ϕ. Therefore, if we were to measure γ under the old and the new technologies, we would indeed find $\gamma_H > \gamma_L$.

D. Dynamics of Market Shares

Consider finally the case where, after entry, firms are subject to demand and productivity shocks. In the general case, we have $j \in [0, 1]$ industries and $i \in [0, N_j]$ firms in each industry. The output of industry j is aggregated as $Y_{j,t}^{((\sigma_j-1)/\sigma_j)} = \int_0^{N_j} h_{i,j,t}^{1/\sigma} (y_{i,j,t})^{((\sigma_j-1)/\sigma_j)} di$, where σ_j is the elasticity between different firms in the same industry and $h_{i,j,t}$ are firm-level demand shocks. The demand for good (i, j) is given by

$$y_{i,j,t} = h_{i,j,t} Y_{j,t} \left(\frac{p_{i,j,t}}{P_{j,t}}\right)^{-\sigma_j},$$

where $P_{j,t}$ is the industry price index. The nominal revenues of firm i are

$$p_{i,j,t} y_{i,j,t} = p_{i,j,t}^{1-\sigma_j} h_{i,j,t} P_{j,t}^{\sigma_j} Y_{j,t}$$

and the market share of firm i in industry j is

$$s_{i,j,t} = \frac{p_{i,j,t} y_{i,j,t}}{P_{j,t} Y_{j,t}} = \frac{h_{i,j,t}}{N_j} \left(\frac{(1 + \mu_j) a_{i,j,t}}{(1 + \mu_{i,j}) A_{j,t}}\right)^{\sigma_j-1},$$

where μ_j is the industry average markup and $A_{j,t}$ is the industry average productivity, as defined earlier. If we track the market shares of firms over time, we have the following proposition.

Proposition 4. The volatility of log-market shares is

$$\sum_{\log s}^{2} = \sum_{\log h}^{2} + (\sigma_j - 1)^2 \sum_{\log a}^{2},$$

where $\Sigma_{\log a}^2$ is the volatility of idiosyncratic productivity shocks.

Therefore,

Corollary 2. All else equal, an increase in σ_j leads to an increase in the volatility of market shares in industry j.

In summary, we have established that an increase in σ leads to an increase in concentration, productivity, exit, the volatility of market shares, and investment. Similarly, an increase in γ results in more concentration, higher profits, and higher productivity for surviving firms.[7] Finally, an increase in κ leads to an increase in concentration and a decrease in productivity, exit rates, market share volatility, and investment (relative to Q).

II. Measurement Issues

Before testing our predictions, we discuss two important issues related to the measurement of concentration and markups.

A. Foreign Competition and Concentration

First, when computing industry concentration, it is important to control for imports. We compute import-adjusted concentration measures ($CR8^{IA}$) and use them throughout the paper. Figure 3 shows the importance of the correction, focusing on manufacturing industries that are highly exposed to foreign competition. While domestic concentration increased by 6.7 percentage points in these industries, import-adjusted

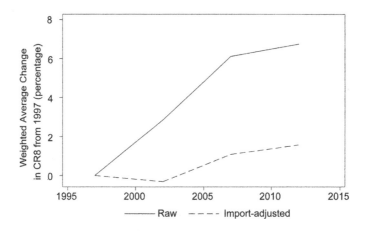

Fig. 3. Domestic versus import-adjusted concentration for high import manufacturing industries. Weighted average absolute change in domestic (solid line) and import-adjusted (dotted line) eight-firm concentration ratio (CR8) across North American Industry Classification System (NAICS)-6 manufacturing industries in the top three quantiles of import shares as of 2012. Imports accounted for 29% of sales plus imports in these industries, on average. Domestic concentration from US Economic Census. Import adjusted concentration defined as $CR8^{IA}_{jt} = CR8_{jt} \times (\text{sale}_{jt}/(\text{sale}_{jt} + \text{imp}_{jt})) = CR8_{jt} \times \text{US Share}_{jt}$. NAICS-6 industries are included if they are consistently defined from 1997 to the given year. See appendix (available online) for details.

concentration (dotted line) increased by only 1.6 points.[8] Foreign competition, therefore, plays an important role in manufacturing. But import-exposed industries only account for about 10% of the private economy, so foreign competition cannot explain the aggregate trends that we have presented earlier.

B.   Markup Measurement

The second issue relates to measurement of markups. De Loecker et al. (2019) estimate markups using the methodology of De Loecker and Warzynski (2012). The idea is to compare the elasticity of output to a variable input, with the cost share of that input. De Loecker et al. (2019) implement this methodology using cost of goods sold (COGS) as their main measure of variable input. While this approach is promising in theory, the question is whether it provides a reliable measure of market power. There are measurement issues with COGS that we discuss in appendix A (apps. A–E are available online; see https://www.nber.org/data-appendix/c14237/appendix.pdf). Our main concern, however, is that technology can change over time in a way that creates challenges for COGS-based markup measures.

Identification: The China Shock

We use the China shock to illustrate this issue, following Autor et al. (2016) and Pierce and Schott (2016). Chinese competition led to a strong replacement effect. Figure 4 shows the normalized number of firms in industries with high and low Chinese import penetration.[9] Both groups have the same preexisting trends, including during the dot-com boom, but start to diverge after 2000. In unreported tests, we confirm that this relationship is strongly statistically significant.

Realized imports are endogenous so, in the rest of the section, we use the instrument proposed by Pierce and Schott (2016). The instrument exploits changes in barriers to trade following the US granting permanent normal trade relations (PNTR) to China.[10] Pierce and Schott (2016) show that industries facing larger NTR gaps experienced a larger increase in Chinese imports and a larger decrease in US employment. We follow Pierce and Schott (2016) and quantify the impact of granting PNTR on industry j as the difference between the non-NTR rate (to which tariffs would have risen if annual renewal had failed) and the NTR rate as of 1999:

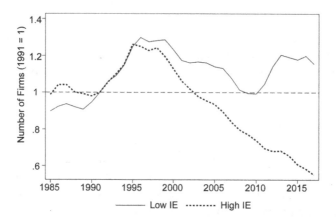

Fig. 4. Number of firms by Chinese exposure. Annual data. Number of firms from Compustat; import penetration based on data from NBER Center for Economic Studies and Peter Schott. Manufacturing industries only, split into "high" (above-median) and "low" (below-median) import exposure (IE) based on import penetration from 1991 to 2015. See appendix E (available online) for details.

$$\text{NTR Gap}_j = \text{Non NTR Rate}_j - \text{NTR Rate}_j.$$

This measure is plausibly exogenous to industry demand and technology after 2001. The vast majority of the variation in NTR gaps is due to variation in non-NTR rates set 70 years prior to passage of PNTR. See Pierce and Schott (2016) for additional discussion.

Profits versus Markups

Figure 5 reports results of the following regressions across firms i in industry j

$$\pi_{i,j,t} = \sum_{y=1991}^{2007} \beta_t \times \text{NTR Gap}_j + \delta_i + \gamma_t + \varepsilon_{i,j,t}, \qquad (2)$$

where π_{ijt} denotes a given outcome variable (profits, etc.). All regressions include firm and year fixed effects and are weighted by firm sales. Standard errors are clustered at the North American Industry Classification System (NAICS)-6 industry level. Consistent with the identification assumption, we see no significant pre-trends before 2000 and strong responses afterward. Consistent with the increase in exits, the operating income of US companies falls upon Chinese accession to the World Trade Organization (WTO; fig. 5a).

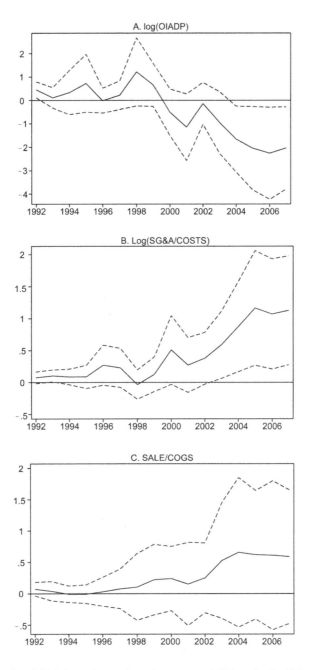

Fig. 5. Profits, SG&A intensity, and markups around China shock. (*a*) log(OIADP). (*b*) log(SG&A/COSTS). (*c*) SALE/COGS. Firm financials from Compustat. Normal trade relations gap from Pierce and Schott (2016). Figure reports regression results following equation (2), including 95% confidence intervals. Only firms that existed before 1997 are included. SALE/COGS and XSGA/XOPR (SG&A/total operating expenses) are winsorized at the 2% and 98% level, by year. See text for details. SG&A = sales, general, and administrative expenses; OIADP = operating income after depreciation; COSTS = total costs; SALE = sales; COGS = cost of goods sold.

What is more remarkable, however, is the increase in the share of sales, general, and administrative expenses (SG&A) in total costs. SG&A is the second major component of costs and includes all intangible-building activities (e.g., R&D, advertising, and IT staff expenses). US firms react to the increased competition by almost doubling their SG&A intensity (fig. 5b), a result consistent with the shift toward intangible capital documented in table 4, as well as the increased product differentiation documented by Feenstra and Weinstein (2017). The increase in SG&A is precisely the type of technological change that may affect the validity of COGS-based markups. Indeed, figure 5c shows that SALE/COGS (ratio of sales to COGS) appears to increase rather than decrease upon the shock.[11] COGS-based markup measures would fail to classify the China shock as an increase in competition, while exit and profit margins do.[12]

We can also get a broad evaluation of the usefulness of markups by studying the evolution across regions. Figure 6 plots the sales-weighted average ratio of sales to COGS against gross profit rates by region.[13]

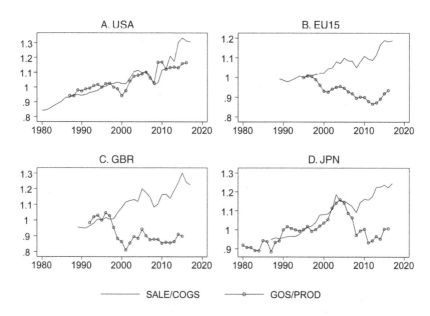

Fig. 6. Weighted average SALE/COGS versus gross profit rates by region (1995 = 1). (a) USA; (b) EU15; (c) GBR; (d) JPN. SALE/COGS equals the sales-weighted average ratio of sales to cost of goods sold across all Compustat firms in a given region. GOS/PROD based on Organization for Economic Cooperation and Development Structural Analysis database for nonagriculture business sector excluding real estate. EU15 = original European Union member states; GBR = Great Britain; JPN = Japan; SALE = sales; COGS = cost of goods sold.

The shift toward intangible expenditures is clearly present across all advanced economies: SALE/COGS rises everywhere as the cost-share of COGS falls. This may suggest a global rise in market power, but profits show us the opposite—especially for the European Union 15 and the United Kingdom. Only in the US do we observe a large increase in profits. In the remaining regions, the decline in COGS is fully offset by a rise in SG&A so that profits remain flat (operating income before depreciation equals sales minus COGS and SG&A). Given the inability of markup estimates to control for technology, we focus on profits and market share dynamics in the rest of the paper.[14]

III.   Aggregate Evidence

A.   Entry, Exit, and Turnover

Having clarified some measurement issues, let us return to the main goal of the paper: differentiating theories of good versus bad concentration. We begin with market share turnover. Industrial organization economists rightly complain about the use of Herfindahl-Hirschman indexes (HHIs) or concentration ratios (CRs) at the broad industry × country level as measures of market power. The limitations of national CRs and HHIs are well understood. NAICS industries and countries are much broader than product markets—and concentration may evolve differently at more granular levels.[15] But there is a more fundamental problem: depending on the nature of competition, technology, and supply and demand primitives, concentration may be positively or negatively correlated with competition and markups. In other words, concentration "is a market outcome, not a market primitive" (Syverson 2019, 4).

Leader Turnover

To obtain an alternate measure of market power, we consider turnover of market shares and market leadership. In particular, one can ask: Given that a firm is at the top of its industry now (top 4, top 10% of market value), how likely is it that it will drop out over the next 5 years? Per proposition 4, increases in σ would result in higher leader turnover, while increases in κ would result in lower turnover.

Figure 7 tests this prediction. We define turnover in industry j at time t as the probability of leaving the top 4 firms of the industry over a 5-year period,

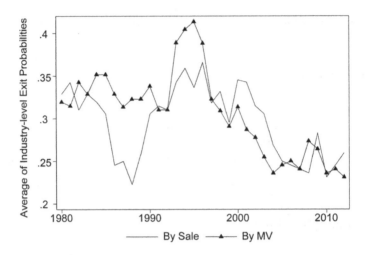

Fig. 7. Turnover of leaders by sale and market value (MV; Compustat North America, following Bureau of Economic Analysis industries). Only industry years with five or more firms are included. See text for details.

$$\text{TopTurn}_{jt} = \Pr\left(z_{i,j,t+5} < z_{j,t+5}^{\#4} \middle| z_{i,j,t} \geq z_{j,t}^{\#4}\right),$$

where $z_{i,j,t}$ denotes either the sales of firm i at time t or its market value of equity, and $z_{j,t}^{\#4}$ is the value of $z_{i,j,t}$ for the fourth largest firm at time t in industry j.[16] We then average turnover across all industries in a given year. We focus on the post-1980 period, after the addition of Nasdaq into Compustat. As shown, the likelihood of a leader being replaced was 35% in the 1980s, rose to 40% at the height of the dot-com bubble, and is only 25% today. Appendix A (available online) presents results by sector.

Persistence of Market Shares

Leader turnover focuses on the right tail of the distribution. Let us now broaden the sample to include all firms and study the persistence of market shares. We follow proposition 4 and estimate an AR(1) model of the log-market share for firm i that belongs to Standard Industrial Classification (SIC)-3 industry j, using a 5-year rolling window:

$$\log s_{i,j,t} = \rho_{j,t} \log s_{i,j,t-1} + \epsilon_{i,j,t}.$$

Figures 8a and 8b plot the sales-weighted average $\rho_{j,t}$ and root mean squared error (RMSE), respectively. In line with the decline in turnover,

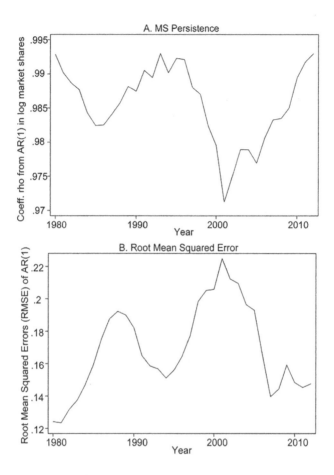

Fig. 8. Persistence and volatility of market shares (MS). (*a*) MS persistence. (*b*) root mean squared error (RMSE). Autocorrelation and RMSE for AR(1) model of firm-level log-market shares, following Standard Industrial Classification-3 industries. Estimates based on a 5-year rolling window. Only industry years with five or more firms and firms with a market share higher than 0.02 are included.

the persistence of market shares increases after 2000, whereas the RMSE falls.[17]

Leaders clearly have less to worry about today than 30 years ago. Their market shares and leadership positions are far more persistent today than even 15 years ago. Why might this be? In Gutiérrez and Philippon (2019), we study competitive pressures directly, focusing on the entry and exit margins. We show that exit rates have remained stable, while the elasticity of entry with respect to Tobin's Q was positive and significant until the late 1990s but fell close to zero afterward. The behavior of entry, exit, and turnover is inconsistent with σ, but consistent with κ.

B.   Concentration, Productivity, and Prices

According to σ and γ, concentration rises as high productivity leaders expand, increasing industry-level productivity and decreasing prices. If more productive firms have lower labor shares, the aggregate labor share also falls. Autor et al. (2017b) document a reallocation from high- to low-labor-share establishments, while Ganapati (2018) finds that changes in concentration are uncorrelated with changes in prices but positively correlated with changes in productivity. Kehrig and Vincent (2017) and Hsieh and Rossi-Hansberg (2019) make similar arguments for manufacturing and service industries, respectively.

BLS and Compustat

We begin our analysis with relatively aggregated data from the Bureau of Labor Statistics (BLS) multifactor productivity (MFP) Tables. This data set includes total factor productivity (TFP), prices, wages, and labor productivity. We complement it with Compustat-based concentration measures to obtain the same industry classification in left- and right-hand side variables. We assess the joint evolution of productivity, prices, and markups using regressions of the form

$$\Delta_5 \log(Z_{j,t}) = \beta \Delta_5 \log(CR4_{j,t}) + \gamma_t + \varepsilon_{jt},$$

where Z is the variable of interest and Δ_5 denotes a 5-year change. We consider TFP, prices, and markups of prices over unit labor costs (ULC): $\Delta_5 \log \mu = \Delta_5 \log P - \Delta_5 \log ULC$, where $\Delta_5 \log(ULC) \equiv \Delta_5 \log(W) - \Delta_5 \log(LP_t)$.

Table 2 summarizes the results. Columns 1, 3, and 5 are based on pre-2000 changes and exhibit correlations in line with σ and γ: positive and significant with TFP and negative (although insignificant) with prices and markups. However, the relationship seems to have collapsed after 2000. The correlation between concentration and TFP turns negative (though insignificant), while the correlation with prices and markups turns positive.

To illustrate the transition, figure 9 plots the evolution of markups and concentration for the telecom and air transportation industries. While they exhibit little (or negative) correlation before 2000, both rise sharply

Table 2
Concentration, TFP, Prices, and Markups: BLS Industries

	$\Delta_5 \log(\text{TFP})$		$\Delta_5 \log(P)$		$\Delta_5 \log(\mu)$	
	Pre-00	Post-00	Pre-00	Post-00	Pre-00	Post-00
	(1)	(2)	(3)	(4)	(5)	(6)
$\Delta_5 \log(\text{CR4}^{IA})$	.186*	−.044	−.093	.077	−.102*	.116⁺
	(.070)	(.051)	(.069)	(.088)	(.047)	(.064)
Cons	.016	.025**	.074**	.097**	.048**	.045**
	(.013)	(.009)	(.013)	(.010)	(.012)	(.011)
Year FE	Y	Y	Y	Y	Y	Y
R^2	.12	.1	.048	.07	.041	.082
Observations	94	141	94	141	94	141

Note: Table shows the results of industry-level ordinary least squares regressions of contemporaneous 5-year changes in TFP, prices (P), markups (μ), and import-adjusted concentration over the periods specified. Data include all industries covered in the BLS multifactor tables. CR4 from Compustat. Standard errors in parentheses are clustered at industry level. TFP = total factor productivity; BLS = Bureau of Labor Statistics; CR = concentration ratio; FE = fixed effects.
⁺$p < .10$.
*$p < .05$.
**$p < .01$.

afterward. This is consistent with the cross-country analyses of Gutiérrez and Philippon (2018).

The BLS MFP tables provide several advantages. They cover the full economy, include TFP estimates, and follow a consistent segmentation that can be mapped to other Bureau of Economic Analysis (BEA) data sets. This allows us to include the evolution of prices, unit-labor costs, and markups in the PCA of Section IV. However, using broad industry definitions limits the power of our regressions, hence the previous large confidence intervals. Let us now bring in more granular data.

BEA, NBER, and Census

We roughly follow Ganapati (2018) and combine concentration data from the US Economic Census with price data from the NBER Center for Economic Studies (NBER-CES) database for the manufacturing sector and the BEA's detailed gross domestic product (GDP) by industry accounts for nonmanufacturing.[18] Combined, these data sets allow us to estimate real labor productivity and analyze the evolution of markups using the previous definitions.

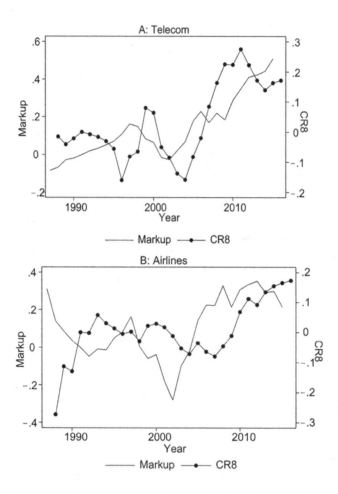

Fig. 9. Change in markup and concentration since 1991: (*a*) telecom and (*b*) airlines (Bureau of Labor Statistics multifactor tables for markups and Compustat for import-adjusted concentration). CR8 = change in eight-firm concentration ratio.

We estimate regressions of the following form:

$$\Delta_5 \log(Z_{jt}) = \beta \Delta_5 \log(CR4_{j,t}) + \gamma_{s,t} + \varepsilon_{jt},$$

where j denotes industries and t denotes years. $\gamma_{s,t}$ denotes sector-year fixed effects. Table 3 reports results for prices and markups. Before 2002, the correlation is small and often insignificant, in line with the results of Ganapati (2018). After 2002, however, increases in concentration are

Table 3
Concentration versus Prices: Pre- and Post-2002

	$\Delta_5 \log(P)$			$\Delta_5 \log(\mu)$			$\Delta_5 \log(\mu)$		
	All (1)	Mfg (2)	NonMfg (3)	All (4)	Mfg (5)	NonMfg (6)	All (7)	Mfg (8)	NonMfg (9)
$\Delta_5 \log(CR4_{jt})$	−.01	.05*	−.03	.02	.10**	−.00	.12*	.12**	.12*
	(.03)	(.02)	(.04)	(.04)	(.03)	(.05)	(.05)	(.04)	(.06)
$\Delta_5 \log(CR4_{jt}) \times 1_{>2002}$	.17**	.20**	.17**	.23**	.13$^+$	.26**			
	(.04)	(.06)	(.05)	(.06)	(.07)	(.07)			
$\Delta_5 \log(CR4_{jt}) \times$ High CR							.18*	.08	.41**
							(.09)	(.07)	(.14)
High CR							.03*	.07**	−.01
							(.02)	(.02)	(.02)
$\Delta_5 \log(LP_{jt})$	−.39**	−.37**	−.39**						
	(.05)	(.07)	(.08)						
$\Delta_5 \log(w_{jt})$	.58**	.74**	.48**						
	(.14)	(.28)	(.12)						
Cons	.05**	.06$^+$	.06**	.05**	.11**	.03**	.04**	.06**	.02$^+$
	(.02)	(.03)	(.02)	(.01)	(.02)	(.01)	(.01)	(.01)	(.01)
Sector × Year FE	Y	Y	Y	Y	Y	Y	Y	Y	Y
R²	.47	.45	.5	.39	.34	.36	.38	.38	.35
Observations	2,083	1,682	401	2,083	1,682	401	2,083	1,682	401

Note: Table shows the results of industry-level OLS regressions of contemporaneous 5-year changes in prices, markups, and concentration over the periods specified. P = prices; μ = markups; Mfg = manufacturing industries; NonMfg = nonmanufacturing industries; CR = concentration ratio; FE = fixed effects. Observations are weighted by sales. Standard errors in parentheses are clustered at industry level.

$^+p < .10.$
$^*p < .05.$
$^{**}p < .01.$

systematically correlated with increases in prices. Columns 7–9 show a similar effect but instead of sorting on time (pre-/post-2002), we sort by ending levels of concentration. When ending concentration is low, there is not much correlation between changes in concentration and changes in markups. When concentration reaches a high level, however, the correlation is much stronger, especially in the nonmanufacturing sector. See appendix B (available online) for additional results, including a decomposition of the correlation between concentration and markups into the underlying components: prices, wages, and labor productivity.

The joint evolution of concentration, TFP, and prices appears consistent with the σ and γ theories before 2000. Over the past 15 years, however, concentration is correlated with lower TFP and higher prices. The evidence is now more closely aligned with the κ theory.

Our data and correlations are consistent with the ones in Ganapati (2018) but our interpretation is quite different. Regarding prices, we agree that the full sample correlation is small, but as we have shown the correlations after 2000 and at high level of concentration are large and positive. The most important disagreement, however, relates to the correlation with productivity. The existing literature has failed to recognize that, given what we know about firm-level data, we should expect a quasi-mechanical correlation between concentration and productivity at the level of detailed industries (NAICS level 4 or 5, for instance). We know that the firm-size distribution is skewed. At NAICS level 5, the top four firms account for about one-third of output. We also know that firm-level shocks are large. Therefore, changes in industry output at level 5 are strongly affected by idiosyncratic firm-level shocks. If a large firm experiences a positive shock, industry output increases and concentration increases at the same time.

Therefore, in the regressions run by Ganapati (2018) or Autor et al. (2017b), one would expect a mechanical positive correlation between changes in CR4 and changes in output or productivity or both (depending on the details of the shocks). At level 4 the kurtosis of log changes in CR4 is 8.8. Once we move to level 2 or level 3, the law of large number kicks in and these effects are muted. At level 2, for instance, log changes in CR4 have a skewness of 0 and a kurtosis of 2.5. In other words, the changes are basically normal. This has nothing to do with synergies or with the value of concentration per se. It is just fat-tail econometrics. Ganapati (2018) claims that, because changes in concentration and changes in industry productivity are positively correlated on average, we need not worry about the (smaller) impact of concentration on prices.[19] The earlier reasoning suggests that this claim is incorrect.

C. Investment and Profits

Under σ and γ, the increase in concentration is driven by technological change linked to the rise of intangibles. In that case, aggregate investment would remain in line with Q, while intangible investment would increase. However, as shown in figure 10, the growth of the capital stock has fallen across all asset types since 2000, notably including intellectual property assets. Moreover, the decline in investment is not explained by Tobin's Q, as shown by figure A24 (available online). In fact, investment is near its historical trough while Q is near its historical peak.

Is the fall in investment pervasive across firms? In table 4, we define leaders by constant shares of market value to ensure comparability over time.[20] Capital K includes intangible capital as estimated by Peters and Taylor (2016). As shown, the leaders' share of investment and capital has decreased, while their profit margins have increased. By contrast, laggards exhibit much more stable investment and profit rates. As shown in figure A25 (available online), the increase in leader profits is not fully

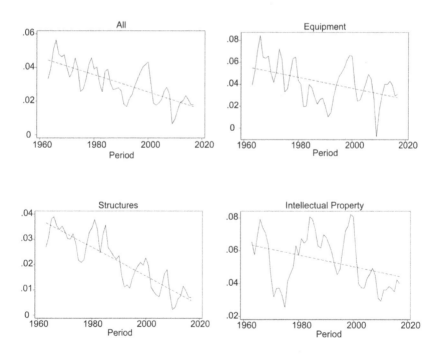

Fig. 10. Growth rates of capital stock. Growth rate of private nonresidential fixed assets, based on section 4.2 of the Bureau of Economic Analysis fixed assets tables.

Table 4
Investment, Capital, and Profits by Leaders and Laggards

	1980–95			1996–2017			Difference		
	Leaders	Mid	Laggards	Leaders	Mid	Laggards	Leaders	Mid	Laggards
	0–33 (%)	33–66 (%)	66–100 (%)	0–33 (%)	33–66 (%)	66–100 (%)	0–33 (%)	33–66 (%)	66–100 (%)
Share of OIBDP	.36	.33	.32	.35	.32	.33	.00	−.01	.01
Share of CAPX + R&D	.36	.32	.32	.33	.30	.36	−.02	−.02	.04
Share of PP&E	.34	.33	.33	.33	.29	.37	.00	−.04	.04
Share of K (CAPX + R&D)/ OIBDP	.33	.33	.33	.32	.31	.36	−.01	−.02	.03
OIADP/ SALE	.59	.58	.60	.43	.44	.52	−.16	−.14	−.08
	.13	.11	.09	.16	.14	.10	.03	.03	.01

Note: Table shows the weighted average value of a broad set of investment, capital, and profitability measures by time period and market value (MV). Leaders (laggards) include the firms with the highest (lowest) MV that combined account for 33% of MV within each industry and year. Annual data from Compustat. See appendix E (available online) for details. OIBDP = operating income before depreciation; CAPX = capital expenditures; R&D = research and development; PP&E = property, plant, and equipment; K = capital; OIADP = operating income before depreciation; SALE = sales.

explained by a reallocation effect with higher profit firms becoming leaders: profits increased within firms for leaders and decreased slightly for laggards.

Is the decline in investment by leaders linked to concentration? According to σ and γ, leaders should increase investment in concentrating industries, reflecting an escape-competition strategy (σ) or their increasing relative productivity (γ). We test this at the firm level by estimating the following regression for firm i that belongs to BEA industry j:

$$\Delta \log(K_{ijt}) = \beta_1 Q_{it-1} + \beta_2 CR8_{jt-1}^{IA} \times \text{Lead}_{i,j,t} + \beta_3 CR8_{jt-1}^{IA}$$
$$+ \beta_4 \text{Lead}_{ijt-1} + \beta_5 \log(\text{Age}_{it-1}) + \eta_t + \delta_i + \varepsilon_{it}, \tag{3}$$

where K_{it} is firm capital (property, plant, and equipment [PP&E], intangibles, or total), $CR8_{jt}^{IA}$ is the import-adjusted Census-based CR8, and $\text{Lead}_{i,j,t}$ is an indicator for a firm having a market value in the top quartile of segment k. We include Q_{it-1} and $\log(\text{Age}_{it-1})$ as controls, along with firm and year fixed effects (η_t and δ_i). β_2 is the coefficient of interest. Table 5

Table 5

Investment by Leaders in Concentrating Industries

	All			Mfg			NonMfg		
	$\Delta \log(\text{PPE})^a$	$\Delta \log(\text{Int}_{PT})^b$	$\Delta \log(K^{PT})^{a+b}$	$\Delta \log(\text{PPE})^a$	$\Delta \log(\text{Int}_{PT})^b$	$\Delta \log(K^{PT})^{a+b}$	$\Delta \log(\text{PPE})^a$	$\Delta \log(\text{Int}_{PT})^b$	$\Delta \log(K^{PT})^{a+b}$
	(1)	(2)	(3)	(4)	(5)	(6)	(7)	(8)	(9)
CR8^{IA}_{jt-1}	-10.98+	.58	-4.82	-17.10+	-3.49	-3.81	-7.06	12.13	-2.35
	(5.96)	(6.00)	(5.38)	(9.21)	(8.29)	(7.52)	(9.19)	(10.75)	(9.18)
$\text{CR8}^{IA}_{jt-1} \times \text{lead}_{it-1}$	-11.95*	-18.92**	-15.14**	1.44	-1.35	-1.15	-13.64*	-23.92**	-17.44**
	(4.66)	(5.80)	(4.51)	(7.20)	(9.58)	(7.25)	(6.10)	(7.53)	(5.90)
$\log Q_{it-1}$	13.45**	11.66**	12.90**	11.99**	9.85**	10.66**	15.60**	14.16**	15.96**
	(.43)	(.37)	(.35)	(.53)	(.42)	(.40)	(.73)	(.67)	(.61)
Lead_{it-1}	4.19**	3.83**	3.03**	3.69**	2.39	2.37+	2.47+	2.99+	1.51
	(.99)	(1.13)	(.91)	(1.42)	(1.67)	(1.32)	(1.38)	(1.72)	(1.38)
$\log \text{age}_{it-1}$	-15.11**	-18.85**	-17.17**	-15.50**	-18.31**	-17.34**	-14.36**	-19.29**	-16.75**
	(.78)	(.72)	(.64)	(1.03)	(.86)	(.83)	(1.18)	(1.25)	(1.00)
Year FE	Y	Y	Y	Y	Y	Y	Y	Y	Y
Firm FE	Y	Y	Y	Y	Y	Y	Y	Y	Y
R^2	.1	.12	.15	.098	.14	.16	.11	.12	.15
Observations	63,680	63,342	65,285	33,700	34,293	34,308	29,980	29,049	30,977

Note: Table shows the results of firm-level panel regressions of the log change in the stock of capital (K; deflated to 2009 prices) on import-adjusted concentration ratios (CR), following equation (3). Regression from 1997 to 2012 given the use of Census concentration measures. We consider three measures of capital: property, plant, and equipment (PP&E), intangibles (Int) defined as in Peters and Taylor (2016; abbreviated as PT), and their sum (total). Leaders (Lead) include firms with market value in the top quartile of the corresponding Bureau of Economic Analysis segment j for the given year. Q and log-age included as controls. As shown, leaders decrease investment with concentration rather than increase it. Annual data, primarily sourced from Compustat. Standard errors in parentheses are clustered at the firm level. Mfg = manufacturing industries; NonMfg = nonmanufacturing industries; FE = fixed effects.

+$p < .10$.

*$p < .05$.

**$p < .01$.

shows that with the exception of manufacturing, leaders in more concentrated industries underinvest. This is inconsistent with σ and γ but consistent with κ.

Case Study: The China Shock Again

Another way of investigating the role of κ for investment is to examine the behavior of leaders and laggards following the China shock. Figure 11 plots the average stock of K across Compustat firms in a given year, split by the 1999 NTR gap (see Section II for details). K includes PP&E as well as intangibles, as estimated by Peters and Taylor (2016). In low exposure industries, leaders and laggards exhibit similar growth rates of capital. By contrast, leaders increase capital much faster than laggards in high exposure industries.

Figure 11 suggests that leaders react to increased competition from China by increasing investment. We confirm this by estimating a generalized difference-in-differences (DiD) regression:

$$\log(K_{i,j,t}) = \beta_1 \text{Post01} \times \text{NTR Gap}_j \times \overline{\Delta \text{IP}_t}$$

$$+ \beta_2 \text{Post01} \times \text{NTR Gap}_j \times \overline{\Delta \text{IP}_t} \times \text{Leader}_{i,j,0} \qquad (4)$$

$$+ X'_{j,t}\gamma + \eta_t + \mu_i + \varepsilon_{it},$$

where the dependent variable is a given measure of capital for firm i in industry j during year t. $\overline{\Delta \text{IP}_t}$ captures time-series variation in Chinese competition averaged across all industries.[21] The first two terms on the right-hand side are the DiD terms of interest. The first one is an interaction between the NTR gap and $\overline{\Delta \text{IP}_t}$ for the post-2001 period. The second term adds an indicator for leader firms to capture differences in investment between leaders and laggards. The third term includes several industry-level characteristics as controls, such as capital and skill intensity.[22] We include year and firm fixed effects η_t and μ_i.

Table 6 reports the results. It shows that leaders increase investment in response to an exogenous increase in competition. We consider three different measures of capital: PP&E, intangibles (from Peters and Taylor 2016) and total capital (equal to the sum of PP&E and intangibles).[23] Columns 1–3 include all US incorporated manufacturing firms in Compustat over the 1991–2015 period. Columns 4–6 focus on continuing firms (i.e., firms that were in the sample before 1995 and after 2009) and show that leaders invested more than laggards, even when compared to firms that survived the China shock.

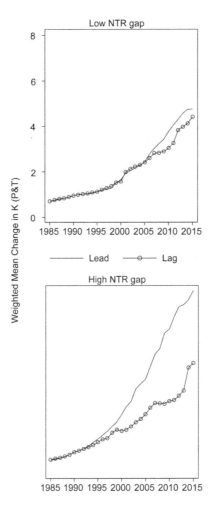

Fig. 11. Change in average firm K^{PT} by Chinese exposure (1991 = 1). Annual data from Compustat, Peters and Taylor (2016; abbreviated as P&T), Schott (2008), and Pierce and Schott (2016). Manufacturing industries only, split into high (above-median) and low (below-median) exposures based on the 1999 normal trade relations (NTR) gap. Leaders (Lead) defined as firms with market value in top quartile of the distribution within each North American Industry Classification System level 6 industry, as of 2001. Only firms-year pairs with non-missing K^{PT} included. K = capital; Lag = laggards.

Our results are consistent with Frésard and Valta (2015) and Hombert and Matray (2015). Frésard and Valta (2015) find a negative average impact of foreign competition in industries with low entry costs and strategic substitutes. They briefly study within-industry variation and find that investment declines primarily at financially constrained firms. Hombert

Table 6

Investment of Leaders and Laggards Following the Accession of China to the WTO

	All Firms			Continuing Firms		
	$\log(PPE_i)^a$ (1)	$\log(\text{Int}_i^{PT})^b$ (2)	$\log(k_i^{PT})^{a+b}$ (3)	$\log(PPE_i)^a$ (4)	$\log(\text{Int}_i^{PT})^b$ (5)	$\log(k_i^{PT})^{a+b}$ (6)
Post01 × NTRGap	-8.035**	-.426	-1.884	-11.214**	-3.284+	-4.670**
	(2.008)	(1.962)	(1.578)	(2.138)	(1.921)	(1.534)
Post01 × NTRGap × Lead	9.267**	6.978**	6.643**	9.601**	8.319**	7.998**
	(2.005)	(1.159)	(1.149)	(2.457)	(1.457)	(1.459)
Firm FE	Y	Y	Y	Y	Y	Y
Year FE	Y	Y	Y	Y	Y	Y
Industry controls	Y	Y	Y	Y	Y	Y
R^2	.14	.52	.49	.18	.57	.54
Observations	34,711	35,043	35,075	15,906	16,017	16,034

Note: Table shows the results of firm-level panel regressions of measures of capital on NTR Gap$_j$ × $\overline{\Delta IP_{jt}^{US}}$, following equation (4). We consider three measures of capital: gross property, plant, and equipment (PPE), intangibles (Int) defined as in Peters and Taylor (2016; abbreviated as PT) and their sum (total). Regression over 1991–2015 period. Leaders (Lead) defined as firms with market value in top quartile of the distribution within each North American Industry Classification System Level 6 industry, as of 2001. All regressions include measures of industry-level production structure as controls (see text for details). Only US-headquartered firms in manufacturing industries with non-missing K^{PT} included. Standard errors in parentheses are clustered at the industry level. WTO = World Trade Organization; NTR = normal trade relations; FE = fixed effects.

+$p < .10$.

**$p < .01$.

and Matray (2015) studies within-industry variation with a focus on firm-level R&D intensity. They show that R&D-intensive firms exhibit higher sales growth, profitability, and capital expenditures than low-R&D firms when faced with Chinese competition, consistent with our finding of increased intangible investment. They find evidence of product differentiation using the index of Hoberg and Phillips (2017). In the appendix of Gutiérrez and Philippon (2017), we study the dynamics of employment and find that leaders increase both capital and employment, while laggards decrease both. Employment decreases faster than capital so that K/Emp increases in both groups of firms. Since initial publication of these results in Gutiérrez and Philippon (2017), Pierce and Schott (2018) obtained similar results using Census data to cover the entire sample of US firms.

In summary, leader profit margins increased while investment relative to Q decreased, in line with κ. The falling growth rate of the capital stock—including intangibles—and the decline in leader investment, particularly in concentrated industries, is inconsistent with σ and γ.

D.   Returns to Scale

So far, we have evaluated the different theories indirectly by looking at their predictions about observable measures. In the case of γ, however, we can test the theory directly.

In Gutiérrez and Philippon (2019), we use industry- and firm-level data to estimate returns to scale. Industry-level estimates are based on BLS capital (K), labor (L), energy (E), materials (M), and service (S; KLEMS) data, following the methodology of Basu et al. (2006) while incorporating the instruments of Hall (2018). These estimates have the advantage of relying on well-measured inputs, outputs, and prices while following an established literature and set of instruments. However, the limited data availability implies that we can only estimate long-run average changes, such as an increase from before to after 2000. We perform this estimation and find a small increase in returns to scale, from 0.78 before 2000 to 0.8 afterward.

We complement industry-level estimates with firm-level estimates based on Compustat, roughly following Syverson (2004) and De Loecker et al. (2019). In particular, we estimate

$$\Delta\log q_{it} = \gamma\left[\alpha_V\Delta\log v + \alpha_K\Delta\log k + \alpha_X\Delta\log x\right] + \omega,$$

where γ measures the average return to scale across all firms. The variables v, k, and x denote COGS, capital costs, and overhead costs (SG&A), respectively. The equation $\alpha_V = P^V V / (P^V V + rK + P^X X)$ denotes the cost share of the COGS (likewise for α_K and α_X).[24] We again find stable estimates since 1970.

The relative stability of returns to scale is consistent with a variety of estimates in the literature, including Ho and Ruzic (2018) for manufacturing in the US, and Salas-Fumás, San Juan, and Vallés (2018) and Diez et al. (2019) across EU industries. Thus, γ cannot explain the aggregate trends, though it likely matters for some industries.

IV.   Industry Evidence

Aggregate trends are interesting, but they obscure the dynamics of individual industries: one size does not fit all. In this section, we perform a PCA on a wide range of variables related to competition (and covering all types of measures in table 1) to obtain a systematic classification of the drivers of industry-level changes. We follow the industry segments in the BLS KLEMS and perform the PCA on the correlation matrix, so all measures contribute equally. Because we include census-concentration ratios, agriculture and mining are excluded from the analysis.

Figure 12 shows the variables included in the analysis and the resulting loadings of the first two principal components. Together, these components explain 34% of the variance. They have an intuitive interpretation. PC1 seems to capture the σ and γ theories of good concentration. It exhibits a positive loading on the level and changes in concentration (cr4_cen) and a high loading on intangible capital intensity (intan_kshare). The corresponding industries face significant import competition (import_share) and exhibit stable or declining profits (profit_margin). TFP increases (dtfp_kl), and unit-labor costs fall (Dlogulc). Prices also fall (Dlogp) but less than unit-labor costs so that markups rise (Dlogmu). Leader turnover falls while the investment gap is close to zero.

PC2, by contrast, seems closely related to the κ theories of bad concentration. It captures a sharp increase in concentration despite limited growth in intangibles and negative import competition. Profits rise and the labor share falls. Markups also rise, but for inefficient reasons: prices rise while productivity and ULC remains largely flat.

Figure 13 contrasts the 2012 loadings on PC1 and PC2 for each industry. We highlight the six industries with the highest score according to

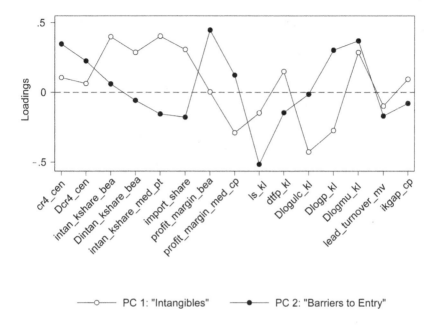

Fig. 12. Principal component (PC) loadings. See text for details and appendix E (available online) for definitions of variables. Cen = Census; BEA = Bureau of Economic Analysis industry accounts; PT = Peters and Taylor (2016); CP = Compustat; KL = capital (K), labor (L), energy (E), materials (M), and service (S; KLEMS); mv = market value; ikgap_cp = investment gap_compustat. See text for further details.

PC1 and PC2. Durable computer manufacturing, computer services, and nondurable apparel exhibit high loadings on PC1 and low loadings on PC2. They appear to remain strongly competitive despite increases in intangibles and concentration, likely as a result of foreign competition as shown in figure 14. In fact, figure 14 confirms the importance of foreign competition for domestic concentration and serves as a comforting validation of our PCA.

Nondurable chemical manufacturing, information (data), and information (publishing) present a mix of intangible-driven concentration and barriers to entry. These industries include Pfizer and Dow DuPont; Google and Facebook; and Microsoft, respectively. They are good examples of industries with large amounts of intangible assets—including patents—where leaders have become more efficient but also more entrenched over time.

Information (telecom), banking, and air transportation score near the top according to PC2. As discussed in Gutiérrez and Philippon (2018), these industries exhibit higher concentration, prices, and profitability

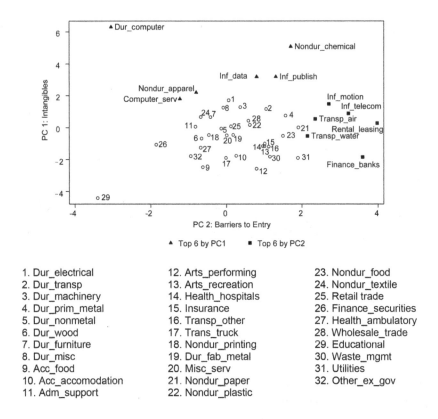

Fig. 13. Principal component (PC) scores, by industry. See text for details and appendix E (available online) for definitions of variables. Dur = durable; Nondur = nondurable; mgmt = management; Adm = administration; Acc = accommodation; Transp = transport; Misc = miscellaneous; Inf = information; serv = server; prim_metal = primary metal; fab_metal = fabricated metal; trans_truck = transportation truck.

in the US than in Europe, despite using similar technologies. Accommodation/food (i.e., restaurants) scores near the bottom according to both measures. This is an industry with limited use of intangible assets that remains largely competitive. The fact that education is the only real outlier is also comforting.

The PCA shows that both the κ theory and a combination of σ and γ are important for explaining the evolution of US industries over the past 20 years. But are they equally important at each point in time? Figure 15 plots the average PC1 and PC2 scores over time. The conclusions are striking. The average PC1 score, reflecting "good" concentration, was substantially higher and increased faster from 1997 to 2002. But PC2 (i.e.,

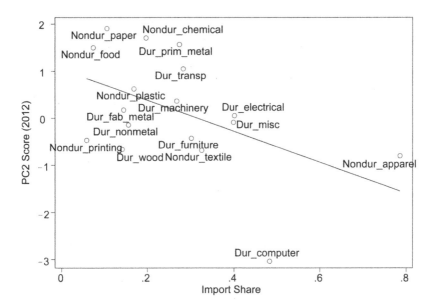

Fig. 14. Principal component (PC2) scores ("barriers to entry") versus import shares. PC2 scores as of 2012 versus industry-level import shares, defined as the ratio of industry-level imports to gross output plus imports. Imports from Peter Schott's website; gross output from the Bureau of Economic Analysis gross domestic product by industry accounts. Dur = durable; Nondur = nondurable; Misc = miscellaneous; transp = transport.

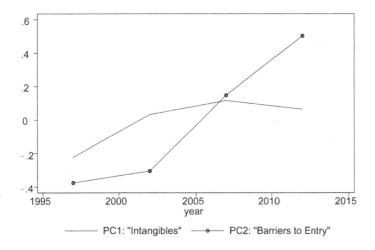

Fig. 15. Evolution of the average scores for principal components PC1 and PC2

barriers to entry) caught up afterward. By 2012, most industries weighted heavily on PC2 while the average PC1 score remained close to zero (with wide dispersion, of course, as shown in fig. 13).

V. Conclusion

A. *Internal Consistency of Macro-market Power Literature*

We have used a wide range of measures of competition throughout this paper, sometimes independently and sometimes jointly, albeit nonparametrically. But all of these measures are connected by economic theory. Let us conclude by bringing together estimates from the macro-market power literature to validate the internal consistency of our conclusions. A decomposition first made by Susanto Basu in his discussion of De Loecker et al. (2019) is useful. We describe the decomposition briefly and refer the reader to Syverson (2019) for a discussion of the underlying assumptions.

Consider a standard profit-maximizing economy, and rewrite the markup by multiplying and dividing by average costs:

$$\mu = \frac{P}{MC} = \frac{P}{AC}\frac{AC}{MC} = \frac{AC}{MC}\frac{\text{Revenue}}{\text{Cost}}.$$

The ratio of average to marginal costs, AC/MC, equals the returns to scale for a cost-minimizing firm taking factor prices as given while Revenue/Cost can be written as $1/(1 - s_\pi)$ using the profit share in revenues s_π. Therefore,

$$\mu = \frac{\gamma}{1 - s_\pi}. \tag{5}$$

Using equation (5) for two time periods, we obtain

$$\frac{\mu_{2016}}{\mu_{1980}} = \left(\frac{1 - s_{\pi,1980}}{1 - s_{\pi,2016}}\right)\frac{\gamma_{2016}}{\gamma_{1980}},$$

which can be used to assess the internal consistency of the macro-market power literature.

Let us begin by reiterating the discrepancy raised by Syverson (2019) and Basu (2019). De Loecker et al. (2019) report an increase in markups from 1.21 to 1.61 between 1980 and 2016 and an increase in returns to scale from 1.03 to 1.08. Barkai (2017) estimates rising profit shares from 3% to 16% of value added over the same period, which (roughly) equate to 1.5% and 8% of sales. Plugging in these values, we obtain

$$\frac{1.61}{1.21} = \left(\frac{1 - 0.015}{1 - 0.08} \right) \frac{1.08}{1.03},$$

$$1.33 = 1.12.$$

The relationship appears widely inconsistent but there is an issue with this comparison. The markup estimates of De Loecker et al. (2019) are based on public firms, which likely have higher intangible (and SG&A) intensity than private firms—certainly more than small and medium enterprises. For the reasons discussed in Section II, this leads to an overestimation of the rise in markups for the full economy. As a rough approximation, let us assume that markups of private firms remained stable, in line with the median Compustat firm as reported in figure 8a of De Loecker et al. (2019). This is valid if the distribution of high intangible firms, and therefore markup increases, is concentrated at the top. We can then obtain a rough estimate of the change in economy-wide markups as the product of the Compustat markup increase (33%) times the Compustat share of sales in the total economy (40% as reported by Grullon et al. 2019). The resulting markup increase is then 13.2%, which seems consistent with the estimates above. Using our return to scale estimates, the last term would be 0.8/0.78—again broadly in agreement.[25]

B. Explaining the Rise in κ

Estimates from the macro-market power literature appear reasonably consistent with each other. They include a sharp increase in profits unique to the US, concentrated in the post-2000 period and explained mostly by rising barriers to entry. The next question is, of course: What might explain the rise in κ in the US? Gutiérrez and Philippon (2018) argue that this is partly explained by weakening competition policy (i.e., antitrust and regulation) compared to Europe. Gutiérrez and Philippon (2019) show that the decline in the elasticity of entry to Q is partly explained by lobbying and increasing federal and state-level regulations.[26] Last, Jones et al. (2019) combine a rich structural dynamic stochastic general equilibrium model with cross-sectional identification from firm and industry data. They use the model to structurally estimate entry cost shocks and show that model-implied entry shocks correlate with independently constructed measures of entry regulation and merger and acquisition activities.

Endnotes

Author email addresses: Covarrubias (mc5851@nyu.edu), Gutiérrez (ggutierr@stern .nyu.edu), Philippon (tphilipp@stern.nyu.edu). This paper was prepared for the *NBER Macroeconomics Annual* 2019. Some of the results presented in the text were first published in Gutiérrez and Philippon (2017). We are grateful to the Smith Richardson Foundation for a research grant, to Janice Eberly and Chad Syverson for their discussion, and to Erik Hurst and participants at the NBER Macro Annual conference for helpful comments and suggestions. For acknowledgments, sources of research support, and disclosure of the authors' material financial relationships, if any, please see https://www.nber.org/chapters /c14237.ack.

1. See Autor et al. (2017a) for a longer time-series of US Census–based concentration measures under a consistent segmentation. The series in Autor et al. (2017a) exhibit similar trends: concentration begins to increase between 1992 and 1997 for retail trade and services and between 1997 and 2002 for the remaining sectors.

2. One could entertain other hypotheses, such as weak demand or credit constraints, but previous research has shown that they do not fit the facts. See Gutiérrez and Philippon (2016) for detailed discussions and references.

3. Furman (2015) also emphasizes the weakness of corporate fixed investment and points out that low investment has coincided with high private returns to capital, implying an increase in the payout rate (dividends and share buybacks).

4. For figure 2, we measure concentration as the ratio of sales by the eight largest firms in Compustat that belong to a given capital (K), labor (L), energy (E), materials (M), and service (S; KLEMS) industry × region to total Gross Output reported in OECD STAN. Corporate consolidation is therefore accounted for, as dictated by accounting rules. Appendix A (available online) provides additional details on the calculation, while Gutiérrez and Philippon (2018) provide a detailed comparison across a wide range of concentration measures for the US and Europe. Bajgar et al. (2019) use Orbis data to include private firms and take into account that some firms are part of larger business groups. When they measure concentration at the business group level within two-digit industries, they find a moderate increase in concentration in Europe, with the unweighted average CR8 increasing from 21.5% to 25.1%. In North America, CR8 increases from 30.3% to 38.4%.

5. These comparisons aggregate across industry categories and may therefore be affected by changes in industry mix. However, Gutiérrez and Philippon (2018) reach similar conclusions using industry-level data. Moreover, in Gutiérrez and Philippon (2017), we compare the evolution of the five industries that concentrate the most in the US against Europe. We find that concentration, profits, and Q increased in the US, while investment decreased. By contrast, concentration and investment remained (relatively) stable in Europe, despite lower profits and lower Q. This is true even though these industries use the same technology and are exposed to the same foreign competition. For more details on the labor share, see Gutiérrez and Piton (2019) and Cette, Koehl, and Philippon (2019).

6. We derive most but not all of these in Section I. For predictions on leader investment, see Gutiérrez and Philippon (2017).

7. In this model, an increase in returns to scale corresponds to a shift toward a high productivity, high fixed cost technology.

8. Gutiérrez and Philippon (2017) report similar results using Herfindahls and the data of Feenstra and Weinstein (2017).

9. We follow Autor et al. (2016) and define import penetration for industry j at time t as $\Delta IP_{jt} = \Delta M_{jt}^{UC}/(Y_{j,91} + M_{j,91} - E_{j,91})$, where ΔM_{jt}^{UC} denotes the change in US imports from China from 1991 to t; and $Y_{j,91} + M_{j,91} - E_{j,91}$ denotes the initial absorption (defined as output,

$Y_{j,91}$, plus imports, $M_{j,91}$, minus exports, $E_{j,91}$). $Y_{j,91}$ is sourced from the NBER-CES database and $M_{j,91}$ and $E_{j,91}$ are based on Peter Schott's data. Only NAICS level 6 industries where data are available across all sources are included in the analyses.

10. Until 2001, China was considered a nonmarket economy. It was subject to relatively high tariff rates (known as "non-normal trade relations" tariffs or "non-NTR rates") as prescribed in the Smoot-Hawley Tariff Act of 1930. From 1980 onward, US presidents began temporarily granting NTR tariff rates to China but required annual reapproval by Congress. The reapproval process introduced substantial uncertainty around future tariff rates and limited investment by both US and Chinese firms (see Pierce and Schott 2016 for a wide range of anecdotal and news-based evidence). This ended in 2001, when China entered the WTO and the US granted PNTR. The granting of PNTR removed uncertainty around tariffs, leading to an increase in competition.

11. SALE/COGS is related to the benchmark measure of De Loecker et al. (2019) up to a measurement error correction and a (time-varying) industry-level scaling factor, which measures the elasticity of SALES to COGS. Both the measurement error correction and the elasticity of output remain largely stable even in the long run so that SALE/COGS dominates the evolution of markups.

12. In unreported tests, we find similar conclusions using the firm-level user-cost markups first reported in the appendix of Gutiérrez and Philippon (2017), and studying regulatory shocks (the entry of Free Mobile in France and the implementation of large product market regulations, as compiled by Duval et al. 2018).

13. See De Loecker and Eeckhout (2018) for actual markup estimates globally. As expected, their results closely follow the SALE/COGS series.

14. This is not to say that profits are a perfect measure. Accounting rules often deviate from economic concepts, and estimates of economic profits are prone to errors given the difficulty in measuring the capital stock and the user cost of capital. We can gain some comfort, however, by comparing a wide range of measures from alternate sources. In Gutiérrez and Philippon (2018), for example, we show that accounting profits from Compustat and national accounts, economic profits in the style of Barkai (2017) and firm-level user-cost implied profits are consistent with each other in both the US and Europe.

15. See Rossi-Hansberg, Sarte, and Trachter (2018), among others, for related evidence, but note that their conclusions are controversial (Ganapati 2018).

16. We use a constant number of leaders because they account for a roughly stable share of sales. In unreported tests, we consider the top 10% of firms and obtain similar results, though this broader group accounts for a rising share of sales.

17. Figure A20 (available online) presents an additional test, based on the correlation of firm rankings over time. It yields consistent results.

18. For manufacturing, the NBER-CES database includes nominal output, prices, wages, and employment. For nonmanufacturing, the concentration accounts include nominal output, payroll, and employment, while the BEA's "detailed" GDP by industry accounts include prices. The detailed GDP by industry accounts include about 400 industries so that our nonmanufacturing data set is more aggregated than that of Ganapati (2018). We use the more aggregated data set given the concerns with skewness described in the text and because, even at that level of aggregation, the BEA cautions of potential measurement error. That said, our results are largely consistent.

19. Ganapati (2018, 9) estimates the following relationship:

$$\Delta_5 \log(P_{jt}) = 0.00992 \times \Delta_5 \log(CR4) - 0.0520 \times \Delta_5 \log(LP) + \gamma_{s,t} + \varepsilon_{jt},$$

which implies that "a one standard deviation increase in monopoly power offsets 1/5 of the price decrease from a one standard deviation increase in productivity." He argues that "the most pessimistic reading is that after controlling for productivity, monopolies do increase prices. But this argument assumes that all other conditions including productivity remain constant. In the light of the close linkage of productivity and concentration, this seems untenable."

20. Operating income before depreciation shares are stable, which is consistent with stable shares of market value and stable relative discount factors. Because firms are discrete,

the actual share of market value in each grouping varies from year to year. To improve comparability, we scale measured shares as if they each contained 33% of market value.

21. Gutiérrez and Philippon (2017) present results excluding $\overline{\Delta IP}_{j,t}$ to mirror the specification of Pierce and Schott (2016) as well as following the approach of Autor et al. (2016)—which instruments $\Delta IP_{j,t}^{US}$ with the import penetration of eight other advanced economies ($\Delta IP_{j,t}^{OC}$).

22. These industry characteristics are sourced from the NBER-CES database. We include the (i) percent of production workers, (ii) log-ratio of capital to employment, (iii) log-ratio of capital to value added, (iv) log-average wage, and (v) log-average production wage.

23. In unreported robustness tests, we confirm that our results are robust to including only balance sheet intangibles or excluding goodwill in the Peters and Taylor (2016) measure.

24. De Loecker et al. (2019) perform the same estimation in levels and find an increase in returns to scale from 0.97 to 1.08. However, levels regressions are likely affected by the inability to control for differences in firm-level prices or to accurately measure intangible capital. For example, an increase in the markups of large relative to small firms would appear as an increase in quantities and result in an overestimation of the increase in returns to scale. The estimation based on changes better controls for this, hence is likely more robust.

25. We can perform a similar exercise since 2000, using the results of Diez et al. (2019), which are based on Orbis data and therefore include private firms. According to their estimates, US markups increased by 12% since 2000 while returns to scale increased from 0.91 to 0.93. Over the same period, Barkai (2017) reports profit shares of value added rising from 4.5% to 16%. We then have

$$1.12 = \left(\frac{1 - 0.023}{1 - 0.08}\right)\frac{0.93}{0.91},$$

$$1.12 = 1.09.$$

We may also want to consider total economy profit shares, instead of nonfinancial corporation profit shares. Gutiérrez (2017) uses BEA data for the nonfinancial private economy. He finds an increase in the profit share from 11% to 21% from 1988 to 2015, which closely aligns with Barkai (2017) over the same period. Last, performing the same exercise for Europe with markup and returns to scale estimates from Diez et al. (2019) and profit share estimates from the appendix of Gutiérrez and Philippon (2018; accounting only for the cost of debt to mirror Barkai [2017]), we obtain

$$1.06 = \left(\frac{1 - 0.036}{1 - 0.038}\right)\frac{0.93}{0.91},$$

$$1.06 = 1.03.$$

Again, broadly in agreement.

26. In unreported tests, we confirm there is a positive relationship between PC2 and industry-level lobbying intensity.

References

Aghion, P., A. Bergeaud, T. Boppart, P. J. Klenow, and H. Li. 2019. "A Theory of Falling Growth and Rising Rents." Working Paper no. 26448 (November), NBER, Cambridge, MA.

Akcigit, U., and S. Ates. 2019. "Ten Facts on Declining Business Dynamism and Lessons from Endogenous Growth Theory." Working Paper no. 25755 (January), NBER, Cambridge, MA.

Alexander, L., and J. Eberly. 2018. "Investment Hollowing Out." *IMF Economic Review* 66 (1): 5–30.

Autor, D. H., D. Dorn, and G. H. Hanson. 2013. "The China Syndrome: Local Labor Market Effects of Import Competition in the United States." *American Economic Review* 103 (6): 2121–68.

———. 2016. "The China Shock: Learning from Labor-Market Adjustment to Large Changes in Trade." *Annual Review of Economics* 8 (1): 205–40.

Autor, D. H., D. Dorn, G. H. Hanson, G. Pisano, and P. Shu. 2016. "Foreign Competition and Domestic Innovation: Evidence from US Patents." Working Paper no. 22879 (December), NBER, Cambridge, MA.

Autor, D., D. Dorn, L. Katz, C. Patterson, and J. Van Reenen. 2017a. "Concentrating on the Fall of the Labor Share." *American Economic Review* 107 (5): 180–85.

———. 2017b. "The Fall of the Labor Share and the Rise of Superstar Firms." Working Paper no. 23396, NBER, Cambridge, MA.

Bain, J. S. 1951. "Relation of Profit Rate to Industry Concentration: American Manufacturing, 1936–1940." *Quarterly Journal of Economics* 65 (3): 293–324.

Bajgar, M., G. Berlingieri, S. Calligaris, C. Criscuolo, and J. Timmis. 2019. "Industry Concentration in Europe and North America." OECD Productivity Working Paper no. 18, OECD Publishing, Paris.

Barkai, S. 2017. "Declining Labor and Capital Shares." Working paper, University of Chicago.

Basu, S. 2019. "Are Price-Cost Markups Rising in the United States? A Discussion of the Evidence." Working Paper no. 26057, NBER, Cambridge, MA.

Basu, S., J. G. Fernald, and M. S. Kimball. 2006. "Are Technology Improvements Contractionary?" *American Economic Review* 96 (5): 1418–48.

Basu, S., J. G. Fernald, N. Oulton, and S. Srinivasan. 2003. "The Case of the Missing Productivity Growth." *NBER Macroeconomics Annual* 18:9–63.

Bernard, A. B., J. B. Jensen, S. J. Redding, and P. K. Schott. 2012. "The Empirics of Firm Heterogeneity and International Trade." *Annual Review of Economics* 4 (1): 283–313.

Bernard, A. B., J. B. Jensen, and P. K. Schott. 2006. "Survival of the Best Fit: Exposure to Low-Wage Countries and the (Uneven) Growth of US Manufacturing Plants." *Journal of International Economics* 68 (1): 219–37.

Bessen, J. 2017. "Information Technology and Industry Concentration." Law and Economics Paper no. 17-41, Boston University School of Law.

Blanchard, O. 2003. "Comment on Basu et al." *NBER Macroeconomics Annual* 18:64–71.

Bloom, N., M. Draca, and J. Van Reenen. 2016. "Trade Induced Technical Change: The Impact of Chinese Imports on Innovation, Diffusion and Productivity." *Review of Economic Studies* 83 (1): 87–117.

CEA (Council of Economic Advisors). 2016. "Benefits of Competition and Indicators of Market Power." Issue Brief (April). https://obamawhitehouse.archives.gov/sites/default/files/page/files/20160414_cea_competition_issue_brief.pdf.

Cette, Gilbert, Lorraine Koehl, and Thomas Philippon. 2019. "Labor Shares in Some Advanced Economies." Working Paper no. 26136 (August), NBER, Cambridge, MA.

Crouzet, N., and J. Eberly. 2018. "Understanding Weak Capital Investment: The Role of Market Concentration and Intangibles." Paper prepared for Federal Reserve Bank of Kansas City's Jackson Hole Economic Policy Symposium.

De Loecker, J., and J. Eeckhout. 2018. "Global Market Power." Working Paper no. 24768, NBER, Cambridge, MA.

De Loecker, J., J. Eeckhout, and G. Unger. 2019. "The Rise of Market Power and the Macroeconomic Implications." Working Paper no. 23687, NBER, Cambridge, MA.

De Loecker, J., and F. Warzynski. 2012. "Markups and Firm-Level Export Status." *American Economic Review* 102 (6): 2437–71.

Decker, R. A., J. Haltiwanger, R. S. Jarmin, and J. Miranda. 2015. "Where Has All the Skewness Gone? The Decline in High-Growth (Young) Firms in the US." Research Paper no. 15-43, Center for Economic Studies, US Census Bureau, Washington, DC.

Demsetz, H. 1973. "Industry Structure, Market Rivalry, and Public Policy." *Journal of Law and Economics* 16 (1): 1–9.

Diez, F. J., J. Fan, and C. Villegas-Sanchez. 2019. "Global Declining Competition." IMF Working Paper no. 19/82, International Monetary Fund, Washington, DC.

Duval, R., D. Furceri, B. Hu, J. T. Jalles, and H. Nguyen. 2018. "A Narrative Database of Major Labor and Product Market Reforms in Advanced Economies." IMF Working Paper no. 18/19, International Monetary Fund, Washington, DC.

Eggertsson, G. B., J. A. Robbins, and E. G. Wold. 2018. "Kaldor and Piketty's Facts: The Rise of Monopoly Power in the United States." Working Paper no. 24287 (February), NBER, Cambridge, MA.

Elsby, M., B. Hobijn, and A. Sahin. 2013. "The Decline of the US Labor Share." *Brookings Papers on Economic Activity* 44 (2): 1–63.

Feenstra, Robert, Hong Ma, and Yuan Xu. 2017. "The China Syndrome: Local Labor Market Effects of Import Competition in the United States: Comment." Unpublished Manuscript, University of California, Davis.

Feenstra, R. C., and D. E. Weinstein. 2017. "Globalization, Markups and US Welfare." *Journal of Political Economy* 125 (4): 1040–74.

Fernald, J. G., R. E. Hall, J. H. Stock, and M. W. Watson. 2017. "The Disappointing Recovery of Output after 2009." Brookings Papers on Economic Activity (Spring), Brookings Institution, Washington, DC.

Frésard, L., and P. Valta. 2015. "How Does Corporate Investment Respond to Increased Entry Threat?" *Review of Corporate Finance Studies* 5 (1): 1–35.

Furman, J. 2015. "Business Investment in the United States: Facts, Explanations, Puzzles, and Policies." Working paper (September 30), Progressive Policy Institute, Washington, DC.

Ganapati, S. 2018. "Growing Oligopolies, Prices, Output, and Productivity." Research Paper no. 18-48, Center for Economic Studies, US Census Bureau, Washington, DC.

Grullon, G., Y. Larkin, and R. Michaely. 2019. "Are US Industries Becoming More Concentrated?" *Review of Finance* 23 (4): 697–743.

Gutiérrez, G. 2017. "Investigating Global Labor and Profit Shares." Unpublished Working Paper, SSRN.

Gutiérrez, G., and T. Philippon. 2016. "Investment-less Growth: An Empirical Investigation." Working Paper no. 22897, NBER, Cambridge, MA.

———. 2017. "Declining Competition and Investment in the US." Working Paper no. 23583, NBER, Cambridge, MA.

———. 2018. "How EU Markets Became More Competitive Than US Markets: A Study of Institutional Drift." Working Paper no. 24700, NBER, Cambridge, MA.

———. 2019. "The Failure of Free Entry." Working Paper no. 26001, NBER, Cambridge, MA.

Gutiérrez Gallardo, German and Sophie Piton. 2019. "Revisiting the Global Decline of the (Non-Housing) Labor Share." Bank of England Working Paper

No. 811 (19 July). https://ssrn.com/abstract=3422923; http://dx.doi.org/10.2139/ssrn.3422923.

Hall, R. E. 2015. "Quantifying the Lasting Harm to the US Economy from the Financial Crisis." *NBER Macroeconomics Annual* 29:71–128.

———. 2018. "New Evidence on the Markup of Prices over Marginal Costs and the Role of Mega-Firms in the US Economy." Working Paper no. 24574, NBER, Cambridge, MA.

Haltiwanger, J., R. Jarmin, and J. Miranda. 2011. "Historically Large Decline in Job Creation from Startup and Existing Firms in the 2008–2009 Recession." Business Dynamics Statistics Briefing (March), US Census Bureau, Washington, DC.

Haskel, J., and S. Westlake. 2017. *Capitalism without Capital: The Rise of the Intangible Economy*. Princeton, NJ: Princeton University Press.

Ho, S. J., and D. Ruzic. 2018. "Returns to Scale, Productivity Measurement, and Trends in US Manufacturing Misallocation." 2018 Meeting Papers No. 119, Society for Economic Dynamics. https://ideas.repec.org/p/red/sed018/119.html.

Hoberg, G., and G. Phillips. 2017. "Text-Based Network Industries and Endogenous Product Differentiation." *Journal of Political Economy* 124 (5): 1423–65.

Hombert, J., and A. Matray. 2015. "Can Innovation Help US Manufacturing Firms Escape Import Competition from China?" Research Paper no. FIN-2015-1075, HEC Paris.

Hopenhayn, H. 1992. "Entry, Exit, and Firm Dynamics in Long Run Equilibrium." *Econometrica* 60 (5): 1127–50.

Hortacsu, A., and C. Syverson. 2015. "The Ongoing Evolution of US Retail: A Format Tug-of-War." *Journal of Economic Perspectives* 29 (4): 89–112.

Hsieh, C.-T., and E. Rossi-Hansberg. 2019. "The Industrial Revolution in Services." Working Paper no. 25968, NBER, Cambridge, MA.

IMF (International Monetary Fund). 2014. "Private Investment: What's the Holdup?" In *World Economic Outlook: Legacies, Clouds, Uncertainties*, chap. 4. Washington, DC: International Monetary Fund.

Jones, C., G. Gutiérrez, and T. Philippon. 2019. "Entry Costs and the Macroeconomy." Working Paper no. 25609, NBER, Cambridge, MA.

Karabarbounis, L., and B. Neiman. 2014. "The Global Decline of the Labor Share." *Quarterly Journal of Economics* 129 (1): 61–103.

Kehrig, M., and N. Vincent. 2017. "Growing Productivity without Growing Wages: The Micro-level Anatomy of the Aggregate Labor Share Decline." ERID Working Paper no. 244, Economic Research Initiatives at Duke, Durham, NC.

Lee, D., H.-H. Shin, and R. M. Stulz. 2016. "Why Does Capital No Longer Flow More to the Industries with the Best Growth Opportunities?" Working Paper no. 2016-15, Fisher College of Business, Columbus, OH.

Peters, R. H., and L. A. Taylor. 2016. "Intangible Capital and the Investment-q Relation." *Journal of Financial Economics* 123 (2): 251–72.

Pierce, J. R., and P. K. Schott. 2016. "The Surprisingly Swift Decline of US Manufacturing Employment." *American Economic Review* 106 (7): 1632–62.

———. 2018. "Investment Responses to Trade Liberalization: Evidence from US Industries and Establishments." *Journal of International Economics* 115:203–22.

Ridder, M. D. 2019. "Market Power and Innovation in the Intangible Economy." Discussion Paper no. CFM-DP2019-07, Centre for Macroeconomics, London.

Rossi-Hansberg, E., P.-D. Sarte, and N. Trachter. 2018. "Diverging Trends in National and Local Concentration." Working Paper no. 25066, NBER, Cambridge, MA.

Salas-Fumás, V., L. San Juan, and J. Vallés. 2018. "Corporate Cost and Profit Shares in the Euro Area and the US: The Same Story?" Working Paper no. 1833, Banco de España, Madrid.

Schmalensee, R. 1987. "Collusion versus Differential Efficiency: Testing Alternative Hypotheses." *Journal of Industrial Economics* 35 (4): 399–425.

Schott, P. 2008. "The Relative Sophistication of Chinese Exports." *Economic Policy* 23 (53): 6–49.

Syverson, C. 2004. "Market Structure and Productivity: A Concrete Example." *Journal of Political Economy* 112 (6): 1181–222.

———. 2019. "Macroeconomics and Market Power: Facts, Potential Explanations, and Open Questions." Report, Brookings Economic Studies (January), Brookings Institution, Washington, DC.

Van Reenen, J. 2018. "Increasing Differences Between Firms: Market Power and the Macro-Economy." CEP Discussion Paper no. 1576, Centre for Economic Performance, London.

Comment

Janice Eberly, *Kellogg School of Management, Northwestern University, and NBER*

The paper by Covarrubias, Gutiérrez, and Philippon provides many useful insights into the rapidly emerging literature on rising concentration in US industries. Importantly, it catalogs some important empirical shortcomings in the literature. It also provides clarity on conceptual issues that have created confusion. The paper goes on to make two types of original empirical contributions. In the first, it focuses on two categories of explanations for rising concentration: "good" and "bad." The former is associated with technological change that increases the elasticity of substitution among goods (σ, and hence greater competition) or increases firms' accumulation of intangible capital (γ, perhaps associated with network externalities and returns to scale). Bad concentration is instead associated with rising barriers to entry, κ. The authors argue that the data tend to favor good concentration earlier in their data sample—through 2000. Thereafter, there is increasing evidence of barriers to competition. The collection of evidence, while not dispositive, moves the weight of the evidence toward market power explanations, especially later in the sample. The last part of the paper takes a different tack. Instead of looking for indicators of market power to explain a broad range of facts, the paper looks at combinations of explanations by industry and argues that there is merit in several of them and that the results vary by industry. I will argue that these last insights are especially helpful, as the macroeconomic data are unlikely to be captured by a single simple narrative.

I. Rising Concentration

The paper first documents the fact that has captured the imagination of many authors: concentration seems to have risen in many US industries. This tendency has been found using various measures, in different data sets, at varying levels of aggregation. Using Compustat data, for example, we find (Crouzet and Eberly 2019) that the Herfindahl index of sales in Compustat firms has increased by at least 50% in 75% of US industries since mid-1990s. Similar results are cited in the paper. What to make of that finding is much less clear, and the explanation for rising concentration is important. Some explanations, such as rising market power, may give rise to economic inefficiencies (though they need not), whereas others, such as the rise of more productive "superstar" firms, may be efficient. Observing concentration alone is not sufficient to know.

A growing body of research has developed to understand the reasons behind the rise in concentration. This paper first does a service to this literature by codifying methodological points. The first is on measuring markups, which are often used as a way of measuring market power. The simple point is that fixed costs make it difficult to measure markups. If the researcher wants to measure the markup over variable cost, the presence of fixed costs can confound the estimate, especially in accounting data where fixed and variable costs are not well differentiated. In practice, using Compustat accounting data for publicly traded firms, a simple measure of markups is the retail value of output (sales) over the cost of goods sold (COGS), treating COGS as the measure of variable cost. The other component of costs in Compustat is sales, general, and administrative expenses (SG&A). Some researchers treat this as a fixed cost, which is therefore excluded from the denominator of the markup calculation. Using that approach, the estimated markup is large and rising, as the components of SG&A have risen over time, reflecting the growing role of intangible capital, marketing expenses, and other expenses. Covarrubias et al. argue that these expenses are entirely variable and instead add them to the denominator of the markup. Using this approach, they find a smaller, though still rising, markup. In practice, the truth is likely in between, as the SG&A category includes some expenses, such as human resources, branding, and marketing, that have some element of overhead or fixed costs. But the discussion in the paper frames the issue and scales it quantitatively. The ultimate answer to the data quandary probably lies in getting better measures of market power than allowed by currently available accounting data.

The second methodological improvement of the paper is moving beyond macro data and using industries to measure concentration. This is the approach used in Crouzet and Eberly (2019), recognizing that firms' markets (and hence market power) are likely defined at a disaggregated level. I expect that economists and lawyers who focus on antitrust issues would find the Standard Industrial Classification (SIC) and North American Industry Classification System (NAICS) industry definitions to be frustratingly crude and only tangentially related to the true nature of competition between firms. However, if these industry classifications were arbitrary, then we would expect to find little when examining concentration and the characteristics of these industries. To the contrary, the authors find much. Nonetheless, it is worth remembering that firms compete across industries; for example, Google and Amazon are increasingly competing for advertising dollars, but they are in quite different industries based on the SIC and NAICS definitions (internet search versus electronics retailing).

II. Why Has Concentration Risen? Looking at Individual Explanations

The first part of the empirical section focuses on the potential explanations for the rise in concentration. These explanations are mapped into parameters of the model laid out in the paper: the demand elasticity and the returns to scale (σ and γ that lead to "good concentration" from substitutability and intangibles), and barriers to entry (κ that leads to "bad concentration," from barriers to entry). Although the paper has a useful model that can give rise to concentration, the mapping to the data is less clear in two dimensions. First, as the authors note, the explanations are not mutually exclusive, so they could be operating in concert and even interacting. Intangibles, such as software and intellectual property, are not simply substitutes with physical capital in the production function, and may have properties, such as scalability and excludability, that are more connected to increasing returns and network externalities, for example. Second, the empirical tests generally focus on objects such as market leaders and churn that may not connect directly to a single parameter or property of the model. Hence, it can be hard to interpret the empirical findings as evidence for a single driver of concentration or even a category such as good or bad. They are more generally associated with market power and hence indicative of a root cause.

A. Measurement Questions

The paper implements a battery of tests to examine the relationship between concentration, markups, and various metrics, such as market share, entry/churn, and investment. Measurement is always a concern, but I would note two relevant issues in this line of research. The paper reasonably uses investment as an indicator of firm outcomes. However, with intangibles, there are a number of potential measures at the firm, industry, and aggregate level. Aggregation can be problematic empirically, as these measures have different trends: intangibles are generally growing, while physical capital has tended to stagnate or even decline. Hence, for example, the choice of numerator and denominator in investment rates requires some care, and it is not hard to induce mechanical trends by using different measures of investment. In particular, the capitalized spending on SG&A, as in Peters and Taylor (2017), has no counterpart in the industry and aggregate data, and its trends can be very large. These choices can have consequences for how we view industry leaders, for example, as they tend to be intangibles intensive.

The analysis of market leaders is one of the most novel and interesting parts of the empirical analysis. One concern, though, is the substantial evidence (Stulz and Kahle 2017) documenting the shrinking number of public firms. Because the Compustat data include only publicly traded firms, the denominator is shrinking in all of the concentration measures. This decline is also relevant for the entry and turnover analysis in the paper, suggesting some caution in interpreting these results.

B. Multiple Rather Than Single Explanations

A final question is how to interpret the individual empirical tests examining one hypothesis at a time, even if grouped into good versus bad. There is an Occam's razor appeal to finding a single explanation, such as market power, for a panoply of facts. In contrast, as the authors acknowledge, these explanations are not mutually exclusive and describe a broad set of interrelated macroeconomic outcomes over decades. For example, intangible capital, such as patents, may create barriers to entry. Similarly, firms may invest in barriers to entry, which are then endogenous. It may be more fruitful to think of the empirical evidence presented here as more of a collage of evidence than single "smoking gun" that favors a particular explanation at a point in time.

As an example, a recent paper by Farhi and Gourio (2018) allows for a changing capital share, intangible capital, and a rising risk premium simultaneously in a macro growth model. They find that several forces, especially the rising risk premium, are necessary to explain the macro data. Notably, the rising risk premium needed to match the cost of capital (when the risk-free rate is low) already puts downward pressure on capital accumulation. Hence, rents from market power and intangible capital actually work to raise the capital stock to measured levels. This is quite a different mechanism than emphasized in Covarrubias et al. It may or may not be correct, but it illustrates the potentially complex forces when more than one explanation is allowed. This is particularly important when the question is quantitative, not just directional.

Modeling multiple explanations can also produce quantitatively important interactions. In current work with Nicolas Crouzet (Crouzet and Eberly 2019), we allow for both market power and intangible capital in a Q model of investment. We specify a revenue function for firm j to allow market power and two types of capital, K_1 and K_2, which we think of as physical and intangible capital:

$$\Pi_{j,t} = \mu D_t^{\frac{\mu-1}{\mu}} (Z_{j,t})^\mu ((1 - \eta)K_{1,j,t}^\rho + \eta K_{2,j,t}^\rho)^{\frac{\mu}{\rho}},$$

where $Z_{j,t}$ is the firm-level productivity, D_t is the industry-wide demand shifter, $\epsilon \geq 1$ is the demand elasticity, and $\mu = (\epsilon/(\epsilon - 1)) \geq 1$ is the markup.

In this setting, we can decompose average Q_1, which is empirical average Q for physical capital, into the marginal q_1 that determines physical capital investment, and three "wedge" terms. The first two measure the value of intangible capital and the rents from market power, respectively, and the last one measures their interaction.

$$Q_{1,j} = q_{1,j} + \underbrace{q_{2,j}\nu_j}_{\text{intangibles}} + \underbrace{\frac{1}{r - g_j}(\mu - 1)R_{1,j}}_{\text{market power}} + \underbrace{\frac{1}{r - g_j}(\mu - 1)\nu_j R_{2,j}}_{\text{intangibles} \times \text{market power}}.$$

Intuitively, the first wedge term captures the value of intangibles that contribute to the value of the firm. The second term calculates the value of the rents from market power. The third term captures the present value of market power rents to intangible capital, hence the interaction between intangibles and market power. This term can be quite large because the cost of capital for intangibles tends to be large due to their high depreciation rates. Simple calculations suggest this last term can be the largest wedge, and hence very important for understanding weak investment. Examining either market power or intangibles individually would find a large effect, but miss that there is the important role and interaction with the other.

III. Why Has Concentration Risen? One Size Does Not Fit All

The second empirical section of the paper takes a different approach, and rather than looking at individual explanations, looks at many. The authors employ a principal components analysis which, importantly, allows for different loadings by industry. Here the authors identify (ex post) two principal components: one they define as "good concentration," which is intangibles-related, and the second as "bad concentration," related to barriers to entry. The results demonstrate both multiple factors at play and much heterogeneity by industry. These results are novel and interesting, and a conceptual and empirical pivot from the first part of the paper.

Principal components are notoriously difficult to interpret, so one has to be careful of falling into a "Rorschach test" in which we tend to see our priors in the data. That being said, the patterns are interesting. Figure A26 (in Covarrubias et al., available online) reports the loadings by industry on the first two principal components, described by the authors as "intangibles" and "barriers to entry," respectively. The weightings are reminiscent of the industry patterns in Alexander and Eberly (2018), which report the share of aggregate investment accounted for by industry groups over time, reproduced in figure 1. The striking fact apparent there is that the share of physical capital has shifted away from production industries, like manufacturing, and toward geographically stationary industries, like utilities and energy extraction, which put in place pipelines and towers. The industries that have seen the most growth in value, such as high tech, have a flat share of physical investment. Instead, these industries

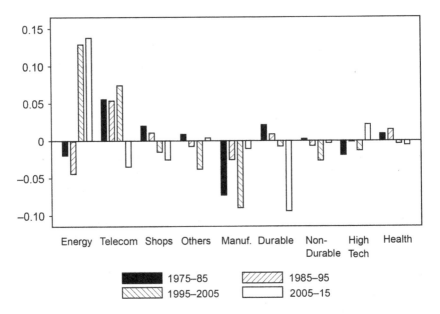

Fig. 1. The distribution of investment across industries, over time. Physical investment is increasingly allocated toward "fixed" industries such as energy and telecom. High-growth industries, such as tech and health, show little growth in their share of physical capital. Units in vertical axis represent the change in the share of aggregate investment (Alexander and Eberly 2018).

have rising intangibles investment. This evidence complements the industry ranking for PC1 in Figure A26 (in Covarrubias et al., available online), showing the highest loadings in computer and data industries, as well as chemicals (which includes pharmaceuticals—a high-patent field). The lowest loadings are on pipelines and utilities, which have more fixed capital. The highest loadings for PC2, which focuses on barriers to entry, are in telecommunications, information (movies), and finance. However, some of the "new economy" industries, such as information (data) and information (publishing), as well as chemicals, have high loadings on both PC2 and PC1, as shown in figure 13 in the paper. These may be industries in which the rise in intangibles generates growth but also creates excludability, for example by patent protections, which act as barriers to entry.

Although this analysis is not dispositive, it does point in the direction of looking for complementary explanations for the rise in concentration. The data here are thought provoking and will hopefully give rise to more detailed examination.

IV. Conclusions

Covarrubias et al. have written a conceptually clarifying and helpful paper. They make clear that the rise in concentration on which much research has been focused is consistent with many economic models, which may give rise to efficient or inefficient concentration. Moreover, they provide a guide to pitfalls in measuring markups using accounting data, and while they may not have the ultimate measure at this point, their work suggests caution in interpreting the measures we have. The empirical work tends to move the weight of the evidence toward a role for market power, especially over time. But the principal components analysis makes clear that a single, across-the-economy story is unlikely to capture the richness of the data. However, by providing this lens to focus our view, the results with heterogeneity and complementary hypotheses are actually more convincing because we more readily see how market power, technological change, and other forces may interact to generate big trends in the macro data.

Endnote

Author email address: Eberly (eberly@kellogg.northwestern.edu). For acknowledgments, sources of research support, and disclosure of the author's material financial relationships, if any, please see https://www.nber.org/chapters/c14238.ack.

References

Alexander, L., and J. Eberly. 2018. "Investment Hollowing Out." *IMF Economic Review* 66 (1): 5–30.

Crouzet, N., and J. Eberly. 2019. "Understanding Weak Capital Investment: The Role of Market Concentration and Intangibles." May 2019 version of paper prepared for Federal Reserve Bank of Kansas City's Jackson Hole Economic Symposium 2018.

Farhi, E., and F. Gourio. 2018. "Accounting for Macro-Finance Trends: Market Power, Intangibles, and Risk Premia." *Brookings Papers on Economic Activity* (Fall): 1–50.

Peters, R. H., and L. A. Taylor. 2017. "Intangible Capital and the Investment-q Relation." *Journal of Financial Economics* 123 (2): 251–72.

Stulz, R., and K. Kahle. 2017. "Is the US Public Corporation in Trouble?" *Journal of Economic Perspectives* 31 (3): 67–88.

Comment

Chad Syverson, *University of Chicago and NBER*

Macro's Newfound Interest and This Paper

Macroeconomics has become interested in market power. A series of studies over the past few years has documented a set of possibly interrelated, broad-based, and decades-long trends: increased market concentration, higher profit rates, higher measured price-cost markups, decreased investment rates, reduced firm entry and factor market dynamism, and a fall in labor's share of income. If one wanted to offer a single, plausible-on-its-face explanation for these trends, it would be reasonable to argue that there has been a broad increase in market power among producers in the economy. This interest in market power extends beyond just product markets. Characterizing the role of monopsony, especially in the labor market, is an active research area as well.

However, there are potential alternative explanations for many of the trends described earlier. These include a growing role for intangible capital in production, increases in product market substitutability due to the expansion of trade or decreases in consumer search costs, and other shifts in production technologies that have increased returns to scale. Moreover, a set of studies has offered evidence for these mechanisms—in case studies, certainly, but in more broadly scoped empirical settings as well.

I view the goal of the Covarrubias, Gutiérrez, and Philippon paper as trying to bring together and make sense of those many data patterns and conflicting stories. On the theory side, the paper shows how a commonly used class of models captures many of the proposed explanations for the aforementioned data trends, and it uses such models to point to possible empirical tests to discriminate among these explanations. On the empirical side, it applies these tests in an attempt to identify the most likely explanation for the data trends. (Though as I note later, the collage of statistical analyses ultimately tells a multicausal story, so in the end I might say the paper points toward the more likely explanations.)

This Is a Useful Class of Models

This paper employs a very useful class of models, with substantial "empirical bang for the theoretical buck." Key elements of this class include heterogeneous-type producers, a demand system that allows for product differentiation and interactions among firms that hold market power (this power is parameterized or microfounded depending on the setting), a zero-cutoff-profit condition that selects on heterogeneity (i.e., a firm must be of sufficiently high type to operate profitably), and free entry among ex ante homogenous potential entrants that pay a sunk entry cost to learn their type. The combination of the zero-cutoff-profit and free entry conditions endogenously determines the equilibrium set of producers. This structure allows considerable richness in the patterns of industry outcomes that it admits as possible while remaining tractable and transparent.

The Problem with Concentration

It is heartening to see the paper's recognition of the problematic nature of using concentration to measure competition. As the field of industrial organization realized several decades ago, concentration is a market outcome, not a market primitive. Depending on the setting, concentration can be associated with less competition or with more. For example, under Cournot competition among heterogeneous-cost firms selling a homogenous output, the share-weighted price-cost margin is proportional to the Herfindahl-Hirschman index of concentration. In this case, concentration is associated with less competition (higher price-cost margins and lower welfare). On the other hand, in the differentiated-product class of models used in this paper, increased competition due to greater product substitutability leads to more concentration but lower price-cost margins and higher welfare. Thus concentration is not just a noisy barometer of competition; we do not even know which end of the barometer should be pointed up. Nor is this just a theoretical issue. Hundreds of studies have found that increases in substitutability (whether through reduced costs of trade, transport, search, or switching) resulted in both lower margins and greater concentration, as the more capable firms become larger in response to increased substitutability. Even studies within the newer macro market power literature have found, at least for some sectors, simultaneous concentration and productivity growth.

This causal inference problem holds generally but is perhaps especially dangerous if one is making comparisons across different markets, when there is considerable scope for variation in primitives to drive concentration and competition in multiple directions. If one wants to study differences in competition, one should look at the primitives.

The paper recognizes this issue and nicely elucidates it with its conceptual framework. It then frames the empirical patterns as indicating mechanisms working in both directions. The paper argues that early in the sample period (before the 2000s), increases in concentration reflected greater competition. On the other hand, the new millennium saw further concentration associated with changes in primitives that reduced competition. I would characterize the underlying evidence as suggestive but not dispositive; still, it certainly points the literature in useful directions.

The Macro of Markups

Given the problems with using concentration to measure market power, a natural question is how one should then measure it. Price-cost markups are the textbook definition and measure of market power; as such, I view them as the most direct measure of that power.

The use of markups highlights three quantitative issues with results found so far in the macro market power literature: the alignment of aggregate price, markup, and cost growth; the relationship between markup, profit share, and scale elasticity; and the fact that factor market power implies the same marginal-product-to-marginal-cost wedge often used to measure markups.

I describe the first two issues in detail in Syverson (2019) and refer interested readers there. In short, one involves the seeming inconsistency between historically low inflation growth on the one hand and unusually high markups growth and either steady or perhaps unusually high growth in costs. Given that the latter two sum to the first, there is a question as to how these relative trends all add up, so to speak. The other issue is that there is a very general relationship that should hold at the firm level among the markup, pure profit's share of income, and the scale elasticity. Because these objects are often measured using at least somewhat independent data and sources of variation, this relationship offers empirical discipline that I believe the literature would find useful. The authors address this relationship in the final section of the paper.

The third issue involves the relationships among product market power, factor market power, and a common measure of markups. This measure, the ratio of the estimated marginal product of a variable input to its revenue share, is a standard metric of product market power in the literature. This is because this ratio equals the price-cost markup of output under the assumptions of imperfect competition in the product market and a perfectly competitive market for the variable input. However—and here is the inference problem—the same ratio equals the monopsony markdown in the wage of the variable factor if the product market is perfectly competitive and producers have market power in the factor market. If firms have market power in both the product and factor markets, then the ratio mixes these two effects in its sum. Therefore reading the ratio as reflecting solely product market monopoly or factor market monopsony could misattribute one for the other. Moreover, even when recognizing that the measured ratio may reflect both market power effects, additional variation and empirical metrics are necessary to separately quantify each component.

Churn

Much of the empirical work in the paper involves the helpful collection and presentation of patterns that have been shown elsewhere in the literature, including in earlier work by the authors. One of the more novel empirical results here regards competition dynamics. The paper documents several notable trends since the late 1990s: a decline in the hazard rate of one of the top four firms in an industry (whether measured by revenues or market value) falling out of that position; a rise in the persistence of sales and market value ranks and shares (among all firms, not just the top four); and in a separate paper by the authors, a reduction in the responsiveness of entry to Tobin's Q.

I agree that exploring the dynamic implications of the market power hypothesis is a potentially very fruitful research channel, and results of this type might bolster the case for market power. However, there is reason to be careful about drawing strong conclusions from the particular results in this paper. They are obtained from Compustat data, which of course comprise publicly listed firms. As is well known, publicly listed firms in the US have experienced certain trends that are notably different from the broader universe of firms. In particular, the number of listed firms has been in secular decline since peaking in the latter half of the 1990s. The implications for the paper's empirical tests on churn are apparent. Listed firms are an increasingly selected and, likely, increasingly stable set of firms. It is therefore perhaps not surprising that the dynamism of this sample (and entry in particular) would have declined, even if market power effects were absent. Indeed, it is interesting that the time series patterns of churn obtained in the paper show a similar rise-and-fall pattern over the past 30–40 years to that of the number of publicly listed firms.

All that said, it is useful to remember that there is separate evidence in the literature that dynamism has fallen even among privately held firms. However, that also seems to reflect an ongoing trend since at least the early 1980s, which means it has run through both the increase and decrease in churn measured in the paper.

Sutton's Endogenous Sunk Costs

The paper treats sunk costs as exogenous and argues increasing sunk costs are the best explanation for several patterns in data. A sunk cost story that might be an even better description of what is going on is the endogenous sunk cost of Sutton (1991, 1997).

In Sutton's framework, incumbents employ an "escalation mechanism" to raise the sunk costs that a firm must pay to enter the industry. If this mechanism is potent enough, then little or no additional entry may occur despite substantial market expansion. In the limit, the number of industry firms can be bounded from above even if the market grows several times over. In Sutton (1991), the escalation mechanism is advertising and marketing. Suppose brand capital is necessary to compete effectively in a market. If brand is sufficiently responsive to investment, entry may stall even as the market continues to grow. An example of this might be the carbonated soft drinks industry, where two firms have dominated even as total consumption grew several times over. The duopolists' continuous brand investments (to the tune of billions of dollars per year), interacting with consumers' particular responsiveness to brand effects in this market, have combined to keep out any entrants. In Sutton (1997), the escalation mechanism is research and development (R&D) and vertical product improvements. Here, commercial aircraft is an example industry where R&D-driven endogenous sunk costs have limited entry into an ever-expanding market.

It is plausible that network effects or lobbying might be other kinds of escalation mechanisms. The paper discusses lobbying in particular. Pursuing these and related phenomena as possible shapers of equilibrium market structure would be a worthwhile use of research effort.

As with the relationship between the markup, profit's share of income, and the scale elasticity I mentioned earlier, endogenous sunk costs are another mechanism that might connect what the paper's framework treats as independent. Here, these connections might be especially strong among the intensity of intangible capital in production, the scale elasticity (ν), and sunk entry costs (κ). For example, network effects are often linked to intangible capital, can create a type of scale elasticity, and surely raise sunk entry costs for later potential entrants.

Multicausality

While emphasizing the increasing entry cost story as the primary explanation for the patterns described earlier, the paper takes a bit of a turn in Section IV and acknowledges, conceptually and empirically, that ultimately the patterns may be multicausal. This is wise. It seems quite plausible that the observed trends reflect a combination of greater intangible intensity, changing product-market substitutability, greater scale economies, and higher entry costs (all with potential implications for market power, though in possibly different directions). Equally important is that the relative contribution of each can vary across sectors. Again, the multicausal nature may not be just coincident effects. The connections mentioned earlier may tie them together directly.

The paper conducts a principal components decomposition to address this issue empirically. This is a very useful step, as it reduces the dimensionality of outcomes in informative ways. And while factor analysis can sometimes lead to not-so-helpful ex post theorizing, the authors avoid drawing too strong a conclusion about specific drivers in specific instances.

I think what will ultimately be required is a series of case studies that puts faces on the facts. I realize readers might roll their eyes at someone who has worked in the industrial organization literature calling for more case studies, but I recently spoke at an industrial organization conference and told them they need to do more macroeconomics. Perhaps we can meet in the middle and learn something from each other.

To conclude, I believe the empirical case is not yet definitive that across-the-board increases in market power have led to the several trends noted earlier. However, my priors have moved relative to 5 years ago, and this paper has helped nudge them. To warrant stronger conclusions, I believe market power and alternatives need to be better quantified, not just qualified, and patterns of heterogeneity in such effects more richly characterized.

Endnote

Author email address: Syverson (chad.syverson@chicagobooth.edu). For acknowledgments, sources of research support, and disclosure of the author's material financial relationships, if any, please see https://www.nber.org/chapters/c14239.ack.

References

Sutton, John. 1991. *Sunk Costs and Market Structure*. Cambridge, MA: MIT Press.
———. 1997. *Technology and Market Structure*. Cambridge, MA: MIT Press.
Syverson, Chad. 2019. "Macroeconomics and Market Power: Context, Implications, and Open Questions." *Journal of Economic Perspectives* 33 (3): 23–43.

Discussion

Martin Eichenbaum interpreted the rising concentration in the banking industry through the lens of the authors' framework. He noted that several regional banks in the Southwest had recently merged to form a super-regional bank. According to banking professionals, increasing returns play an important role in this industry, he said. Eichenbaum argued that this form of concentration seems consistent with increasing sunk costs or barriers to entry. He asked the authors about their thoughts on the subject. The authors clarified that most of their analysis excludes financial services. They agreed that a rise in barriers to entry could explain mergers in the banking industry, together with an increase in efficiency from mergers. They noted, however, that the evidence on increasing returns to scale in the banking industry remains mostly inconclusive. The emergence of "fintech" might potentially create more scope for such efficiency gains, they argued. The authors emphasized the role of lobbying by the banking industry. As an example, they mentioned data portability, which allows a client to share her portfolio information with another institution to obtain financial advice. Banks defeated calls for increased data portability in the US, the authors pointed out. On the contrary, they lost in the European Union, where their lobbying power is smaller. This illustrates the role of increased lobbying for the rise in barriers to entry in the US, according to the authors.

Laura Veldkamp noted that uncertain revenue streams should command risk premia when investors or managers are risk averse. She pointed out that markups could be the firms' compensation for that revenue risk and might not reflect market power at all. Veldkamp wondered how the authors took this into account in their analysis. The authors said that they measure firms' value using market values, which should address concerns related to risk premia. On the relation between firms' value and entry into an industry, they referred to another paper of theirs. Fixing barriers to entry across industries, a standard efficiency condition would predict a positive correlation between the share of entries and Tobin's Q across industries, they argued. In Germán Gutiérrez and Thomas Philippon ("Investment-less Growth: An Empirical Investigation" [Working Paper no. 22897, December, NBER, Cambridge, MA, 2017]), they found that this correlation was positive and strong in the data until the late 1990s but is zero now. This fact is consistent with a substantial increase in the variance of "competition" shocks (σ) and "barriers" shocks (κ) in their model, they noted.

Two topics dominated the rest of the discussion: the decline in firm entry and the rise in barriers to entry since the 2000s, and the role of lobbying.

On the first topic, Erik Hurst noted that various series related to technology and employment feature an inflection point in the early 2000s. This coincides with the apparent sudden increase in barriers to entry. He was curious about the source of these structural changes and asked the authors their opinion. They responded by referring to a recent paper of theirs. In Germán Gutiérrez, Callum Jones, and Thomas Philippon ("Entry Costs and the Macroeconomy" [Working Paper no. 25609, February, NBER, Cambridge, MA, 2019]), they used a structural model with dynamic entry-exit, risk premia, and firm heterogeneity to back out implied time-series entry rates. The corresponding barriers to entry do not feature any discontinuity in the early 2000s. Instead, they rise smoothly since the mid-2000s. Other shocks contributed to the decrease in entry rate at that time. The rise in lobbying is an important source of higher barriers to entry in the US, according to the authors. However, they admitted that they do not have an explanation yet for the increase in lobbying in the US over the past 20 years, and why it did not occur in Europe.

Kristin Forbes offered an alternative explanation for the decline in firm entry since the early 2000s. She noted that China's entry into the World Trade Organization in 2001 disrupted global supply chains and international competition, which might have affected firm entry. The authors referred to evidence of theirs on the effect of the China shock, which they said contributed to an increase in exit rates and an increase in investment and markups. However, the exposure to China only affected a limited part of the economy, they argued. Furthermore, the China shock fails to explain the increase in concentration for airlines and telecom or the different experiences in the US and Europe.

Antoinette Schoar emphasized instead the role of the bursting tech bubble in the early 2000s. She argued that existing firms in broad segments of the economy acquired new technologies after the crash. This contributed to changes in production and distribution technologies, she suggested. The authors agreed with the importance of accounting for technological change. This motivated their comparative approach between the US and Europe, they explained. By comparing industries that use the same technology on each side of the Atlantic, such as airlines or telecoms, the authors found divergent trends for profits, markups, and prices. This is suggestive of a US-specific source of rising barriers to entry, according to the authors.

Robert Gordon shared Schoar's view. He mentioned that investment collapsed between 2000 and 2003, while productivity growth was higher during the 2000–4 period compared with the 1996–99 period. Gordon argued that this evidence is suggestive of lagged learning and a late adoption of digital technologies developed in the 1990s. Janice Eberly joined the discussion. She referred to recent work by Robert J. Gordon and Hassan Sayed ("The Industry Anatomy of the Transatlantic Productivity Growth Slowdown" [Working Paper no. 25703, March, NBER, Cambridge, MA, 2019]), which documents different trends in productivity between the US and Europe. Eberly wondered whether these differences could affect the authors' comparative approach between the two continents. Gordon followed up on Eberly's comment. He pointed out that productivity growth at the industry level was highly correlated between the US and Europe during the period 1995–2005. He argued that this correlation masks an important difference in trends: productivity growth in Europe was roughly half that in the US in every industry over that period. Gordon found this lack of productivity revival in Europe puzzling. He asked the authors about their thoughts on the subject. They disputed the view that productivity is diverging between the US and Europe. The authors suggested instead that differences in productivity growth in the early 2000s between the US and Europe were mostly transitory and reflected different life-cycle compositions of firms within industries. Growth in gross domestic product per capita over the period 1999–2019 was very similar on both sides of the Atlantic, they argued.

On the topic of lobbying, Chad Syverson agreed that a rise in lobbying and an increase in barriers to entry were intrinsically related. He suggested that increased lobbying is the consequence of higher barriers to entry rather than its cause. Syverson also pointed out that lobbying expenditures typically amount to a few billion dollars only. These figures are low compared with other forms of entry cost such as building a new plant. The authors pointed out that the estimates of lobbying costs found in the political economy literature have evolved significantly over the past decade. Factoring in all relevant costs, including political campaign financing, current estimates are now substantially higher, they argued. The authors noted that returns to lobbying seem high nevertheless so that part of the puzzle remains.

Schoar inquired about the institutional context in Europe to better understand differences in lobbying on both sides of the Atlantic. Specifically, she wondered whether European regulators were more prone to regulate certain industries when those industries were supplied mostly by US firms. The authors suggested that lobbying seems to have very little influence on the decisions of European regulatory agencies. They referred to the example of the Alstom-Siemens merger, which was blocked by the European Commission despite intense pressures from France and Germany.

Finally, Silvana Tenreyro asked whether differences in inflation between the US and Europe might affect the measurement of markups. Syverson seconded Tenreyro, admitting that the measurement of markups is notoriously difficult. The authors noted that price inflation over the past 15 years has been 15 percentage points (pp) higher in the US than in Europe, while wage inflation has been 8 pp higher. At the same time, productivity growth has been 3 pp higher in the US. As a result, the average markup in the US increased by 10 pp compared with Europe. The authors argued that this back-of-the-envelope calculation falls within the 10–15 pp range documented in the literature and that this figure is rather small on an annual basis.

2

The Lost Ones: The Opportunities and Outcomes of White, Non-College-Educated Americans Born in the 1960s

Margherita Borella, *University of Torino and CeRP-Collegio Carlo Alberto*

Mariacristina De Nardi, *University of Minnesota, Federal Reserve Bank of Minneapolis, CEPR, and NBER*

Fang Yang, *Louisiana State University*

I. Introduction

Much of macroeconomics studies policies have to do with either business cycle fluctuations or growth. Business cycle fluctuations are typically short-lived, do not affect a cohort's entire life cycle, and tend to have smaller welfare effects. Growth, however, drastically improves the outcomes and welfare of successive cohorts over their entire lives compared with previous cohorts. Yet, recent evidence indicates that while we are still experiencing growth at the aggregate level, many people in recent cohorts are worse off and have not benefited from aggregate growth. It is important to study and better understand these cohort-level shocks and their consequences before trying to evaluate to what extent current government policies attenuate these kinds of shocks and whether we should redesign some policies to reduce their impacts.

Recent research suggests that it is important to understand these cohort-level shocks and their consequences. Guvenen et al. (2017) find that the median lifetime income of men born in the 1960s is 12%–19% lower than that of men born in the 1940s, whereas Roys and Taber (2019) document that the wages of low-skilled men have stagnated over a similar time period. Hall and Jones (2007) highlight that the share of medical expenses to consumption has approximately doubled every 25 years since the 1950s, and Case and Deaton (2015, 2017) have started an important debate by showing that the mortality rate of white, less-educated, middle-aged men has been increasing since 1999. In contrast with men's, the median lifetime income of women born in the 1960s is 22%–33% higher than that of women born in the 1940s (Guvenen et al. 2017). The latter change, however, occurred in conjunction with women's increased participation in the labor market.

Although very suggestive, the changes in lifetime income tell us little about what happened to wages. In addition, depending on how wages, medical expenses, and mortality changed for married and single men and women, they can have weaker or stronger effects on couples, single men, and single women. Given the size of these changes and the large number of people that they affect, more investigation of their consequences is warranted.

The goal of this paper is to better measure these important changes in the lifetime opportunities of white, single and married, less-educated American men and women and to uncover their effects on the labor supply, savings, and welfare of a relatively recent birth cohort. To do so, we start by picking two cohorts of white, non-college-educated Americans for whom we have excellent data,[1] those born in the 1940s and those born in the 1960s, and by using data from the Panel Study of Income Dynamics (PSID) and the Health and Retirement Study (HRS) to uncover several new facts.

First, we find that, across these two cohorts, men's average wages have decreased in real terms by 9% whereas women's average wages have increased by 7% but that the increase in wages for women is due to higher human capital of women in the 1960s cohort rather than to higher wages per unit of human capital.[2] Second, we document a large increase in out-of-pocket medical expenses later in life: average out-of-pocket medical expenses after age 66 are expected to increase across cohorts by 82%. Third, we show that in middle age, the life expectancy of both female and male white, non-college-educated people is projected to go down by about 2 years from the 1940s to the 1960s cohort. All of these changes are thus large and have the potential to substantially affect behavior and welfare.

We then calibrate a life-cycle model of couples and singles to match the labor market outcomes for the 1960s cohort. Our calibrated model is a version of the life-cycle model developed by Borella, De Nardi, and Yang (2017),[3] which, in turn, builds on the literature on female labor supply, including Eckstein and Liftshitz (2011); Fernández and Wong (2014, 2017); Blundell et al. (2016); Blundell, Pistaferri, and Saporta-Eksten (2016); Borella, De Nardi, and Yang (2018); and Eckstein, Keane, and Liftshitz (2019). Our model is well suited for our purposes for two important reasons. First, it is a quantitative model that includes single and married people (with single people meeting partners and married people risking divorce), which matters because most people are in couples. Second, it allows for human capital accumulation on the job, which our findings indicate is important, and includes medical expenses and life span risk during retirement.

Our calibrated model matches key observed outcomes for the 1960s cohort very well. To evaluate the effects of the observed changes that we consider, we give the wage schedules, medical expenses, and life expectancy of the 1940s cohort to our 1960s cohort, starting at age 25, and then study the effects of these changes on the 1960s cohort's labor supply, savings, and welfare.

We find that, of the three changes that we consider (the observed changes in the wage schedule, an increase in expected out-of-pocket medical expenses during retirement, and a decrease in life expectancy), the change in the wage schedule had by far the largest effect on the labor supply of both men and women. In particular, it depressed the labor supply of men and increased that of women. The decrease in life expectancy mainly reduced retirement savings, but the expected increase in out-of-pocket medical expenses increased them by more.

We also find that the welfare costs of these changes are large. Specifically, the onetime asset compensation required at age 25 to make the 1960s households indifferent between the 1940s and 1960s health and survival dynamics, medical expenses, and wages, expressed as a fraction of their average discounted present value of earnings, are 12.5%, 8.0%, and 7.2%, for single men, couples, and single women, respectively.[4] The costs are thus largest for single men and smallest for single women. Looking into the sources of these costs, we find that 47%–58% of them are due to changes in the wage structure, 25%–34% are due to changing life expectancy, and that medical expenses explain the remaining losses.

Our results thus indicate that the group of white, non-college-educated people born in the 1960s cohort, which comprises about 60% of the population of the same age, experienced large negative changes in wages, large increases in medical expenses, and large decreases in life expectancy and would have been much better off if they had faced the corresponding lifetime opportunities of the 1940s birth cohort.

Our paper contributes to the previous literature along several important dimensions. First, it uncovers new facts on wages (and wages per unit of human capital), expected medical expenses during retirement, and life expectancy in middle age, for white, non-college-educated American men and women born in the 1940s and 1960s. Second, it recognizes that most people are not single, isolated individuals, but rather part of a couple, and changes in lifetime opportunities for one member of the couple could be either reinforced or weakened by the changes faced by their partner.

Third, it documents these changes and introduces them in a carefully calibrated model that matches the lifetime outcomes of the 1960s cohort well. Fourth, it studies the effects of these changes in opportunities over time on the savings, labor market outcomes, and welfare of this cohort.

The paper is organized as follows. Section II discusses our sample selection and the main characteristics of our resulting sample. Section III documents the changing opportunities for the 1940s and 1960s cohorts in terms of wages, medical expenses, and life expectancy. Section IV describes the outcomes for our 1960s cohort in terms of labor market participation, hours worked by the workers, and savings. Section V discusses our structural model and thus the assumptions that we make to interpret the data. Section VI explains our empirical strategy and documents the processes that we estimate as inputs of our structural model, including our estimated wages as a function of human capital and our estimated medical expenses and mortality as a function of age, gender, health, and marital status. Section VII describes our results and Section VIII concludes.

II.   The Data and Our Sample

We use the PSID and the HRS to construct a sample of white, non-college-educated Americans. We pick the cohort born in the 1940s (which is composed of the 1936–45 birth cohorts) as our comparison older cohort because it is the oldest cohort for which we have excellent data over most of their life cycle (first covered in the PSID and then in the HRS). We then pick our more recent cohort, the 1960s one (which is composed of the 1956–65 birth cohorts), to be as young as possible, conditional on having available data on most of their working period, which we require our structural model to match. We then compare the lifetime opportunities between these two cohorts. Appendix A (apps. A–D, tables A1–A13, and figs. A1–A3 are available online; see https://www.nber.org/data-appendix/c14249/appendix .pdf) reports more details about the data and our computations.

To be explicit about the population that we are studying, we now turn to discussing our sampling choices for these cohorts and the resulting composition of our sample in terms of marital status and education level. We focus on non–college graduates for two reasons. First, we want to focus on less-educated people, but we need a reasonable number of observations over the life cycle for both single and married men and women. Second, college graduates (and above) is the only group for which Case and Deaton (2017) find continued decreases in middle-age mortality over time.

Table 1
Panel Study of Income Dynamics Sample Selection

Selection	Individuals	Observations
Initial sample (observed at least twice)	30,587	893,420
Heads and spouses (if present)	18,304	247,203
Born between 1935 and 1965	7,913	137,427
Age between 20 and 70	7,847	135,117
White	6,834	116,810
Non–missing education	6,775	116,619
Non–college graduates	5,039	73,944

Table 1 displays sample sizes before and after we apply our selection criteria. We start from 30,587 people and 893,420 observations. We keep household heads and their spouses, if present, and restrict the sample to the cohorts born between 1935 and 1965, to whites, and to include observations reporting their education. Our sample before performing the education screens comprises 6,775 people and 116,619 observations. Dropping all college graduates and those married to college graduates results in a sample of 5,039 people and 73,944 observations.[5]

Turning to our resulting PSID sample, at age 25, 90% and 77% of people in the 1940s and 1960s birth cohorts are married, respectively. To understand how education changed within our sample of interest, table 2 reports the education distribution at age 25 for our non–college graduates in the 1940s and 1960s cohorts. It shows that the fraction of people without a high school diploma decreased by 40% for men and 43% for women from the 1940s to the 1960s cohort. Our model and empirical strategy take into account education composition within our sample because they control for people's human capital, both at labor market entry and over the life cycle.

One might worry about a different type of selection; that is, the one coming from the fact that we drop people who completed college from

Table 2
Fractions (%) of Individuals by Education Level in Our Two Birth Cohorts

	Men		Women	
	1940	1960	1940	1960
Less than high school	.29	.17	.23	.13
High school	.32	.33	.37	.39
More than high school	.39	.50	.40	.48

our sample for all of our cohorts. If college completion rates were rising fast between the 1940s and 1960s, with the most able going into college, our 1960s cohort might be much more negatively selected than our 1940s cohort. Table A12 in appendix D (available online) shows that, in the PSID, the fraction of the population having less than a college degree dropped from 83.1% in the 1940s to 77.2% in the 1960s. This corresponds to a 5.9 percentage point drop in non–college graduates in the population across our two cohorts (5.6 and 6.7 percentage points for men and women, respectively). Appendix D (available online) also compares the implications of our PSID and HRS samples for our model inputs with those of the corresponding samples in which we keep a constant fraction of the population for both cohorts. All of these comparisons show that our model inputs are very similar for both types of samples and that our results are thus not driven by selection out of our sample.

Because the HRS contains a large number of observations and high-quality data after age 50, we use it to compute our inputs for the retirement period. The last available HRS wave is for 2014, which implies that we do not have complete data on the life cycle of the two cohorts that we are interested in. In fact, individuals' ages were, respectively, 69–78 and 49–58 in the 1936–45 and 1956–65 cohorts as of year 2014. We use older cohorts to extrapolate outcomes for the missing periods for our cohorts of interest, and we start estimation at age 50 so that the 1960s cohort is observed for a few waves in our sample.

Thus, our sample selection for the HRS is as follows. Of the 449,940 observations initially present, we delete those missing crucial information (e.g., on marital status), and we select waves since 1996. We then select individuals in the age range 50–100. Given that we use years from 1996 to 2014, these people were born between 1906 and 1964. After keeping white and non–college graduate individuals and their spouses, we have 19,377 individuals and 110,923 observations, as detailed in table 3.

Table 3
Health and Retirement Survey Sample Selection

Selection	Individuals	Observations
Initial sample	37,495	449,940
Non–missing information	37,152	217,574
Wave 1996 or later	35,936	204,922
Ages 50–100	34,775	197,431
White	25,693	152,688
Non–college graduates	19,377	110,923

III.   Changes in Wages, Medical Expenses, and Life Expectancy across Cohorts

In this section, we describe the observed changes in wages, medical expenses, and life expectancy experienced by white, non-college-educated Americans born in the 1960s compared with those born in the 1940s.[6] We show that the wages of men went down by 7%, whereas the wages of women went up by 9%. These changes do not condition on human capital within an education group (we report wages per unit of human capital in Sec. VI.A after we make explicit how we model human capital). We also show that, during retirement, out-of-pocket medical spending increased by 82%, whereas life expectancy decreased by 1.6–2 years.

A.   Wages

Figure 1 displays smoothed average real wage profiles for labor market participants.[7] We deflate all nominal variables using the Consumer Price Index for All Urban Consumers (CPI-U). Appendix B (available online) shows that the CPI-U is very close to the price indexes that have been constructed for lower-income people and that, given our focus on the non-college-educated population, are most appropriate for our analysis.

The *left panel* displays wages for married men and women in the 1940s and 1960s cohort, whereas the *right panel* displays the corresponding wages for single people. Several features are worth noticing. First, the wages of men were much higher than those of women in the 1940s birth cohort. Second, the wages of men, both married and single, went down

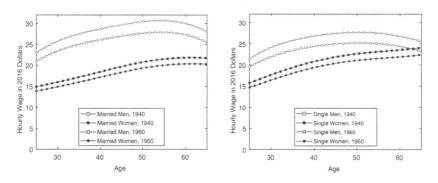

Fig. 1.   Wage profiles, comparing 1960s and 1940s for married people (*left panel*) and single people (*right panel*).

by 9%. Third, the wages of married and single women went up by 7% across these two cohorts.

Our model, however, requires potential wages as an input. Because the wage is missing for those who are not working, we impute missing wages (see details in app. C, available online). Figure 2 shows our estimated potential wage profiles. Potential wages for men are similar to observed wages for labor market participants, except that potential wages drop faster than observed wages after age 55. Potential wages for women not only drop faster after middle age than observed wages but also tend to be lower and grow more slowly at younger ages due to positive selection of women in the labor market.

Both figures display overall similar patterns and, in particular, imply that the large wage gap between men and women in the 1940s cohort significantly decreased for the 1960s cohort because of increasing wages for women and decreasing wages for men.

B. Medical Expenses

We use the HRS data to compute out-of-pocket medical expenses during retirement for the 1940s and 1960s cohorts.[8] Figure 3 indicates a large increase in real average expected out-of-pocket medical expenses across cohorts. For instance, at age 66, out-of-pocket medical expenses expressed in 2016 dollars are $2,878 and $5,236, respectively, for the 1940s and 1960s birth cohorts. The corresponding numbers for someone who survives to age 90 are $5,855 and $10,655. Thus, average out-of-pocket medical expenses after age 66 are expected to increase across cohorts by 82%. These are dramatic increases for two cohorts that are only 20 years apart.

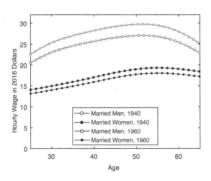 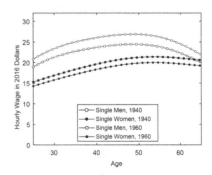

Fig. 2. Potential wage profiles, comparing 1960s and 1940s for married people (*left panel*) and single people (*right panel*).

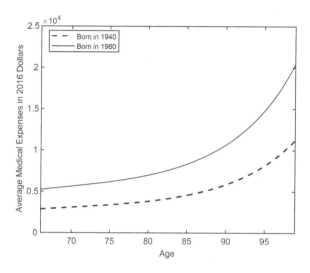

Fig. 3. Average out-of-pocket medical expenses for the cohorts born in the 1940s and 1960s.

C. Life Expectancy

Case and Deaton (2015, 2017) use data from the National Vital Statistics to study mortality by age over time and find that, interrupting a longtime trend in mortality declines, the mortality of white, middle-aged, and non-college-educated Americans went up during the 1999–2015 time period. In particular, they found that individuals ages 55–59 in 2015 (and thus born in 1956–60) faced a 22% increase in mortality with respect to individuals ages 55–59 in 1999 (and thus born in 1940–44). Looking at a younger group, they find that individuals ages 50–54 in 2015 (thus born in 1961–65) experienced a 28% increase in mortality compared with individuals in the same age group and born 16 years earlier.

Using the HRS data, we find that mortality at age 50 increased by about 27% from the 1940s to the 1960s cohort.[9] Thus, the increases in mortality in the HRS data are in line with those found by Case and Deaton.

To further understand the HRS's data implications about mortality and their changes across our two cohorts, we also report the life expectancies that are implied by our HRS data. Table 4 shows that life expectancy at age 50 was age 79.6 and 83.5 for men and women, respectively, in the cohort born in the 1940s. Conditional on being alive at age 66, men and women in this cohort expect to live until age 82.5 and 85.7, respectively. It also shows that the life expectancy of men at age 50 declined

Table 4
Life Expectancy for White and Non-College-Educated Men and Women Born
in the 1940s and 1960s Cohorts

| | Men | | Women | |
	1940	1960	1940	1960
At age 50	79.6	77.5	83.5	81.5
At age 66	82.5	80.9	85.7	84.0

Source: Health and Retirement Survey data.

by 2 years across our two cohorts, which is a large decrease for cohorts
that are 20 years apart and during a period of increasing life expectancy
for people in other groups. The table also reveals two other interesting
facts. First, the life expectancy of 50-year-old women in the same group
also decreased by 2 years. Second, life expectancy at age 66 fell slightly
less than life expectancy at age 50 (by 1.6 years for men and 1.7 for
women).[10]

As a comparison, for the year 2005, the life tables provided by the US
Department of Health and Human Services (Arias, Rostron, and Tejada-
Vera 2010) report a life expectancy at age 66 (and thus for people born in
the 1940s) of 82.1 and 84.7 for white men and women, respectively.
Compared with the official life tables, we thus slightly overestimate life
expectancy, especially for women, a result that possibly reflects that the
HRS sample is drawn from noninstitutionalized, and thus initially
healthier, individuals. After the initial sampling, people ending up in
nursing homes in subsequent periods stay in the HRS data set.

One might wonder whether people born in the 1960s were aware that
their life expectancy was shorter than that of previous generations. To
evaluate this, we use the HRS question about one's subjective probability
of being alive at age 75. As table 5 shows, people born in the 1960s did adjust their life expectancy downward compared with those born in the
1940s. That is, men aged 55 and born in the 1940s report, on average, a subjective probability of being alive at age 75 of 61%, compared with 56% for

Table 5
Average Subjective Probability (in %) of Being Alive at Age 75 Reported
by People Ages 54–56 Who Are White and Non–College Educated

	Men	Women
Born in 1940s	61	66
Born in 1960s	56	58

Source: Health and Retirement Survey data.

those born in the 1960s. For women, the drop is even larger, going from 66% for those born in the 1940s to 58% for those born in the 1960s.

IV.   Labor Market and Savings Outcomes for the 1960s Cohort

Figure 4 displays the smoothed life-cycle profiles of participation, hours worked by workers, and assets for the 1960s cohort, by gender and marital status. Figure 4a highlights several important patterns.[11] First, married men have the highest labor market participation. Second, the participation of single men drops faster by age than that of married men. Third, single women have a participation profile that looks like a shifted-down version of that of married men. Last, married women have the lowest participation until age 40, but it then surpasses that of single men and single women up to age 65.

Figure 4b displays hours worked conditional on participation, with married men working the most hours, followed by single men, single

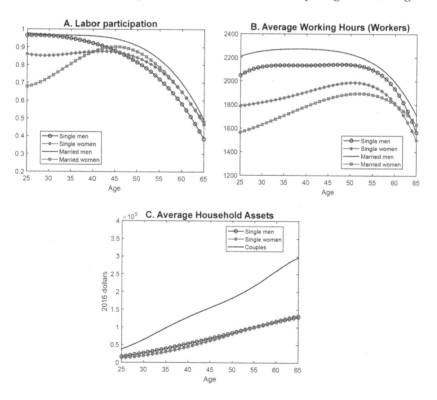

Fig. 4. Participation, hours by workers, and average assets for the cohort born in 1960. (a) Labor participation. (b) Average working hours (workers). (c) Average household assets.

women, and married women until age 60. Figure 4c displays savings accumulation up to age 65 and shows that couples start out with more assets than singles and that this gap widens with age, to peak at about two by retirement time.

We see these outcomes as important aspects of the data that we require our model to match to trust its implications about the effects of the changes in their lifetime opportunities that we consider.

V. The Model

We use a model based on Borella et al. (2017) and closely follow their exposition. A model period is 1 year long. People start their economic life at age 25, stop working at age 66 at the latest, and live up to age 99.

During the working stage, people choose how much to save and how much to work, face wage shocks and, if they are married, divorce shocks. Single people meet partners. For tractability, we make the following assumptions. People who are married to each other have the same age. Marriage, divorce, and fertility are exogenous. Women have an age-varying number of children that depends on their age and marital status. We estimate all of these processes from the data.

During the retirement stage, people face out-of-pocket medical expenses that are net of Medicare and private insurance payments and are partly covered by Medicaid. Married retired couples also face the risk of one of the spouses dying. Single retired people face the risk of their own death. We allow mortality risk and medical expenses to depend on gender, age, health status, and marital status.

We allow for both time costs and monetary costs of raising children and running households. In terms of time costs, we allow for available time to be split between work and leisure and to depend on gender and marital status. We interpret available time as net of home production, childcare, and elderly care that one has to perform whether working or not (and that is not easy to outsource). In addition, all workers have to pay a fixed cost of working, which depends on their age.

The monetary costs enter our model in two ways. There is an adult-equivalent family size that affects consumption. In addition, when women work, they have to pay a childcare cost that depends on the age and number of their children and on their own earnings. We assume that childcare costs are a normal good: women with higher earnings pay for more expensive childcare.

We assume that households have rational expectations about all of the stochastic processes that they face. Thus, they anticipate the nature of the uncertainty in our environment starting from age 25, when they enter our model.

A.   Preferences

Let t be age $\in \{t_0, t_1, \ldots, t_r, \ldots, t_d\}$, with $t_0 = 25, t_r = 66$ being retirement time, and $t_d = 99$ being the maximum possible life span. For simplicity of notation, think of the model as being written for one cohort; thus, age t also indexes the passing of time for that cohort. We solve the model for our 1960s cohort and then perform our counterfactuals by changing some of its inputs to those of the 1940s cohort.

Households have time-separable preferences and discount the future at rate β. The superscript i denotes gender, with $i = 1, 2$ being a man or a woman, respectively. The superscript j denotes marital status, with $j = 1, 2$ being single or in a couple, respectively.

Each single person has preferences over consumption and leisure, and the period flow of utility is given by the standard constant relative risk aversion (CRRA) utility function:

$$v^i(c_t, l_t) = \frac{\left(\left(\frac{c_t}{\eta_t^{i,j}}\right)^\omega l_t^{1-\omega}\right)^{1-\gamma} - 1}{1 - \gamma} + b,$$

where c_t is consumption, $\eta_t^{i,j}$ is the equivalent scale in consumption (which is a function of family size, including children), and $\eta_t^{i,1}$ corresponds to that for singles, and $b \geq 0$ is a parameter that ensures that people are happy to be alive, as in Hall and Jones (2007). The latter allows us to properly evaluate the welfare effects of changing life expectancy.

The term $l_t^{i,j}$ is leisure, which is given by

$$l_t^{i,j} = L^{i,j} - n_t - \Phi_t^{i,j} I_{n_t},$$

where $L^{i,j}$ is available time endowment, which can be different for single and married men and women and should be interpreted as available time net of home production. Leisure equals available time endowment less n_t, hours worked on the labor market, less the fixed time cost of working. That is, the term I_{nt} is an indicator function that equals 1 when hours worked are positive and zero otherwise, and the term $\Phi_t^{i,j}$ represents the fixed time cost of working.

The fixed cost of working should be interpreted as including commuting time, time spent getting ready for work, and so on. We allow it to depend on gender, marital status, and age because working at different ages might imply different time costs for married and single men and women. We assume the following functional form, whose three parameters we calibrate using our structural model:

$$\Phi_t^{i,j} = \frac{\exp(\phi_0^{i,j} + \phi_1^{i,j}t + \phi_2^{i,j}t^2)}{1 + \exp(\phi_0^{i,j} + \phi_1^{i,j}t + \phi_2^{i,j}t^2)}.$$

We assume that couples maximize their joint utility function:

$$w(c_t, l_t^1, l_t^2) = \frac{\left(\left(\frac{c_t}{\eta_t^{i,2}}\right)^\omega \left(l_t^1\right)^{1-\omega}\right)^{1-\gamma} - 1}{1-\gamma} + b + \frac{\left(\left(\frac{c_t}{\eta_t^{i,2}}\right)^\omega \left(l_t^2\right)^{1-\omega}\right)^{1-\gamma} - 1}{1-\gamma} + b.$$

Note that for couples, the economy of scale term $\eta_t^{i,2}$ is the same for both genders.

B.   The Environment

Households hold assets a_t, which earn rate of return r. The timing is as follows. At the beginning of each working period, each single individual observes his or her current idiosyncratic wage shock, age, assets, and accumulated earnings. Each married person also observes their partner's labor wage shock and accumulated earnings. At the beginning of each retirement period, each single individual observes his or her current age, assets, health, and accumulated earnings. Each married person also observes their partner's health and accumulated earnings. Decisions are made after everything has been observed, and new shocks hit at the end of the period after decisions have been made.

Human Capital and Wages

We take education at age 25 as given but explicitly model human capital accumulation after that age. To do so, we define human capital, $\bar{y}_t^i$, as one's average past earnings at each age. Thus, our definition of human capital implies that it is a function of one's initial wages and schooling and subsequent labor market experience and wages.[12]

There are two components to wages. The first is a deterministic function of human capital: $e_t^{i,j}(\bar{y}_t^i)$. The second component is a persistent earnings shock ϵ_t^i that evolves as follows:

$$\ln \epsilon_{t+1}^i = \rho_\epsilon^i \ln \epsilon_t^i + \nu_t^i, \ \nu_t^i \sim N(0, (\sigma_\nu^i)^2).$$

The product of $e_t^{i,j}(\cdot)$ and ϵ_t^i determines an agent's hourly wage.

Marriage and Divorce

During the working period, a single person gets married with an exogenous probability that depends on his or her age and gender. The probability of getting married at the beginning of next period is v_{t+1}^i.

Conditional on meeting a partner, the probability of meeting a partner p with wage shock ϵ_{t+1}^p is

$$\xi_{t+1}(\cdot) = \xi_{t+1}(\epsilon_{t+1}^p | \epsilon_{t+1}^i, i). \tag{1}$$

Allowing this probability to depend on the wage shock of both partners generates assortative mating. We assume random matching over assets a_{t+1} and average accumulated earnings of the partner $\bar{y}_{t+1}^p$, conditional on the partner's wage shock. We estimate the distribution of partners over these state variables from the PSID data (see app. C [available online], marriage and divorce probabilities subsection, for details) and denote it by

$$\theta_{t+1}(\cdot) = \theta_{t+1}(a_{t+1}^p, \bar{y}_{t+1}^p | \epsilon_{t+1}^p), \tag{2}$$

where the variables a_{t+1}^p, $\bar{y}_{t+1}^p$, and ϵ_{t+1}^p stand for the partner's assets, human capital, and wage shock, respectively.

A working-age couple can be hit by a divorce shock at the end of the period that depends on age, ζ_t. If the couple divorces, they split the assets equally, and each of the ex-spouses moves on with those assets and their own wage shock and Social Security contributions.

After retirement, single people do not marry. People in couples no longer divorce and can lose their spouse only because of death. This is consistent with the data because in this cohort, marriages and divorces after retirement are rare.

The Costs of Raising Children and Running a Household

Consistently with the data for this cohort, we assume that single men do not have children. We keep track of the total number of children and children's ages as a function of mother's age and marital status. The total number of children by one's age affects the economies of scale of single women and couples. We denote by $f^{0,5}(i, j, t)$ and $f^{6,11}(i, j, t)$ the number of children from 0 to 5 and from 6 to 11, respectively.

The term $\tau_c^{0,5}$ is the childcare cost for each child ages 0–5, whereas $\tau_c^{6,11}$ is the childcare cost for each child ages 6–11. Both are expressed as a fraction of the earnings of the working mother.

The number of children between ages 0 and 5 and between 6 and 11, together with the per child childcare costs by age of child, determines the childcare costs of working mothers ($i = 2$). Because we assume that childcare costs are proportional to earnings, if a woman does not work outside the home, her earnings are zero and so are her childcare costs. This amounts to assuming that she provides the childcare herself.

Medical Expenses and Death

After retirement, surviving people face medical expenses, health shocks, and death shocks. At age 66, we endow people with a distribution of health that depends on their marital status and gender (see app. C [available online], Health Status at Retirement subsection).

Health status ψ_t^i can be either good or bad and evolves according to a Markov process $\pi_t^{i,j}(\psi_t^i)$ that depends on age, gender, and marital status. Medical expenses $m_t^{i,j}(\psi_t^i)$ and survival probabilities $s_t^{i,j}(\psi_t^i)$ are functions of age, gender, marital status, and health status.

Initial Conditions

We take the fraction of single and married people at age 25 and their distribution over the relevant state variables from the PSID data. We list all of our state variables in Section V.D.

C. The Government

We model taxes on total income Y as in Gouveia and Strauss (1994), and we allow them to depend on marital status as follows:

$$T(Y, j) = (b^j - b^j(s^j Y + 1)^{-\frac{1}{p^j}})Y.$$

The government also uses a proportional payroll tax τ_t^{SS} on labor income, up to a Social Security cap $\tilde{y}_t$, to help finance old-age Social Security benefits. We allow both the payroll tax and the Social Security cap to change over time for the 1960 cohort, as in the data.

We use human capital $\bar{y}_t^i$ (computed as an individual's average earnings at age t) to determine both wages and old-age Social Security payments. While Social Security benefits for a single person are a function of one's average lifetime earnings, Social Security benefits for a married person are the highest of one's own benefit entitlement and half of the spouse's entitlement while the other spouse is alive (spousal benefit).

After the death of one's spouse, one's Social Security benefits are given by the highest of one's benefit entitlement and the deceased spouse's (survival benefit).

The insurance provided by Medicaid and Supplemental Security Income (SSI) in old age is represented by a means-tested consumption floor, $\underline{c}(j)$.[13]

D. Recursive Formulation

We define and compute six sets of value functions: the value function of working-age singles, the value function of retired singles, the value function of working-age couples, the value function of retired couples, the value function of an individual who is of working age and in a couple, and the value function of an individual who is retired and in a couple.

The Singles: Working Age and Retirement

The state variables for a single individual during one's working period are age t, gender i, assets a_t^i, the persistent earnings shock ϵ_t^i, and average realized earnings $\bar{y}_t^i$. The corresponding value function is

$$W^s(t, i, a_t^i, \epsilon_t^i, \bar{y}_t^i) = \max_{c_t, a_{t+1}, n_t^i}(v^i(c_t, l_t^{i,j}) + \beta(1 - \nu_{t+1}(i))E_t W^s(t + 1, i, a_{t+1}^i, \epsilon_{t+1}^i, \bar{y}_{t+1}^i)$$

$$+ \beta\nu_{t+1}(i)E_t[\hat{W}^c(t + 1, i, a_{t+1}^i + a_{t+1}^p, \epsilon_{t+1}^i, \epsilon_{t+1}^p, \bar{y}_{t+1}^i, \bar{y}_{t+1}^p)]), \quad (3)$$

$$l_t^{i,j} = L^{i,j} - n_t^i - \Phi_t^{i,j} I_{n_t^i}, \quad (4)$$

$$Y_t^i = e_t^{i,j}(\bar{y}_t^i)\epsilon_t^i n_t^i, \quad (5)$$

$$\tau_c(i, j, t) = \tau_c^{0.5} f^{0.5}(i, j, t) + \tau_c^{6,11} f^{6,11}(i, j, t), \quad (6)$$

$$T(\cdot) = T(ra_t + Y_t, j), \quad (7)$$

$$c_t + a_{t+1} = (1 + r)a_t^i + Y_t^i(1 - \tau_c(i, j, t)) - \tau_t^{SS}\min(Y_t^i, \tilde{y}_t) - T(\cdot), \quad (8)$$

$$\bar{y}_{t+1}^i = \frac{(\bar{y}_t^i(t - t_0) + (\min(Y_t^i, \tilde{y}_t)))}{(t + 1 - t_0)}, \quad (9)$$

$$a_t \geq 0, \quad n_t \geq 0, \quad \forall\, t. \quad (10)$$

The expectation of the value function next period if one remains single integrates over one's wage shock next period. When one gets married, we not only take a similar expectation but also integrate over the distribution of the state variables of one's partner: $\xi_{t+1}(\epsilon_{t+1}^p | \epsilon_{t+1}^i, i)$ is the distribution of the partner's wage shock defined in equation (1), and $\theta_{t+1}(\cdot)$ is the distribution of the partner's assets and human capital defined in equation (2).

The value function $\hat{W}^c$ is the discounted present value of the utility for the same individual, once he or she is in a married relationship with someone with given state variables, not the value function of the married couple, which counts the utility of both individuals in the relationship. We discuss the computation of the value function of an individual in a marriage later in this section.

Equation (5) shows that the deterministic component of wages is a function of age, gender, marital status, and human capital.

Equation (9) describes the evolution of human capital, which we measure as average accumulated earnings (up to the Social Security earnings cap $\tilde{y}_t$) and that we use as a determinant of future wages and Social Security payments after retirement.

During the last working period, a person takes the expected values of the value functions during the first period of retirement. The state variables for a retired single individual are age t, gender i, assets a_t^i, health ψ_t^i, and average realized lifetime earnings $\bar{y}_r^i$. Because we assume that the retired individual can no longer get married, his or her recursive problem can be written as

$$R^s(t, i, a_t, \psi_t^i, \bar{y}_r^i) = \max_{c_t, a_{t+1}}(v^i(c_t, L^{i,j}) + \beta s_t^{i,j}(\psi_t^i)E_t R^s(t + 1, i, a_{t+1}, \psi_{t+1}^i, \bar{y}_r^i)), \qquad (11)$$

$$Y_t = SS(\bar{y}_r), \qquad (12)$$

$$T(\cdot) = T(Y_t + ra_t, j), \qquad (13)$$

$$B(a_t, Y_t, \psi_t^i, \underline{c}(j)) = \max\left\{0, \underline{c}(j) - [(1 + r)a_t + Y_t - m_t^{i,j}(\psi_t^i) - T(\cdot)]\right\}, \qquad (14)$$

$$c_t + a_{t+1} = (1 + r)a_t + Y_t + B(a_t, Y_t, \psi_t^i, \underline{c}(j)) - m_t^{i,j}(\psi_t^i) - T(\cdot), \qquad (15)$$

$$a_{t+1} \geq 0, \qquad \forall t \qquad (16)$$

$$a_{t+1} = 0, \quad \text{if} \quad B(\cdot) > 0. \qquad (17)$$

The term $s_t^{i,j}(\psi_t^i)$ is the survival probability as a function of age, gender, marital status, and health status. The expectation of the value function next period is taken with respect to the evolution of health.

The term $SS(\bar{y}_r^i)$ represents Social Security, which for the single individual is a function of the income earned during their work life, $\bar{y}_r^i$, and the function $B(a_t, Y_t^i, \psi_t^i, \underline{c}(j))$ represents old-age means-tested government transfers such as Medicaid and SSI, which ensure a minimum consumption floor $\underline{c}(j)$.

The Couples: Working Age and Retirement

The state variables for a married couple in the working stage are $(t, a_t, \epsilon_t^1,$ $\epsilon_t^2, \bar{y}_t^1, \bar{y}_t^2)$, where 1 and 2 refer to gender, and the recursive problem for the married couple ($j = 2$) before t_r can be written as

$$W^c(t, a_t, \epsilon_t^1, \epsilon_t^2, \bar{y}_t^1, \bar{y}_t^2) = \max_{c_t, a_{t+1}, n_t^1, n_t^2} \left(w\left(c_t, l_t^{1,j}, l_t^{2,j}\right) \right.$$

$$+ (1 - \zeta_{t+1})\beta E_t W^c(t + 1, a_{t+1}, \epsilon_{t+1}^1, \epsilon_{t+1}^2, \bar{y}_{t+1}^1, \bar{y}_{t+1}^2) \quad (18)$$

$$+ \zeta_{t+1}\beta \sum_{i=1}^{2} \left(E_t W^s\left(t + 1, i, \frac{a_{t+1}}{2}, \epsilon_{t+1}^i, \bar{y}_{t+1}^i \right) \right),$$

$$l_t^{i,j} = L^{i,j} - n_t^i - \Phi_t^{i,j} I_{n_t^i}, \quad (19)$$

$$Y_t^i = e_t^{i,j}(\bar{y}_t^i)\epsilon_t^i n_t^i, \quad (20)$$

$$\tau_c(i, j, t) = \tau_c^{0,5} f^{0,5}(i, j, t) + \tau_c^{6,11} f^{6,11}(i, j, t), \quad (21)$$

$$T(\cdot) = T(ra_t + Y_t^1 + Y_t^2, j), \quad (22)$$

$$c_t + a_{t+1} = (1 + r)a_t + Y_t^1 + Y_t^2(1 - \tau_c(2, 2, t)) - \tau_t^{SS}(\min(Y_t^1, \tilde{y}_t) \quad (23)$$

$$+ \min(Y_t^2, \tilde{y}_t)) - T(\cdot),$$

$$\bar{y}_{t+1}^i = \frac{(\bar{y}_t^i(t - t_0) + (\min(Y_t^i, \tilde{y}_t)))}{(t + 1 - t_0)}, \quad (24)$$

$$a_t \geq 0, \quad n_t^1, n_t^2 \geq 0, \quad \forall t. \quad (25)$$

The expected value of the couple's value function is taken with respect to the conditional probabilities of the two ϵ_{t+1}s, given the current values of the ϵ_ts for each of the spouses (we assume independent draws). The expected values for the newly divorced people are taken using the appropriate conditional distribution for their own labor wage shocks.

During their last working period, couples take the expected values of the value functions for the first period of retirement. During retirement—that is, from age t_r on—each of the spouses is hit with a health shock ψ_t^i and a realization of the survival shock $s_t^{i,2}(\psi_t^i)$. Symmetrically with the other shocks, $s_t^{1,2}(\psi_t^1)$ is the after-retirement survival probability of the husband, whereas $s_t^{2,2}(\psi_t^2)$ is the survival probability of the wife. We assume that the health shocks of each spouse are independent of each other and that the death shocks of each spouse are also independent of each other.

In each period, the married couple's ($j = 2$) recursive problem during retirement can be written as

$$R^c(t, a_t, \psi_t^1, \psi_t^2, \bar{y}_r^1, \bar{y}_r^2) = \max_{c_t, a_{t+1}} (w(c_t, L^{1,j}, L^{2,j})$$

$$+ \beta s_t^{1,j}(\psi_t^1) s_t^{2,j}(\psi_t^2) E_t R^c(t + 1, a_{t+1}, \psi_{t+1}^1, \psi_{t+1}^2, \bar{y}_r^1, \bar{y}_r^2)$$

$$+ \beta s_t^{1,j}(\psi_t^1)(1 - s_t^{2,j}(\psi_t^2)) E_t R^s(t + 1, 1, a_{t+1}, \psi_{t+1}^1, \bar{\bar{y}}_r)$$

$$+ \beta s_t^{2,j}(\psi_t^2)(1 - s_t^{1,j}(\psi_t^1)) E_t R^s(t + 1, 2, a_{t+1}, \psi_{t+1}^2, \bar{\bar{y}}_r)),$$

$$(26)$$

$$Y_t = \max\left\{ (SS(\bar{y}_r^1) + SS(\bar{y}_r^2), \frac{3}{2} \max(SS(\bar{y}_r^1), SS(\bar{y}_r^2)) \right\}, \quad (27)$$

$$\bar{\bar{y}}_r = \max(\bar{y}_r^1, \bar{y}_r^2), \quad (28)$$

$$T(\cdot) = T(Y_t + ra_t, j), \quad (29)$$

$$B(a_t, Y_t, \psi_t^1, \psi_t^2, \underline{c}(j)) = \max\left\{ 0, \underline{c}(j) - [(1 + r)a_t + Y_t - m_t^{1,j}(\psi_t^1) - m_t^{2,j}(\psi_t^2) - T(\cdot)] \right\}, \quad (30)$$

$$c_t + a_{t+1} = (1 + r)a_t + Y_t + B(a_t, Y_t, \psi_t^1, \psi_t^2, \underline{c}(j))$$
$$- m_t^{1,j}(\psi_t^1) - m_t^{2,j}(\psi_t^2) - T(\cdot), \quad (31)$$

$$a_{t+1} \geq 0, \quad \forall t, \quad (32)$$

$$a_{t+1} = 0, \quad \text{if} \quad B(\cdot) > 0. \quad (33)$$

In equation (27), Y_t mimics the spousal benefit from Social Security, which gives a married person the right to collect the higher of his or her own benefit entitlement and half of the spouse's entitlement. In equation (28), $\bar{\bar{y}}_r$ represents survivorship benefits from Social Security in case of death of one of the spouses. The survivor has the right to collect the higher of his or her own benefit entitlement and the deceased spouse's entitlement.

The Individuals in Couples: Working Age and Retirement

We have to compute the joint value function of the couple to appropriately compute joint labor supply and savings under the married couple's available resources. However, when computing the value of getting married for a single person, the relevant object for that person is his or her discounted present value of utility in the marriage. We thus compute this object for a person of gender i who is married to a specific partner,

$$\hat{W}^c(t, i, a_t, \epsilon_t^1, \epsilon_t^2, \bar{y}_t^1, \bar{y}_t^2) = v^i(\hat{c}_t(\cdot), \hat{l}_t^{i,j})$$
$$+ \beta(1 - \zeta_{t+1})E_t\hat{W}^c(t + 1, i, \hat{a}_{t+1}(\cdot), \epsilon_{t+1}^1, \epsilon_{t+1}^2, \bar{y}_{t+1}^1, \bar{y}_{t+1}^2)$$
$$+ \beta\zeta_{t+1}E_tW^s\left(t + 1, i, \frac{\hat{a}_{t+1}(\cdot)}{2}, \epsilon_{t+1}^i, \bar{y}_{t+1}^i\right), \quad (34)$$

where $\hat{c}_t(\cdot)$, $\hat{l}_t^{i,j}(\cdot)$, and $\hat{a}_{t+1}(\cdot)$ are, respectively, optimal consumption from the perspective of the couple, leisure, and saving for an individual of gender i in a couple with the given state variables.

During the retirement period, we have

$$\hat{R}^c(t, i, a_t, \psi_t^1, \psi_t^2, \bar{y}_r^1, \bar{y}_r^2)$$
$$= v^i(\hat{c}_t(\cdot), L^{i,j}) + \beta s_t^{i,j}(\psi_t^i)s_t^{p,j}(\psi_t^p)E_t\hat{R}^c(t + 1, i, \hat{a}_{t+1}(\cdot), \psi_{t+1}^1, \psi_{t+1}^2, \bar{y}_r^1, \bar{y}_r^2)$$
$$+ \beta s_t^{i,j}(\psi_t^i)(1 - s_t^{p,j}(\psi_t^p))E_tR^s(t + 1, i, \hat{a}_{t+1}(\cdot), \psi_{t+1}^i, \bar{\bar{y}}_r), \quad (35)$$

where $s_t^{p,j}(\psi_t^p)$ is the survival probability of the partner of the person of gender i. This continuation utility is needed to compute equation (34) during the last working period, when $\hat{W}^c(\cdot)$ is replaced by $\hat{R}^c(\cdot)$.

VI.   Estimation and Calibration

We calibrate our model to match the data for the 1960s birth cohort by using a two-step strategy, as in Gourinchas and Parker (2002) and De Nardi, French, and Jones (2010, 2016). Then, in a third step, as in De Nardi, Pashchenko, and Porapakkarm (2017), we calibrate the parameter b, which affects the utility of being alive. It is important to note that this parameter does not change our decision rules and the data that we match and can thus be calibrated after the other parameters are calibrated. Nonetheless, it is necessary to calibrate it to properly evaluate welfare when life expectancy changes.

More specifically, in the third step, we choose b so that the value of statistical life (VSL) implied by our model is in the middle of the range estimated by the empirical literature. The VSL is defined as the compensation that people require to bear an increase in their probability of death, expressed as "dollars per death." For example, suppose that people are willing to tolerate an additional fatality risk of $1/10,000$ during a given period for a compensation of \$500 per person. Among 10,000 people there will be one death, and it will cost the society 10,000 times \$500 = \$5 million, which is the implied VSL.

A. First-Step Calibration and Estimation for the 1960s Cohort

In the first step, we use the data to compute the initial distributions of our model's state variables and estimate or calibrate the parameters that can be identified outside our model. For instance, we estimate the probabilities of marriage, divorce, health transitions, and death, the number and age of children by maternal age and marital status, the wage processes, and medical expenses during retirement.

Our calibrated parameters are listed in table 6. We set the interest rate r to 4% and the utility curvature parameter, γ, to 2.5. The equivalence scales are set to $\eta_t^{i,j} = (j + 0.7 \times f_t^{i,j})^{0.7}$, as estimated by Citro and Michael (1995). The term $f_t^{i,j}$ is the average total number of children for single and married men and women by age.

We use the tax function for married and single people estimated by Guner, Kaygusuz, and Ventura (2012). The retirement benefits at age 66 are calculated to mimic the Old Age and Survivor Insurance component of the Social Security system. The most recent paper estimating the consumption floor during retirement is the one by De Nardi et al. (2016) in a rich model of retirement with endogenous medical expenses. In their framework, they estimate a utility floor that corresponds to consuming \$4,600 a year when healthy. However, they note that Medicaid recipients are guaranteed a minimum income of \$6,670. As a compromise, we use \$5,900 as our consumption floor for elderly singles, which is \$8,687 in 2016 dollars, and the one for couples to be 1.5 the amount for singles, which is the statutory ratio between benefits of couples to singles.

Table 6
First-Step Inputs Summary

	Source
Calibrated parameters:	
Preferences and returns:	
r: Interest rate	4%; De Nardi et al. (2016)
$\eta_t^{i,j}$: Equivalence scales	PSID
γ: Utility curvature parameter	2.5; see text
Government policy:	
b^j, s^j, p^j: Income tax	Guner et al. (2012)
$SS(\bar{y}_r)$: Social Security benefit	See text
τ_t^{SS}: Social Security tax rate	See text
$\tilde{y}_t$: Social Security cap	See text
$\underline{c}(1)$: Minimum consumption, singles	$8,687; De Nardi et al. (2016)
$\underline{c}(2)$: Minimum consumption, couples	$13,031; Social Security rules
Estimated processes:	
Wages:	
$e_t^{i,j}(\cdot)$: Endogenous age-efficiency profiles	PSID
ϵ_t^i: Wage shocks	PSID
Demographics:	
$s_t^{i,j}(\psi_t^i)$: Survival probability	HRS
ζ_t: Divorce probability	PSID
ν_t: Probability of getting married	PSID
ξ_t: Matching probability	PSID
θ_t: Partner's assets and earnings	PSID
$f^{0,5}(i, j, t)$: Number of children ages 0–5	PSID
$f^{6,11}(i, j, t)$: Number of children ages 6–11	PSID
Health shock:	
$m_t^{i,j}(\psi_t^i)$: Medical expenses	HRS
$\pi_t^{i,j}(\psi_t^i)$: Transition matrix for health status	HRS

Note: PSID = Panel Study of Income Dynamics; HRS = Health and Retirement Survey.

In the subsections that follow, we describe the estimation of our wage functions, medical expenses, and survival probabilities. More details about all of our first-step inputs are in appendix C (available online).

Wage Schedules

We estimate wage schedules using the PSID data and regressing the logarithm of potential wage for person k at age t,

$$\ln \overline{wage}_{kt} = d_k + f^i(t) + \sum_{g=1}^{G} \beta_g D_g \ln(\bar{y}_{kt} + \delta_y) + u_{kt},$$

on a fixed effect d_k, a polynomial f in age t for each gender i, gender-cohort dummies D_g interacted with human capital $\bar{y}_{kt}$, and a shift parameter δ_y

(to be able to take logs). Thus, we allow all coefficients to be gender-specific and for the coefficient on human capital to also depend on cohort.

We then regress the sum of the fixed effects and the residuals for each person on cohort and marital status dummies and their interactions, separately for each gender, and use the estimated effects for gender, marital status, and cohort as shifters for the wage profiles of each demographic group and cohort.

Table 7 reports the results of our estimated equation for potential wages.[14] It shows that the effects of age on potential wages are small, especially for men.[15] The largest age effect for men is at age 60, when their potential wage declines by 1.3%. Women's potential wages, instead, grow on average by half a percentage point until age 50 and decline only mildly around age 60.

In terms of the position of the age profile, the effect of being born in the 1960s cohort instead of the 1940s cohort is large and negative, especially for married and single men. Because these declines depend on one's human capital level, we discuss their magnitudes when illustrating the interaction between wages and human capital for the two cohorts in figure 5. In contrast to this decline, however, returns to human capital went up for the 1960s cohort compared with the 1940s cohort, as our estimated elasticity of wages to human capital increases from 0.256 and 0.363 for the 1940s cohort to 0.347 and 0.413 for the 1960s one, respectively, for men and women.

Table 7
Estimation Results for Potential Wages

	Men	Women
Age overall	.0015	.0017***
Age = 30	.0043	.0012***
Age = 40	.0039	.0056***
Age = 50	−.0018	.0044***
Age = 60	−.013**	−.0025**
Married and born in 1960s versus 1940s	−.642***	−.395***
Single and born in 1960s versus 1940s	−.660***	−.381***
$\ln(\bar{y}_t + \delta_y)$ and born in 1940s	.256***	.363***
$\ln(\bar{y}_t + \delta_y)$ and born in 1960s	.347***	.413***

Note: Results are reported as percentage changes in potential wages due to one-unit increases in the relevant variables (or changes from zero to one in case of dummy variables). In the case of $\bar{y}_t$ we report the elasticity.
**$p < .05$.
***$p < .01$.

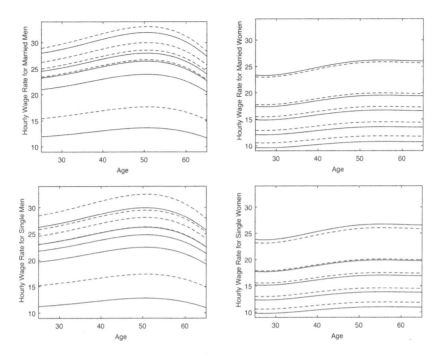

Fig. 5. Wages as a function of human capital levels. *Top*: married people. *Bottom*: single people. *Left*: men. *Right*: women. The dashed lines refer to the cohort born in 1940 and the solid lines to that born in 1960, conditional on a fixed gender-specific level of human capital, measured at the 0th, 25th, 50th, 75th, and 99th percentiles of the distributions of average accumulated earnings in our sample.

To better understand the implications of our estimates by cohort and subgroup, figure 5 reports our estimated average wage profiles by age conditional on a fixed level of human capital during all of the working period. The human capital levels over which we condition are the 0th, 25th, 50th, 75th, and 99th percentiles of the distributions of average accumulated earnings of men and women in our sample. They correspond to, respectively, $0, $30,100, $41,300, $51,600, and $79,100 for men and to $0, $5,000, $13,900, $23,700, and $55,900 for women (expressed in 2016 dollars). In these graphs, therefore, human capital is held fixed by age. The *top graphs* are for married people, and the bottom ones refer to singles. The graphs on the *left* are for men, and those on the *right* for women. The solid lines refer to the 1960s cohort and the dashed ones to the 1940s cohort.

In sum, these graphs display wages as a function of age for single and married men and women in our two cohorts for five fixed levels of human capital. Hence, they illustrate the changes in the returns to human capital across cohorts and marital status for various human capital levels.

Focusing on married men with zero human capital (the lowest two lines in the *top left* graph), the effect of the lower position of the age profile for the 1960s cohort is apparent: married men entering the labor market receive an average potential hourly wage that is 3.5 dollars lower than that received by the same men in the 1940s cohort. At higher levels of human capital, the disadvantage is progressively reduced by the higher returns to human capital but is still not enough to counterbalance the drop in the level of all wages. Even at the highest level of human capital within the non–college graduate group, the hourly wage for married men born in the 1960s is still 90 cents lower than that received by the same men in the 1940s. The *bottom left* graph displays the wages of single men and shows that their drops are even larger than those for married men at all human capital levels.

The graphs on the *right* refer to the wages of women. The wages of married women (*top* graph) with zero human capital went down by about 0.9 dollars, a much smaller decrease across cohorts than that for men, both in absolute value and in percentage terms. As a consequence of the increased returns to human capital, at the median human capital level for women, their wage is 0.6 dollars lower, while it is actually higher for the high-human-capital women in the 1960s than the 1940s cohort, by 0.3 dollars. The main difference between married and single women is that, from the 1940s to the 1960s, only married women in the top 1% of the human capital distribution experienced a wage increase, whereas single women in the top 15% of the human capital distribution experienced a wage increase.

In sum, we find that men and women in the 1960s cohort had a higher return to human capital but lower cohort-and-gender-age wage profiles compared with those born in the 1940s. The latter drop was especially large for men. These changes imply that men and women with lower human capital had the largest drop, that wages dropped for men at all human capital levels, and that the wages of the highest human capital women increased. As a result of these changes in the wage structure and a larger increase in women's human capital (partly due to more years of education and partly due to more labor market experience), average wages over the life cycle, shown in figure 2, were higher for women and lower for men in the 1960s cohort.

Medical Expenses

We estimate out-of-pocket medical expenses using the HRS data and regressing the logarithm of medical expenses for person k at age t,

$$\ln(m_{kt}) = X_{kt}^{m\prime}\beta^m + \alpha_k^m + u_{kt}^m,$$

where the explanatory variables include a third-order polynomial in age fully interacted with gender, current health status, and interactions between these variables.[16] The term α_k^m represents a fixed effect and takes into account all unmeasured fixed-over-time characteristics that may bias the age profile, such as differential mortality, as discussed in De Nardi et al. (2010). We then regress the residuals from this equation on cohort, gender, and marital status dummies to compute the average effect for each group of interest. Hence, the profile of the logarithm of medical expenses is constant across cohorts up to a constant.

Table 8 reports the results from our estimates for medical expenses[17] and shows that after age 66, real medical expenses increase with age on average by 2.4% and 2.6% for men and women, respectively, with the growth for women being much faster than for men after age 76, reaching, for example, 5.8% at age 96. Finally, those born in the 1960s cohort face medical expenses that are 48.6% higher than those born in the 1940s cohort, even after conditioning on health status.

Life Expectancy

As described in our model section, we allow mortality to depend on health, gender, marital status, and age, and we have health evolving over time, depending on previous health, age, gender, and marital status. We allow cohort effects to affect all of these dynamics and their initial conditions, both in our estimation of these inputs and in our model.

Table 8
Estimation Results for Medical Expenses for Men and Women

	Men	Women
Age overall	.024***	.026***
At age 66	.022***	.019***
At age 76	.017***	.014***
At age 86	.017***	.027***
At age 96	.023***	.058***
Bad health	.201***	.209***
Married	.327***	.327***
Born in 1960s	.486***	.486***

Source: Health and Retirement Survey data.
Note: Results are reported as percentage changes in medical expenses due to marginal increases in the relevant variables (or changes from zero to one in case of dummy variables).
***$p < .01$.

More specifically, we model the probability of being alive at time t as a logit function:

$$s_t = \text{Prob}(\text{Alive}_t = 1 \mid X_t^s) = \frac{\exp(X_t^{s\prime}\beta^s)}{1 + \exp(X_t^{s\prime}\beta^s)},$$

which we estimate using the HRS data. Among the explanatory variables, we include a third-order polynomial in age, gender, marital status, and health status in the previous period, as well as interactions between these variables and age, whenever they are statistically different from zero. We also include cohort dummies and use coefficients relative to the cohort of interest to adjust the constant accordingly.[18]

To investigate the implications of the cohort effects that we estimate through these pathways, table 9 reports the model-implied life expectancy at age 66 and their changes when we add, in turn, the changes in mortality, health dynamics, initial health at age 66, and initial fractions of married and single people that are driven by cohort effects on each of those components.

The first row of table 9 reports life expectancy using all of the inputs that we estimate for the 1960s cohort. The model-implied life expectancy is very close to the one we have computed using the data and a much simpler regression for mortality, reported in Section III.C. The second row changes the observed relationship between mortality and health and demographics from the one we estimate for the 1960s cohort to the one we estimate for the 1940s cohort. It shows that this change alone implies an increase of 0.8 and 0.7 years of life for men and women, respectively. In the third row, we switch from the 1960s to the 1940s health dynamics, and there is no noticeable change in life expectancy because the health dynamics are very similar. In the fourth row, we change the fraction of

Table 9
Life Expectancy at Age 66 for White and Non-College-Educated Men and Women Born in the 1940s and 1960s Cohorts as We Turn On Various Determinants of Mortality

	Men	Women
1960s inputs	80.8	84.5
1940s survival functions	81.6	85.3
1940s survival and health dynamics	81.6	85.3
1940s survival, health dynamics, initial health	81.7	85.4
1940s survival, health dynamics, initial health, and marital status	82.0	85.6

Source: Health and Retirement Survey data.

people who are in bad health at age 66, conditional on marital status, to that of the 1940s cohort. This change implies a further increase of 0.1 years of life expectancy for both men and women, indicating that a smaller part of the observed decrease in life expectancy at age 66 is captured by changing health conditions at age 66. The last row of the table not only changes initial health at age 66 but also allows for the fact that more people were married in the 1940s cohort compared with the 1960s cohort. This change in the fraction of married people at age 66 explains an additional change of 0.3 and 0.2 years of life for men and women, respectively.

Our decomposition thus shows that the biggest change in life expectancy in our framework comes from a change in the relationship between mortality and health dynamics after age 66, whereas a smaller one stems from a worsening of initial health status at age 66. Finally, the reduction in the fraction of married people also has a nonnegligible effect on life expectancy of both men and women. In our experiments changing life expectancy, we do not change marital status at age 25, and we thus abstract from the effects of the small changes in life expectancy coming from that channel.

B. Second-Step Calibration

In the second step, we calibrate 19 model parameters (β, ω, ($\phi_0^{i,j}$, $\phi_1^{i,j}$, $\phi_2^{i,j}$), ($\tau_c^{0,5}$, $\tau_c^{6,11}$), $L^{i,j}$) so that our model mimics the observed life-cycle patterns of labor market participation, hours worked conditional on working, and savings for married and single men and women that we report in figure 4.

Table 10 presents our calibrated preference parameters for the 1960s cohort. Our calibrated discount factor is 0.981, and our calibrated weight on consumption is 0.416.

We normalize available time for single men to 5,840 hours a year (112.3 hours a week) and calibrate available time for single women and married women and men. Our calibration implies that single women have the same time endowment as single men (112 hours a week). The corresponding time endowments for married men and women are, respectively, 105 and 88 hours. This implies that people in the latter two groups spend 7 and 24 hours a week, respectively, in nonmarket activities such as running households, raising children, and taking care of aging parents. Our estimates of nonmarket work time are similar to those reported by Aguiar and Hurst (2007) and by Dotsey, Li, and Yang (2014).

Table 10
Second-Step Calibrated Model Parameters

Calibrated Parameters	1960s Cohort
β: Discount factor	.981
ω: Consumption weight	.416
$L^{2,1}$: Time endowment (weekly hours), single women	112
$L^{1,2}$: Time endowment (weekly hours), married men	105
$L^{2,2}$: Time endowment (weekly hours), married women	88
$\tau_c^{0,5}$: Prop. childcare cost for children ages 0–5 (%)	35
$\tau_c^{6,11}$: Prop. childcare cost for children ages 6–11 (%)	3.0
$\Phi_t^{i,j}$: Participation cost	Figure 6

Our estimates for the 1960s cohort imply that the per child childcare cost of having a child ages 0–5 and 6–11 are, respectively, 35% and 3.0% of a woman's earnings. In the PSID data, childcare costs are not broken down by age of the child, but per child childcare costs (for all children in the age range 0–11) of a married woman are 33% and 19% of her earnings at ages 25 and 30, respectively. Computing our model's implications, we find that per child childcare costs (for all children in the age range 0–11) of a married woman are 30% and 23% of her earnings, respectively, at ages 25 and 30. Thus, our model infers childcare costs that are similar to those in the PSID data.

Figure 6 shows the calibrated profiles of labor participation costs by age, expressed as a fraction of the time endowment of single men.

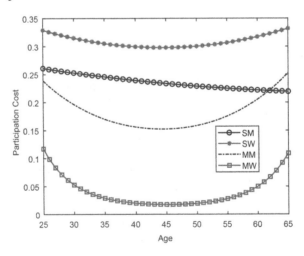

Fig. 6. Calibrated labor participation costs, expressed as a fraction of the time endowment of single men. SM = single men, SW = single women, MM = married men, MW = married women. Model estimates.

Participation costs are relatively high when young, decrease in middle age, and with the exception of single men, increase after 45.

C.   Third-Step Calibration

To match the VSL, we proceed as follows. Because in our model we do not have mortality until age 66, we review the VSL estimated for older people in previous empirical work. Within this literature, O'Brien (2013) estimates the VSL by examining consumer automobile purchases by individuals up to 85 years old. He finds that the VSL is respectively $8 million for the 65–74 age group and $7 million for the 75–85 age group (expressed in year 2009 dollars). Alberini et al. (2004) instead use contingent valuation surveys, which elicited respondents' willingness to pay for reductions of mortality risk of different magnitudes, and find values between $1 million and $5 million for the 40–75 age group (expressed in year 2000 dollars). Thus, the range from these two papers, expressed in year 2016 dollars (the base year that we use in this paper), is between $1 million and $9 million. Then, we choose $b = 0.009$ so that when we increase mortality after retirement and compute a compensation that makes them indifferent between this counterfactual case and our benchmark mortality, we obtain an average VSL at age 66 of $5 million.

D.   Model Fit

Figures 7 and 8 report our model-implied moments, as well as the moments and 95% confidence intervals from the PSID data for our 1960s cohort. They show that our parsimoniously parameterized model (19 parameters and 448 targets) fits the data well and reproduces the important patterns of participation, hours conditional on participation, and asset accumulation for all four demographic groups.

VII.   The Effects of Changing Wages, Medical Expenses, and Life Expectancy

We now turn to evaluating the effects of the changes in wages, medical expenses, and life expectancy that we have documented. Because we want to isolate the effects of these changes on the 1960s cohort (while keeping everything else constant for this cohort), we only replace these three sets of inputs with those experienced by the 1940s cohort, first one

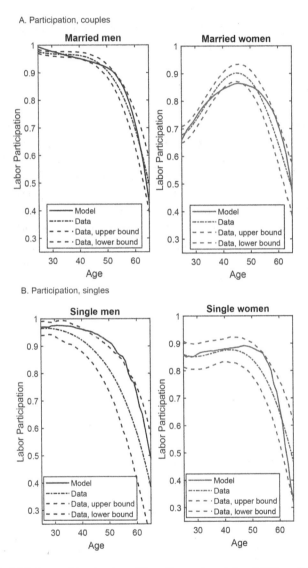

Fig. 7. Model fit for participation (*a* and *b*) and hours (*c* and *d*) and 95% confidence intervals from the Panel Study of Income Dynamics data. (*a*) Participation, couples. (*b*) Participation, singles. (*c*) Hours for workers, couples. (*d*) Hours for workers, singles.

at a time and then all at the same time. In doing so, we assume that, as of age 25, the 1960s cohort have rational expectations about all of the stochastic processes that they face over the rest of their lives, including when we switch some of them to their 1940s counterparts.

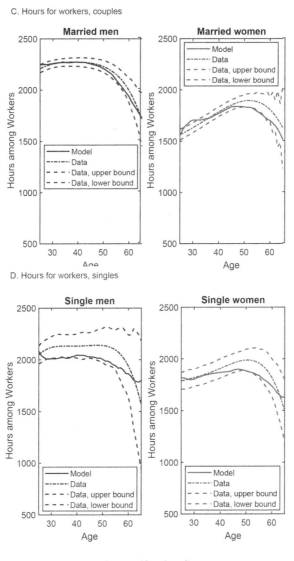

Fig. 7.   (*Continued*)

We start by studying the implications of these changes for labor participation, hours worked by workers, and savings for single and married men and women. Then, to evaluate welfare, we compute a onetime asset compensation to be given upon entering the model—that is, at age 25—that makes a household endowed with a given set of state variables indifferent between facing the 1960s input and the 1940s input.[19] Finally,

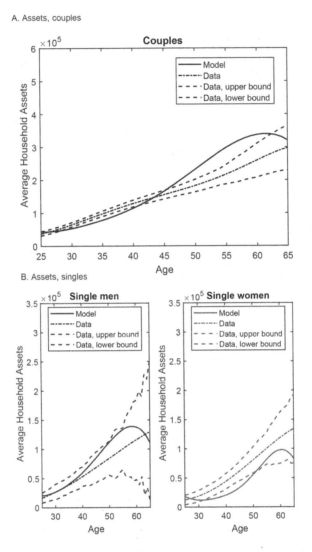

Fig. 8. Model fit for assets and 95% confidence intervals from the Panel Study of Income Dynamics data. (*a*) Assets, couples. (*b*) Assets, singles.

we compute the fraction of people that have lost or gained as a result of these changes and report the average welfare loss experienced by single men, single women, and married couples expressed as the average compensation that makes each of these groups indifferent between the two set of inputs.

A. Changing Wages

Figure 9 compares the participation, hours worked by workers, and savings for the 1960s cohort under their own wage schedule and under the wage schedule of the 1940s cohort. It shows that, according to our model,

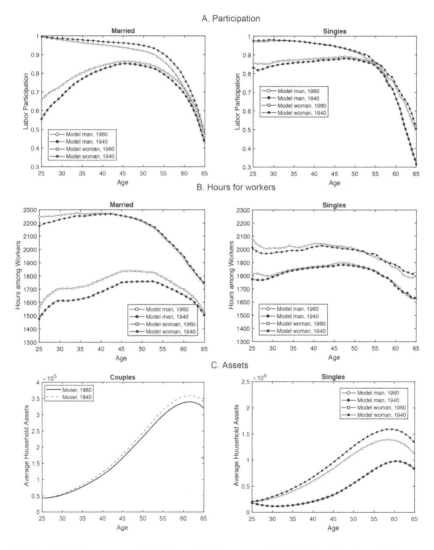

Fig. 9. Model outcomes with 1960s and 1940s wage schedule. (*a*) Participation. (*b*) Hours for workers. (*c*) Assets.

all of these economic outcomes would have been rather different under the 1940s wage schedule.

The largest effects occurred for married couples, with many more married women participating and working more hours under the 1960s wage schedule, while their husbands dropped out of the labor force at younger ages. At age 25, for instance, the participation of married women was 8 percentage points higher. Married men's participation started dropping faster after age 30 and was 4 percentage points lower than under the 1940s wage schedule at age 55. Hours worked by young married women were about 100 hours a year higher, whereas hours worked by young married men were only slightly higher. These changes were due to much lower wages for men, in conjunction with increasing returns to human capital. The latter, in particular, increased the returns to working when young.

Single people were affected too. They were experiencing lower wages, for the most part, and in the case of single women, they were also expecting to get married to lower-wage husbands. This negative wealth effect makes them invest more in their own human capital, work harder when young, and receive higher wages because of higher human capital accumulation. Single men reacted little to these changes by marginally reducing their participation, increasing hours worked while young, and reducing them after age 50.

As a result of the changing wage schedule and endogenous labor market decisions, average discounted lifetime income decreased by $115,000 (10%) for single men and $108,000 (9%) for married men but increased by $28,000 (5%) for single women and $36,000 (7%) for married women. As households experienced the large negative wealth effect coming from lower wages and earnings, retirement savings were much lower. Assets at age 66 dropped by 21% for single men, 1.1% for single women, and 6.1% for couples, respectively.

We now turn to evaluating how much worse (or better) people fared under the 1960s rather than the 1940s wage schedule.[20] We start by studying the effects of the wage changes for men only. In this case, everyone loses, and the onetime asset compensation that we should give to 25-year-olds to make them indifferent between the two wage schedules for men is $68,300 for single men, $17,800 for single women, and $64,800 for couples. The first row of table 11 reports this compensation as a fraction of the present value of lifetime income for each group. It amounts to 6.8%, 2.9%, and 4.0% for single men, single women, and couples, respectively.

We then turn to the welfare effects of having the wages of both men and women set to the 1960s instead of 1940s wage schedules. Again, virtually

Table 11
Welfare Compensation for the 1960s Cohort for Facing the 1960s Wage Schedule Instead of the 1940s Wage Schedule, Computed as a Onetime Asset Compensation at Age 25 and Expressed as a Fraction of the Present Discounted Value of One's Income

Compared with 1940 Wage Schedule	Single Men (%)	Single Women (%)	Couples (%)
Men only[a]	6.8	2.9	4.0
Men and women[a]	7.3	3.4	4.5
No marriage and divorce economy:			
Men only[b]	11.1	.0	4.3
Men and women[b]	11.1	.7	4.9

[a]Our benchmark economy.
[b]An economy without marriage and divorce after age 25.

everyone loses as a result. The onetime asset compensation that we should give to 25-year-olds to make them indifferent between the 1940s and the 1960s wages is $72,900 for single men, $20,400 for single women, and $73,600 for couples. The second row of table 11 reports this compensation as a fraction of lifetime income for each group. It amounts to 7.3%, 3.4%, and 4.5% for single men, single women, and couples, respectively. Thus, everyone loses, and the welfare losses are big, both in absolute value and when compared with the discounted value of lifetime income in each group.

To isolate the welfare effects coming from marriage and divorce dynamics, we also compute an economy in which there is no marriage and divorce after age 25. In it, a 25-year-old single person stays single forever, and a 25-year-old married couple stays married forever.[21] The last two rows of table 11 report the welfare losses of the losers as a fraction of the present discounted value of lifetime income for each group.

When men's wages drop in this economy, all men and couples lose as a result. The onetime asset compensation that we should give to 25-year-olds to make them indifferent between the 1940s and the 1960s men's wages when there is no marriage and divorce is $98,800 for single men, $0 for single women, and $72,000 for couples, respectively. When the wages of both men and women change, all single men and almost all couples lose and 38% of single women gain. The single women who gain are the high-human-capital ones who end up with higher wages. The welfare compensation for those who lose when all wages change is, respectively, $98,800 for single men, $5,400 for single women, and $80,500 for couples, respectively. The average welfare gain among the 38% of single women who gain is $6,400.

Compared with our benchmark economy, in an economy without marital dynamics after age 25, single men experience a larger welfare loss due to their much lower wages and their inability to benefit from a future working spouse. In contrast, 38% of single women gain when their wage goes up (those with high human capital), whereas the remaining single women experience a smaller welfare loss because although their wage goes down, they no longer marry a husband with much lower wages and thus do not work as hard to help support their families.

B.   Changes in Medical Expenses

We now turn to studying the effects of replacing the out-of-pocket medical expenses faced by the 1960s cohort with those faced by the 1940s cohort. The present discounted value of medical expenses at age 25 for the 1960s cohort went up by $5,000, $7,000, and $12,300 for single men, single women, and couples, respectively, compared with the 1940s cohort. This corresponds to a 76% increase for single men, single women, and couples.

Figure 10 shows that the main effects of these changes are that hours worked by married women in the 1960s cohort under the 1960s inputs are slightly higher after age 30, whereas those of single women, who are poorer and rely on the consumption floor more, go down after age 55. Also, savings at age 66 were 14%, 11%, and 16% higher for single men, single women, and couples in the 1960s cohort than they would have been under the lower medical expenses experienced by the 1940s cohort.

Turning to our welfare computations, the resulting onetime asset compensation that we should give to 25-year-olds to make them indifferent between the 1940s and 1960s medical expenses is $14,000 for single men, $6,000 for single women, and $14,900 for couples. These numbers correspond, respectively, to 1.4%, 1.0%, and 0.9% of the present discounted value of their lifetime income. Despite the similar change in medical expenses for single men and women, the compensation is smaller for single women because they are poorer and rely on the consumption floor more. Thus, to the extent that they are at the consumption floor, the size of their medical expenses is not very important to them.

C.   Changes in Life Expectancy

We endow the 1960s cohort with the mortality—that is, health initial, health transition, and survival function, and thus life expectancy—of

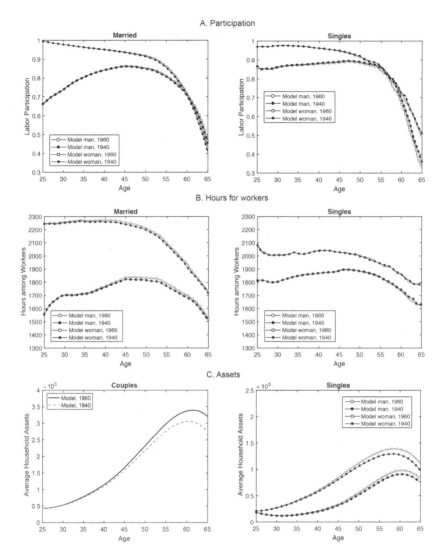

Fig. 10. Model outcomes with 1960s and 1940s medical expenses. (*a*) Participation. (*b*) Hours for workers. (*c*) Assets.

the 1940s cohort. Because we estimate out-of-pocket medical expenses as a function of age, gender, and health, changing a cohort's health and survival dynamics also changes its medical expenses. In fact, moving from the 1940s to the 1960s health and survival dynamics not only lowers survival, but, because people die off faster, also decreases the present discounted value of medical expenses at age 25 by $600 (4.5%)

for single men, by \$670 (4.0%) for single women, and by \$1,300 (4.3%) for couples. Thus, both life expectancy and medical expenses go down as a result of these changes across cohorts.

Figure 11 compares the participation and hours of married and single men and women under the two scenarios. It shows that participation and hours would have been very similar under the two scenarios but that retirement savings would have been 6.4%, 6.0%, and 4.1% higher

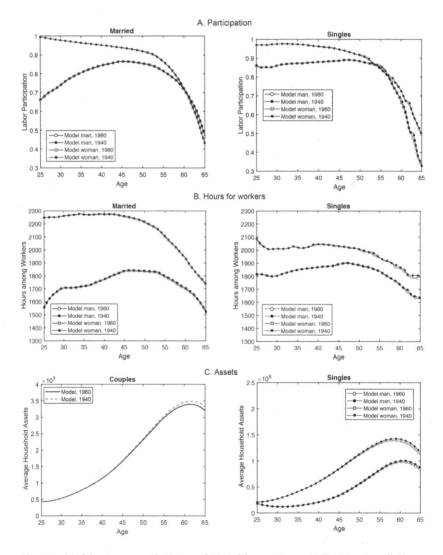

Fig. 11. Model outcomes with 1960s and 1940s life expectancy. (*a*) Participation. (*b*) Hours for workers. (*c*) Assets.

for single men, single women, and couples, respectively, at retirement time under the 1940s health and survival dynamics. Thus, savings go down, as one might expect, because of the shorter time period over which people expect to have to finance retirement consumption and decreased medical spending. Given that, in contrast, the life expectancy of the college educated (and their medical expenses) went up over time, this change contributes to increasing the gap in their retirement savings and thus wealth inequality across these education groups.

Hall and Jones (2007) and De Nardi et al. (2017) find that changes in life expectancy can have large effects on welfare. One mitigating factor in our framework is that this lower life expectancy occurred together with lower medical expenses. In our model, medical expenses are a shock reducing available resources; thus, reducing them increases welfare. This counters the loss in welfare due to a shorter life span.

We find the welfare cost due to a shorter life expectancy dominates the welfare gain from reduced medical expenses and that all single men and women and married couples lose welfare as a result. More specifically, the onetime asset compensation that we have to give 25-year-old households to make them indifferent between the 1940s and the 1960s health and survival dynamics is $32,000 for single men, $15,000 for single women, and $36,000 for couples. These numbers correspond, respectively, to 3.2%, 2.4%, and 2.2% of the present discounted value of their lifetime income.[22]

D. All Three Changes Together

As we have seen from our previous three decomposition exercises, changes in the wage schedule had the largest effects on participation, hours, savings, and welfare. The other two changes that we consider, the decrease in life expectancy and increase in expected out-of-pocket medical costs, mostly affect retirement savings and partly offset each other. They still have very sizeable welfare costs.

Figure 12 shows that the effects of all of these changes imply large increases in the participation of both married and single women, noticeable decreases in the participation of married men after age 40, and almost no changes in the participation of single men. Hours worked by married men and women changed in opposite directions, whereas the hours of single men and women displayed some increases earlier on in their working period. On net, these changes depressed the retirement savings of single men while leaving those of couples and single women roughly unchanged.

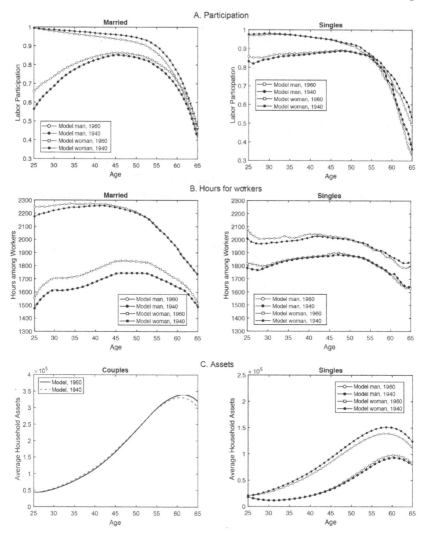

Fig. 12. Model outcomes with all changes we consider. (*a*) Participation. (*b*) Hours for workers. (*c*) Assets.

Table 12 compares outcomes for the 1960s cohort. Under the 1960s inputs (wage schedules, medical expenses, and life expectancies), the participation rates of married women over their working period were 3.12 percentage points higher than under the 1940s wage schedule, whereas those of married men were 2.42 percentage points lower. Overall, participation was only 0.12 percentage points higher due to offsetting changes across groups. Hours worked conditional on participation, however, were higher for all groups and especially for married women, resulting in an additional 1.95% of hours worked over the life cycle for this group.

Table 12
Changes in Participation Rates (in Percentage Points) and Hours (in %) for the 1960s
Cohort When Facing the 1960s Inputs (Wage Schedules, Medical Expenses, and Life
Expectancies) Compared with the 1940s Ones

All Changes Considered	SM	SW	MM	MW	All
Average participation change	−1.15	−.23	−2.42	3.12	.12
Average hours change	.48	.21	.70	4.82	1.95

Note: SM = single men; SW = single women; MM = married men; MW = married women;
All = everyone.

As a result of all three changes together, the present discounted value
of income went down, by 9.9%, 4.6%, and 4.0% for single men, single
women, and couples, and the onetime welfare loss experienced by people in the 1960s cohort amounts to $126,000 for single men, $44,000 for
single women, and $132,000 for couples. The fourth row of table 13 re-
ports that these numbers expressed as a fraction of their average present discounted value of earnings are 12.5%, 7.2%, and 8.1%, respectively.
Thus, the resulting welfare loss due to the changes between the 1940s and
the 1960s birth cohort is very large.

Table 13 summarizes key information about the welfare losses and
their sources. The first column shows, for instance, that 58.4% of the total
welfare loss that we consider for single men comes from wage changes
and 25.6% comes from their decrease in life expectancy. The second column shows that, for single women, 47.2% of the welfare loss for single
women comes from wage changes (their own and those of their prospective husbands) and 33.3% of it comes from decreased life expectancy.
The last column refers to couples and shows that 55.6% of the welfare

Table 13
Welfare Compensation for the 1960s Cohort When Facing the 1960s Wage Schedules,
Medical Expenses, and Life Expectancies Instead of the 1940s Ones, Computed as
Onetime Asset Compensation at Age 25 and Expressed as a Fraction of the Present
Discounted Value of One's Income

Compared with 1940 Inputs	SM (%)	SW (%)	Couples (%)
Wages	7.3	3.4	4.5
Medical expenses	1.4	1.0	.9
Life expectancy	3.2	2.4	2.2
All changes considered	12.5	7.2	8.1
All changes considered, no marriage and divorce	15.2	2.1	8.7

Note: SM = single men; SW = single women.

loss for couples comes from wage changes and 25.3% comes from decreased life expectancy.

The last row of the table considers all changes together in an economy without marital dynamics after age 25 and finds that the welfare loss of single men is higher and that of single women lower when they have no expectations of getting married in the future. When couples no longer divorce, their welfare loss is higher because the wife works harder and no longer gets divorced.

VIII. Conclusions and Directions for Future Research

Of the three changes that we consider—that is, wages, out-of-pocket medical expenses during retirement, and life expectancy—we find that the observed changes in the wage schedule had by far the largest effect on the labor supply of men and women born in the 1960s cohort. Specifically, it depressed the labor supply of men and increased that of women, especially in married couples. The decrease in life expectancy mainly reduced retirement savings, whereas the expected increase in out-of-pocket medical expenses increased them. On net, these two changes taken together had overall modest effects on all of the outcomes that we consider, including savings.

We also find that the combined effect of the changes has large welfare costs. In fact, the onetime asset compensation required to make 25-year-old households indifferent between the 1940s and 1960s health and survival dynamics, medical expenses, and wages is $126,000 for single men, $44,000 for single women, and $132,000 for couples. The corresponding numbers expressed as a fraction of their average present discounted value of earnings are 12.5%, 7.2%, and 8.1%, respectively. Lower wages explain 47%–58% of these losses, shorter life expectancies explain 26%–34%, and higher medical expenses account for the rest.

Other interesting changes took place for the same cohorts, including in the number of children, marriage and divorce patterns, assortative mating, childcare costs, initial conditions at age 25, and time spent in home production and raising children. Our paper suggests that studying the opportunities and outcomes of people in different cohorts and across different groups is a topic worthy of investigation, including from a macroeconomic standpoint.

We focus on the population of white and non-college-educated Americans to bring to bear a large and relatively homogeneous population to our structural model and study its implications. However, white non-college-educated Americans are hardly the only disadvantaged population losing ground over time in the United States. Neal (2011) extensively documents that while black-white skill gaps diminished over most of the 20th century, important measures of these gaps have not dropped since the late 1980s. A significant literature also documents a dramatic decline in employment rates and a lack of wage growth among less-skilled black men over the past 4 decades or more (see Neal and Rick 2016; Bayer and Charles 2018). However, this literature does not employ structural models that facilitate analyses of trends in aggregate welfare or overall inequality.

Although employment rates for less-skilled black and white men were falling, incarceration rates were rising. However, these rising incarceration rates did not reflect rising levels of criminal activity. Neal and Rick (2014, 2016) show that the prison boom, which began around 1980, was primarily the result of policy changes that increased the severity of punishment for all types of criminal offenders. These changes more than doubled the incarceration rates of both young black men and young white men. As a result, a much larger fraction of the current generation of less-educated Americans have spent time in prison, and only the future can reveal the total impact of these prison experiences on their lifetime earnings and consumption (Holzer 2009). Thinking about crime and related policies and their effects in the context of structural models is an important extension to better understand the economic outcomes of disadvantaged populations.

Fella and Gallipoli (2014) estimate a rich life-cycle model with endogenous education and crime choices to study the effects of two large-scale policy interventions aimed at reducing crime by the same amount: subsidizing high school education and increasing the length of prison sentences. They find that increases in high school graduation rates entail large efficiency and welfare gains, which are absent if the same crime reduction is achieved by increasing the length of sentences. Intuitively, the efficiency gains of the subsidy come from its effect on the education composition of the labor force. No such effect is present in the case of a longer prison term.

Another important observation is that low-income individuals are both more likely to develop a severe work-limiting disability and more likely to apply for disability insurance when they are not severely disabled. Low and Pistaferri (2015) find that by age 60, the low educated are 2.5 times more likely to be disability insurance claimants than the high educated (17% vs. 7%). In addition, a large increase in disability enrollment has been taking place over time, going from 2.2% in the late 1970s to 3.5% in the years immediately preceding the 2007–9 recession and 4.4% in 2013 (Liebman 2015). Michaud and Wiczer (2018) study the increase in disability claims of men over time in the context of a structural model and evaluate the importance of changing macroeconomic conditions in driving it. They find the secular deterioration of economic conditions concentrated in populations with high health risks accounts for a third of the increase in aggregate disability claims for men. These changes occurred in conjunction with the rise in participation (and disability claiming) of women. Gallipoli and Turner (2011) show that marriage interacts with health and disability shocks in an important way and that single workers' labor supply responses to disability shocks are larger and more persistent than those of married workers. Thus, enriching our framework to allow for health shocks during the working period and disability insurance is an important area of research to better understand the changing opportunities and outcomes of the most disadvantaged groups.

Endnotes

Author email addresses: Borella (margherita.borella@unito.it), De Nardi (denardim@nber.org), Yang (fyang@lsu.edu). Borella gratefully acknowledges financial support from the Italian Ministry of Education, University and Research (MIUR), Dipartimenti di Eccellenza grant 2018–2022. De Nardi gratefully acknowledges financial support from the NORFACE Dynamics of Inequality across the Life-Course (TRISP) grant 462-16-122. We thank Jonathan Parker, Marty Eichenbaum, and Erik Hurst, who encouraged us to investigate the changes in opportunities and outcomes across cohorts and provided us with valuable feedback. We also thank our discussants, Richard Blundell and Greg Kaplan, for sharing their views and thus helping us strengthen our work. We are grateful to Daron Acemoglu, Marco Bassetto, Joan Gieseke, John Bailey Jones, Rory McGee, Derek Neal, Gonzalo Paz-Pardo, Richard Rogerson, Rob Shimer, and seminar participants at various institutions for useful comments. The views expressed herein are those of the authors and do not necessarily reflect the views of NBER, Center for Economic and Policy Research, any agency of the federal government, the Federal Reserve Bank of Minneapolis, or the Federal Reserve System. For acknowledgments, sources of research support, and disclosure of the authors' material financial relationships, if any, please see https://www.nber.org/chapters/c14249.ack.

1. Because the finding of lower life expectancy is confined to less-educated whites, we focus on this group, and to have a sample size that is large enough, we focus on non–college graduates.

2. We measure human capital at a given age as average past earnings at that age. Thus, our measure of human capital incorporates the effects of both years of schooling and work experience.

3. Borella et al. (2017) develop and estimate this model to study the effects of marriage-based income taxes and Social Security benefits on the whole population, regardless of education.

4. These computations are performed for each household one at a time, keeping fixed the assets of their potential future partners in our benchmark.

5. Thus, we also drop people with less than 16 years of education but married to someone with 16 or more years of education. Before making this selection, nongraduate husbands with a graduate wife were 5% of the sample, whereas nongraduate wives with a graduate husband were 9.7% of the sample.

6. All amounts in the paper are expressed in 2016 dollars.

7. To compute these average wage profiles, we first regress log wages on fixed effect regressions with a flexible polynomial in age, separately for men and women. We then regress the sum of the fixed effects and residuals from these regressions on cohort and marital status dummies to fix the position of the age profile. Finally, we model the variance of the shocks by fitting age polynomials to the squared residuals from each regression in logs and use it to compute the level of average wages of each group as a function of age (by adding half the variance to the average in logs before exponentiating).

8. To generate this graph, we regress the logarithm of out-of-pocket medical expenses on a fixed effect and a third-order polynomial in age. We then regress the sum of the fixed effects and residuals from this regression on cohort dummies to compute the average effect for each cohort of interest, and we add the cohort dummies into the age profile. Finally, we model the variance of the shocks fitting an age polynomial and cohort dummies to the squared residuals from the regression in logs and use it to construct average medical expenses as a function of age.

9. We obtain the results in this section by estimating the probability of being alive conditional on age and cohort and by assuming that the age profiles entering the logit regression are the same across cohorts up to a constant. We then compute the mortality rate for the cohorts of interest using the appropriate cohort dummy.

10. Our estimated increases for medical expenses and mortality are consistent with the data that we currently observe at the aggregate level and the individual level, respectively, and forecast trends in these variables for the remaining periods of the lives of our cohorts.

11. The smoothed profiles of participation and hours are obtained by regressing each variable on a fourth-order polynomial in age fully interacted with marital status, and on cohort dummies, also interacted with marital status, which pick up the position of the age profiles. For assets, the profiles are obtained by fitting age polynomials separately for single men, single women, and couples to the logarithm of assets plus shift parameter, also controlling for cohort. The variance of the shocks is modeled by fitting age polynomials to the squared residuals from the regression in logs and is used to obtain the average profile in levels. Our figures display the profiles for the 1960s cohort.

12. It also has the important benefit of allowing us to have only one state variable keeping track of human capital and Social Security contributions.

13. Borella, De Nardi, and French (2018) discuss Medicaid rules and observed outcomes after retirement.

14. We report the percentage changes in potential wages by exponentiating the relevant marginal effect for each variable, β_x, and reporting it as $\exp(\beta_x) - 1$. In the case of $\bar{y}_t$, the estimated coefficient is an elasticity, and we report it without any transformations.

15. As we do not observe the complete profile for those born in the 1960s, the shape of the age profile is assumed to be the same across generations.

16. We experimented with adding marital status, but it is not statistically different from zero.

17. We report the percentage changes in medical expenses by exponentiating the relevant marginal effect for each variable, β_x, and reporting it as $\exp(\beta_x) - 1$.

18. We are thus assuming that the age profiles entering our estimated equation are the same across cohorts up to a constant. We then compute the mortality rate for the cohorts of interest using the appropriate cohort dummy.

19. These computations are performed for each household while keeping fixed the assets of their potential future partners to those that we estimate in the data.

20. When changing the wage schedule, we keep everything else (including initial conditions and prospective spouses) fixed at the levels experienced by the 1960s cohort.

21. To isolate the effect of wage changes, we eliminate marriage and divorce dynamics after age 25 from both the baseline and the counterfactual economies when performing these welfare comparisons.

22. Decreasing the VSL by 40% (i.e., reducing it from $5 million to $3 million) decreases the welfare costs of reduced life expectancy from 3.18% to 1.60% for single men, from 2.43% to 1.19% for single women, and from 2.21% to 1.11% for couples. Increasing the VSL by 40% (i.e., from $5 million to $7 million) raises the corresponding welfare costs from 3.18% to 4.80% for single men, from 2.43% to 3.72% for single women, and from 2.21% to 3.36% for couples.

References

Aguiar, Mark, and Erik Hurst. 2007. "Measuring Trends in Leisure: The Allocation of Time over Five Decades." *Quarterly Journal of Economics* 122 (3): 969–1006.

Alberini, Anna, Maureen Cropper, Alan Krupnick, and Nathalie B. Simon. 2004. "Does the Value of Statistical Life Vary with Age and Health Status? Evidence from the US and Canada." *Journal of Environmental Economics and Management* 48 (1): 769–92.

Arias, Elizabeth, Brian L. Rostron, and Betzaida Tejada-Vera. 2010. "United States Life Tables, 2005." *National Vital Statistics Reports* 58 (10): 1–132.

Bayer, Patrick, and Kerwin Kofi Charles. 2018. "Divergent Paths: A New Perspective on Earnings Differences Between Black and White Men since 1940." *Quarterly Journal of Economics* 133 (3): 1459–501.

Blundell, Richard, Monica Costa Dias, Costas Meghir, and Jonathan Shaw. 2016. "Female Labor Supply, Human Capital, and Welfare Reform." *Econometrica* 84 (5): 1705–53.

Blundell, Richard, Luigi Pistaferri, and Itay Saporta-Eksten. 2016. "Consumption Inequality and Family Labor Supply." *American Economic Review* 106 (2): 387–435.

Borella, Margherita, Mariacristina De Nardi, and Eric French. 2018. "Who Receives Medicaid in Old Age? Rules and Reality." *Fiscal Studies* 39 (1): 65–93.

Borella, Margherita, Mariacristina De Nardi, and Fang Yang. 2017. "The Effects of Marriage-Related Taxes and Social Security Benefits." Working Paper no. 23972, NBER, Cambridge, MA.

———. 2018. "The Aggregate Implications of Gender and Marriage." *Journal of the Economics of Ageing* 11 (C): 6–26.

Case, Anne, and Angus Deaton. 2015. "Rising Morbidity and Mortality in Midlife among White Non-Hispanic Americans in the 21st Century." *Proceedings of the National Academy of Sciences* 112 (49): 15078–83.

———. 2017. "Mortality and Morbidity in the 21st Century." *Brookings Papers on Economic Activity* (Spring): 397–476.

Citro, Constance F., and Robert T. Michael, eds. 1995. *Measuring Poverty: A New Approach.* Washington, DC: National Academy Press.

De Nardi, Mariacristina, Eric French, and John B. Jones. 2010. "Why Do the Elderly Save? The Role of Medical Expenses." *Journal of Political Economy* 118 (1): 39–75.

———. 2016. "Medicaid Insurance in Old Age." *American Economic Review* 106 (11): 3480–520.

De Nardi, Mariacristina, Svetlana Pashchenko, and Ponpoje Porapakkarm. 2017. "The Lifetime Costs of Bad Health." Working Paper no. 23963, NBER, Cambridge, MA.

Dotsey, Michael, Wenli Li, and Fang Yang. 2014. "Consumption and Time Use over the Life Cycle." *International Economic Review* 55 (3): 665–92.

Eckstein, Zvi, Michael Keane, and Osnat Liftshitz. 2019. "Career and Family Decisions: Cohorts Born 1935–1975." *Econometrica* 87 (1): 217–53.

Eckstein, Zvi, and Osnat Liftshitz. 2011. "Dynamic Female Labor Supply." *Econometrica* 79 (6): 1675–726.

Fella, Giulio, and Giovanni Gallipoli. 2014. "Education and Crime over the Life Cycle." *Review of Economic Studies* 81 (4): 1484–517.

Fernández, Raquel, and Joyce Cheng Wong. 2014. "Divorce Risk, Wages and Working Wives: A Quantitative Life-Cycle Analysis of Female Labour Force Participation." *Economic Journal* 124 (576): 319–58.

———. 2017. "Free to Leave? A Welfare Analysis of Divorce Regimes." *American Economic Journal: Macroeconomics* 9 (3): 72–115.

Gallipoli, Giovanni, and Laura Turner. 2011. "Household Responses to Individual Shocks: Disability and Labor Supply." University of British Columbia and University of Toronto mimeo.

Gourinchas, Pierre-Olivier, and Jonathan A. Parker. 2002. "Consumption Over the Life Cycle." *Econometrica* 70 (1): 47–89.

Gouveia, Miguel, and Robert P. Strauss. 1994. "Effective Federal Individual Income Tax Functions: An Exploratory Empirical Analysis." *National Tax Journal* 47 (2): 317–39.

Guner, Nezih, Remzi Kaygusuz, and Gustavo Ventura. 2012. "Income Taxation of US Households: Facts and Parametric Estimates." Discussion Paper no. 9078, Center for Economic and Policy Research, Washington, DC.

Guvenen, Fatih, Greg Kaplan, Jae Song, and Justin Weidner. 2017. "Lifetime Incomes in the United States over Six Decades." Working Paper no. 23371, NBER, Cambridge, MA.

Hall, Robert E., and Charles I. Jones. 2007. "The Value of Life and the Rise in Health Spending." *Quarterly Journal of Economics* 122 (1): 39–72.

Holzer, Harry J. 2009. "Collateral Costs: Effects of Incarceration on Employment and Earnings among Young Workers." In *Do Prisons Make Us Safer? The Benefits and Costs of the Prison Boom*, ed. Steven Raphael and Michael A. Stoll, 239–66. New York: Russell Sage Foundation.

Liebman, Jeffrey B. 2015. "Understanding the Increase in Disability Insurance Benefit Receipt in the United States." *Journal of Economic Perspectives* 29 (2): 123–50.

Low, Hamish, and Luigi Pistaferri. 2015. "Disability Insurance and the Dynamics of the Incentive Insurance Trade-Off." *American Economic Review* 105 (10): 2986–3029.

Michaud, Amanda, and David Wiczer. 2018. "The Disability Option: Labor Market Dynamics with Economic and Health Risks." Working Paper no. 2018-12, Stony Brook University.

Neal, Derek. 2011. "Why Has Black–White Skill Convergence Stopped?" In *Handbook of the Economics of Education*, vol. 1, ed. Eric A. Hanushek and Finis Welch, 511–76. Amsterdam: North-Holland.

Neal, Derek, and Armin Rick. 2014. "The Prison Boom and the Lack of Black Progress after Smith and Welch." Working Paper no. 20283, NBER, Cambridge, MA.

———. 2016. "The Prison Boom and Sentencing Policy." *Journal of Legal Studies* 45 (1): 1–41.

O'Brien, James. 2013. "The Age-Adjusted Value of a Statistical Life: Evidence from Vehicle Choice." Photocopy, Georgetown University.

Roys, Nicolas, and Christopher Taber. 2019. "Skills Prices, Occupations and Changes in the Wage Structure for Low Skilled Men." Working Paper no. 26453, NBER, Cambridge, MA.

Comment

Richard Blundell, *University College London and Institute for Fiscal Studies*

Introduction

Individuals without a college degree in the United States have experienced a relative decline in labor market and other opportunities. This is especially the case for lower-educated white men who entered the labor market in the early 1980s and after. These trends are not exclusive to the United States; in the United Kingdom and elsewhere, those without a college degree have fared poorly since the early 1980s.

For the United States, the raw statistics point to one of the largest declines for developed economies. There has been a fall in (relative) real earnings for the low educated, especially white men. There appears to be almost no wage progression over the working life for low-educated men and women. There is strong assortativeness by wages in marriage such that the increasing labor market participation of women has not offset the growth in earnings inequality for couple households. In addition, medical costs have risen, especially in terms of social care, and perhaps most surprisingly, mortality has risen.

Motivated by these trends, the authors specify a life-cycle model that includes marriage and divorce, human capital accumulation, medical expenditures, and changing life expectancy. They use data from the Panel Study of Income Dynamics and the Health and Retirement Survey to construct a sample of white, non-college-educated Americans. Sample moments are then used to estimate the model. Counterfactual simulations are then used to ask: What if the 1940s cohort of non-college-educated white Americans had experienced the wages, the medical expenses, and the mortality of the 1960s cohort? The "what if" is for labor market participation, hours, savings, and welfare.

In this discussion, I first examine the trends in outcomes for these different groups over this period in the United States. I then briefly run through the modeling framework for the counterfactual simulations. Finally, I raise a number of issues concerning the data and the interpretation of the changes across cohorts.

Setting the Scene

The strong relative decline in real earnings for the low educated is not just true of the United States; it is a phenomenon that has occurred elsewhere. For example, the 90-to-10 ratio for male earnings in the United Kingdom has risen continuously from 2.5 to around 5.5 over the period from 1980 to the present with male real earnings at the 10th percentile seeing almost no increase. In the United States, the 90-to-10 ratio for male earnings has also grown and stands at more than 6.5, while male earnings below the median has fared even more poorly (see Blundell et al. 2018).[1]

Perhaps what stands out most is the relative decline of low-educated white men in the United States. Figure 1, from the Current Population Survey (CPS), shows the decline of the position of white men with less than a high school education. Although in absolute terms they are faring no less well than similarly educated black men, the relative decline is striking. To avoid issues relating to schooling and early retirement, these figures are median average hourly wages for men aged 25 to 55. The relative decline is clear.[2] Women have fared better in terms of real growth in earnings but from a low base, and again the lower-educated women have had relatively low earnings growth (see fig. 1b).

Figure 1 focuses on the group with less than a high school education. Figure 2 shows this relative decline for men is true across all lower-education groups over this period.

These changes in earnings, coupled with strong sorting by wages in marriage, point to a large relative decline in real earnings for families of the lower educated. Increased female earnings have not offset the inequality growth nor the decline in the relative position of the lower-educated couples over this period (see Blundell et al. 2018).

What is even more poignant is the lack of wage progression over the working life for those without college education. Figure 3a shows the average profiles by age, sex, and education, whereas figure 3b suggests these profiles may have been widening over the period. Especially noticeable is the difference between the 1940s and 1960s cohorts, precisely the groups being compared in this study.

Added to this is a fallback in longevity documented in the recent work of Case and Deaton (2015). Figure 4 presents the descriptive statistics

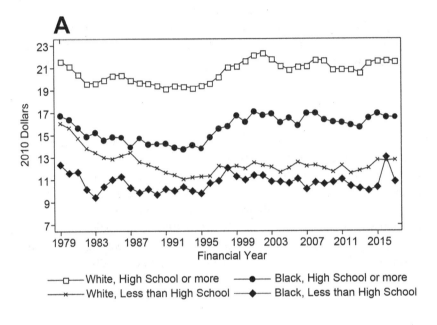

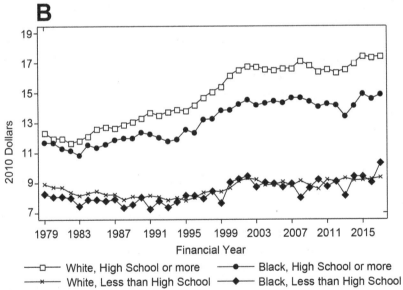

Fig. 1. Real wages in the United States by education, race, and sex. (*a*) Men. (*b*) Women. Current Population Survey, real median earnings 1976–2014, personal consumption expenditure deflator, ages 25–55 (author's calculations).

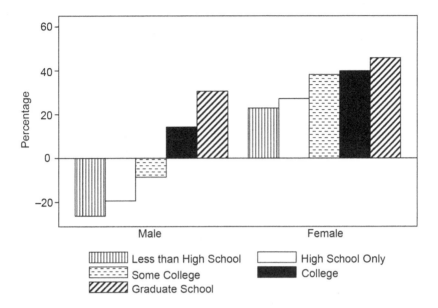

Fig. 2. Earnings changes in the United States by education and sex. Current Population Survey, real median earnings 1976–2014, personal consumption expenditure deflator, ages 25–55 (author's calculations).

for all-cause mortality. Case and Deaton show that it is poisoning (mainly opioids) and suicide that drive this change in direction.

These statistics provide motivation for this paper. The lower educated in the 1960s cohort saw a strong decline in wages and longevity relative to the position of the lower educated in the 1940s cohort.

The Quantitative Approach to Counterfactual Simulations

The framework used by the authors is to place individuals in a life-cycle model that includes single and married people with single people meeting partners and married people facing a risk of divorce. Human capital accumulation occurs on the job, medical expenditures are incorporated that change across the lifetime, and life expectancy is allowed to differ by education group.

The drawback of such a quantitative model for counterfactual simulations is the inevitability of strong assumptions. The authors are clear about these. Marriage, divorce, and fertility are exogenous, and married people are assumed to have the same age. One strong assumption I will return to later is that the lifetime wage profiles for each education group are assumed parallel across the two birth cohorts. The authors also assume

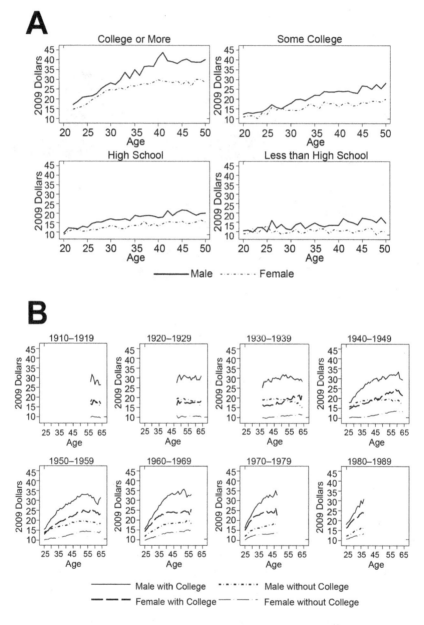

Fig. 3. (*a*) Wage profiles by education and age in the United States (real average hourly wage-age profile of male and female workers in the United States, 2016). Current Population Survey (CPS), real median earnings 2016, personal consumption expenditure (PCE) deflator, ages 25–64 (author's calculations). (*b*) Wage profiles by education, cohort, and age in the United States (real median hourly wage-age profile of male and female workers ages 25–64 in the United States by birth cohort). CPS, real median earnings, PCE deflator, ages 25–64 (author's calculations).

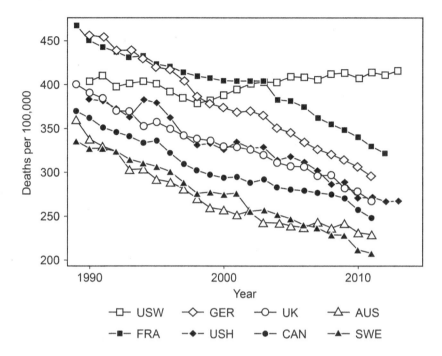

Fig. 4. All-cause mortality among those aged 45–54 in the United States (Case and Deaton 2015).

that households have rational expectations about all of the stochastic processes that they face. Thus, they anticipate the nature of the uncertainty following the time when they enter the model at age 25. In some ways these assumptions, or something similar, are inevitable given the ambition of the authors to provide counterfactuals but they are strong nonetheless.

There are three main counterfactual simulations examined by the authors: (1) a change in the wage schedule, (2) an increase in expected out-of-pocket medical expenses during retirement, and (3) a decrease in life expectancy. These are for the group of white, non-college-educated people born in the 1960s cohort, which comprises about 60% of the population of the same age.

The change in the wage schedule is found to have by far the largest effect on the labor supply of both men and women. In particular, it depresses the labor supply of men and increases that of women. The decrease in life expectancy mainly reduces retirement savings, but the expected increase in out-of-pocket medical expenses increases them by more.

Relative to the same group born in the 1940s, the results suggest that the group of white, non-college-educated people born in the 1960s cohort, which comprises more than 60% of the population, experienced large negative changes in wages, large increases in medical expenses, and large decreases in life expectancy. It seems they would have been much better off if they had faced the corresponding lifetime opportunities of the 1940s birth cohort.

Selection of Non-College-Educated White Americans across the Two Birth Cohorts

How Important Are Sample Selection and Changes in Composition?

The selection of non-college-educated white people in the 1940s and 1960s birth cohorts provides the focus for this paper. It is a large group, even for the 1960s cohort, but it is still selective. College enrollment increased by more than a third over this period, from 17% to 23%. There could be clear implications for wages and mortality. It is possible that the low educated had "better" underlying productivity and health in the 1940s cohort. It would be useful to compute worse case bounds that would imply the highest wages and lowest mortality are selected out. It is likely though that at this level of selection would have little impact.

On a related matter, why not split out high school dropouts from the noncollege group? The model does allow some differences across people in each cohort by accumulated/average earnings (human capital), but figure 2, for example, suggests it would be very useful to split out dropouts.

Finally, changes in cohort size could have equilibrium effects on wages. It might be useful to see what the impact would be in a Katz-Murphy framework. Again, this is likely to be small, but worth ruling out.

Does the Reason behind the Decline Matter?

The reason for the decline in relative real wages for the non-college-educated white population is taken as exogenous in the paper and is not discussed. But the cause of the decline could inform the model and change the welfare implications of the results. For example, there is evidence that the decline is related to the fall in unionized employment in the United States; see Farber et al. (2018). This probably reflects a change in occupational structure and changes in product demand. It suggests a change in the bargaining strength of blue-collar workers and changes in the competitive nature of the labor market. Alternatively, the decline in wages could be driven purely by a decline in productivity within a largely competitive market.

In both of these cases, there would be implications for the college-educated wages and for rents going to the owners of capital. These changes in rents and returns (to those with more human capital and more physical and financial capital) would surely change the counterfactuals in the model. Maybe not the overall conclusion, though?

Should We Worry about Changes in Wage Progression as Well as Wage Levels?

The authors find that wages are key in driving differences across cohorts in terms of overall family labor supply and earnings. The analysis suggests three components to this. First, the wages of men were much higher than those of women in the 1940s birth cohort. Second, the wages of men, both married and single, went down by 9%. Third, the wages of married and single women went up by 7% across these two cohorts.

Wages (log) are specified to have an age profile term, a human capital term, a persistent shock term, and a fixed effect term. Differences across cohorts occur in all these terms. But is it enough? The age profiles are assumed to be parallel shifts across cohorts. Does this look reasonable? Figure 3*b* suggests there may be a "fanning out" of wage profiles across education groups.

There is also an issue as to whether these changes are known at the beginning of working life for each cohort. The model assumes each cohort expects the same age profile.

What Are the Implications of Sorting for Family Earnings and Labor Supply?

Marital sorting by education and wages appears to have increased in the United States over this period, especially for lower-wage workers (see Blundell et al. 2018). At the same time, the relative earnings of women have risen, but it seems earnings inequality among women has risen too. The implication is that inequality within families has fallen but overall inequality between families has risen. How does this play out for the 1960s cohort?

In terms of marriage and divorce, the authors specify a nice Markov structure for the arrival of partners and for marital breakups. What about marital matches across education groups? There are more college-educated males in earlier cohorts, so some non-college educated women will match with college-educated men. How does this work in the model?

How large are cross-Marshallian female labor supply elasticities effects from persistent shocks to male wages on labor supply of spouses? Blundell, Pistaferri, and Saporta-Eksten (2016) suggest this could be an important source of earnings response within the family, especially for low-asset, low-educated couples, who are the focus in this study.

How Important Are Deaths of Despair and the Value of Life?

Specifying the value of life is key in this world of increasing mortality, but what is the value of an extra year for the low educated in the 1940s? How sensitive are the results to the assumptions on the additive utility value of life?

The adverse health issues and increased mortality identified in Case and Deaton (2015) arise at working ages (see fig. 4). It would be useful to allow mortality and the changes across cohorts to occur during working life. To an extent the authors acknowledge this and note that enriching their framework to allow for health shocks during the working period and disability insurance is an important area of research to better understand the changing opportunities and outcomes of the most disadvantaged groups.

Does the Tax Function Adequately Capture Welfare and Tax Credits?

Getting the tax and welfare system right would seem a first-order issue. To what extent does the tax function accurately reflect changes to food stamps and Aid to Families with Dependent Children/Temporary Assistance to Needy Families (eligibility restrictions), Earned Income Tax Credit (EITC) (work conditions), or Medicaid (child and income conditions)?

In the counterfactuals, it would be useful to know the implications for tax revenues and welfare expenditures, especially due to the changes induced by the wage changes. What would it take to offset growth in inequality of family incomes using taxes, EITC, and food stamps, for example?

What Should Be the Price Deflator for Wages?

What is the appropriate price index to use and should this index differ across education groups? Although the figures mentioned earlier adopt the same deflator for all education groups, they do use the PCE deflator.

Because this is a chain-weighted index, by accounting for substitution and new goods, it typically records a larger rise in real earnings. Even so, the figures support the analysis in the paper, suggesting that real wages and earnings for less-educated white men across these birth cohorts do seem to have fallen.

These indices may still overestimate the rise in living costs because they account for neither the different shares of consumption goods across education groups nor the changing quality of new goods. There are also changes in homeownership, house prices, and the tax advantage of housing in the US tax system. It is probable that the higher educated gain more from quality change because these goods are often luxuries. They may also have gained from changes in the housing market and in overall price changes.

Overall, it is difficult to deny the strong decline in the relative economic position of the lower educated in the 1960s cohort.

Conclusion

The rise and fall of less-educated white men in the United States in the postwar period is bound to attract increasing attention as the political fallout and the impact on economic and health inequalities become more evident. This is a thought-provoking paper that deserves a wide readership.

Endnotes

Author email address: Blundell (r.blundell@ucl.ac.uk). Thanks to Jim Ziliak for comments and help in constructing the CPS series. Support from the UK Economic and Social Research Council through the Centre for the Microeconomic Analysis of Public Policy (CPP) at the Institute for Fiscal Studies, grant reference ES/M010147/1, is gratefully acknowledged. Any errors and all views expressed are mine. For acknowledgments, sources of research support, and disclosure of the author's material financial relationships, if any, please see https://www.nber.org/chapters/c14250.ack.

1. Of course, the deflator matters in calculations of real earnings levels but not for ratios unless the price changes have had a systematically differential effect favoring low earners over this period.

2. These figures are for men who do not have their hours or earnings imputed by the Census Bureau. Moreover, for each year and gender we trim the top and bottom 1% of the hourly wage distribution. Nominal earnings are deflated using the personal consumption expenditure deflator with 2010 base year.

References

Blundell, Richard, Robert Joyce, Agnes Norris Keiller, and James P. Ziliak. 2018. "Income Inequality and the Labour Market in Britain and the US." *Journal of Public Economics* 162 (March): 48–62.

Blundell, Richard, Luigi Pistaferri, and Itay Saporta-Eksten. 2016. "Consumption Inequality and Family Labor Supply." *American Economic Review* 106 (2): 387–435.

Case, Anne, and Angus Deaton. 2015. "Rising Morbidity and Mortality in Midlife among White Non-Hispanic Americans in the 21st Century." *Proceedings of the National Academy of Sciences* 112 (49): 15078–83.

Farber, Henry S., Daniel Herbst, Ilyana Kuziemko, and Suresh Naidu. 2018. "Unions and Inequality over the Twentieth Century: New Evidence from Survey Data." NBER Working Paper no. 24587, National Bureau of Economic Research, Cambridge, MA.

Comment

Greg Kaplan, *University of Chicago and NBER*

Borella, De Nardi, and Yang (2019) tackle an important question. They consider two cohorts of white, non-college-educated Americans: (i) those born between 1936 and 1945 (referred to as the 1940s cohort), and (ii) those born between 1956 and 1965 (referred to as the 1960s cohort). They consider three differences in the opportunities afforded to these cohorts: (i) potential wages, (ii) life expectancy, and (iii) out-of-pocket medical expenses. And they ask how these three differences in opportunities affected three differences in outcomes across the two cohorts: (i) labor supply, (ii) savings, and (iii) welfare.

The authors reach a provocative conclusion. They write: "Our results thus indicate that the group of white, non-college-educated people born in the 1960s cohort, which comprises about 60% of the population of the same age, experienced large negative changes in wages, large increases in medical expenses, and large decreases in life expectancy and would have been much better off if they had faced the corresponding lifetime opportunities of the 1940s birth cohort." If correct, this finding is worth repeating. Despite all the technological advances in health care, communication, and transportation; despite the progress that has been made on gender equality; despite the massive increase in international trade; despite iPhones and the internet; despite the fact that real gross domestic product per capita has grown by more than a factor of 2.5 in the 50 years from 1965 to 2015; and despite all these perceived improvements in life, more than half of the US population would have been better off had they been born 20 years earlier.

In the following section, I will offer some casual observations of changes in the US economy over this time period that might make one skeptical that the 1940s cohort really was better off than the 1960s cohort. To shed light on the authors' pessimistic conclusions, I will then explain why the authors' assumptions about each of the three changing opportunities that they take as inputs into their analysis—potential wages, life expectancy, and medical expenses—might be considered pessimistic lower bounds. Regarding potential wages, I will highlight the importance of choosing an appropriate price index to deflate nominal wage growth. Regarding life expectancy, I will highlight the importance of assumptions regarding the calibration of the value of a statistical life (VSL). Regarding medical expenses, I will suggest that the benefits of higher medical expenditures need to be weighed against these higher costs. I will end the discussion by offering some more methodological thoughts, about how to identify the most important features of the model around which to perform sensitivity analysis.

Were the 1940s Cohort Really Better Off?

Smith, Son, and Schapiro (2015) offer a first hint that maybe life is not so terrible compared with 2 decades ago. They report responses to a question in the General Social Survey that asks a representative sample of Americans whether they think that their own standard of living is better or worse compared with their parents' standard of living at the same age. In 2014, 60% of respondents said that their own living standards were better than their parents and only 15% said that their living standards were worse. Moreover, this pattern of responses has been relatively stable over the past 20 years. In 2004 and 1994, 70% and 65% of respondents, respectively, believed their living standards were better than their parents, and 12% and 13%, respectively, said they were worse.

Of course, stated beliefs about quality of life should be taken with a grain of salt. But a number of tangible of measures of quality of life also suggest that things might not be so bad. Meyer and Sullivan (2011) examine various dimensions of the material well-being of poor and middle-class households and show improvement among many dimensions. For example, for households in the bottom quartile of the income distribution, they report increases in the number of rooms (adjusted for household size), average house size, and the fraction of households with air conditioning, dishwashers, washing machines, and dryers, between 1981 and 2009. It is not just about housing; they show that car ownership, on both the extensive and intensive margin, also increased substantially for this group of households.

Patterns of expenditures on nondurables also suggest growth in real incomes among this population. Furth (2017) makes the important observation that Engel's Law can be used to inform us about changes in real income. Engel's Law—about which Houthakker (1987) remarks, "of all the empirical regularities observed in economic data, Engel's Law is probably the best established"—states that as real incomes rise, the proportion of income spent on food declines. And indeed, Furth (2017) shows that between 1979 and 2014, the percentage of disposable personal income spent on food declined from over 13% to under 10%. Moreover, the proportion of total household food expenditures spent on food away from home, which is well known to be a luxury good, increased from just under 32% to over 43%. Both of these observations are inconsistent with generational real wage stagnation.

So what explains the authors' finding that the majority of the US population in the 1960s cohort would have been better off had they been born 20 years earlier? This finding about welfare can be decomposed into approximately orthogonal components arising from each of the three changes in lifetime opportunities. The largest factor, accounting for roughly half of the decline in welfare, is the decline in potential wages. The decline in life expectancy and the increase in medical expenses account for the other half of the decline in welfare, in roughly equal parts. In the following sections, I highlight some caveats regarding each of these sources.

Measuring Changes in Real Wages

Figure 1*a* reproduces the authors' assumed life-cycle profiles for mean potential hourly wages for married men and women in each of the two cohorts. The main driver of the wage component of the decline in welfare is the fact that, at all ages, mean potential wages for men in the 1960s cohort (solid line with filled squares) is about 9% lower than for men in the 1940s cohort (solid line with open squares). When this lower potential wage profile is fed through the structural model, it generates lower welfare for the later cohort. The authors construct real wages (which they report in 2016 dollars) by adjusting nominal wages for inflation using the Consumer Price Index for All Urban Consumers (CPI-U), produced by the Bureau of Labor Statistics (BLS). I will argue that adjusting for inflation using CPI-U provides only a very low bound on implied real wage growth and that using other price indexes that adjust for some of the biases in CPI-U paints a different picture of mean real wage growth across these cohorts.

Over the past half century, the BLS has made numerous changes to the way it calculates the CPI, most of which took place prior to 2000. Although these changes are intended to improve accuracy, the historical CPI-U series is not retroactively adjusted to reflect these improvements,

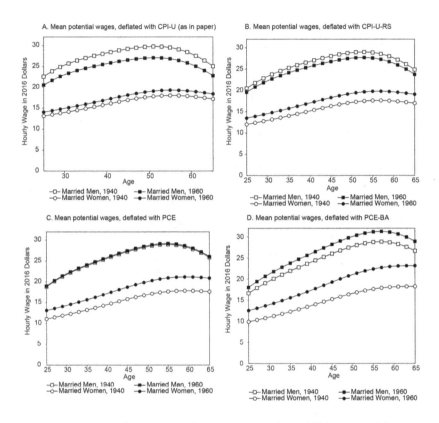

Fig. 1. Mean potential wages with alternative price indexes. (*a*) Mean potential wages, deflated with CPI-U (as in paper). (*b*) Mean potential wages, deflated with CPI-U-RS. (*c*) Mean potential wages, deflated with PCE. (*d*) Mean potential wages, deflated with PCE-BA. CPI-U = Consumer Price Index for All Urban Consumers; CPI-U-RS = Consumer Price Index Research Series Using Current Methods; PCE = personal consumption expenditure; PCE-BA = bias-adjusted personal consumption expenditure.

and hence the CPI-U is not consistent over time. Accordingly, the BLS makes available the Consumer Price Index Research Series Using Current Methods (CPI-U-RS), which adjusts CPI-U from 1978 onward to incorporate most of the recent improvements into the entire series. From 2000 onward, the CPI-U and CPI-U-RS series are almost identical, but between 1978 and 2000 they differ substantially. In particular, inflation according to the CPI-U is on average 0.4% per annum (p.a.) higher than inflation according to the CPI-U-RS. Figure 1*b* shows that simply using the CPI-U-RS rather than CPI-U to construct life-cycle profiles eliminates about one-half of the decline in mean potential wages for men across cohorts.

There are also a number of well-known biases in the CPI-U-RS series (see Furth 2017, for an excellent summary). The CPI-U-RS is constructed by first estimating 8,018 separate item-area indexes and then aggregating these using a Laspeyres index. First, an upward small-sample bias arises because geometric averages are used to compute price indexes for about two-thirds of the item-areas. This bias has been estimated by the BLS to be about 0.15 percentage points per year. Second, a substitution bias arises because the Laspeyres index used to aggregate across item-areas does not account for households substituting toward lower priced goods. This bias has been estimated by the BLS to be about 0.10 percentage points per year. Both of these biases can be mitigated by using a chain-weighted index, such as the C-CPI-U or the personal consumption expenditure (PCE) deflator produced by the Bureau of Economic Analysis (BEA). Furth (2017) also notes a third bias specific to the CPI that is due to the fact that the BLS uses the Consumer Expenditure Survey to construct item weights. Because households have better recall for large and repeated purchases, the weights on housing and utilities, which happen to be high inflation items, are biased upward. Furth (2017) estimates this bias to be about 0.07–0.1 percentage points per year.

These biases in the CPI-U-RS can mostly be avoided by using the PCE deflator. The BEA uses a Fisher index to construct the PCE, which mitigates the small-sample and substitution biases, and computes weights using business sales data, which suffer less from the weighting bias. Over the 50 years from 1967 to 2017, the period covered by the authors' analysis, inflation as measured by the PCE is on average 0.3% p.a. lower than inflation as measured by the CPI-U-RS. Moreover, the PCE covers a different basket of goods than the CPI-U-RS. If the PCE were reweighted to reflect the same bundle of goods as the CPI, it would yield even lower inflation over this period. Figure 1c shows that using the PCE yields mean potential wage profiles that are actually slightly higher for the 1960s cohort than for the 1940s cohort.

But it is likely that even the PCE still overstates inflation because there are a number of biases that are common to both the PCE and CPI. These include (i) outlet-substitution bias, which reflects the fact that consumers can save money by shopping around and purchasing larger quantities from lower-price sellers; (ii) new-product bias, which reflects the fact that the introduction of new products is essentially a price reduction from infinity to a finite price; (iii) quality-adjustment bias, which reflects the fact that both the BEA and BLS can only partially adjust for the effects of products being replaced by higher quality versions; and (iv) consumer-valuation bias, which reflects the fact that when preferences change over time, households substitute toward preferred goods. Furth (2017) provides an overview of the various attempts to quantify the size of each of these biases and concludes that a conservative lower bound on the upward bias is around 0.4% p.a. (0.1% p.a. of outlet-substitution bias and 0.3% p.a. of new-product bias and quality-adjustment bias). He labels the resulting price index as a bias-adjusted personal consumption expenditure deflator (PCE-BA). The PCE-BA also generates very similar inflation to the preferred measure of Meyer and Sullivan (2011), which is to subtract 0.8% p.a. from CPI-U-RS to account for these biases.

Figure 1d shows the effects of deflating nominal wages with the PCE-BA on the authors' potential wage profiles for married men and women. Two features stand out. First, rather than showing a large decline in potential wages for men across cohorts, the data now show a substantial increase for both men and women. Second, the implied potential wage profiles are much steeper with respect to age than the original versions, suggesting that much of the flatness of the authors' wage-age profiles is due to the choice of price index.

Overall, these comparisons suggest that about half of the decline in welfare across cohorts is directly due to the choice of price index for deflating nominal wages. The authors' chosen price index (CPI-U) implies substantially higher inflation, and hence lower real wage growth, than more appropriate price indexes, such as the PCE.

Interpreting Changes in Life Expectancy

To understand how changes in life expectancy drive the differences in welfare across the two cohorts, it is useful to recap the way that the authors model mortality. In the authors' model, dying is exogenous. The probability of dying depends on which of two health states an individual is in, so the death shock might be considered a "hit-by-a-bus shock, with a little bit of warning." There is nothing that an individual can do about mortality risk because not even health care affects the probability of being hit by the death shock.

Because the value attached to death is additively separable from the value of consumption and leisure while alive, the welfare effect of an increase in the probability of dying is effectively pinned down by the calibrated value of the parameter (b) that governs the value of being alive. The authors choose this parameter to match a target VSL of $5 million. By choosing different values for this target, the authors' model could have delivered almost any desired implied welfare effect of the assumed change in life expectancy. In other words, the conclusions about the welfare effects of a change in life expectancy, once expressed in dollar terms, are determined almost entirely by the assumption about the target VSL.

Empirical estimates of VSL come with a very large degree of uncertainty. The authors cite two studies that report values for VSL from $1 million to $9 million, but the reality is that we know very little about this number, particularly for the subpopulation of low-educated white men that is the focus of the paper (the studies cited by the authors refer to the entire US population in a given age range, not low-educated white men, for whom one might expect to find lower values of VSL). Even small variations within this range yield large (almost one-to-one) differences in the welfare effects of changes in life expectancy. For example, the authors report that increasing (decreasing) the target VSL by 40% leads to an increase (decrease) in the welfare costs of approximately 40%.

Moreover, even if we take the calibration target for VSL at face value, the hit-by-a-bus nature of mortality in the authors' model is another reason why we should think of the welfare effects of the decline in life expectancy as an upper bound. Modeling mortality in this way means that we should interpret the increase in mortality risk as referring to increases in causes of death that are purely exogenous and over which individuals have no control. But Case and Deaton (2015) show that the mortality increase that motivates the paper is explained mostly by so-called deaths of despair—drug use and suicides. One might reasonably argue that these causes of death are not well captured by the hit-by-a-bus model of mortality.

Finally, Currie and Schwandt (2016) remind us that focusing too heavily on low-educated white males is somewhat misrepresentative of more general trends in life expectancy across the 1940s and 1960s cohorts. They show that the increase in mortality among white men is barely visible when viewed alongside the massive declines in mortality that have been experienced by other groups over this same period, most notably nonwhites (see Currie and Schwandt 2016, fig. 5).

Modeling Changes in Medical Expenses

The remaining quarter of the decline in welfare across the two cohorts is due to the higher medical expenses incurred by the 1960s cohort. The authors write, "those born in the 1960s cohort face medical expenses that are 48.6% higher than those born in the 1940s cohort, even after conditioning on health status." This is indeed a large increase in expenditures, and presumably using one of the aforementioned alternative price indexes instead of CPI-U would yield an even larger increase.

Such a large increase in expenditures naturally raises the question of what people are getting in return for these much higher payments. The most pessimistic possibility is nothing. Yet this is exactly what the authors assume. Their model treats medical expenditures as a purely exogenous shock. Individuals cannot choose whether or not to pay these costs nor take any actions to avoid them. And when they are incurred, they bring no benefits in terms of health or otherwise. The upshot of modeling medical expenditures in this way is that it is guaranteed from the outset of the exercise that the observed increases in medical expenditures must have a negative effect on welfare.

Such an approach to measuring changes in welfare stands in contrast to a long economic tradition based on revealed preference and price theory. When an economist observes higher expenditure on a particular good—in this case, medical services—we typically do not jump to the conclusion that it must be bad for welfare. Rather, we seek to explain what has changed about preferences, technology, or market structure so that either the resulting equilibrium price or quantity of medical services (or both) has increased. Although it is indeed plausible that the utility benefits of the 48.6% increase in health expenditure do not outweigh the costs, I find it implausible that those benefits are zero. As such, I think of the authors' conclusions about the decline in welfare brought about by higher medical expenses as a very loose upper bound.

Optimization and Sensitivity

Over the past few decades, quantitative heterogeneous-agent models with incomplete markets have become a widely used tool to evaluate the welfare effects of changes in technology, policy, and demographics. One of the (valid) critiques that is routinely levied on this approach is that the exercise is something of a "black box." It is hard for a reader to digest all the workings of the model; it is hard to know which assumptions matter for the ultimate conclusions about welfare and which do not; and it is hard to know whether the welfare conclusions are hardwired into the model structure, hardwired from the calibrated inputs, or arise from viewing a particular feature of the data through the lens of a particular feature of the model. Hence, it is important for the authors of such papers to give guidance to their readers on what drives their conclusions.

Fortunately, this paper is one where it is relatively simple to understand which features of the data and model are most important for the quantitative conclusions about welfare. To see this, note that there are only two endogenous decisions in the model: (i) savings and (ii) labor supply. Now consider how each of the three changes that the authors feed into the model would affect welfare, if we were to hold the savings and labor supply policy functions fixed—in other words, if we did not allow individuals in the model to reoptimize in response to the changes in potential wages, life expectancy, and medical expenses. The effect of lower potential wages and higher medical expenses is simply to lower lifetime consumption. The effect of lower life expectancy is to lower the value of being alive (the discounted value of b), without altering lifetime consumption. Hence, under the assumption of no change in behavior, only two features of the model matter for the quantitative conclusions about welfare: the assumed utility function and the calibration target for VSL. This suggests that it would be useful to perform sensitivity analysis along these two dimensions.

This assumes that individuals do not change their savings or labor supply decisions behavior in response to the three changes in their environment, so one might worry that such a thought experiment misses important features of individual adjustment. Such changes in behavior might exacerbate or mitigate the changes in welfare and might depend on other features of the model and calibration beyond the utility function and VSL target. However, the envelope condition strongly suggests that this is unlikely to be the case. In fact to a first order, the welfare effects under the thought experiment above will be exactly the same as the welfare effects in the full model in which individuals reoptimize their savings and labor supply decisions.

Final Thoughts

The authors have written a provocative paper on a very important question. It got me thinking hard about several difficult issues: (i) how to compare real incomes over long time periods, (ii) why medical expenses have increased so much, (iii) how to value human life, and (iv) how to model mortality and health care in economic models. No doubt this paper will spur much future work on these and related topics.

Endnote

Author email address: Kaplan (gkaplan@uchicago.edu). In preparing this discussion, I have drawn heavily on other people's work, in particular Furth (2017). I make no claims as to the originality of the ideas put forth here. For acknowledgments, sources of research support, and disclosure of the author's material financial relationships, if any, please see https://www.nber.org/chapters/c14251.ack.

References

Borella, Margherita, Mariacristina De Nardi, and Fang Yang. 2019. "The Lost Ones: The Opportunities and Outcomes of Non-College-Educated Americans Born in the 1960s." Working Paper no. 25661 (March), NBER, Cambridge, MA.

Case, Anne, and Angus Deaton. 2015. "Rising Morbidity and Mortality in Mid-life among White Non-Hispanic Americans in the 21st Century." *Proceedings of the National Academy of Sciences* 112 (49): 15078–83.

Currie, Janet, and Hannes Schwandt. 2016. "Mortality Inequality: The Good News from a County-level Approach." *Journal of Economic Perspectives* 30 (2): 29–52.

Furth, Salim. 2017. "Measuring Inflation Accurately." Backgrounder 3213, Heritage Foundation, Washington, DC.

Houthakker, H. 1987. "Engel's Law." In *The New Palgrave Dictionary of Economics*, ed. J. Eatwell, M. Milgate, and P. Newman. Vol. 2, 143–4. London: McMillan.

Meyer, Bruce D., and James X. Sullivan. 2011. "The Material Well-Being of the Poor and the Middle Class since 1980." Working Paper no. 2011-04, American Enterprise Institute for Public Policy Research, Washington, DC.

Smith, Tom W., Jaesok Son, and Benjamin Schapiro. 2015. *General Social Survey Final Report: Trends in Public Evaluations of Economic Well-Being, 1972–2014.* Chicago: NORC at the University of Chicago.

Discussion

Daron Acemoglu contextualized the authors' paper as part of an ongoing debate about the origins of intercohort trends in labor market outcomes. He argued that differences across education groups have been studied extensively, whereas differences across cohorts are less understood. He contrasted two views on the subject. According to the first one, which he labeled the "early labor view," intercohort trends stem from differences in protections and unionization across cohorts. The second view, which Acemoglu labeled the "Card-Lemieux (2001) view" (David Card and Thomas Lemieux ["Can Falling Supply Explain the Rising Return to College for Younger Men? A Cohort-Based Analysis," *Quarterly Journal of Economics* 116, no. 2 (2001): 705–46]), imputes these trends to differences in educational attainments across cohorts. Acemoglu downplayed the importance of the first view. He suggested instead that a decrease in the relative supply of educated workers across cohorts is the most plausible explanation for the rise in the skill premium observed in the data. He noted that college graduation rates rose steadily for cohorts born before 1950, but educational attainments stagnated or even declined afterward. Acemoglu argued that the literature still does not have a good understanding of the source of this structural break. The authors agreed that the decline in educational achievements across cohorts is striking, especially because the skill premium rose over the relevant period. They would not speculate about the reasons underlying this trend but suggested that skill-biased technical changes might also have played a role for the rising skill premium.

Valerie Ramey followed up on the subject and offered a tentative explanation for the decline in educational achievements across cohorts. She highlighted the role of expectations for investment in human capital. She noted that the 1960s cohort (studied in the paper) turned 18 in the late 1970s, when the college premium was low and strong unions guaranteed favorable labor market outcomes to low-educated workers. Ramey suggested that education choices based on backward-looking outcomes might have led the 1960s cohort to underinvest in education. The authors were sympathetic to this idea.

Silvana Tenreyro spoke next and suggested that deviations from rational expectations might play an important role when modeling decisions related to education and health. She offered the rise in opioid use as an example. The authors acknowledged that the determinants of health outcomes are complex. In particular, they argued that there is much uncertainty in the first place about whether health outcomes are endogenous (i.e., a result of investment decisions) or mostly exogenous, as in their model. For illustration, they cited the work of Rachel Griffith, Rodrigo Lluberas, and Melanie Lührmann ("Gluttony and Sloth? Calories, Labor Market Activity and the Rise of Obesity," *Journal of the European Economic Association* 14, no. 6 [2016]: 1253–86) on the source of the rise in obesity in England. Although this increase in obesity had long been largely attributed to an increase in calorie consumption, Griffith et al. (2016) found that the change in the nature of jobs (an external change) was an important factor. In the case of opioid use, the authors pointed out that prescriptions by doctors (again, an external change) might also have played a role. This uncertainty about the endogenous or exogenous nature of health outcomes justifies their modeling choice, they argued, addressing a point raised by one of the discussants, Greg Kaplan.

Erik Hurst offered two comments. The first was related to positive selection into employment, and to the work of Richard Blundell, Luigi Pistaferri, and Itay Saporta-Eksten ("Consumption Inequality and Family Labor Supply," *American Economic Review* 106, no. 2 [2016]: 387–435) and Richard Blundell et al. ("Female Labor Supply, Human Capital, and Welfare Reform," *Econometrica* 84, no. 5 [2016]: 1705–53). Hurst noted that selection might be particularly important for female education and labor supply. Excluding the bottom 5%–6% of the education distribution would provide a conservative robustness check, he argued. Second, Hurst inquired about the role of medical expenses in the model because they are assumed to be exogenous. On selection into employment, the authors agreed that more robustness checks were warranted and welcomed Hurst's suggestion. On the modeling of medical expenses, they reiterated that a substantial part of medical expenses seems exogenous. For instance, doctors might prescribe newer, more expensive treatments due to fear of lawsuits, even if those treatments do not have a significant effect on life expectancy.

Chad Syverson noted that health shocks only take place after retirement in the authors' model. He suggested an extension with preretirement health shocks and disability shocks. The authors were very receptive to this comment. The evidence suggests that marriage affects the response to health and disability shocks, they argued. Allowing for preretirement health and disability, and for an interaction with marriage, is a promising avenue for future research, according to the authors.

James Poterba offered a comment on measurement. Referring to the work of Bruce D. Meyer and Nikolas Mittag ("Combining Administrative and Survey Data to Improve Income Measurement" [Working Paper no. 25738, NBER, Cambridge, MA, 2019]), Poterba noted that survey data might be inaccurate for individuals at the lower end of the income distribution. Furthermore, the share of individuals reporting no income in surveys far exceeds that observed in administrative data, and the survey response rates have decreased over time, he argued. Poterba suggested that taking these measurement issues seriously is particularly important when comparing outcomes across cohorts, citing the work of Fatih Guvenen et al. ("Lifetime Incomes in the United States over Six Decades" [Working Paper, University of Minnesota, November 2018]). The authors agreed that measurement across cohorts is crucial. They noted that intercohort trends have far-reaching consequences, including political polarization and attitudes toward trade and immigration policies. Measuring outcomes accurately is a required first step toward making progress on those issues, they argued. The authors also emphasized the need to account for changes in consumption baskets across cohorts to measure price indices accurately, following up on a point raised by one of the discussants, Greg Kaplan.

Benjamin Friedman concluded the discussion with a remark on assortative mating, a feature of the authors' model. Friedman noted that the degree of assortative mating has actually increased over time. He suggested that higher education institutions might have played an important role in this trend. Although university attendance has remained stable over time, he noted, individuals now tend to study farther away from their hometown. As a consequence, the pool of individuals remaining in towns without major colleges is less qualified, contributing to increased assortative mating.

3

On the Empirical (Ir)Relevance of the Zero Lower Bound Constraint

Davide Debortoli, *Universitat Pompeu Fabra, CREI, and Barcelona Graduate School of Economics*

Jordi Galí, *CREI, Universitat Pompeu Fabra, Barcelona Graduate School of Economics, and NBER*

Luca Gambetti, *Collegio Carlo Alberto, Università di Torino, Universitat Autònoma de Barcelona, and Barcelona Graduate School of Economics*

I. Introduction

The magnitude of the global financial crisis of 2007–8 and the recession that it triggered led many central banks to lower their policy rates down to values near zero, their theoretical lower bound.[1] In the United States, the target for the federal funds rate remained at zero for 7 years, from January 2009 through December 2015. During that period, the short-term interest rate stopped playing its role as an instrument of macroeconomic stabilization. Was the performance of the US economy affected by the binding zero lower bound (ZLB)? The present paper seeks to provide an answer to that question. More specifically, our goal is to evaluate the merits of what we refer to as the "ZLB empirical irrelevance hypothesis" (or the "irrelevance hypothesis," for short), that is, the hypothesis that the economy's performance was not affected by the binding ZLB constraint, in practice, during the recent US episode. In particular, we focus on two dimensions of that performance that were ex ante likely to have experienced the impact of a binding ZLB: (i) the volatility of macro variables and (ii) the economy's response to shocks.

We start our empirical exploration with an assessment of the possible changes in the volatility of macro variables during the period in which the ZLB constraint was binding. A rise in volatility could have been expected as a result of the Fed's hands being tied because of the federal funds rate having hit the ZLB, since this prevented the "usual" stabilizing policy response to aggregate shocks. Yet we find little evidence of such an increase in volatility of either real or nominal US macro variables over the period during which the federal funds rate attained its ZLB. The previous finding is at odds with the predictions of a baseline New Keynesian (NK) model, as we show by means of a number of simulations, under the assumption that the central bank follows a simple interest rate rule that embeds the ZLB assumption.

In the second part of the paper, we ask ourselves whether the response of a variety of US macro variables (other than the policy rate itself) to different aggregate shocks changed during the binding ZLB episode. Our empirical approach involves the estimation of a structural vector autoregressive model with time-varying coefficients (TVC-SVAR), driven by four shocks that are identified by means of a combination of long-run and sign restrictions. Under the irrelevance hypothesis, there should not be any significant change in the estimated responses over the binding ZLB period relative to period before the ZLB was binding. This is indeed what we find. In particular, we show that the estimated response of the long-term interest rate during the ZLB period is very similar to its counterpart for the pre-ZLB period. Furthermore, when we estimate a "rule" for the long-term rate, we find little evidence of a break during the ZLB period.

The previous findings are consistent with (but not a proof of) the notion that the adoption and fine-tuning of unconventional monetary policies (UMPs) may have been highly effective during the ZLB period in steering the long rate as desired, despite an unchanged policy rate. To illustrate that interpretation, we show how the previous findings can be reconciled with the predictions of a baseline NK model when we assume an interest rate rule based on a shadow interest rate. That rule can be interpreted as capturing the role of forward guidance (i.e., the management of expectations on the future path of the policy rate) in getting around the constraints imposed by the ZLB.

We want to warn the reader at the outset against two possible misinterpretations of our findings. First, one may be tempted to view those findings as suggesting that, contrary to what mainstream economic theory implies in the presence of nominal rigidities, the ZLB is irrelevant "always and everywhere." Instead, our evidence focuses on a specific economy (the United States) and episode (the 2009Q1–2015Q4 period). Several unconventional programs were adopted by the Federal Reserve during that period, which may account for our evidence. A binding ZLB could very well have a different impact in a different context if unaccompanied by such unconventional policies.

Second, our "irrelevance" findings should not be interpreted as downplaying the significance of the Great Recession and the slowness of the subsequent recovery. Together with the associated deflationary pressures, they were undoubtedly the main factors behind the sharp reduction in the federal funds rate down to its ZLB. Our findings suggest, however, that no special role should be attributed to the ZLB constraint as explanation for the depth and persistence of the recession. Instead, the size, persistence, and financial nature of the shocks experienced by the US economy (before the start of the ZLB episode) are more likely explanations of the severity of the downturn, as had been the case for many other financial crises experienced by different countries in the past, and which did not generally involve a binding ZLB constraint.[2]

The remainder of the paper is organized as follows. Section II discusses the related literature. Section III provides evidence on the impact of the binding ZLB on macroeconomic volatility. Section IV contrasts that evidence with the predictions of a baseline NK model. Section V studies how the binding ZLB constraint may have affected the economy's response to a variety of shocks. Section VI analyzes the ability of a modified interest rate rule to account for the empirical evidence. Section VII summarizes and concludes.

II. Related Literature

Our work is close in spirit to papers that seek to evaluate, using different approaches, some form of ZLB irrelevance hypothesis. Thus, Swanson and Williams (2014) estimate the time-varying sensitivity of yields to macroeconomic announcements using high-frequency data and conclude that long-term yields were essentially unconstrained throughout 2008–12 and short-term yields seemed to be constrained only by late 2011. Similarly, Campbell et al. (2012) provide evidence suggesting that forward guidance announcements by the Federal Open Market Committee have been successful in moving interest rates that are relevant for households' and firms' decisions, despite the binding ZLB constraint.

The recent works of Wu and Xia (2016) and Wu and Zhang (2017) are also closely related to our paper. Thus, Wu and Xia (2016) propose a shadow rate indicator as a measure of the monetary policy stance that also applies to binding ZLB periods. They embed their shadow rate in an identified factor-augmented vector autoregressive model similar to that in Bernanke, Boivin, and Eliasz (2005) and find that (exogenous) changes in the shadow rate have an effect on the economy during the ZLB period similar to the federal funds rate in the pre-ZLB period. A counterfactual simulation, in which the shadow rate is prevented from becoming negative, points to large real effects of having a persistently negative shadow rate during the ZLB period, which they attribute to the adoption of UMPs. Wu and Zhang (2017) study a NK model where aggregate demand is a function of a shadow rate that is not subject to a ZLB constraint and that is determined according to a conventional Taylor-type rule. The equilibrium dynamics are thus equivalent to those of the standard NK model without a ZLB constraint. Wu and Zhang discuss alternative channels through which the central bank can lower the shadow rate below zero, including purchases of assets by the central bank (combined with a preferred habitat-like assumption), direct lending to firms, and/or changes in tax rates on interest income. They conclude that a binding ZLB constraint on the policy rate does not have to alter the responses of aggregate variables to supply and demand shocks relative to periods with a nonbinding ZLB, as long as the central bank manages to adjust the shadow rate suitably.

Christiano, Eichenbaum, and Trabandt (2015) estimate and analyze a dynamic stochastic general equilibrium (DSGE) model that incorporates a truncated shadow rule similar to the one considered later. They use the estimated model to interpret the Great Recession. They attribute the bulk of the fall in output to a drop in total factor productivity and a rise in the cost of working capital, with counterfactual simulations without a ZLB constraint suggesting that the latter played a small role in accounting for the drop in output. That finding contrasts with Gust et al. (2017), who carry out a similar counterfactual experiment and find that 30% of the output contraction observed during the Great Recession can be attributed to the constraint imposed by the ZLB on the ability of monetary policy to stabilize the economy, with that constraint playing an even larger role in accounting for the slow recovery. Those estimates are, however, subject to large uncertainty.[3] A similar finding was obtained in Del Negro et al. (2017), whose counterfactual simulations of a DSGE model with financial frictions suggest that the ZLB constraint can explain about one-half of the 6% decline in output that would have been observed in the absence of unconventional interventions.

Our findings point to the benefits of adopting a shadow rule with sufficient inertia, which we interpret as a shortcut for UMPs. A number of papers have also uncovered a similar result using alternative models and assumptions, including Reifschneider and Roberts (2006), Kiley and Roberts (2017), and Bernanke, Kiley, and Roberts (2019).

Cochrane (2018) notes the absence of a break in the dynamics of US inflation and, in particular, the absence of a rise in inflation volatility during the binding ZLB episode. He argues that such an observation is inconsistent with the NK model, unless the fiscal theory of the price level is invoked. Our analysis in Section VI provides an alternative explanation for that observation, based on the use of forward guidance as a stabilizing tool.

Other authors have uncovered a change in asset price dynamics associated with the binding ZLB episode. Thus, Gourio and Ngo (2018) document a switch in the sign of the correlation between inflation and stock returns after 2008, which they attribute to the binding ZLB. Using a standard NK model, they show how the binding ZLB amplifies (dampens) the impact of demand (supply) shocks, lowering both inflation and term premia in long-term interest rates, which may partly account for the latter's unusually low levels since 2008. Similarly, Datta et al. (2019) document a substantial rise in the correlation between oil and equity returns, as well as a large responsiveness of those variables to news announcements, during the binding ZLB episode and show that finding can be reconciled with a NK model embedding the ZLB constraint.

Our paper, and the literature described earlier, can be seen as complementing the extensive work aimed at assessing the effects of UMPs and, in particular, the effects of UMP announcements or their implementation on financial variables. Examples of that work include Krishnamurthy and Vissing-Jorgensen (2011), Hamilton and Wu (2012), D'Amico and King (2013, 2017), and Swanson (2018), among many others.

Throughout the paper, we maintain the assumption of an unchanged inflation target, which we take as exogenously given. A branch of the literature has instead focused on the determination of the optimal inflation rate in the presence of the ZLB constraint, given the trade-off between the distortions associated with a higher average inflation and the benefits from it in the form of a smaller incidence of a binding ZLB. Contributions to that branch of the literature include Coibion, Gorodnichenko, and Wieland (2012), Dordal-i-Carreras et al. (2016), Blanco (2019), Kiley and Roberts (2017), and Andrade et al. (2018).

III.   Macroeconomic Volatility and the ZLB: Some Evidence

We start with an empirical assessment of the impact of the binding ZLB constraint on US macroeconomic volatility. We report statistics for gross domestic product (GDP) and total hours in the nonfarm business sector (both in log first differences), as well as three measures of quarterly inflation based, respectively, on the GDP deflator, the core consumer price index (CPI), and the core personal consumption expenditure (PCE) deflator. All data are quarterly. The first column of table 1 reports the standard deviation of several macro variables over the ZLB episode (2009Q1–2015Q4) relative to the corresponding standard deviation during the period 1984Q1–2018Q2 but excluding the binding ZLB episode (henceforth, the no-ZLB period). Note that 1984 is often viewed as the date marking the beginning of the Great Moderation. The second column reports an analogous statistic, but excluding from both the no-ZLB and ZLB periods the observations corresponding to the Great Recession (2008Q1–2009Q2, according to the NBER chronology).

The previous statistics show little evidence of an increase in macro volatility during the ZLB period. Many of the ratios of standard deviations are below 1, suggesting if anything a decline in volatility during the ZLB period. The previous statistics contrast starkly with the volatility in the pre-1984 period relative to the same benchmark, shown in the last column. In the latter case, the ratio of standard deviations is well above 1 for all the variables considered.[4]

Table 2 provides additional evidence pertaining to potential changes in volatility during the ZLB episode. It reports the estimates from an ordinary least squares (OLS) regression of the absolute value of the deviation of each variable (i.e., GDP growth, hours growth, and each of the three inflation measures) from a (period-specific) mean, on a constant and a dummy variable for the ZLB episode.[5] Together with each point estimate, we report the corresponding standard errors, computed using the Newey-West estimator with a four-lag window. As a robustness check, we also report estimates from regressions that include a dummy for the

Table 1
Ratio of Standard Deviations

	ZLB (1)	ZLB (2)	Pre-84
GDP	.92	.89	2.19
Hours	1.32	.74	1.60
GDP deflator	1.02	.88	3.11
Core CPI	.52	.54	3.03
Core PCE	.52	.50	2.52
Great Recession?	Yes	No	No

Note: Standard deviations are computed relative to the no-ZLB period given by 1984Q1–2008Q4 and 2016Q1–2018Q2. The ZLB period is 2009Q1–2015Q4. When the Great Recession is excluded, the pre-ZLB sample period ends in 2007Q4 and the ZLB period starts in 2009Q3. The Pre-84 period starts in 1960Q1 and ends in 1983Q4. ZLB = zero lower bound; GDP = gross domestic product; CPI = consumer price index; PCE = personal consumption expenditure.

Table 2
Volatility Regressions

	CONST	ZLB	GR
GDP	.41*	.01	
	(.04)	(.05)	
	.37*	−.01	.94*
	(.03)	(.05)	(.19)
Hours	.47*	.05	
	(.05)	(.16)	
	.42*	−.00	1.39*
	(.04)	(.09)	(.42)
GDP deflator	.70*	(.12)	
	(.07)	.03	
	.69*	.02	.37
	(.07)	(.11)	(.26)
Core CPI	.91*	−.47*	
	(.10)	(.13)	
	.91*	−.47*	−.05
	(.10)	(.13)	(.13)
Core PCE	.83*	−.41*	
	(.08)	(.10)	
	.83*	−.42*	(.23)
	(.09)	(.10)	.13

Note: The table reports the estimated coefficients from an ordinary least squares regression of the absolute value of the deviation of each variable's growth rate from its mean, on a constant (CONST) and a dummy for the zero lower bound (ZLB) period (2009Q1–2015Q4), with and without a control dummy for the Great Recession (GR) period (2008Q1–2009Q2). The sample period is 1984Q1–2018Q2. Standard errors obtained using a Newey-West estimator (4 lags). GDP = gross domestic product; CPI = consumer price index; PCE = personal consumption expenditure. *denotes statistical significance at the 5% level.

Great Recession in addition to the ZLB period. The eventual impact of the binding ZLB on the volatility of each variable should be captured by the estimated coefficient of the ZLB dummy in the corresponding regression. As the estimates reported in table 2 indicate, there is no evidence of a significant volatility increase during the ZLB period in any of the variables considered, for any specification. By contrast, we find two instances of a significant reduction in volatility during that episode: this is the case for core CPI and core PCE inflation.

The evidence reported in tables 1 and 2 is reflected graphically in figure 1, which shows the evolution of GDP growth and inflation (based on the GDP deflator) over the period 1984Q1–2018Q2, with the binding ZLB episode marked with a shaded area. It is not obvious at all to the naked

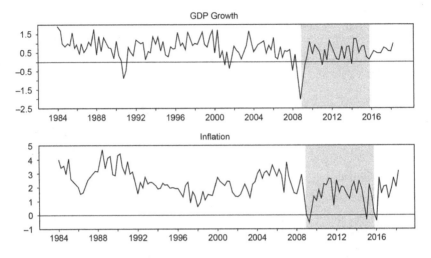

Fig. 1. Macroeconomic volatility and the zero lower bound. GDP = gross domestic product.

eye that the volatility of either variable was affected one way or another during the ZLB episode.

The evidence provided earlier contrasts with much of the literature on the effects of a binding ZLB constraint. The next section illustrates that contrast.

IV. Macroeconomic Volatility and the ZLB: Predictions of a Benchmark Model

Next, we analyze the predictions of a baseline NK model regarding the implications of a binding ZLB constraint for the equilibrium behavior of different macroeconomic variables. Needless to say, we are not the first to carry out an analysis of this kind. Examples of related earlier work include Christiano, Eichenbaum, and Rebelo (2011), Eggertsson (2011), and Wieland (2019), among many others. In contrast with those papers, our focus here is on the implications of the binding ZLB constraint for macro volatility relative to "normal" times.

Our model is fully standard, so we restrict ourselves to describing its main elements. We assume an infinitely lived representative household with expected utility given by

$$\mathbb{E}_0 \left\{ \sum_{t=0}^{\infty} \beta_{0,t} \left(\log C_t - \frac{N_t^{1+\varphi}}{1+\varphi} \right) \right\},$$

where C_t is a constant elasticity of substitution function (with elasticity of substitution $\epsilon > 1$) of the quantities consumed of a continuum of differentiated goods and N_t denotes hours worked. The discount factor $\beta_{0,t}$ is defined recursively by $\beta_{0,t} = \beta_{0,t-1} \exp\{-z_t\}$, for $t = 1, 2, 3, \ldots$ with $\beta_{0,0} \equiv 1$. Variable z_t is the implied discount rate, which is assumed to follow a stochastic process with two components:

$$z_t = \rho_t + \eta_t.$$

The first component, ρ_t, is a two-state Markov process, switching between a normal value $\rho > 0$ and a low value $\rho_L < 0$. The realization of the latter, which we interpret as a large adverse demand shock, pulls the short-term interest rate against the ZLB constraint, given the assumed policy rule. The second component, η_t, is meant to capture "regular" or "recurrent" demand shocks and is assumed to follow an AR(1) process:

$$\eta_t = \rho_\eta \eta_{t-1} + \varepsilon_t^\eta,$$

where $\rho_\eta \in [0, 1)$, and ε_t^η is a white noise process with variance σ_η^2. For concreteness, in the simulations that follow, we restrict ourselves to shifts in the discount rate z_t as a source of aggregate fluctuations.

The supply side is fully standard. We assume a continuum of identical monopolistically competitive firms, each facing a constant Calvo probability θ of not being able to reoptimize its price in any given period. Technology is given by $Y_t = N_t^{1-\alpha}$. All output is consumed. The labor market is perfectly competitive.

The log-linearized equilibrium conditions describing the private sector of this economy are given by the familiar NK Phillips curve and dynamic investment/saving equations:

$$\hat{\pi}_t = \beta \mathbb{E}_t\{\hat{\pi}_{t+1}\} + \kappa \hat{y}_t$$

$$\hat{y}_t = \mathbb{E}_t\{\hat{y}_{t+1}\} - (i_t - \mathbb{E}_t\{\pi_{t+1}\} - z_t)$$

where $\hat{\pi}_t \equiv \pi_t - \pi$ and $\hat{y}_t \equiv y_t - y$ respectively denote the deviation of inflation and (log) output from their steady-state values, i_t is the short-term (one-period) nominal interest rate, $\beta \equiv \exp\{-\rho\}$ and $\kappa \equiv (1 - \theta)(1 - \beta\theta)$ $(1 + \varphi)/\theta(1 - \alpha + \alpha\epsilon)$.[6] It can be easily checked that under our assumptions the natural (flexible price) level of output is constant (and corresponds to the steady state), and z_t has the interpretation of the natural (flexible price) rate of interest.

The model is closed by assuming a monetary policy rule. As an empirically plausible baseline, we consider the following "truncated" version of a Taylor-type rule with inertia:

$$i_t = \max\left[0, \phi_i i_{t-1} + (1 - \phi_i)(\rho + \pi + \phi_\pi \hat{\pi}_t + \phi_y \Delta \hat{y}_t)\right], \tag{1}$$

Next, we analyze the equilibrium behavior of a long-term interest rate, which we define as the yield on a pure discount bond with stochastic maturity. More precisely, the long-term bond is assumed to mature each period with probability $1 - \gamma$, in which case it pays one unit of the *numéraire* (and yielding no payoff otherwise). The (normalized) yield of that bond, denoted by i_t^L, can be shown to satisfy the following difference equation in equilibrium (and up to a first-order approximation):

$$i_t^L = (1 - \beta\gamma)i_t + \beta\gamma E_t\{i_{t+1}^L\}.$$

We adopt a quarterly calibration of the model. We assume $\theta = 0.75$, which implies an average price duration of four quarters. The coefficients of the policy rule are set to $\phi_\pi = 1.5$, $\phi_y = 0.5$, and $\phi_i = 0.7$, in line with the empirical evidence. Steady-state inflation π is set to 0.005, consistent with an (annual) inflation target of 2%. We assume $\alpha = 0.25$ and $\varphi = 1$, both conventional values. We set $\epsilon = 6$, implying a flexible price markup of 20%. We assume $\rho_\eta = 0.8$ and $\sigma_\eta = 0.001$. Under the previous settings, the standard deviation of quarterly output growth when the ZLB is not binding is about 0.7%, consistent with that of US GDP growth over the 1984Q1–2008Q4 period. We set $\rho = 0.005$, implying an average real rate of 2% in normal times. We assume $\rho_L = -0.01$ so that a large adverse demand shock implies a natural rate of –4% in annual terms (and in the absence of other recurrent shocks). The probability of remaining in the normal regime is 0.994, whereas the probability of remaining in the low demand regime is 0.66. These values imply that ZLB episodes occur on average once every 140 quarters, with each episode expected to last 3 quarters. Under the previous settings, the contemporaneous impact on output of a large adverse demand shock (i.e., a Markov transition to ρ_L) is about –4%, which roughly corresponds to the observed decline in US GDP over the Great Recession. Most importantly for our purposes, the realization of a large adverse demand shock generally brings the policy rate down to zero, where it remains until the normal Markov state is restored again. Finally, we set $\gamma = 0.975$, consistent with an expected maturity for the long-term bond of 40 quarters (i.e., 10 years).

Similarly to Fernández-Villaverde et al. (2015), we solve the model using a global projection method to accurately account for the uncertainty and the nonlinearities associated with the presence of the occasionally binding ZLB constraint. In particular, we approximate the policy functions for inflation, output, and interest rates with Chebyshev polynomials (or splines) through a collocation method on a discrete grid for the four state variables (lagged output and interest rate, and the two components of the demand shocks).

Figure 2 shows the dynamic responses of several macro variables to a negative η_t shock, under the two possible states of the economy, namely, normal times (i.e., when the ZLB is nonbinding, shown in lines with filled circles) and under a binding ZLB regime (shown in lines with open diamonds). The figure illustrates clearly the destabilizing role of a binding ZLB in the face of an adverse demand shock relative to normal times: the inability to bring down the policy rate leads to much larger declines of output and inflation. Note that the long-term rate responds in opposite directions to the negative demand shock under the two scenarios. It declines in normal times, reflecting the expectations of a persistently lower short-term rate. In contrast, when the negative demand shock hits the economy during a binding ZLB episode, the long-term rate increases, reflecting the expectations of a (transitorily) higher path of short-term rates in the future, when the ZLB stops being binding, because in that case the economy would experience higher output growth in its transition to the new steady state, having started from a lower output level due to the current adverse demand shock. Note also that the contractionary effect of

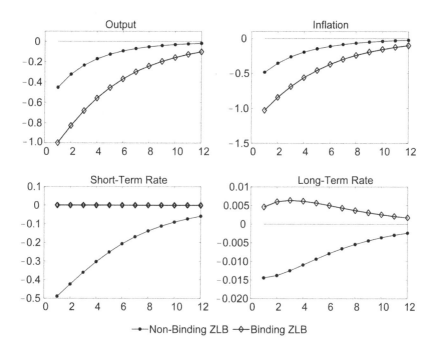

Fig. 2. The impact of a binding zero lower bound (ZLB) on the dynamic effects of a demand shock, baseline interest rate rule.

higher expected nominal short-term rates (reflected in the higher long-term nominal rate) is further amplified by the deflationary expectations caused by the shock, leading to an even larger increase in the long-term real rate (not shown).

Figure 3 displays the time series for output growth and inflation around the time of a large adverse demand shock, based on a simulation of the calibrated model described earlier. The timing of the large adverse shock and its eventual undoing is indicated with two vertical dashed lines. The "tunnel" within which the time series evolves represents, for each period, a 95% confidence interval for the realizations of the plotted variable across 1,000 simulations. The figure illustrates the increase in the volatility of output and inflation during the binding ZLB period relative to the earlier and later periods when the ZLB constraint is not binding. The model's predictions in that regard seem to conflict with the patterns of volatility observed in the US economy discussed in the previous section. Tables 3 and 4 formalize that visual intuition.

Table 3 reports the mean, across 1,000 model simulations, of the ratio of standard deviations of output growth and inflation over the binding ZLB episodes relative to normal times, together with a 95% confidence interval. In computing that ratio, we use simulations of the calibrated model for which the realized length of the binding ZLB period is equal to that observed in the recent US episode, namely, 28 quarters. As the

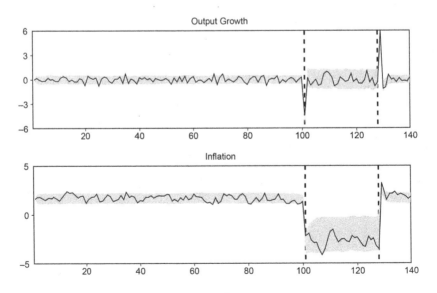

Fig. 3. Macroeconomic volatility and the zero lower bound: model simulations, baseline interest rate rule.

Table 3
Relative Volatility: Simulations

	Baseline Interest Rate Rule	
	(1)	(2)
Output	1.49	2.29
	[.86, 2.37]	[1.69, 2.95]
Inflation	1.94	2.39
	[.91, 3.38]	[1.02, 3.86]
Markov transitions?	Yes	No

Note: For each variable, the table reports the mean of the standard deviation in the ZLB period relative to the no-ZLB period over 1,000 model simulations under the baseline interest rate rule. The no-ZLB period is given by the first 100 observations and the last 8 observations in the simulation. The ZLB period corresponds to the intermediate 28 observations. Statistics are calculated both including all the observations (column 1) and excluding the two Markov transition observations into and out of the ZLB period (column 2). Brackets indicate 95% confidence intervals.

values reported in the table make clear, and in a way consistent with the impulse responses of figure 2 and the evidence in figure 3, the binding ZLB episode is characterized by a much larger average volatility, especially when we exclude the Markov transition observations from the computation of the standard deviation (column 2).

Table 4
Volatility Regressions: Simulations

	Baseline Interest Rate Rule			
	CONST	ZLB	MT	%REJ
Output	.32*	.35*		.86
	[.27, .36]	[.16, .56]		
	.26*	.34*	4.15*	.98
	[.23, .3]	[.19, .50]	[3.34, 4.92]	
Inflation	.27*	.47*		.98
	[.23, .32]	[.21, .79]		
	.26*	.47*	.61*	.98
	[.22, .30]	[.22, .79]	[.02, 1.31]	

Note: For each variable, the table reports the mean, over 1,000 model simulations under the baseline interest rate rule, of the estimated coefficients from an ordinary least squares regression of the absolute value of the demeaned growth rate of each variable on a constant (CONST), a dummy indicating the zero lower bound (ZLB) period, and, when it applies, a dummy for the two periods when a Markov transition (MT) occurs. Brackets indicate 95% confidence bands. %REJ is the fraction of simulations for which the estimated coefficient on the ZLB dummy is positive and statistically significant using the Newey-West estimate of the standard error (4 lags).
*denotes statistical significance at the 5% level.

Table 4 shows the estimated coefficients, using simulated data, from a regression of the absolute value of (demeaned) output growth and inflation on a ZLB dummy, with and without a control dummy for the two periods when a Markov transition occurs.[7] The regression uses time series generated by 1,000 simulations of the calibrated model. Each time series has 138 observations, with a binding ZLB episode taking place between periods 101 and 128, that is, a pattern that corresponds to that observed in the empirical sample period used in the previous section. In addition to the mean estimated coefficients, we report the 95% confidence band across simulations (shown in brackets), as well as the fraction of simulations for which we reject the null of a zero coefficient on the ZLB dummy at the 5% significance level, using the Newey-West estimate of standard errors. Note that the means (as well as the 95% confidence band) of the estimated coefficients on the ZLB dummy are systematically positive, reflecting the increase in volatility associated with ZLB episodes. This is true for both output growth and inflation, and independently of whether we control for the periods with "large shocks," corresponding to the Markov transitions. The previous finding contrasts with the estimates of the corresponding regressions using US data and reported in table 2, and where most of the estimated coefficients on the ZLB dummy were insignificant, with the exception of a few instances in which they were significantly negative (thus pointing to a reduction in volatility). Finally, note that the large fraction of simulations (ranging between 86% and 98%, depending on the variable and specification) for which the null of no change in volatility during the ZLB episode is rejected at the 5% significance level. The previous finding suggests that the relatively short ZLB period is not an obstacle for the changing volatility test to have a high power when the data are generated by our baseline calibrated model.

V.   Did the Binding ZLB Affect the Economy's Response to Shocks?

In the present section, we use a TVC-SVAR to estimate the dynamic responses of a number of macro variables to several identified aggregate shocks. The main motivation for using a model with TVC lies in our interest in assessing the extent to which the binding ZLB episode implied a change in the way the economy responded to different shocks. In addition, the use of a TVC-SVAR provides a flexible specification that allows for other structural changes that the US economy may have experienced over the sample period used in the estimation.[8]

A. Our Empirical Approach

Let $\mathbf{x}_t = [\Delta(y_t - n_t), n_t, \pi_t, i_t^L]'$, where y_t is (log) output in the nonfarm business sector, n_t denotes (log) hours of all persons in the nonfarm business sector, π_t is GDP deflator inflation, and i_t^L is the 10-year Treasury bond yield. Both output and hours are normalized by civilian population. All data are for the US economy, at a quarterly frequency, and cover the period 1953Q2 through 2015Q4.[9] We assume that the evolution of $\mathbf{x}_t$ is described by the following TVC-VAR model:

$$\mathbf{x}_t = \mathbf{A}_{0,t} + \mathbf{A}_{1,t}\mathbf{x}_{t-1} + \mathbf{A}_{2,t}\mathbf{x}_{t-2} + \ldots + \mathbf{A}_{p,t}\mathbf{x}_{t-p} + \mathbf{u}_t, \tag{2}$$

where $\mathbf{A}_{0,t}$ is a vector of time-varying intercepts, $\mathbf{A}_{i,t}$, for $i = 1, \ldots, p$, are matrices of TVCs, and $\mathbf{u}_t$ is a Gaussian white noise vector process with covariance matrix $\mathbf{\Sigma}_t$. We assume the reduced-form innovations $\mathbf{u}_t$ are a linear transformation of the underlying structural shocks ε_t given by

$$\mathbf{u}_t \equiv \mathbf{Q}_t\varepsilon_t,$$

where $\mathbb{E}\{\varepsilon_t\varepsilon_t'\} = I$ and $\mathbb{E}\{\varepsilon_t\varepsilon_{t-k}'\} = 0$ for all t and $k = 1, 2, 3, \ldots$ It follows that $\mathbf{Q}_t\mathbf{Q}_t' = \mathbf{\Sigma}_t$.

Following Primiceri (2005), we assume that the coefficients of the autoregressive matrices $\{\mathbf{A}_{i,t}\}$ and the covariance matrix $\mathbf{\Sigma}_t$ follow random walks, as described in detail in the appendix. The resulting reduced-form model is estimated as in Del Negro and Primiceri (2013). Given the estimated reduced-form VAR for any given period t, we recover the reduced-form moving average (MA) representation

$$\mathbf{x}_t = \boldsymbol{\mu}_t + \mathbf{B}_t(L)\boldsymbol{u}_t,$$

where $\boldsymbol{\mu}_t$ is a vector of time-varying means and $\mathbf{B}_t(L)$ is a polynomial of (time-varying) matrices.

The identifying restrictions assumed in the following allow us to determine the linear mapping $\mathbf{Q}_t$. Given the latter, we can write the structural MA representation as

$$\mathbf{x}_t = \boldsymbol{\mu}_t + \mathbf{C}_t(L)\varepsilon_t, \tag{3}$$

where $\mathbf{C}_t(L) \equiv \mathbf{B}_t(L)\mathbf{Q}_t$ describes the dynamic responses of the economy in period t. The possible changes over time in those responses are the focus of our analysis. Next, we turn to the determination of $\mathbf{Q}_t$, that is, to the issue of identification.

B. Identification

We assume fluctuations in $\mathbf{x}_t$ are driven by four structural shocks, represented by the elements of vector ε_t: technology, demand, monetary policy, and temporary supply shocks. We use a mix of long-run and sign restrictions to identify those shocks as follows: (i) the technology shock is the only one with a permanent effect on labor productivity; (ii) a demand shock generates a positive comovement of prices, GDP, and the long-term interest rate; (iii) a monetary policy shock generates a positive comovement between prices and GDP, but a negative one between the previous variables and the long-term interest rate; (iv) a transitory supply shock (e.g., a markup shock) implies a negative comovement of inflation and GDP. All the restrictions on the sign of comovements refer to a 1-year horizon. The long-run restriction used to identify technology was first proposed in Galí (1999). The sign restrictions are consistent with the predictions of a standard NK model under a plausible policy rule and are generally satisfied by estimated DSGE models (e.g., Smets and Wouters 2007). In the appendix, we discuss how the previous identification strategy is implemented in practice.

C. Evidence

Figure 4a displays the estimated impulse responses of output, inflation, and the long rate (in both nominal and real terms) to the four shocks considered. The responses plotted correspond to the averages of the estimated responses for the pre-ZLB period 2002Q1–2008Q4 (shown in lines with filled circles) and the ZLB period 2009Q1–2015Q4 (lines with open diamonds). Note that both subsamples contain 28 periods. We also display 68% and 95% confidence bands for the average impulse responses in the pre-ZLB period, based on 500 draws from the posterior distribution of the estimated model.[10]

The differences in the estimated responses between the two periods are very small for all variables and shocks considered. In particular, the estimated responses of output and inflation for the two periods lie almost on top of each other. Most importantly, note that the lack of a significant gap between the responses in the two periods carries over to both the nominal and real long-term yields, which are arguably more relevant in the determination of aggregate demand than the short-term nominal rate (which does not adjust during the binding ZLB period). Although the response of both the nominal and real long-term rates over the ZLB period

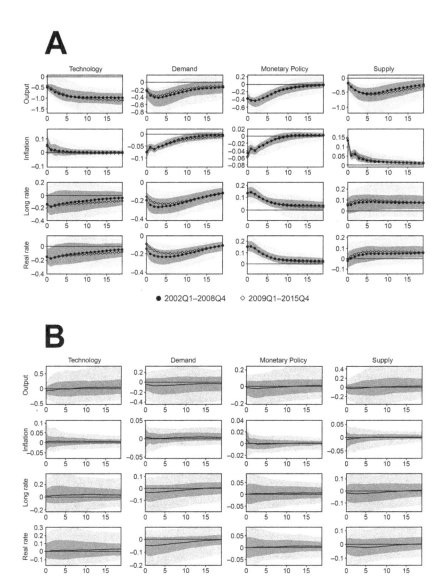

Fig. 4. (a) Dynamic responses: the impact of the binding zero lower bound (ZLB), short sample. (b) Dynamic response differentials: the effect of the binding ZLB, short sample. (c) Dynamic responses: the effect of the binding ZLB, short sample excluding the Great Recession. (d) Dynamic responses: the effect of the binding ZLB, extended pre-ZLB sample.

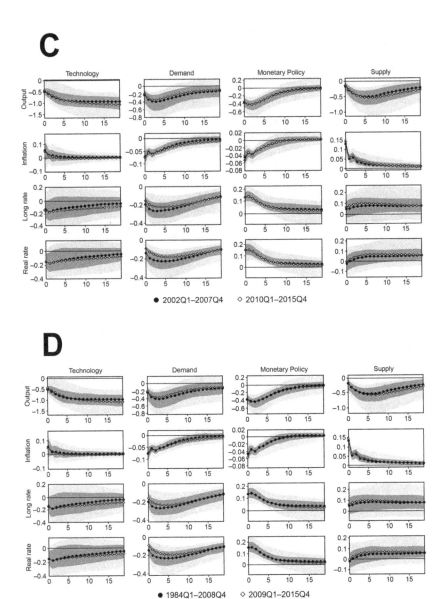

Fig. 4. *Continued.*

appears slightly muted relative to the pre-ZLB period, the difference is quantitatively very small and statistically insignificant. Figure 4*b* displays the corresponding impulse response differentials with their associated confidence bands. One cannot reject the null of a zero differential response for any variable, even at a 32% significance level.

The finding of similar responses of the long-term rate across the two subsample periods is consistent with our irrelevance hypothesis. Though we do not offer any direct evidence in that regard, that finding suggests that—possibly through the use of unconventional policies like forward guidance and quantitative easing—the Fed managed to steer long-term rates "as in normal times" in response to shocks hitting the economy during the ZLB period, thus leading to similar responses of output and inflation.

A caveat that might be raised regarding the evidence reported in figure 4a and 4b is that the estimated impulse responses may be somehow distorted by the Great Recession, which overlaps with both the pre-ZLB and ZLB periods. Figure 4c reports estimates of average impulse responses for the pre-ZLB and ZLB periods but excluding from the respective averages the estimated responses for the Great Recession quarters (i.e., those between 2008Q1 and 2009Q2). None of the qualitative findings discussed earlier seem to be affected by the exclusion of that episode.

An additional potential caveat is that the methodology used may not be able to capture changes in dynamics that take place suddenly, as opposed to gradually over time. Figure 4d seeks to dispel that concern by comparing the average impulse responses over the ZLB period with the median estimated average response across 500 draws, with each draw corresponding to a sample period of 28 consecutive observations, drawn randomly from the set {1984Q1:1990Q4, ..., 2002Q1:2008Q4}.[11] The resulting estimates are once again very similar across the two periods, suggesting a relatively uniform response over the entire post-1984 period.

We conclude this section by providing an alternative perspective on the irrelevance hypothesis and the possible role played by the long-term interest rate in getting around the ZLB constraint. Consider the following (admittedly ad hoc) descriptive rule for the long-term interest rate

$$i_t^L = \phi_0 + \phi_i i_{t-1}^L + (1 - \phi_i)[\phi_\pi \pi_t + \phi_y \Delta y_t] + \varepsilon_t^m, \qquad (4)$$

where ε_t^m is interpreted as an exogenous monetary policy shock. We estimate equation (4) and try to uncover changes in the coefficients on inflation and output growth by including as right-hand variables multiplicative dummies for the binding ZLB period and examining their significance. Furthermore, and to overcome the likely endogeneity of the regressors with respect to the policy shock $\{\varepsilon_t^m\}$, we estimate equation (4) using the time series for $\{i_t^L, \pi_t, \Delta y_t\}$, obtained after subtracting from each of them the corresponding component associated with the monetary policy shock in the estimated TVC-SVAR model described earlier.[12]

Table 5
Estimated Long-Term Interest Rate Rules

	(1)	(2)	(3)	(4)
π_t	2.42*	2.82*	2.26*	2.61*
	(.61)	(.82)	(.23)	(.32)
$\pi_t \times ZLB_t$	−.08	−.01	−.17*	−.45
	(.08)	(.06)	(.06)	(.50)
Δy_t			3.52*	4.43*
			(.42)	(.58)
$\Delta y_t \times ZLB_t$			−.16	−.60
			(.08)	(.89)
ϕ_0 and ϕ_i dummies?	Yes	No	Yes	No

Note: The table reports the ordinary least squares estimates of the long-term rate rule described in the text, both without output growth (first two columns) and with output growth (last two columns), with multiplicative dummies for the binding zero lower bound (ZLB) period. Column (2) and (4) also include ZLB dummies for the constant term (ϕ_0) and the coefficient on the lagged interest rate (ϕ_i). All the estimates are obtained using the nonmonetary component of the long-term interest rate, inflation, and output growth obtained from the estimated time-varying vector autoregressive model with time-varying coefficients.
*denotes statistical significance at the 5% level.

Under our assumptions, the resulting "cleansed" variables should be uncorrelated with the monetary policy shock, so that equation (4) can be estimated consistently using OLS. Table 5 reports the corresponding estimated coefficients, using two alternative specifications (with and without output growth in the rule). The reported estimates of the inflation and output growth coefficients point to a strong and highly significant response to both variables. In particular, the estimate of ϕ_π is well above 1, implying that the estimated rule satisfies the so-called Taylor principle. Most interesting, however, is the insignificance of the estimated coefficient on the multiplicative dummies associated with the binding ZLB period, suggesting the absence of a discernable change in the systematic response of the long-term interest rate to inflation and output growth as a consequence of the ZLB constraint becoming binding.

VI. Reconciling Theory and Evidence

The earlier empirical findings lend support, overall, to the irrelevance hypothesis. One possible explanation for our findings is that the implementation of UMPs during the binding ZLB episode made it possible to steer the long-term interest rate as in normal times in response to developments in the economy. The absence of unconventional policies in the baseline NK model analyzed in Section IV may thus account for the discrepancy between our evidence and the model predictions.

In the present section, we study whether modifying the specification of monetary policy in our baseline model can help reconcile theory and evidence. In particular, and following Christiano et al. (2015), Gust et al. (2017), and Andrade et al. (2018), among others, we replace the baseline interest rate rule (eq. [1]) with the following "shadow rate rule":

$$i_t = \max[0, \tilde{i}_t^s], \tag{5}$$

where $\tilde{i}_t^s$ is a shadow interest rate that is not subject to any lower bound and that evolves according to

$$\tilde{i}_t^s = \phi_i \tilde{i}_{t-1}^s + (1 - \phi_i)(\rho + \pi + \phi_\pi \hat{\pi}_t + \phi_y \Delta \hat{y}_t). \tag{6}$$

Figure 5 displays the dynamic responses to an adverse demand shock (i.e., a negative η_t realization) under the previous rule, with all the parameters of the model (including the coefficients in the rule) calibrated

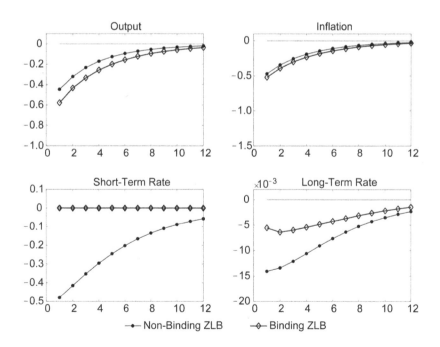

Fig. 5. The impact of a binding zero lower bound (ZLB) on the dynamic effects of a demand shock, shadow rate rule.

as before. Impulse responses are displayed under the two regimes, characterized by a binding and a nonbinding ZLB. As the figure makes clear, the responses of output and inflation under the two regimes are now very similar, despite the large discrepancy in the responses of the short-term rate (also displayed in the figure) due to the central bank's inability to lower that rate when the ZLB is binding. By contrast, the central bank manages to bring down the long-term nominal rate in response to the adverse demand shock, albeit not as much as under the nonbinding ZLB regime, and despite the lack of an adjustment in the short-term rule. The channel through which the shadow rate rule (eq. [6]) manages to stabilize the economy is one typically associated with forward guidance policies: the inertial term in equation (6), which is not bounded below, implies that the short-term rate will be kept "lower for longer" relative to the baseline rule (eq. [1]) in the aftermath of a binding ZLB episode, with the expected length of that additional stimulus being commensurate to the size of the decline in inflation and output, as well as the size of the inertial coefficient ϕ_i.

Tables 6 and 7, based on simulations of the calibrated NK model with the shadow rate rule in place, report evidence on the implied changes in volatility during the binding ZLB period, in a way analogous to tables 3 and 4 for the baseline rule. Note that the estimates of the standard deviation of output growth and inflation in the binding ZLB period relative to the nonbinding ZLB period, shown in table 6, are noticeably lower than those in table 3, reflecting the gains in stability from the adoption

Table 6
Ratio of Standard Deviations: Simulations

	Shadow Rate Rule	
Output	1.01	1.50*
	[.65, 1.9]	[1.03, 1.94]
Inflation	.82	1.0
	[.50, 1.38]	[.59, 1.41]
Markov transitions?	Yes	No

Note: For each variable, the table reports the mean of the standard deviation in the zero lower bound (ZLB) period relative to the pre-ZLB period over 1,000 model simulations under the baseline interest rate rule. The no-ZLB period is given by the first 100 observations and the last 8 observations in the simulation. The ZLB period corresponds to the intermediate 28 observations. Brackets indicate 95% confidence intervals. *denotes statistical significance at the 5% level.

Table 7
Volatility Regressions: Simulations

	Shadow Rate Rule			
	CONST	ZLB	MT	%REJ
Output	.31*	.1		.15
	[.28, .35]	(−.03, .27)		
	.26*	.14*	3.11*	.49
	[.23, .3]	[.02, .26]	[2.66, 3.6]	
Inflation	.28*	.03		.07
	[.24, .32]	[−.06, .14]		
	.26*	.05	1.37*	.16
	[.22, .29]	[−.04, .14]	[1.07, 1.69]	

Note: For each variable, the table reports the mean over 1,000 simulations under the shadow rate rule of the estimated coefficients from an ordinary least squares regression of the absolute value of the demeaned growth rate of the variable on a constant (CONST), a dummy indicating the zero lower bound (ZLB) period, and, when it applies, a dummy for the period of a Markov transition (MT). Brackets indicate 95% confidence bands. %REJ is the fraction of simulations for which the estimated coefficient on the ZLB dummy is positive and statistically significant using the Newey-West estimate of the standard error (4 lags).
*denotes statistical significance at the 5% level.

of the shadow rate rule. Furthermore, the reported relative standard deviations are comparable to some of the estimates in table 1, obtained using actual US data. Similarly, the estimated volatility regressions reported in table 7 show very limited evidence of an increase in volatility during the binding ZLB episodes, with the implied fraction of simulations for which the null of no change in volatility is rejected at the 5% significance level being very small for most specifications (with a largest value of 49%). The previous findings are visually captured by figure 6, which displays the time series for output growth and inflation around the time of a large adverse demand shock, based on a simulation of our calibrated model under the shadow rate rule. In contrast to figure 3, which was based on simulations under the baseline rule, neither the volatility of the simulated series nor the width of the tunnel appear to change in a discernible way during the binding ZLB episode (the period between the two vertical dashed lines).

VII.   Concluding Comments

The ZLB empirical irrelevance hypothesis implies that an economy's performance is not affected, in practice, by a binding ZLB episode. The

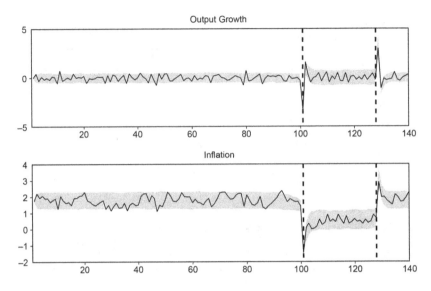

Fig. 6. Macroeconomic volatility and the zero lower bound: model simulations, shadow rate rule.

objective of the present paper was to evaluate that hypothesis for the recent ZLB episode experienced by the US economy (2009Q1–2015Q4). We have focused on two dimensions of performance that were ex ante likely to have experienced the impact of a binding ZLB: (i) the volatility of macro variables and (ii) the economy's response to a variety of macro shocks. Using several empirical approaches, we find little evidence against the irrelevance hypothesis, with our estimates suggesting that macro volatility did not increase significantly as a result of the binding ZLB constraint. Similarly, the responses of output, inflation, and the long-term interest rate to different shocks do not appear to have been much affected by that constraint. Our empirical findings can be reconciled with the predictions of a simple NK model under the assumption of a shadow interest rate rule, which can be viewed as capturing the effects of forward guidance policies that commit to lower for longer interest rates.

We interpret our findings as being consistent with (though not a proof of) the hypothesis that the UMPs implemented during the ZLB years may have succeeded, at least to some extent, at getting around the constraints imposed by the ZLB on conventional monetary policy.

Under that hypothesis, the unusual magnitude of the Great Recession and the slowness of the subsequent recovery in the US economy would be just the consequence of the large size, high persistence, and financial nature of the shock that triggered that recession, with no special amplifying role attributed to the binding ZLB constraint.

One should not interpret our evidence as suggesting that the ZLB constraint is irrelevant always and everywhere. A binding ZLB could very well have a much larger impact in a context different from the one that has been the object of analysis here.

Appendix

Let $\theta_t = vec(\mathbf{A}'_t)$, where $\mathbf{A}_t = [\mathbf{A}_{0,t}, \mathbf{A}_{1,t} \dots, \mathbf{A}_{p,t}]$ and $vec(\cdot)$ is the column stacking operator. We assume θ_t evolves over time according to the following equation:

$$\theta_t = \theta_{t-1} + \omega_t, \tag{7}$$

where ω_t is a Gaussian white noise vector process with covariance matrix Ω.

Time variation of Σ_t is modeled in the standard way. Let $\Sigma_t = \mathbf{F}_t \mathbf{D}_t \mathbf{F}'_t$, where $\mathbf{F}_t$ is lower triangular, with ones on the main diagonal, and $\mathbf{D}_t$ is a diagonal matrix. The vector containing the diagonal elements of $\mathbf{D}_t^{1/2}$, denoted by σ_t, is assumed to evolve according to the process

$$\log \sigma_t = \log \sigma_{t-1} + \zeta_t. \tag{8}$$

Moreover, let $\phi_{i,t}$ denote the column vector with the nonzero elements of the $(i+1)$th row of $\mathbf{F}_t^{-1}$. We assume

$$\phi_{i,t} = \phi_{i,t-1} + v_{i,t}, \tag{9}$$

where ζ_t and $v_{i,t}$ are Gaussian white noise vector processes with zero mean and (constant) covariance matrices Ξ and Ψ_i, respectively. We further assume that $v_{i,t}$ is independent of $v_{j,t}$, for all $j \neq i$, and that $\omega_t, \varepsilon_t, \zeta_t,$ and $v_{i,t}$ (for all i) are mutually independent. Estimation is carried out as in Del Negro and Primiceri (2013).[13]

Reduced-form impulse response functions (IRFs) can be derived from the local moving average (MA) representation of the model. First, let us consider the companion form representation of equation (2):

$$\tilde{\mathbf{x}}_t = \mathbf{a}_t + \tilde{\mathbf{A}}_t \tilde{\mathbf{x}}_{t-1} + \tilde{\mathbf{u}}_t$$

where $\tilde{\mathbf{x}}_t \equiv [\mathbf{x}'_t, \mathbf{x}'_{t-1}, \dots, \mathbf{x}'_{t-p+1}]'$, $\tilde{\mathbf{u}}_t \equiv [\mathbf{u}'_t, 0, \dots, 0]'$, $\mathbf{a}_t \equiv [\mathbf{A}'_{0,t}, 0, \dots, 0]'$, and $\tilde{\mathbf{A}}_t$ is the corresponding companion matrix. The (local) time-varying reduced-form MA representation of the model is given by

$$\mathbf{x}_t = \boldsymbol{\mu}_t + \sum_{j=0}^{\infty} \mathbf{B}_{t,j} \mathbf{u}_{t-j},$$

where $\mathbf{B}_{t,j} = [\tilde{\mathbf{A}}_t^j]_{n,n}$, for $j = 1, 2, \ldots$, where $[M]_{n,n}$ represents the first n rows and n columns of any matrix M, and where $\mathbf{B}_{t,0} = \mathbf{I}$.

The identification is implemented as follows. Let

$$\mathbf{H}_t^n = \begin{pmatrix} 1 & \mathbf{0}' \\ \mathbf{0} & \mathbf{H}_t^{n-1} \end{pmatrix},$$

where $\mathbf{0}$ is an n-dimensional column vector of zeros and $\mathbf{H}_t^n$ and $\mathbf{H}_t^{n-1}$ are orthogonal matrices of dimension $n \times n$ and $n - 1 \times n - 1$, The identification is implementedespectively. To impose the restrictions, we use the standard algorithm; see Uhlig (2005) and Rubio-Ramirez, Waggoner, and Zha (2010). We draw $\mathbf{H}_t^{n-1}$ using the QR decomposition and compute the implied structural IRFs as in equation (3) with $\mathbf{Q}_t = \mathbf{B}_t(1)^{-1} \mathbf{S}_t \mathbf{H}_t^n$, where $\mathbf{S}_t$ is the Cholesky factor of $\mathbf{B}_t(1)\Sigma_t \mathbf{B}_t'(1)$. We retain the draw if the sign restrictions are satisfied. We collect a total of 500 draws at each point in time. With no loss of generality, we order the shocks as follows: technology, demand, monetary policy, and supply.

Sign restrictions for set identification require only qualitative implications from the theory. This can be seen as an advantage with respect to standard methods because contemporaneous exclusion restrictions are often arbitrary or hard to justify. The sign restriction approach, however, also presents a few drawbacks. As Baumeister and Hamilton (2015) show, the previous approach implies informative priors for the structural parameters and this might have implications for the analysis and the interpretation of the results. See also Watson's discussion of our paper in the present volume.

The average IRFs over the full pre-ZLB period are computed as follows:

1. Draw an integer between 1 and 78 with equal probabilities over the set of possible starting periods. Call it $t_0(j)$.
2. Take a draw from the distribution of IRFs (at all the horizons) from $t_0(j)$ up to $t_0(j) + 27$, call it $x(t, j)$ with $t = t_0(j), \ldots, t_0(j) + 27$ and $j = 1, 2, \ldots, 500$ (number of draws).
3. Compute the average IRF over the sample period drawn, $\bar{x}(t) = (1/28)\Sigma_{t=t_0(j)}^{t_0(j)+27} x(t, j)$.
4. Repeat 1–3, 500 times. Compute the median and the percentiles of the corresponding $\bar{x}(t)$.

Endnotes

Author email addresses: Debortoli (davide.debortoli@upf.edu), Galí (jgali@crei.cat), Gambetti (luca.gambetti@uab.cat). We have benefited from comments from Ben Bernanke, Christian Brownlees, John Cochrane, Marty Eichenbaum, Mark Gertler, Barbara Rossi, Paolo Surico, and Mark Watson and by participants at the NBER Summer Institute, Bicocca University, Universitat Pompeu Fabra, Bucharest International Network for Economic Research Workshop, Shanghai University of Finance and Economics, European Central Bank, Stockholm School of Economics, Sveriges Riksbank, Finnish Economic Association Congress, and NBER Macroeconomics Annual Conference. We acknowledge the financial support of the Spanish Ministry of Economy and Competitiveness through grants RyC-2016-20476 and ECO-2017-82596-P (Debortoli), ECO-2017-87827 (Galí), and ECO2015-67602-P (Gambetti), and through the Severo Ochoa Programme for Centres of Excellence in R&D (SEV-2015-0563), and the Barcelona Graduate School of Economics. For acknowledgments, sources of research support, and disclosure of the authors' material financial relationships, if any, please see https://www.nber.org/chapters/c14241.ack.

1. Several central banks lowered their policy rates down to values below zero, thus proving that the latter should be seen a soft lower bound. From the point of view of our paper, what matters is the existence of a "perceived" value below which a given central bank is not willing to lower the policy rate, that is, an effective lower bound. In the case of the US economy, which is the focus of the present paper, zero appears to be the Fed's effective lower bound.

2. Many empirical papers have provided evidence on the unusual depth and persistence of downturns caused by financial crises. See, for example, Cerra and Saxena (2008), IMF (2009), and Reinhart and Rogoff (2009). Romer and Romer (2018) provide evidence suggesting that the degree of monetary and fiscal policy space greatly affects the macroeconomic performance in the aftermath of financial crises.

3. As Gust et al. (2017) themselves acknowledge, their estimates "are subject to considerable uncertainty as the 68 percent credible region does not exclude the possibility that the estimated effects of the ZLB constraint were much smaller or much larger" (2000).

4. Changes in volatility between the Great Moderation and the pre-Great Moderation periods have been uncovered by many authors (e.g., McConnell and Pérez-Quirós 2000; Stock and Watson 2002).

5. A similar methodology was used by Stock and Watson (2002) to test for a change in volatility during the Great Moderation.

6. See, for example, Galí (2015) for a derivation. By allowing for a nonzero steady-state inflation, we are implicitly assuming that prices are indexed to that variable. We also solved and simulated a fully nonlinear version of the model with price adjustment cost à la Rotemberg, obtaining very similar results to the linearized version considered here.

7. As in table 3, we allow for a period-specific mean during the binding ZLB episode.

8. These may include the change in the cyclical behavior of productivity emphasized in Galí and Gambetti (2009) as well as the change in monetary policy starting with Paul Volcker's tenure at the Fed uncovered in Clarida, Galí, and Gertler (2000).

9. We construct our data set using the following time series drawn from the Federal Reserve Economic Data database: real output per hour of all persons (nonfarm business sector; OPHNFB), hours of all persons (nonfarm business sector; HOANBS), civilian non-institutional population (CNP16OV), GDP deflator (GDPDEF), and 10-Year Treasury Constant Maturity Rate (GS10).

10. It is worth noting that the reported bands take into account the uncertainty associated with the estimates of the reduced-form coefficients as well as the width of the set-identified impulse responses using sign restrictions.

11. See the appendix for a detailed description of the algorithm used.

12. Note that the monetary policy shock component for the ith element of $\mathbf{x}_t$ is given by $\mathbf{C}_t^{i3}(L)\varepsilon_t^m$.

13. We refer the reader to Galí and Gambetti (2009) for details.

References

Andrade, Philippe, Jordi Galí, Hervé Le Bihan, and Julien Matheron. 2018. "The Optimal Inflation Target and the Natural Rate of Interest." *Brookings Papers on Economic Activity*, forthcoming.

Baumeister, C., and J. D. Hamilton. 2015. "Sign Restrictions, Structural Vector Autoregressions, and Useful Prior Information." *Econometrica* 83 (5): 1963–99.

Bernanke, Ben S., Jean Boivin, and Piotr Eliasz. 2005. "Measuring the Effects of Monetary Policy: A Factor-Augmented Vector Autoregressive (FAVAR) Approach." *Quarterly Journal of Economics* 120:387–422.

Bernanke, Ben S., Michael T. Kiley, and John M. Roberts. 2019. "Monetary Policy Strategies for a Low Rate Environment." Finance and Economics Discussion Series 2019-009, Board of Governors of the Federal Reserve System, Washington, DC. https://doi.org/10.17016/FEDS.2019.009.

Blanco, Andrés. 2019. "Optimal Inflation Target in an Economy with Menu Costs and Zero Lower Bound." *American Economic Journal: Macroeconomics*, forthcoming.

Campbell, Jeffrey R., Charles L. Evans, Jonas D. M. Fisher, and Alejandro Justiniano. 2012. "Macroeconomic Effects of Federal Reserve Forward Guidance." *Brookings Papers on Economic Activity* 43 (1): 1–54.

Cerra, Valerie, and Sweta C. Saxena. 2008. "Growth Dynamics: The Myth of Economic Recovery." *American Economic Review* 98 (1): 439–57.

Christiano, Lawrence, Martin Eichenbaum, and Sergio Rebelo. 2011. "When Is the Government Spending Multiplier Large?" *Journal of Political Economy* 119 (1): 78–121.

Christiano, Lawrence, Martin Eichenbaum, and Mathias Trabandt. 2015. "Understanding the Great Recession." *American Economic Journal: Macroeconomics* 7 (1): 110–67.

Clarida, Richard, Jordi Galí, and Mark Gertler. 2000. "Monetary Policy Rules and Macroeconomic Stability: Evidence and Some Theory." *Quarterly Journal of Economics* 105 (1): 147–80.

Cochrane, John H. 2018. "Michelson-Morley, Fisher, and Occam: The Radical Implications of Stable Quiet Inflation at the Zero Bound." *NBER Macroeconomics Annual* 2017 (32): 113–226.

Coibion, Olivier, Yuriy Gorodnichenko, and Johannes Wieland. 2012. "The Optimal Rate of Inflation in New Keynesian Models: Should Central Banks Raise Their Inflation Target in Light of the Zero Lower Bound?" *Review of Economic Studies* 20:1–36.

D'Amico, Stefania, and Thomas B. King. 2013. "Flow and Stock Effects of Large-Scale Treasury Purchases: Evidence on the Importance of Local Supply." *Journal of Financial Economics* 108 (2): 425–48.

———. 2017. "What Does Anticipated Monetary Policy Do?" Working Paper 2015-10, Federal Reserve Bank of Chicago.

Datta, Deepa, Benjamin K. Johannsen, Hannah Kwon, and Robert J. Vigfusson. 2019. "Oil, Equities, and the Zero Lower Bound." Finance and Economics Discussion Series 2018-058, Board of Governors of the Federal Reserve System, Washington, DC.

Del Negro, Marco, Gauti Eggertsson, Andrea Ferrero, and Nobuhiro Kiyotaki. 2017. "The Great Escape? A Quantitative Evaluation of the Fed's Liquidity Facilities." *American Economic Review* 107 (3): 824–57.

Del Negro, Marco, and Giorgio Primiceri. 2013. "Time-Varying Structural Vector Autoregressions and Monetary Policy: A Corrigendum." Staff Report No. 619, Federal Reserve Bank of New York.

Dordal-i-Carreras, Marc, Olivier Coibion, Yuriy Gorodnichenko, and Johannes-Wieland. 2016. "Infrequent but Long-Lived Zero-Bound Episodes and the Optimal Rate of Inflation." *Annual Review of Economics* 8 (1): 497–52.

Eggertsson, Gauti. 2011. "What Fiscal Policy Is Effective at Zero Interest Rates?" *NBER Macroeconomics Annual* 2010:59–112.

Fernández-Villaverde, Jesús, Grey Gordon, Pablo Guerrón-Quintana, and Juan F. Rubio-Ramírez. 2015. "Nonlinear Adventures at the Zero Lower Bound." *Journal of Economic Dynamics and Control* 57 (C): 182–204.

Galí, Jordi. 1999. "Technology, Employment and the Business Cycle: Do Technology Shocks Explain Aggregate Fluctuations?" *American Economic Review* 89:249–71.

———. 2015. *Monetary Policy, Inflation and the Business Cycle. An Introduction to the New Keynesian Framework and Its Applications*. 2nd ed. Princeton, NJ: Princeton University Press.

Galí, Jordi, and Luca Gambetti. 2009. "On the Sources of the Great Moderation." *American Economic Journal: Macroeconomics* 1 (1): 26–57.

Gourio, François, and Phuong Ngo. 2018. "Risk Premia at the ZLB: A Macroeconomic Interpretation." Working Paper 2020-01, Federal Reserve Bank of Chicago.

Gust, Christopher, Edward Herbst, David López-Salido, and Matthew E. Smith. 2017. "The Empirical Implications of the Interest-Rate Lower Bound." *American Economic Review* 107 (7): 1971–2006.

Hamilton, James, and Jing Cynthia Wu. 2012. "The Effectiveness of Alternative Monetary Policy Tools in Zero Lower Bound Environments." *Journal of Money, Credit and Banking* 44 (s1): 3–46.

IMF (International Monetary Fund). 2009. *World Economic Outlook, April 2009: Crisis and Recovery*. Washington, DC: IMF.

Kiley, Michael T., and John M. Roberts. 2017. "Monetary Policy in a Low Interest Rate World." *Brookings Papers on Economic Activity* 2017 (1): 317–89.

Krishnamurthy, Arvind, and Annette Vissing-Jorgensen. 2011. "The Effects of Quantitative Easing on Interest Rates." *Brookings Papers on Economic Activity* 43:215–87.

McConnell, Margaret M., and Gabriel Pérez-Quirós. 2000. "Output Fluctuations in the U.S.: What Has Changed since the 1980s?" *American Economic Review* 90 (5): 1464–76.

Primiceri, Giorgio E. 2005. "Time Varying Structural Vector Autoregressions and Monetary Policy." *Review of Economic Studies* 72:821–52.

Reifschneider, David L., and John M. Roberts. 2006. "Expectations Formation and the Effectiveness of Strategies for Limiting the Consequences of the Zero Bound on Interest Rates." *Journal of the Japanese and International Economies* 20 (3): 314–37.

Reinhart, Carmen M., and Ken S. Rogoff. 2009. "The Aftermath of Financial Crises." *American Economic Review: Papers and Proceedings* 99 (2): 466–72.

Romer, Christina D., and David H. Romer. 2018. "Why Some Times Are Different: Macroeconomic Policy and the Aftermath of Financial Crises." *Economica* 85 (337): 1–40.

Rubio-Ramirez, J., D. Waggoner, and T. Zha. 2010. "Structural Vector Autoregressions: Theory of Identification and Algorithms for Inference." *Review of Economic Studies* 77:665–96.

Smets, Frank, and Raf Wouters. 2007. "Shocks and Frictions in US Business Cycles: A Bayesian DSGE Approach." *American Economic Review* 97 (3): 586–606.

Stock, James, and Mark Watson. 2002. "Has the U.S. Business Cycle Changed and Why?" *NBER Macroeconomics Annual* 17:159–218.

Swanson, Eric T. 2018. "The Federal Reserve Is Not Very Constrained by the Lower Bound on Nominal Rates." *Brookings Papers on Economic Activity* 2018 (2): 555–72.

Swanson, Eric T., and John C. Williams. 2014. "Measuring the Effect of the Zero Lower Bound on Medium- and Longer-Term Interest Rates." *American Economic Review* 104 (10): 3154–85.

Uhlig, Harald. 2005. "What Are the Effects of Monetary Policy on Output? Results from an Agnostic Identification Procedure." *Journal of Monetary Economics* 52:381–419.

Wieland, Johannes. 2019. "Are Negative Supply Shocks Expansionary at the Zero Lower Bound?" *Journal of Political Economy* 127 (3): 973–1007.

Wu, Jing Cynthia, and Fan Dora Xia. 2016. "Measuring the Macroeconomic Impact of Monetary Policy at the Zero Lower Bound." *Journal of Money Credit and Banking* 48 (2–3): 253–91.

Wu, Jing Cynthia, and Ji Zhang. 2017. "A Shadow Rate New Keynesian Model." Working Paper no. 22856, NBER, Cambridge, MA.

Comment

Ben S. Bernanke, *Brookings Institution*

In 2008, for the first time since the Great Depression, the Federal Reserve encountered the zero lower bound (ZLB) on the nominal interest rate. The Fed's target rate, the overnight federal funds rate, fell effectively to zero in the fall as the central bank's emergency lending programs rapidly increased the supply of bank reserves. Then at its December 2008 meeting, the Federal Open Market Committee (FOMC), the Fed's monetary policy-making body, formally set the target range for the funds rate at 0 to 25 basis points—effectively zero. With the economy in free fall and little scope for additional rate cuts, the FOMC then turned to nonstandard policy tools, including forward guidance (communication about the likely or intended forward path of the policy rate) and large-scale asset purchases, also known as quantitative easing. Both tools were used actively during the Great Recession and the subsequent recovery.

Did the nonstandard tools work? The current consensus of central bankers and economists is that forward guidance and asset purchases eased financial conditions and supported the economy, with fewer adverse side effects than many predicted. Accordingly, these policies appear to have become permanent components of the monetary tool kit, both in the United States and abroad. However, the prevailing view also holds that the overall response of monetary policy was effectively constrained by the ZLB; that is, although nonstandard policies evidently mitigated the downturn, their use did not fully compensate for the inability of the Fed to cut short-term rates significantly further. This view, and the concern that in a world of low neutral interest rates future encounters with the ZLB may be frequent, has led the Fed and other central banks to actively consider new tools and new policy frameworks for dealing with the ZLB constraint.

In contrast to this prevailing view, however, a small literature has adduced indirect evidence to argue that the Fed's response to the Great

Recession was actually "normal," despite the ZLB. In other words, according to this literature, by applying its nonstandard tools the FOMC was able to provide about the same amount of countercyclical stimulus as it would have if, hypothetically, the ZLB had not been binding. For example, Swanson and Williams (2014) find that 2- and 5-year Treasury interest rates responded to economic data releases in a historically normal way during the ZLB period, especially prior to the FOMC's strengthening of its forward guidance in August 2011. (At that meeting, the FOMC announced its intention to hold rates at zero "through mid-2013," implementing date-based forward guidance for the first time.) If the ZLB was effectively constraining the monetary policy response, these authors argue, the response of longer-term rates to economic news would instead have been attenuated. In another interesting paper, Wu and Xia (2014) infer the extent of monetary stimulus from the entire term structure rather than from the target funds rate alone. They use an affine term structure model to construct a "shadow" short-term interest rate, which can be negative, and find that, judging by the behavior of the shadow rate, US monetary policy provided about the normal degree of stimulus despite the ZLB, especially later in the ZLB period (when the estimated shadow rate becomes significantly negative).

The present paper adds to the indirect evidence on the extent to which the ZLB limited the monetary response to the Great Recession. The authors perform several exercises comparing the volatility and dynamics of key macro variables during the recent ZLB episode to a non-ZLB period that includes the earlier "Great Moderation" era. Their intuition, confirmed in a simple model, is that, if the ZLB constrained monetary policy in the recent episode, then volatility should have increased, and macro dynamics changed, relative to the benchmark of the Great Moderation. Contrary to that prediction, they find that the behavior of key economic variables (including longer-term interest rates) did not change much in the ZLB period, implying that the ZLB was not an effective constraint on monetary policy. Needless to say, these findings are good news if true. If, even in the face of a very severe downturn, the Fed was able to overcome the ZLB and provide a normal degree of countercyclical stimulus, then concerns about future encounters with the ZLB may be overblown.

Before commenting on the paper's results, I will add one suggestive result of my own. Figure 1 shows the pace of labor market recovery from recessions since 1960. Figure 1a shows the unemployment gap, the difference between the civilian unemployment rate and the Congressional Budget Office's estimate of the natural rate of unemployment. Shaded

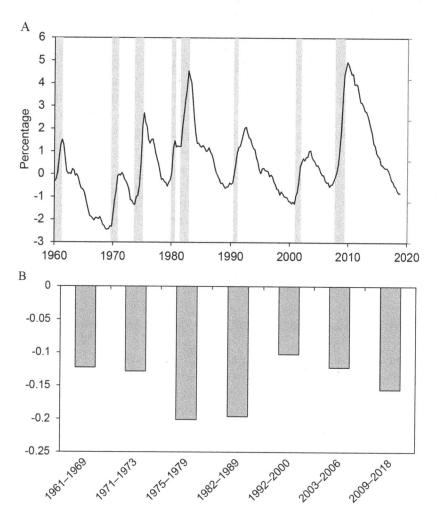

Fig. 1. Pace of labor market recovery from recessions since 1960: (*a*) unemployment gap; (*b*) average change in unemployment gap during recoveries.

lines show periods of recession. As the reader can observe, unemployment tends to lag the cycle, peaking later than output before declining.

Figure 1*b* shows the average quarterly change in the unemployment gap between the peak and the trough of the unemployment rate. As the figure shows, the pace of labor market recovery from the Great Recession was faster than in the previous two recessions and only modestly slower than the most severe prior postwar recessions, in 1973–75 and 1981–82. On this metric, then, the recovery from the Great Recession seems relatively normal, consistent with the conclusions of the present paper.

Fernald et al. (2017), who display a figure similar to my figure 1, develop this point further.

Turning to the present paper, I consider two questions. First, the evidence presented by the authors, though interesting, is indirect and drawn from a single episode. How persuasive is it? Are there other plausible explanations for their findings? Second, the indirect evidence of this paper is silent about exactly how, and with what policies, the Fed overcame the ZLB constraint. It is worth asking whether their findings are consistent with what we know about the effectiveness of nonstandard policies. Is it quantitatively plausible that, using forward guidance and asset purchases, the Fed was able fully to overcome the constraint posed by the ZLB?

On the first question, the paper's comparison of the recent ZLB episode with the non-ZLB period is not a controlled experiment. It is possible that the ZLB did constrain monetary policy, which all else equal would have led to the predicted changes in macro volatility and dynamics, but that other differences between the periods obscure the comparison. Here are some possible confounding factors: First, the Great Recession, which was caused by a severe financial crisis, may differ on important dimensions from previous postwar recessions (Ng and Wright 2013). For example, consumption or investment may have been affected by adverse financial shocks in ways not typical in recession. Second, productivity growth was slow following the financial crisis; if the crisis suppressed variation in productivity as well, standard real-business-cycle arguments would suggest that cyclical dynamics would also be affected. Third, even if monetary policy was constrained by the ZLB, fiscal policy may have compensated, particularly early in the recovery. Finally, the authors' finding that volatility was no higher in the ZLB episode than earlier could conceivably be the result of declining trends in volatility unrelated to the ZLB or the Great Recession.

Table 1 provides simple evidence on the first three of these possibilities. The table shows the ratio of standard errors of key macroeconomic variables during the ZLB episode (2009Q1–2015Q4) to the non-ZLB period (1984Q1–2018Q2 excluding the ZLB period and the Great Recession). The top five entries replicate (to a close approximation) the results of the authors' table 1, confirming their finding that these macroeconomic variables were less volatile during the ZLB episode than before, contrary to what we would expect if the ZLB had constrained monetary policy. The table shows the same comparison for five additional variables: personal consumption expenditures (PCEs), nonresidential fixed investment, nonfarm business productivity, industrial production, and the full-employment federal deficit.

Table 1
Ratio of Standard Errors in ZLB Periods to Non-ZLB Periods

Variable	Ratio of Standard Errors
GDP	.88
Hours	.73
GDP deflator	.89
Core CPI inflation	.59
Core PCE inflation	.49
PCE	.71
Nonresidential fixed investment	.85
Nonfarm business productivity	1.02
Industrial production	.95
Full-employment federal deficit	1.34

Note: Zero lower bound (ZLB) period is 2009Q1–2015Q4; non-ZLB period is 1984Q1–2018Q2 less ZLB period. The Great Recession, which covers the period from 2008Q1 to 2009Q2, is excluded. All variables are in percent quarterly annualized growth rates with the following exceptions: inflation rates are in percent levels and the full-employment deficit is a percent of potential gross domestic product (GDP). CPI = consumer price index; PCE = personal consumption expenditure.

In brief, table 1 does not provide evident support for the idea that unusual behavior of consumption or investment, arising perhaps from the unusual mix of shocks underlying this recession, can explain the relatively low volatility of the economy during the ZLB period. Rather, the volatility of consumption and nonresidential fixed investment behaved similarly to that of overall gross domestic product (GDP). Nor is there evidence that differences in the behavior of productivity account for lower overall volatility, as the volatility of nonfarm business productivity growth is about the same in the ZLB period as in the non-ZLB period. There is, however, some evidence in table 1 that fiscal policy was unusual during the recent episode: the standard error of the full-employment federal deficit (Congressional Budget Office) is 34% larger in the ZLB episode than during the non-ZLB period. A possible story is that expansionary fiscal policy, including major fiscal actions in 2009, compensated for constrained monetary policy early in the ZLB period. Later in the recovery, fiscal policy became more restrictive, but monetary policy may also have been relatively more aggressive after, say, 2011, as suggested by the evidence in Swanson and Williams (2014) and Wu and Xia (2014). In short, fiscal activism, rather than the irrelevance of the ZLB, may help explain why macroeconomic volatility did not increase.

Figure 2 provides some evidence on the fourth possibility that the relatively low volatility during the ZLB episode reflected longer-term volatility trends. The figure shows 10-year rolling standard deviations of annualized growth rates for five macro variables studied in the paper. Prior to 1994, the data include observations from before the Great Moderation and do exhibit a downward trend, but from 1994 on there is little evidence of a trend in volatility. The exception is core PCE inflation, whose volatility does decline over time, which may partially account for the low volatility of inflation variables in the ZLB episode. Otherwise, though, the authors' result does not appear to be an artifact of longer-term volatility trends.

Continuing with an evaluation of the paper's findings, I turn next to a basic prediction underlying the paper's empirical test that periods in which the ZLB constrains monetary policy will exhibit higher output and inflation volatility. The authors derive that prediction from a small, calibrated macro model, under the assumption that monetary policy (if unconstrained) would follow a simple Taylor rule with an inertial interest rate adjustment. To test the robustness of their analysis, in lieu of their small theoretical model, we used stochastic simulations of the Fed's large-scale macro model, known as FRB/US. We conducted 500 simulations of the model using shocks drawn from the period 1970–2015. In each run, the model was simulated for 200 quarters, with the first 100 quarters

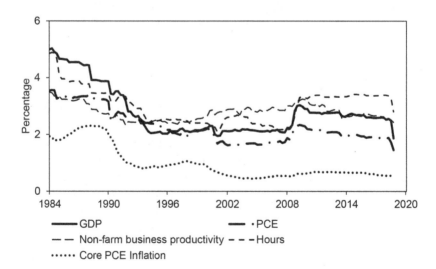

Fig. 2. Ten-year rolling standard deviations of annualized growth rates. GDP = gross domestic product; PCE = personal consumption expenditure.

used to establish initial conditions, then discarded. For these simulations, agents were assumed to have model-consistent (essentially, rational) expectations. Importantly, the simulations also assume that the real neutral interest rate is 1% so that the nominal neutral rate is about 3%. That assumption, common to recent studies of the effects of the ZLB, implies in these simulations that the ZLB is binding about one-third of the time. In contrast, the authors assume a 2% real neutral rate for their simulations, which in their model implies that the ZLB is binding only about 2% of the time. Our assumption seems the better one for studying the effects of the ZLB.

We performed the simulations for three alternative policy rules: (1) a standard Taylor rule with inertial rate adjustment; (2) the same Taylor rule, but in which the lagged interest rate is a shadow rate, allowed to be negative (the policy rate itself must be nonnegative, however); and (3) a temporary price-level targeting (TPLT) rule with 1-year lookback. Under the TPLT rule, the Fed is assumed to commit not to raise its target rate from zero until inflation over the past year is equal to or greater than the inflation target of 2%; away from the ZLB, policy is governed by an inertial Taylor rule. Bernanke, Kiley, and Roberts (2019) show that the TPLT rule with 1-year lookback—essentially, an inflation threshold rule—performs well in FRB/US simulations when the neutral interest rate is low and the ZLB is, accordingly, a potential significant constraint. See that paper for more details on the simulation approach and the alternative policy rules.

Table 2 shows the simulation results from FRB/US. For each policy rule, the table shows the relative volatility (ZLB vs. non-ZLB periods) of the output gap and inflation, under assumptions to be specified in a moment. The last column shows the mean duration of ZLB episodes in the simulations under each policy assumption.

The first two columns of table 2 calculate the relative volatilities by the same method as the authors do in their simulations. Specifically, we first calculate the relative volatilities of ZLB versus non-ZLB periods within each 100-period simulation, then average this ratio across the 500 simulations. For the baseline policy rule (inertial Taylor), the relative volatilities are lower than those found by the authors (compare their table 3). For the Taylor rule with a lagged shadow rate, we find, like the authors, that volatility in ZLB and non-ZLB periods is about the same (see the authors' table 6). For the TPLT rule, volatilities are lower in the ZLB period.

The finding that, even under the baseline policy rule, simulated volatilities are not much greater during ZLB periods would appear to weaken a

Table 2
Relative Volatility (ZLB vs. Non-ZLB) in FRB/US Simulations

	Relative Volatility (Mean within-Simulation)		Relative Volatility (Pooled Simulation Periods)		Relative Volatility (Pooled Simulation Periods, ZLB Episodes of 24–32 Quarters)		
Policy Rule	Output Gap	Inflation	Output Gap	Inflation	Output Gap	Inflation	Mean ZLB Duration
Inertial Taylor	1.22	1.04	1.62	1.27	1.36	1.05	20.70
Inertial Taylor, with shadow rate	1.07	.96	1.50	1.14	1.31	1.01	19.80
TPLT, 1-year lookback	.77	.72	1.27	.80	1.58	.73	9.4

Note: For each policy rule, the table reports the ratio of the standard deviation of the output gap and demeaned inflation in zero lower bound (ZLB) periods to that in non-ZLB periods. The first two columns report the mean ratio across 500 simulations of 100 periods each. The second two columns report this ratio calculated for 50,000 pooled simulation periods. The next two columns report this ratio where the numerator is the standard deviation for the pool of ZLB periods in which the episode is between 24 and 32 quarters in length. Simulations assume agents have model-consistent expectations and that the real neutral interest rate is 1%. TPLT = temporary price-level targeting.

key premise of the paper. Indeed, for the baseline policy rule, we found that in more than half of the simulations the observed relative volatilities for both inflation and the output gap were less than 1, suggesting low power for tests based on these ratios. However, inspection of the simulation results also showed that the distribution of ZLB durations is highly skewed, with many episodes being very short; moreover, observed volatilities tend to be much higher for long ZLB episodes. These observations are illustrated by the third and fourth columns of table 2, which show relative volatilities calculated by pooling the 500 simulations (yielding 50,000 simulation periods). This means of aggregating effectively gives greater weight to longer ZLB episodes, leading to higher relative volatilities.

Because volatilities are correlated with the length of the ZLB episode, the right way to make an inference about the recent experience would seem to be to consider simulated episodes of similar length. The actual ZLB episode of the past decade was 28 quarters long, and so the fifth and sixth columns of table 2 calculate volatilities, relative to all non-ZLB periods, of simulated ZLB episodes of between 24 and 32 quarters. We find that relative volatility of the output gap is well above 1 for all three policy rules, whereas inflation volatility is not much affected by the ZLB. These results seem qualitatively similar to those of the paper, except that the shadow-rate version of the Taylor rule does not reduce relative volatility of the output gap in our simulations as it does in those of the paper. We also find surprisingly high volatility of the output gap for the TPLT rule—surprising, because we know that that rule in general does a good job of overcoming the ZLB. One reason may be sample size: ZLB episodes in the range of 24–32 quarters are only about 3% of simulation periods under the TPLT rule.

Overall, my investigation has not turned up any obvious reasons for the surprisingly low volatility of the ZLB period, other than the authors' hypothesis that monetary policy was able to overcome much of the effect of the ZLB constraint. A possibility worthy of further investigation is that fiscal policy offset to some extent the effects of the ZLB on monetary policy. I also find in simulations that the duration and severity of ZLB episodes is highly skewed toward shorter and less-damaging episodes, which should be considered in assessing the power of this paper's test.

My second broad question, which I'll entertain here briefly, is whether the paper's findings are consistent with the available direct evidence on the power of nonstandard monetary tools. There is something of a puzzle here. Consider, for example, the recent paper by Chung et al. (2019), which assesses the Fed's current policy tool kit. Using the FRB/US model, this group of Federal Reserve authors examine the ability of forward guidance and asset purchases/quantitative easing, the Fed's main nonstandard tools, to respond effectively to a deep recession scenario. Table 3 shows a few selected results from their paper.

Table 3
Simulation Results from Chung et al. (2019)

	Unemployment Peak	Inflation Trough
Inertial Taylor (1999):		
With ZLB	10	.75
Assuming no ZLB	8.5	1.5
Forward guidance:		
Threshold of $u < 3.5$	9.8	1.25
LSAPs:		
$85 billion per month until ff > 0, $u < 5.5$,		
or $\pi > 1.75$	9.5	1.25

Note: Under the large-scale asset purchase program, assets peak at 33% of gross domestic product, lowering the term premium by 200 basis points at this peak. ZLB = zero lower bound, u = unemployment rate, ff = federal funds rate, π = inflation.

In their baseline scenario, Chung et al. (2019) assume that policy is described by an inertial Taylor (1999) rule, constrained by the ZLB. They calibrate the recessionary shocks so that, in their simulation of FRB/US, the unemployment rate peaks at 10% and inflation troughs at 0.75% (table 3)—in other words, a deep recession broadly comparable to the Great Recession. They then calculate that, if short-term rates could go indefinitely negative (so the ZLB does not bind), the same shocks in FRB/US would produce a peak unemployment rate of about 8.5% and a trough inflation rate of about 1.5%. The differences from the baseline case—about 1.5 percentage points of unemployment and 0.75 percentage points of inflation at the extreme points—suggest that the costs of the ZLB constraint are high, at least in this simulation.

Can nonstandard policies overcome the ZLB constraint? Chung et al. (2019) examine this issue through simulations that incorporate such policies. Importantly, these authors assume that the nonstandard policies used are credible (they assume that agents in the model generally understand and believe the Fed's policy promises), aggressive, and effective. For example, the results reported in table 3 assume that the Fed can credibly promise to keep the short-term rate at zero at least until the unemployment rate falls to 3.5%. The quantitative easing program considered involves asset purchases of up to $85 billion per month, securities holdings that peak at 33% of GDP, and a reduction of the term premium on longer-term Treasuries by as much as 200 basis points. Overall, these assumptions are on the optimistic end of the conventional range of views about nonstandard policy effectiveness.

Do these policies make the ZLB irrelevant? As table 3 suggests, in the Chung et al. (2019) simulations, forward guidance and asset purchases each reduce the simulated decline in inflation substantially, indicating that on this dimension perhaps a combination of the two policies would overcome the ZLB. However, for unemployment the outcome is not so good. Even added together, the two nonstandard policies appear able to reduce the peak unemployment rate by only about half of the effect of the ZLB (although they are collectively more effective at later stages of the recovery). The authors argue that lags in the effectiveness of nonstandard policies help explain their inability to fully offset the effects of the ZLB. In this regard, it is interesting that the Wu and Xia (2014) estimate of the shadow rate does not fall much below zero for some time after the beginning of the ZLB period.

Of course, these results are specific to the FRB/US models and the choices the Fed authors use in their simulations. Still, to make more credible the present paper's conclusion that the ZLB did not constrain monetary policy in the recent episode, future research will need to provide a more detailed accounting of the policies the Fed actually adopted during this period and how they could have plausibly offset the constraint imposed by the ZLB.

Endnote

Author email address: Bernanke (bbernanke@brookings.edu). Michael Ng and Sage Belz provided excellent research assistance. For acknowledgments, sources of research support, and disclosure of the author's material financial relationships, if any, please see https://www.nber.org/chapters/c14242.ack.

References

Bernanke, Ben S., Michael T. Kiley, and John M. Roberts. 2019. "Monetary Policy Strategies for a Low-Rate Environment." Finance and Economics Discussion Series 2019-009, Board of Governors of the Federal Reserve System, Washington, DC. https://doi.org/10.17016/FEDS.2019.009.

Chung, Hess, Etienne Gagnon, Taisuke Nakata, Matthias Paustian, Bernd Schlusche, James Trevino, Diego Vilán, and Wei Zheng. 2019. "Monetary Policy Options at the Effective Lower Bound: Assessing the Federal Reserve's Current Policy Toolkit." Finance and Economics Discussion Series 2019-003, Board of Governors of the Federal Reserve System, Washington, DC. https://doi.org/10.17016/FEDS.2019.003.

Fernald, John, Robert Hall, James Stock, and Mark W. Watson. 2017. "The Disappointing Recovery of Output after 2009." *Brookings Papers on Economic Activity* 2017 (1): 1–81. https://www.brookings.edu/bpea-articles/the-disappointing-recovery-of-output-after-2009/.

Ng, Serena, and Jonathan H. Wright. 2013. "Facts and Challenges from the Great Recession for Forecasting and Macroeconomic Modeling." *Journal of Economic Literature* 51 (4): 1120–54. https://doi.org/10.1257/jel.51.4.1120.

Swanson, Eric T., and John C. Williams. 2014. "Measuring the Effect of the Zero Lower Bound on Medium- and Longer-Term Interest Rates." *American Economic Review* 104 (10): 3154–85. https://doi.org/10.1257/aer.104.10.3154.

Taylor, John B., ed. 1999. *Monetary Policy Rules*. Chicago: University of Chicago Press. https://www.nber.org/books/tayl99-1.

Wu, Jing Cynthia, and Fan Dora Xia. 2014. "Measuring the Macroeconomic Impact of Monetary Policy at the Zero Lower Bound." Working Paper no. 20117 (May), NBER, Cambridge, MA. https://doi.org/10.3386/w20117.

Comment

Mark W. Watson, Princeton University and NBER

In this paper, Debortoli, Galí, and Gambetti offer compelling empirical evidence that extraordinary actions taken by the Federal Reserve were able to shield the macroeconomy from many of the policy constraints associated with the zero lower bound (ZLB) on nominal interest rates. As Debortoli et al. argue, if these extraordinary actions had been ineffective, the United States would have witnessed a change in the volatility of macro aggregates and a change in their response to specific nonfinancial shocks. Yet volatility and impulse responses remained largely unchanged during the ZLB period.

There is no one more qualified than the paper's first discussant to discuss the ZLB, the Fed's actions, and their effects on the macroeconomy. With this in mind, I will offer no comments of substance about this excellent paper, beyond the observation that I am in agreement with Debortoli et al.'s overall empirical conclusions. Instead, I will focus my comments on a methodological issue: statistical inference in sign-restricted structural vector autoregressions (SVARs), which is one of the methods used in Debortoli et al.'s paper.

Sign-restricted SVARs are an increasingly popular method for estimating dynamic causal effects in macroeconomics. Many researchers use a variant of Uhlig's (2005) Bayes method for imposing these sign restrictions and conducting inference. This method has both strengths and weaknesses. The strengths are widely recognized by macroeconomists but the weaknesses far less so. This discussion explains and highlights these weaknesses.

I make two initial comments. First, Debortoli et al. use a sophisticated time-varying SVAR identified by both long-run equality restrictions and shorter-run sign restrictions. To keep things simple, I will focus on a time-invariant SVAR. Second, there is nothing original in my comments beyond a few numerical calculations. Sign-restricted SVARs are a special case of "set identification," which is well studied in econometrics (Manski 2003 is a classic reference). The issues I highlight for Bayes inference in sign-restricted SVARs are derived and discussed in Baumeister and Hamilton (2015); many of my comments are simply a nontechnical summary of their analysis.

Why Sign-Restricted SVARs Are Different from Standard SVARs

I begin by introducing some familiar notation. Let Y_t denote the vector of observed data. (In the Debortoli et al. paper, $Y_t = (\Delta(y_t - n_t), n_t, \Delta p_t, i_t^{\text{Long}})'$, where (y, n, p) denote the logarithms of output, employment, and the price level, and i^{Long} is the 10-year Treasury bond rate, all for the United States.) The VAR for Y_t is

$$Y_t = A_0 + A(L)Y_{t-1} + u_t, \tag{1}$$

where A_0 is the intercept, $A(L)$ is the VAR lag polynomial, and u_t is the VAR's one-period-ahead forecast error ("innovation"), which is serially uncorrelated with covariance matrix Σ_u. The forecast errors u_t are linearly related to a vector structural shocks ε_t,

$$u_t = Q\varepsilon_t, \tag{2}$$

where Q is nonsingular. (In the Debortoli et al. paper, the structural shocks are $\varepsilon_t = (\varepsilon_t^{\text{Technology}}, \varepsilon_t^{\text{Demand}}, \varepsilon_t^{\text{Monetary policy}}, \varepsilon_t^{\text{Supply}})'$.) The distributed lag relating the observed data to the structural shocks is $Y_t = \tilde{A}_0 + (I - A(L))^{-1}Q\varepsilon_t$, and the impulse responses, $\partial Y_{t+h}/\partial \varepsilon_t$ correspond to the various elements of the lag polynomial $(I - A(L))^{-1}Q$.

A common parameterization of the SVAR uses standardized structural shocks, so the covariance matrix of ε_t is $\Sigma_\varepsilon = I$. With this "unit-standard deviation" parameterization, equation (2) can be written as

$$u_t = \Sigma_u^{1/2}R\varepsilon_t, \tag{3}$$

where $\Sigma_u^{1/2}$ is the Cholesky factor of Σ_u and R is a "rotation matrix" (i.e., a matrix with $RR' = I$). With this parameterization, the impulse responses are $(I - A(L))^{-1}\Sigma_u^{1/2}R$. The values of $A(L)$ and $\Sigma_u^{1/2}$ can be estimated from the VAR in equation (1), leaving R to be determined by a researcher's a priori restrictions on the way the structural shocks affect the observed data.

In standard SVAR analysis, these a priori restrictions take the form of equality restrictions (e.g., $\partial Y_{i,t+h}/\partial \varepsilon_{j,t} = 0$ for some values of i, j, and h)

that uniquely determine R and the impulse responses. In contrast, sign-restricted SVARs rely on inequality restrictions (e.g., $\partial Y_{i,t+h}/\partial \varepsilon_{j,t} \geq 0$) that place set-valued constraints on R but do not uniquely determine its value. Each value of R in this "identified set" leads to different impulse responses, so the impulse responses are also set-identified. Some SVAR analyses, like the Debortoli et al. paper, use a combination of equality and sign restrictions that determine the value of some elements of R and place set-valued restrictions on other elements.

Some generic notation will streamline the discussion. Let μ denote the set of parameters that characterize the probability distribution of Y_t. In the VAR model, $\mu = (A, \Sigma_u)$ characterizes the data's Gaussian likelihood, where A denotes the parameters in A_0 and $A(L)$. Let θ denote the parameters of interest. In the SVAR, θ might denote a set of impulse responses $\partial Y_{i,t+h}/\partial \varepsilon_{j,t}$ for particular values of i, j, and h. In standard SVAR analysis, the identifying restrictions uniquely determine the value of θ from μ, that is $\theta = g(\mu)$ for some function g. In the jargon of econometrics, the value of θ is "point identified." In contrast, in sign-identified SVAR analysis, the value of θ is restricted to lie in a set that depends on μ, that is, $\theta \in G(\mu)$, where G is a set-valued function. In this case, θ is said to be set identified.

Bayes and Frequentist Inference for Set-Identified Parameters

Set identification presents challenges for statistical inference. In point-identified models, when the value of μ is known, then θ is known. Absent sampling uncertainty, Bayes and frequentist inference are trivially identical. And, when sampling uncertainty in μ is small and approximately normally distributed (as it is when the sample size is large), Bayes and frequentist inference often coincide when standard Bayes priors are used. This rationalizes large-sample Bayes analysis for frequentists and vice versa.

This large-sample Bayes-frequentist coincidence disappears in set-identified models. An example, much simpler than the SVAR, highlights the key issues. Suppose you have data on two variables $Y_t = (Y_{1,t}, Y_{2,t})'$ with

$$Y_t = \begin{bmatrix} Y_{1,t} \\ Y_{2,t} \end{bmatrix} \sim \text{i.i.d. } N\left(\begin{bmatrix} \mu_1 \\ \mu_2 \end{bmatrix}, I_2 \right) \qquad (4)$$

for $t = 1, \ldots, T$, and with $\mu_1 < \mu_2$. In this example, the probability distribution for Y_t is completely determined by $\mu = (\mu_1 \ \mu_2)'$. Suppose interest focuses on a parameter θ, and all that is known is that $\mu_1 \leq \theta \leq \mu_2$, so that θ is set-identified.

Figure 1 summarizes frequentist inference about θ. Figure 1a shows small-sample inference: the estimators $\hat{\mu}_1$ and $\hat{\mu}_2$ are the sample means of the data; they contain sampling error, so the endpoints of the identified set for θ are uncertain. Figure 1b shows large-sample frequentist inference: sampling error disappears when T is large so the values of μ_1 and μ_2 and the identified set for θ are pinned down.

The corresponding figure for Bayes inference is shown in figure 2. Bayes inference requires a prior, say $f(\theta, \mu)$, and a likelihood, say $f(Y|\mu)$. The resulting posterior for θ is

$$f(\theta|Y) = \int f(\theta|\mu)f(\mu|Y)d\mu, \tag{5}$$

where $f(\theta|\mu)$ is the prior for θ conditional on μ and $f(\mu|Y)$ is the posterior for μ. Figure 2a shows the posterior $f(\theta|Y)$ for a hypothetical prior and data. As in equation (5), the posterior is the prior $f(\theta|\mu)$ averaged over the values of μ from the posterior. Figure 2b shows the large-sample posterior: here, as in the frequentist case, uncertainty about the value of μ has vanished, so the Bayes posterior coincides with the Bayes prior, that is, $f(\theta|Y) = f(\theta|\mu)$, where the prior is evaluated at the true value of μ.

For both frequentist and Bayes inference, the data are informative about the value of μ, perfectly so when $T \to \infty$. For frequentist inference, this yields a set of values for θ, $\mu_1 \leq \theta \leq \mu_2$, that are consistent with the data. One of the values in this identified set corresponds to the true value of θ, the other values do not, but nothing can be said about how likely one of these values is relative to another. In contrast, for Bayes inference, the prior $f(\theta|\mu)$ shows that some values of θ may be more likely than other

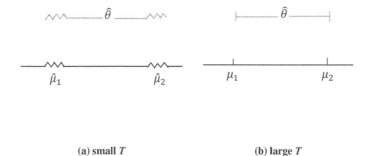

(a) small T (b) large T

Fig. 1. Frequentist inference about θ. Jagged lines in a connote uncertainty about the values of μ_1 and μ_2.

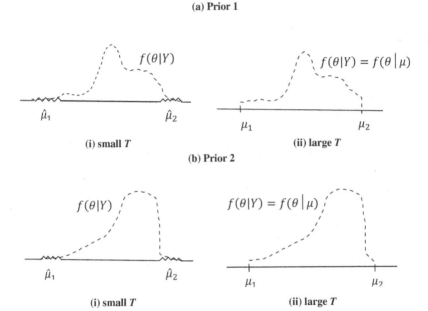

Fig. 2. Bayes inference about θ. (*a*) Prior 1. (*b*) Prior 2. Jagged lines above $\hat{\mu}_1$ and $\hat{\mu}_2$ in *a* and *c* connote uncertainty about the values of μ_1 and μ_2.

values. Importantly, this information comes solely from the prior—not the data—so different priors yield different inference, even when confronted with the same (possibly infinitely large) data set. This is highlighted in figure 2*b*, which uses the same hypothetical data and value of μ as figure 2*a* but uses a different prior $f(\theta|\mu)$. Bayes inference about the value of θ will be different using this new prior, even when confronted with an arbitrarily large sample of data (compare fig. 2*a.ii* and 2*b.ii*).

What are we to make of this simple example? Focusing on the large-sample results, I see three lessons. First, frequentist inference is informative when the identified set is small: if the data indicate that μ_1 is close to μ_2, then the restriction $\mu_1 \leq \theta \leq \mu_2$ says a lot about the value of θ. Second, Bayes inference is potentially more useful than frequentist inference because it informs us about the relative likelihood of values of θ within the identified set. For example, the median, mean, and 95% "credible" intervals for θ can be computed using Bayes methods but have no frequentist counterparts. Third, Bayes inference over the identified set is completely determined by the prior. Thus, conclusions drawn from Bayes analysis are persuasive only to the extent that the prior is credible. A corollary of this third lesson is that it is impossible to evaluate the conclusions from

Bayes analysis without knowing and evaluating the prior used in the analysis.

Identified Sets and Priors in a Version of the Debortoli et al. SVAR

To apply these lessons to the Debortoli et al. SVAR, I conducted a numerical exercise. In my experiment, I estimated a version of the authors' four-variable VAR using data from 1984 to 2008. This yielded estimates of the VAR parameters A_0, $A(L)$, and Σ_u; these are the μ-parameters for this exercise. Holding μ fixed, I then used the Debortoli et al. equality and sign restrictions to compute the identified sets for the impulse response functions (IRFs; θ for this exercise). I also used their prior to compute the posterior $f(\theta|Y)$. Because μ was held fixed in my exercise (i.e., I ignored sampling error in the VAR parameters), the posterior corresponds to the prior, that is, $f(\theta|Y) = f(\theta|\mu)$.

Figure 3 shows the identified sets for the IRFs for the three shocks identified by sign restrictions. The authors' identifying restrictions turn out to be (remarkably) informative about the values of these IRFs. For example, figure 4a shows the identified set for the response of output after 4 quarters (y_{t+4}) to a 1-standard negative demand shock ($\varepsilon_t^{\text{Demand}}$), that is, for the parameter $\theta = \partial y_{t+4} / \partial \varepsilon_t^{\text{Demand}}$. The identified set is $-0.27 \leq \theta \leq 0$. The upper bound of the set ($\theta \leq 0$) is one of the authors' sign restrictions, but the lower bound ($\theta \geq -0.27$) follows from the value of μ computed

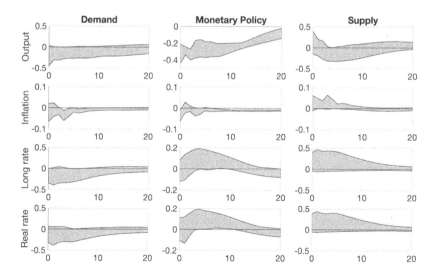

Fig. 3.   Identified sets for the four-variable SVAR.

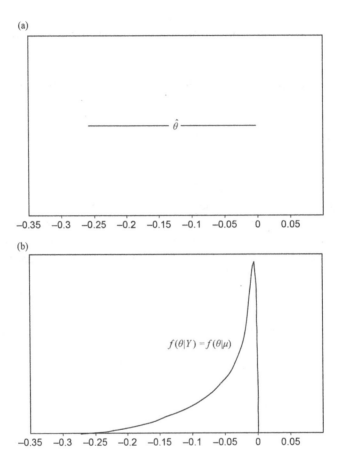

Fig. 4.   Inference about $\theta = \partial \text{Output}_{t+4}/\partial \varepsilon_t^{\text{Demand}}$: (*a*) frequentist inference: the identified set; (*b*) Bayes inference: the truncated prior = posterior for θ.

from the data, together with the equality and sign restrictions. Looking across the panels in figure 3 leads me to conclude that the combination of sign and equality restrictions used by Debortoli et al. impose sufficient structure on the data to greatly narrow the range of IRFs. Frequentist inference is informative.

What more do we learn from Bayes inference? As in the large-sample version of the mean example in the last section, the posteriors for the impulse responses coincide with their priors over the identified sets. Thus, the question becomes what prior was used in the Debortoli et al. SVAR. In this paper, as in many sign-restricted VARs, the authors follow Uhlig (2005) and construct these priors by a flat (Haar) prior on the columns of the rotation matrix R truncated to satisfy the sign restrictions on θ. This prior for R induces a prior for the impulse responses, and this impulse response prior is easily computed using numerical methods.

Figure 4b shows the implied prior for $\theta = \partial y_{t+4}/\partial \varepsilon_t^{\text{Demand}}$ over the the identified set shown in figure 4a. Notice that the prior is quite informative about the effect of the demand shock on output. For example, the prior puts roughly 60% of its mass on $-0.05 \leq \theta \leq 0$ and less than 2% of its mass on values with $-0.27 \leq \theta \leq -0.20$. Comparing figure 4$a$ and 4b, frequentist inference says that $-0.27 \leq \theta \leq 0$ and says nothing more. Bayes inference sharpens this, by saying that it is 30 times more likely that $-0.05 \leq \theta \leq 0$ than $-0.27 \leq \theta \leq -0.20$. Importantly, this latter conclusion follows from the authors' prior, not from any information in the data.

Figure 5 shows the implied priors for the other variables to the other shocks, again at the 4-quarter horizon. Here, too, the "flat" prior on R together with the authors' equality and sign restrictions imply quite informative priors on the impulse responses. For example, the prior implies that demand shocks have relatively small effects on output and prices but large effects on interest rates; in contrast, monetary policy shocks have relatively small effects on interest rates and inflation but large effects on output.

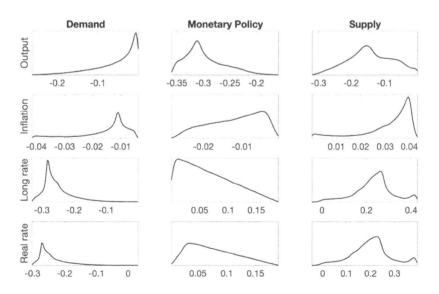

Fig. 5. Truncated priors (= posteriors) for $\partial Y_{t+4}/\partial \varepsilon_t$. The figure shows the prior on the four-period-ahead impulse responses induced by a flat prior on R and the equality and sign restrictions.

Are these priors reasonable? Maybe they are, and maybe they are not. In any event, the credibility of the conclusions reached using Bayes methods depends critically on the answer to this question. Given the key role played by the priors, it is remarkable that priors are not reported in the vast majority of papers using sign-restricted SVARs (including the Debortoli et al. paper). Simply put, it is impossible to evaluate the "point estimates" or "error bands" for IRFs without evaluating the priors.

To complete the numerical calculations, figure 6 shows the identified sets for the impulse responses previously shown in figure 3 together with selected percentiles of Bayes priors/posteriors. I have drawn the figures to highlight the point estimates (prior/posterior median), 68% error bands (prior/posterior 16% and 84% percentiles), and 95% bands. Readers are used to associating error bands with sampling uncertainty, but in large-sample sign-restricted SVARs, these error bands summarize the researchers' prior uncertainty, not sampling uncertainty.

Additional Comments and Recommendations for Practice

Let me end with two additional comments and some recommendations for practice. The first comment involves the unit standard deviation normalization for the structural shocks ($\Sigma_\varepsilon = I$) widely used in SVAR analysis (and in the Debortoli et al. paper). This normalization means that

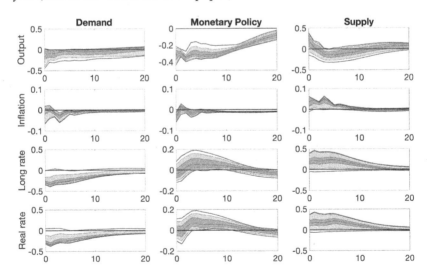

Fig. 6. Impulse responses $\partial Y_{t+h}/\partial \varepsilon_t$. Identified sets and quantiles of truncated prior (= posterior). The outer dark gray lines show the boundaries of the identified sets. The dark (light) error bands show the equal-tail 68% (95%) posterior/prior credible intervals.

the impulse responses show the response of, say $Y_{i,t+h}$, measured in Y_i-units, to a one standard deviation shock in $\varepsilon_{j,t}$. But how large is one standard deviation in $\varepsilon_{j,t}$; for example, how large is a one standard deviation "monetary policy shock" or a one standard deviation "demand shock"? As argued elsewhere (see Stock and Watson 2016), a more interpretable normalization is the "unit-effect" normalization that imposes $\partial Y_{k,t}/\partial \varepsilon_{j,t} = 1$ for some variable $Y_{k,t}$, so that $\varepsilon_{j,t}$ is measured in units of the observed data $Y_{k,t}$. As an example, if $\varepsilon_{j,t}$ is a monetary policy shock, then it is natural to measure its magnitude in terms of basis points of the short-term interest rate. In this case, impulse responses measure the response of macroeconomic variables to a monetary policy shock that, for example, raises short-term interest rates by 100 (or 25) basis points. As a matter of arithmetic, the unit-effect normalized impulse responses can be computed from the unit-standard-deviation normalized impulse responses as the ratio:

$$\frac{\partial Y_{i,t+h}}{\partial \tilde{\varepsilon}_{j,t}} = \frac{\frac{\partial Y_{i,t+h}}{\partial \varepsilon_{j,t}}}{\frac{\partial Y_{k,t}}{\partial \varepsilon_{j,t}}},$$

where $\tilde{\varepsilon}_{j,t}$ is measured in units of $Y_{k,t}$ and $\varepsilon_{j,t}$ is measured in standard deviation units. In point-identified models, this nonlinearity means that care must be taken in computing standard errors for estimated IRFs when translating from one normalization to another. In sign-identified SVARs, the translation is potentially more serious, as for example the identified set for $\partial Y_{k,t}/\partial \varepsilon_{j,t}$ may include values equal to or close to zero. Looking at figure 3, for example, what is the implied effect on output of monetary policy shock that raises interest rates by 25 basis points?

My second comment advertises the work of Wolf (2018), who studies the points in the identified set for some well-known examples of sign-identified SVARs. Wolf is motivated by the observation that only one point in the identified set shows the true impulse response, that is, the response of $Y_{i,t+h}$ to the true structural shock $\varepsilon_{j,t}$. The other points in the identified set implicitly show the response of $Y_{i,t+h}$ to other linear combinations of the structural shocks that also satisfy the sign restrictions. Wolf uses structural models to determine these linear combinations that "masquerade" (his term) for the true structural shock. He uses this to gauge the identifying power of sign restrictions in different classes of models.

Finally, what does all this mean for empirical practice? Sign restrictions can yield valuable identifying information for sorting out cause and effect in macroeconomics. This is particularly the case when these sign restrictions are used in tandem with more traditional equality restrictions (see Arias, Rubio-Ramirez, and Waggoner 2018; Wolf 2018). The narrow identified sets for the Debortoli et al. model (see fig. 3) is an example of the identifying power of these restrictions. That said, the nature of set identification makes inference nonstandard and/or difficult to interpret. One approach is to conduct inference on the identified sets using frequentist methods (e.g., Granziera, Moon, and Schorfheide 2018). This approach usefully summarizes what the data, together with the sign restrictions, have to say about the value of impulse responses. One may be tempted to move beyond these identified sets to produce point estimates, error bands, and so forth, but with set identification this requires Bayes methods, and the associated point estimates, error bands, and so forth merely reproduce the researchers prior over the identified set. Here, "good" priors lead to good inference and conversely for bad priors. Sorting out the good from the bad requires careful presentation and justification for the prior actually used, a point forcefully and convincingly made in theory and practice in Baumeister and Hamilton (2015, 2019). In this regard, the kinds of flat (Haar) priors made on the rotation matrix R in equation (1) seem counterproductive. These flat priors on R produce informative priors on the impulse responses (see figs. 4–6 for examples in a version of the Debortoli et al. SVAR) in ways that are difficult to know a priori, and in any event are rarely, if ever, reported or justified.

Endnote

Author email address: Watson (mwatson@princeton.edu). For acknowledgments, sources of research support, and disclosure of the author's material financial relationships, if any, please see https://www.nber.org/chapters/c14243.ack.

References

Arias, Jonas, Juan Rubio-Ramirez, and Daniel Waggoner. 2018. "Inference Based on SVARs Identified with Sign and Zero Restrictions." *Econometrica* 86 (2): 685–720.
Baumeister, Christine, and James D. Hamilton. 2015. "Sign Restrictions, Vector Autoregressions, and Useful Prior Information." *Econometrica* 83 (5): 1963–99.
———. 2019. "Structural Interpretation of Vector Autoregressions with Incomplete Information: Revisiting the Role of Oil Supply and Demand Shocks." *American Economic Review* 109 (5): 1873–910.
Granziera, Eleonora, Hyungsik Roger Moon, and Frank Schorfheide. 2018. "Inference for VARs Identified with Sign Restrictions." *Quantitative Economics* 9 (3): 1087–121.

Manski, Charles F. 2003. *Partial Identification of Probability Distributions*. New York: Springer.

Stock, James H., and Mark W. Watson. 2016. "Factor Models and Structural Vector Autoregressions in Macroeconomics." In *Handbook of Macroeconomics*, Vol. 2A, ed. John B. Taylor and Harald Uhlig. Amsterdam: North Holland.

Uhlig, Harald. 2005. "What Are the Effects of Monetary Policy on Output? Results from an Agnostic Identification Procedure." *Journal of Monetary Economics* 52:381–419.

Wolf, Christian K. 2018. "SVAR (Mis-)Identification and the Real Effects of Monetary Policy." Manuscript, Princeton University.

Discussion

Mark Gertler and Martin Eichenbaum followed up on comments made by one of the discussants, Ben Bernanke. Gertler noted that the zero lower bound (ZLB) on the nominal interest rate might have played its biggest role from late 2008 to 2010, before quantitative easing and forward guidance produced their full effects. This period was also characterized by a rise in aggregate uncertainty, he argued, which might have interacted with the binding ZLB. Gertler identified two channels through which increased uncertainty could have operated. First, increased precautionary savings further reduce the neutral interest rate, bringing it closer to the ZLB. Second, higher uncertainty raises the spread between short- and long-term interest rates, because the ZLB creates an option value by putting a lower bound on future short-term rates. Gertler encouraged the authors to quantify these channels using their model. Eichenbaum pointed out that the binding ZLB took place during a period of large changes in fiscal spending. According to the Hutchins Center Fiscal Impact Measure, fiscal policy was strongly expansionary until 2011, he argued, before turning very contractionary until 2014. Eichenbaum wondered whether the authors could investigate the interplay between fiscal policy and the ZLB by repeating their empirical exercise using the pre- and post-2011 subsamples. He admitted that there might be power issues with such a short sample. The authors acknowledged that strongly countercyclical fiscal policy could in theory explain the empirical irrelevance of the ZLB that they document in the paper. However, this explanation is hard to reconcile with their evidence on the response of long-term interest rates. Fiscal policy alone could not explain why the behavior of these rates did not change during the ZLB period, they argued. This is suggestive of a dominant role for monetary policy in the form of quantitative easing and forward guidance, according to the authors.

978-0-226-70789-1/2019/2019-0304$10.00

The rest of the discussion focused on three topics: the role of deflation, the open economy implications of a binding ZLB, and the ability of monetary policy to offset shocks using unconventional monetary policy instruments.

On the first topic, Benjamin Friedman noted that deflation might be the major risk associated with the ZLB. He argued that neither the standard New Keynesian model nor the FRB/US model (the Fed's large-scale macro model) used by one of the discussants, Ben Bernanke, creates room for strong deflationary effects. The authors agreed that the incidence of deflation depends on the specifics of the model. In particular, they argued that their New Keynesian model is more forward-looking than the models used by Bernanke in his discussion, namely the FRB/US model and the one of Hess Chung et al. ("Monetary Policy Options at the Effective Lower Bound: Assessing the Federal Reserve's Current Policy Toolkit" [Finance and Economics Discussion Series (Fed Board), No. 2019-003, Board of Governors of the Federal Reserve System, Washington, DC, 2019]). The authors suggested that this fact could explain some of the discrepancies between Bernanke's simulations and the authors', particularly when it comes to the response of long-term interest rates. Bernanke clarified that price and wage setting are forward-looking in the model of Chung et al. ("Monetary Policy Options at the Effective Lower Bound") and so are financial markets. However, consumption and investment are backward-looking. Friedman offered a second comment. The paper's findings suggest that unconventional monetary policy instruments had a powerful effect and helped mitigate the importance of the ZLB, he reminded. This raises the possibility that these instruments could be used as a substitute for the federal funds rate even when the ZLB does not bind, he argued.

Laura Veldkamp emphasized the role of expectations about inflation and the duration of the ZLB episode. Survey evidence and bond-implied inflation risk premia reveal that agents expected this episode to be short-lived and inflation to take off, she mentioned. Veldkamp suggested that these expectations could have mitigated the effect of the binding ZLB. The authors shared Veldkamp's view. They used their model to explore the effect of expectations about the duration of the ZLB episode. The authors noted that these expectations are key for the response to shocks, especially when it comes to movements in long-term rates. They clarified that their baseline simulation assumes that the ZLB is binding for three quarters in expectation. The authors noted that the actual ZLB episode lasted for 28 quarters and that such a long duration was arguably unexpected. A version of their model calibrated with an expected duration of

28 quarters produces unrealistically large responses to shocks. This exercise suggests that expectations about the duration of the ZLB episode play a crucial role, they argued. Thomas Philippon followed up briefly on Veldkamp's comment. He noted that the case of Japan is interesting in that the expected duration of the ZLB episode was much longer than in the United States. This could allow the authors to verify some of their predictions, he suggested.

Turning to the second topic, Philippon emphasized that the authors adopted a closed economy framework. He noted that a binding ZLB typically modulates the exchange rate response to shocks in the class of models that the authors work with. Philippon wondered whether this prediction is verified in the data. They responded by referring to existing work of theirs. In Jordi Galí ("Uncovered Interest Parity, Forward Guidance and the Exchange Rate" [Mimeo, CREI, Barcelona, May 2019]), they found that the exchange rate response to expected changes in interest rates is muted when the ZLB binds, which suggests that the effect of monetary policy is dampened.

Christopher Erceg suggested decomposing the impulse response for output in terms of each component of aggregate demand. A binding ZLB might not affect the response of output to shocks, he argued, but it could affect its composition and the international spillovers. In particular, accommodative monetary policy should mostly operate through domestic demand if the exchange rate response is dampened at the ZLB—as the authors suggested.

On the third topic, Erceg reminded the audience that the issue of the ZLB is not specific to the United States. He agreed with the authors' assessment that quantitative easing had been effective in the United States. However, Erceg noted that the effects of unconventional monetary policy might be more limited in economies where interest rates are low across all maturities, as in Germany. The authors agreed with Erceg's comment. They emphasized that the paper does not claim that the ZLB itself is irrelevant. Rather, it concludes that policy was conducted in such a way that the ZLB was effectively irrelevant.

Gabriel Chodorow-Reich noted that two types of shocks can hit an economy: diffusion shocks and jump shocks. Chodorow-Reich agreed that the monetary authority might be able to offset small diffusion shocks, even when the ZLB binds. However, central banks might lack the proper tools to respond to large jump shocks, he noted. The authors responded that they found that large shocks actually took place when the ZLB was binding. The corresponding responses of inflation, output, and long-term interest rate are still proportional to those obtained for the pre-ZLB period. This finding suggests that monetary policy was able to mitigate the effect of a binding ZLB despite large shocks.

Mark Gertler agreed with the authors' overall conclusion, arguing that policy largely circumvented the ZLB constraint from 2010 onward. However, the ZLB might have been more constraining during the 2008–9 period, according to Gertler. He noted that the decrease in nominal interest rates during the Great Recession relative to the decrease in output was similar to previous recessions. A much larger decrease in nominal interest rates was needed to compensate for the increase in credit costs due to the financial crisis, he argued. This suggests that the ZLB might have played a significant role in the aftermath of the financial crisis, according to Gertler. The authors suggested that they could use long-term rates in their vector autoregression specifications, instead of 10-year government bonds, to investigate this point.

The participants concluded the general discussion with a more informal exchange on the experiences of Europe and Japan at the ZLB. Martin Eichenbaum noted that the European Central Bank's (ECB) response was less aggressive than that of the Federal Reserve. He wondered whether this was responsible for more volatility in Europe. Ben Bernanke and Valerie Ramey pointed out that sovereign debt crises and different fiscal responses in Europe might be confounding factors. Frederic Mishkin argued that the ECB's response was actually as aggressive as the Fed's before 2010 but was more timid afterward. The authors cited the case of Japan as having larger responses to aggregate shocks during the ZLB episode compared with the United States. They suggested that the Bank of Japan was less accommodative than the Fed, which could explain the higher volatility of aggregate variables.

4

Optimal Inflation and the Identification of the Phillips Curve

Michael McLeay, *Bank of England*

Silvana Tenreyro, *Bank of England, London School of Economics, Center for Macroeconomics, and CEPR*

I. Introduction

A number of recent papers have pointed out that inflation can be approximated (and forecast) by statistical processes unrelated to the amount of slack in the economy (Atkeson and Ohanian 2001; Stock and Watson 2007, 2009; Cecchetti et al. 2017; Forbes, Kirkham, and Theodoridis 2017; Dotsey, Fujita, and Stark 2018). The empirical disconnect between inflation and various measures of slack has been interpreted by some commentators as evidence that the Phillips curve (a positive relation between inflation and the output gap) has weakened or even disappeared (Ball and Mazumder 2011; Hall 2013; IMF 2013; Blanchard, Cerutti, and Summers 2015; Coibion and Gorodnichenko 2015).[1] On the face of it, a change in the Phillips curve relationship could have major implications for monetary policy, so the potential causes of any weakening have been an important topic of discussion for policy makers (Carney 2017a; Draghi 2017; Powell 2018).

The Phillips curve is one of the building blocks of the standard macroeconomic models used for forecasting and policy advice in central banks. Its empirical elusiveness could challenge the wisdom of these models and the usefulness of their forecasts. Arguably, it even calls into question part of the rationale for independent, inflation-targeting central banks. Or does it?

In this paper, we use a standard conceptual framework to show why:

- The empirical disconnect between inflation and slack is a result to be expected when monetary policy is set optimally.

- It is also perfectly consistent with an underlying stable and positively sloped Phillips curve.

More specifically, our framework is built under the assumption that the Phillips curve always holds (an assumption we later corroborate in the data). In other words, in our model, inflation depends positively on the degree of slack in the economy. We also allow for cost-push shocks that can lead to deviations from the curve but without altering its slope. Monetary policy is set with the goal of minimizing welfare losses (measured as the sum of the quadratic deviations of inflation from its target and of output from its potential), subject to the Phillips curve or aggregate supply relationship. In that setting, a central bank will seek to increase inflation when output is below its potential. This targeting rule imparts a negative correlation between inflation and the output gap, blurring the identification of the (positively sloped) Phillips curve.[2]

The paper is extended along five dimensions. First, we study differences in the solutions between discretion—our baseline case in which the monetary authority cannot commit to a future path of inflation and the output gap—and the case of commitment, in which the authority credibly commits to a future plan. We show that the main intuition goes through in both cases. The difference lies in the implied properties of the statistical process for inflation generated by the optimal policy in each case. In the simple framework studied here, the greater degree of inertia under optimal commitment also offers one potential solution to the identification problem.

A second extension introduces shocks to the targeting rule. These shocks can be interpreted as lags in monetary transmission, as shocks to the monetary policy instrument rule, or, in a multiregion setting, as idiosyncratic demand shocks affecting different regions or countries within a monetary union. We show that the relative variance of these shocks vis-à-vis the cost-push shocks is key for the empirical identification of the Phillips curve using standard regression analysis. This result also rationalizes the findings of the vast empirical literature that uses identified monetary policy shocks to estimate the transmission of monetary policy. Effectively, well-identified monetary policy shocks should help in retrieving the Phillips curve.

Third, we study a multiregion (multicountry or multisector) setting with a common central bank and discuss conditions under which regional (or sectoral) data can help mitigate the bias from the endogeneity of monetary policy. The discussion, however, also underscores some of the limitations faced by regional analysis.

A fourth extension discusses the estimation of a wage Phillips curve and compares the identification challenges with those faced in the price Phillips curve.

The final extension departs from the stylized New Keynesian model of Clarida, Gali, and Gertler (1999) and studies the aggregate supply constraint in a large-scale dynamic stochastic general equilibrium (DSGE) model of the type designed for forecasting and policy analysis in central banks. In such larger models, the concept of a single, structural relationship between inflation and the output gap is no longer well defined: their reduced-form correlation varies according to which shock hits the economy. Nonetheless, we show that the intuition from the structural Phillips curve in the basic model continues to apply to the reduced-form Phillips curve in larger-scale DSGE models. In the model of Burgess et al. (2013), designed for policy use at the Bank of England, a positively sloped reduced-form Phillips curve is present when policy is set according to an estimated Taylor rule. But under optimal discretionary policy, the slope of the curve changes sign.

We next turn to practical attempts to address the identification issue we raise, focusing on US data. The simultaneity bias arises due to the behavior of monetary policy in partially accommodating cost-push shocks to the Phillips curve. It is magnified because monetary policy seeks to offset any demand shocks that might otherwise help identify the curve. We discuss three practical solutions that attempt to circumvent these issues by isolating the remaining demand-driven variation in inflation.

First, econometricians can attempt to control for cost-push and other trade-off inducing shocks to aggregate supply, in line with the approach proposed by Gordon (1982). This helps to minimize the remaining cost-push driven variance in the error term, leaving only demand shocks that can correctly identify the Phillips curve. In practice, however, the success of this approach requires successfully controlling for each and every trade-off inducing shock affecting the economy. The ability to do this may be limited in the recent past, where energy price shocks are less dominant than in the 1970s.

Second, if econometricians can find suitable instrumental variables, they can purge their output gap data of any cost-push shocks, leaving only the demand variation needed to consistently estimate the Phillips curve. With highly autocorrelated cost-push shocks (precluding the use of lagged variables as instruments), using measures of monetary policy or other demand shocks may be one set of appropriate external instruments (Barnichon and Mesters 2019). But if the variance of monetary policy shocks has fallen since the early 1980s and/or the effect of a shock of a given size has reduced, as suggested by Boivin and Giannoni (2006), then these instruments may be too weak to provide a practical solution in the recent data.

We next present evidence on our third solution, using cross-sectional regional variation in unemployment to identify the Phillips curve. Following Fitzgerald and Nicolini (2014) and concurrently with a recent paper by Hooper, Mishkin, and Sufi (2019), we use US metropolitan area price and unemployment data to estimate a Phillips curve including metropolitan area fixed effects, to control for time-invariant regional heterogeneity in the natural rate of unemployment, as well as time fixed effects to control for variation over time in monetary policy and the aggregate natural rate. Under our preferred specification, a steeper Phillips curve reemerges, with a short-run slope at least twice as large as any of our estimates using aggregate data.

The idea that endogenous stabilization policy can hide structural relationships in the data is an old one, going back at least to Kareken and Solow's (1963) critique of Milton Friedman's evidence on the effect of money on income. They pointed out that a monetary policy that perfectly stabilized nominal income would completely offset any underlying relationship between income and measures of money. Similarly, Brainard and Tobin (1968) present a model in which the lead-lag correlation between money and income following an exogenous change in fiscal policy depends on the endogenous monetary policy response. Goldfeld and Blinder (1972) study the bias arising from reduced-form ordinary least squares (OLS) estimation of fiscal and monetary policy multipliers when both policies are set endogenously. These identification issues are very well known in the context of monetary policy effects: Cochrane (1994) sets out how they were the primary motivation for the literature on identified monetary policy shocks.

Several authors over the years have also highlighted the general result that under an optimal control policy the correlation between a policy target and policy instrument should be driven toward zero, including Worswick (1969), Peston (1972), Goodhart (1989), and, in the context of the Phillips curve, Mishkin (2007).[3] This point is perhaps also a specific example of Goodhart's law "that any observed statistical relationship will tend to collapse once pressure is placed upon it for control purposes" (Goodhart 1984, 96).

In a forecasting context, Woodford (1994) shows that if an indicator is a poor predictor of inflation that may just be because monetary policy is already responding to it appropriately. Similarly, Edge and Gürkaynak (2010) point out that unforecastable inflation is a prediction of DSGE models in which policy makers respond aggressively to stabilize inflation. They suggest that forecasting performance during the Great Moderation is therefore a poor metric of the models' success, because policy makers acted strongly to offset the forecastable component of inflation. Perhaps because measures of slack are one step removed from monetary policy instruments, these issues seem to have been often neglected in discussions of the Phillips curve.

Of course, that the empirical Phillips curve may vary with monetary policy was one of the examples given by Lucas (1976) in his critique. Given their original emphases, both the Lucas critique and Goodhart's law are more often applied to explain suboptimal stabilization policies. Indeed, several authors have explicitly modeled a situation where policy makers set monetary policy based on a misspecified or unidentified Phillips curve (Haldane and Quah 1999; Primiceri 2006; Sargent, Williams, and Zha 2006). In these papers, mistakes or imperfect information on the part of policy makers can lead to changes in inflation expectations that cause the reduced-form Phillips curve to disappear.[4]

In contrast, we show how a disappearing reduced-form Phillips curve is also a natural consequence of successful monetary policy. The idea that improvements in monetary policy have flattened the slope of the reduced-form Phillips curve is often ascribed to researchers and policy makers at the Federal Reserve.[5] Most articulations of this view have tended to focus on the role of improved monetary policy in anchoring inflation expectations (e.g., Williams 2006; Bernanke 2007, 2010; Mishkin 2007).[6]

Our point is closely related but distinct: even in a purely static setting in which expectations play no role, the structural relationship between slack and inflation can be masked by the conduct of monetary policy. This effect of monetary policy on the Phillips curve has also been highlighted at various times over the years in the literature and by policy makers. Roberts (2006), Carlstrom, Fuerst, and Paustian (2009), and recently Bullard (2018) highlight the role of monetary policy on inflation dynamics in simple New Keynesian models with Taylor rules, and Nason and Smith (2008); Mavroeidis, Plagborg-Møller, and Stock (2014); and Krogh (2015) explore Phillips curve identification in detail in similar setups. Haldane and Quah (1999), using a similar model to the one we adopt, show that optimal discretionary policy can flatten or reverse the slope of the reduced-form Phillips curve. Fitzgerald and Nicolini (2014) make the same point using an old Keynesian framework and, like us, use regional data from US metropolitan areas to recover a steeper Phillips curve slope.

Despite these papers, a surprisingly bulky literature has continued searching for a Phillips curve in the data without addressing the key identification challenge. Our first contribution is to frame the issue as simply as possible: as a classical identification problem, and as one that is present in the same standard New Keynesian equations that are taught in graduate economics textbooks. Given that the New Keynesian framework forms the basis for the models used in central banks, it is also a natural platform to respond to criticisms of that framework and of policy makers for their continued reliance on Phillips curve relationships. A second contribution is to show the extent to which these conclusions generalize to a more complex DSGE quantitative framework and to different measures of inflation and slack, including articulating why one should expect to see stronger wage Phillips curve relationships in the data. Our simple analytical framework also enables us to rationalize findings in various strands of the empirical literature and to critically evaluate some of the practical solutions to the identification problem. This discussion motivates our empirical focus on using regional variation to recover a steeper Phillips curve slope for the United States.

The paper is organized as follows. Section II introduces a simple model of optimal policy embedding the Phillips curve and illustrates the "exogeneity result" or disconnect between equilibrium inflation and output gap under the assumption that the monetary authority cannot commit to a future path of inflation (discretion). Section III illustrates the empirical identification problem. Section IV presents and discusses extensions of the model and notes some conceptual solutions to achieve identification. Section V examines the solutions in practice using national and metropolitan area data for the United States. Section VI contains concluding remarks.

II.   Optimal Inflation in the Basic New Keynesian Model

This section uses an optimal monetary policy framework to illustrate why, in equilibrium, one should expect inflation to follow a seemingly exogenous process, unrelated (or even negatively related) to measures of slack.

To explain the intuition as starkly as possible, we use the canonical New Keynesian model, as derived in Clarida et al. (1999), Woodford (2003), and elsewhere. Here we closely follow the textbook exposition from Galí (2008). For now, we dispense with the usual investment/saving (IS) equation determining aggregate demand. This equation is necessary only to determine how policy is implemented. In the basic model it does not constrain equilibrium outcomes, so we can equivalently consider the policy maker as directly choosing the output gap as their policy instrument. Our model therefore consists of just two equations: a Phillips curve and a description of optimal monetary policy.

The (log-linearized) New Keynesian Phillips curve is given by

$$\pi_t = \beta E_t \pi_{t+1} + \kappa x_t + u_t, \tag{1}$$

where π_t is the deviation of inflation from its target; x_t is the output gap, measured as the difference between output and its potential level;[7] and u_t is a cost-push shock that follows an exogenous AR(1) process with persistence ρ ($u_t = \rho u_{t-1} + \epsilon_t$, where ϵ_t are independently and identically distributed [i.i.d.] and mean zero). We assume that the Phillips curve has a strictly positive slope, denoted by $\kappa > 0$.

The Phillips curve is evidently alive and well in the model: it is the only equation making up its nonpolicy block. By construction, we have a positively sloped Phillips curve. Increases in the output gap clearly increase inflation and falls in the output gap reduce it. Nonetheless, once we augment the model with a description of optimal monetary policy, this relationship will not be apparent in the data. Inflation will instead inherit the properties of the exogenous shock process u_t.

To show this, we assume that the policy maker sets monetary policy optimally under discretion. Period by period, the policy maker minimizes the following quadratic loss function:

$$L_t = \pi_t^2 + \lambda x_t^2$$

subject to the constraint (eq. [1]) and taking expectations of future inflation as given.[8] The solution to the minimization problem is the policy maker's optimal targeting rule:

$$\pi_t = -\frac{\lambda}{\kappa} x_t. \tag{2}$$

When faced with a positive cost-push shock that creates a trade-off between the inflation and output stabilization objectives, the policy maker balances them, creating a negative output gap to reduce the degree of above-target inflation. The relative weight placed on each objective depends on the policy maker's preference parameter λ.

The Phillips curve (eq. [1]) and optimal targeting rule (eq. [2]) together completely determine the path of inflation in the model. We can solve for equilibrium inflation by using equation (2) to substitute out for x_t in equation (1) and by iterating forward to obtain

$$\pi_t = \frac{\lambda}{\kappa^2 + \lambda(1 - \beta\rho)} u_t. \tag{3}$$

In equilibrium, inflation deviations are at all times perfectly proportional to the exogenous cost-push shock. In other words, with a constant target, equilibrium inflation itself behaves as an exogenous process. In the limit, when the monetary authority does not put any weight on the output gap ($\lambda = 0$), inflation equals the target rate, a point previously made by Haldane and Quah (1999).

This behavior is entirely consistent with recent empirical work by Cecchetti et al. (2017) and Forbes et al. (2017), suggesting that inflation data in the United States and the United Kingdom can be modeled as an exogenous statistical process, unrelated or negatively related to measures of slack.[9] But crucially, the basic theory is also built under the assumption that monetary policy is at all times constrained by a working Phillips curve. There is no discrepancy between the two results. The Phillips curve may be the correct structural model of the inflation process, but that does not mean that one should observe it in the empirical relationship between (equilibrium levels of) inflation and the output gap.

The reason is simple: the policy maker in the model is able to set policy to achieve any desired level of the output gap. Successful monetary policy should lean against any undesirable deviations in output from potential, which would otherwise cause inflationary or deflationary pressures. Precisely because monetary policy can be used to offset the effect of such output gaps on inflation, their effect on inflation should not be visible in the data.

Optimal monetary policy does not seek to eliminate all output volatility: from equation (2), we can see that in response to cost-push shocks, the policy maker will prefer to tolerate output deviations from potential. But such shocks impart a negative correlation between inflation and output rather than a positive one. Again, the more successful monetary policy is in managing any trade-offs between inflation and output, the more it will blur the underlying positive Phillips curve correlation.

To summarize, we have shown that with an optimizing monetary policy, equilibrium levels of inflation inherit the statistical properties of exogenous cost-push shocks. This does not necessarily tell us that the Phillips curve is not present. In the model, the Phillips curve exists and policy makers are completely aware of its existence. But because they know exactly how the curve operates, they are able to perfectly offset its effects on equilibrium inflation.[10]

III. Phillips Curve Identification

As may already be apparent from the discussion in Section II, regression analysis will have difficulty in recovering the Phillips curve. Figure 1 shows data simulated from the model described by equations (1) and (2), with parameters calibrated as in Galí (2008). Specifically, the slope of the Phillips curve is set at $\kappa = 0.1275$, and the policy maker's weight on output deviations relative to quarterly inflation is set as $\lambda = 0.0213$ or around one-third relative to annualized inflation. The discount factor is set to $\beta = 0.99$ and the persistence of the cost-push shock to $\rho = 0.5$.

Of course, there is no Phillips curve visible in the simulated data. As can be seen from the line of best fit, a naive OLS regression of inflation on the output gap,

$$\pi_t = \gamma_1 x_t + \varepsilon_t, \tag{4}$$

will produce a negative parameter estimate, $\hat{\gamma}_1 = -1/6$, reflecting the targeting rule (eq. [2]), rather than a consistent estimate of the positive slope

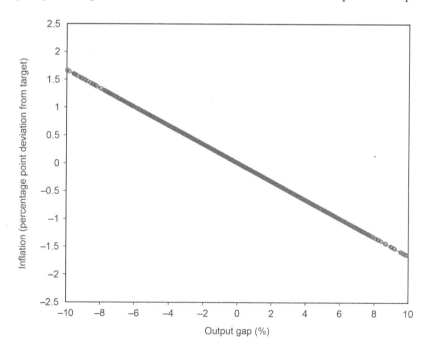

Fig. 1. Inflation/output gap correlation in model-simulated data. One thousand periods of data are simulated from the model described by equations (1) and (2). We draw each ε_t from a standard normal distribution.

of the Phillips curve. Many papers have focused on the difficulty of controlling for inflation expectations in Phillips curve estimation, but the problem here is a more straightfoward one.[11]

The identification problem is a simple case of simultaneity bias. The regressor x_t is correlated with the error term ε_t. The naive econometrician does not observe the Phillips curve in the data. Rather, he or she observes equilibrium inflation and output gap outturns, which are the intersection of the Phillips curve (eq. [1]) and the targeting rule (eq. [2]). In fact, the case here is an extreme one: the regressor and the error are perfectly negatively correlated.[12] The issue is completely analagous to the classic case of simultaneity bias: jointly determined supply and demand equations.

To show the identification challenge, we first plot the two model equations in figure 2.[13] The Phillips curve (eq. [1]) is in light gray, the optimal targeting rule (eq. [2]) in dark gray, and the black circles index the policy maker's loss function at different levels of loss. The observed inflation-output gap pairs are the equilbrium where the two lines intersect. With no cost-push shocks to the Phillips curve, the first-best outcome of at

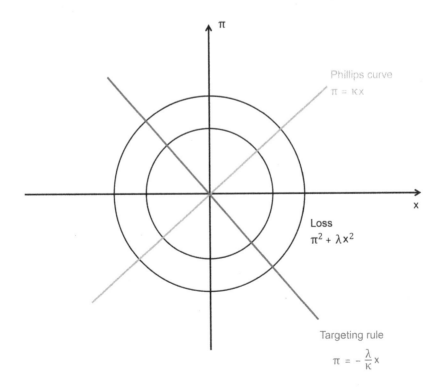

Fig. 2. Graphical illustration of optimal monetary policy under discretion.

target inflation and no output gap is feasible, so the lines intersect at the origin.

When the upward sloping Phillips curve is subject to cost-push shocks, the equilibrium shifts to different points along the optimal targeting path, shown in figure 3. But with monetary policy set optimally, there are no shifts along the Phillips curve: at all times the equilibrium remains on the negatively sloped optimal targeting rule line. As a result, the simulated data trace out the optimal targeting rule, not the Phillips curve. The estimated coefficient is $\hat{\gamma}_1 = -\lambda/\kappa = -1/6$.

The issue is that the Phillips curve is not identified. Our simple setup has no exogenous variables shifting monetary policy. Worse, the only shocks are to the equation of interest, so the estimated parameter is almost entirely unrelated to the slope of the Phillips curve.[14] The problem is the same one that arises when trying to identify a supply curve while only observing equilibrium quantities and prices. Without any exogenous demand shifter, there is no way of doing so.

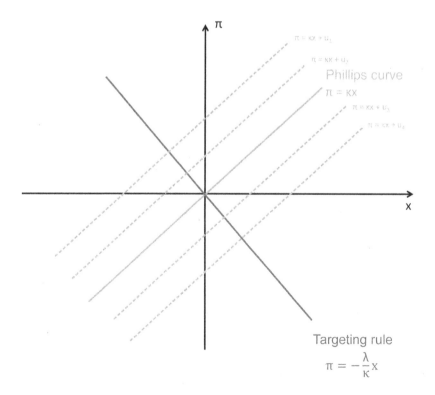

Fig. 3. Graphical illustration of optimal discretionary policy in response to cost-push shocks.

IV. Extensions to the Basic Model and Solutions to the Estimation Challenge

In this section, we study a number of extensions to the basic model. For each extension, we discuss whether and how it can help solving the Phillips curve's empirical identification problem. In Section IV.A, we discuss the case in which the monetary authority can commit to a path of inflation and output gap. In Section IV.B, we allow for shocks to the targeting rule and discuss how they link to the identified monetary policy shocks in the monetary policy transmission literature. In Section IV.C, we study a multiregion setting. In Section IV.D, we discuss the mapping into a wage Phillips curve. In Section IV.E, we extend our analysis to explore the effect of monetary policy on the Phillips curve in larger DSGE models.

A. Commitment

First, we show that our main results are unchanged when the monetary policy maker is able to commit to a future plan for inflation and the output gap. In Sections II and III, we assumed that the policy maker was unable to commit. There are a range of practical issues that may make commitment difficult: monetary policy committees often have changes in membership and future policy makers may not feel bound by prior commitments, and perhaps relatedly, successful commitment requires that promises are credible, even when they are time inconsistent. Nonetheless, the optimal commitment policy is able to achieve better outcomes in the face of cost-push shocks than optimal policy under discretion, so it is important to know how this affects our results.

It turns out that the same intuition holds, although the precise details slightly differ. Again following Galí (2008), when the policy maker instead minimizes the loss function:

$$L = E_0 \sum_{t=0}^{\infty} \beta^t (\pi_t^2 + \lambda x_t^2),\qquad(5)$$

subject to the sequence of Phillips curves given by equation (1) for each period, this gives a pair of optimality conditions

$$\pi_0 = -\frac{\lambda}{\kappa} x_0,\qquad(6)$$

$$\pi_t = -\frac{\lambda}{\kappa}(x_t - x_{t-1}).\tag{7}$$

These can be combined to give the targeting rule under commitment

$$p_t = -\frac{\lambda}{\kappa}x_t,\tag{8}$$

where p_t is the log deviation of the price level from its level in period -1. Substituting $p_t - p_{t-1}$ for π_t in equation (1) and substituting out x_t using equation (8) gives a difference equation in p_t. Galí (2008) shows the solution for this in terms of the previous period's price level and the current period cost-push shock. Iterating backward and then taking the first difference gives equilibrium inflation

$$\pi_t = \frac{\delta}{1 - \delta\beta\rho}(u_t - (1 - \delta)\sum_{i=0}^{t-1}\delta^{t-1-i}u_i),\tag{9}$$

where $\delta \equiv (((\lambda(1 + \beta) + \kappa^2) - ((\lambda(1 + \beta) + \kappa^2)^2 - 4\beta\lambda^2)^{0.5}))/2\lambda\beta$. Substituting into equation (7) and iterating backward gives the equilibrium output gap

$$x_t = \frac{-\delta\kappa}{\lambda(1 - \delta\beta\rho)}\sum_{i=0}^{t}\delta^{t-i}u_i.\tag{10}$$

Equilibrium inflation under optimal commitment policy depends solely on the cost-push shock process. The equilibrium path is quite different to that under discretion, however. At any point in time, inflation displays history dependence, depending on the entire history of cost-push shocks rather than just the one in the current period.

Simple regressions will again fail to uncover the Phillips curve. The only difference is that under commitment, the optimal targeting rule imposes a negative correlation between the output gap and the price level. The relationship between inflation and the output gap in the simulated data shown in figure 4 is noisier but shows no sign of the Phillips curve embedded in the model. The OLS estimate of γ in equation (4) gives the coefficient $\hat{\gamma}_1 = -0.085$.

At least in the simple framework here, the history dependence of optimal commitment policy also suggests a straightforward solution to the identification problem. From equation (10), the equilibrium output gap will be correlated with its own lagged values. This policy-induced persistence means that the lagged output gap can be used as an instrument for

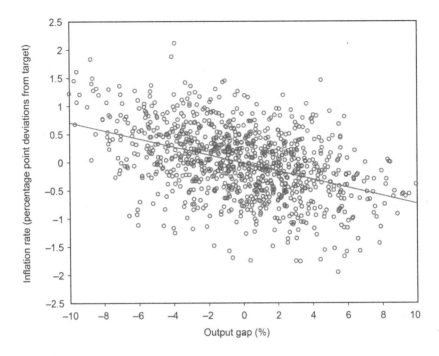

Fig. 4. Inflation/output gap correlation in model-simulated data: optimal commitment. One thousand periods of data are simulated from the model described by equations (1) and (7). We draw each ϵ_t from a standard normal distribution.

the current output gap. Intuitively, policy makers choose to create an output gap even after the cost-push shock has disappeared. They commit to do so to achieve better inflation outcomes when the shock originally occurs. The policy maker therefore optimally reintroduces traces of the positive Phillips curve relation that is absent under optimal discretion. As a result, in the simple case here, a suitable choice of instrument will be able to recover the true Phillips curve slope.

B. Shocks to the Targeting Rule

The previous sections have illustrated how successful monetary policy might mask the underlying structural Phillips curve in the data. We now show that the opposite is also true in our model: if monetary policy is set far from optimally, the Phillips curve is likely to reappear.

So far we have assumed policy makers can implement monetary policy by directly choosing their desired observable output gap each period.

But, alas, in practice, policy making is not quite so simple. In empirical studies, we observe lags between changing policy and its impact on the output gap and inflation, which means that in practice central banks are inflation forecast targeters (Svensson 1997; Haldane 1998). Forecast errors will therefore inject noise into the targeting rule. Potential output is unobservable, so the output gap must be estimated (with error). And the effect of the policy instruments actually available (typically the central bank policy rate and forward guidance on its future path, as well as quantitative easing) on the target variables is also uncertain. Errors from any of these sources will insert noise into the desired balance between inflation and output gap deviations. These various shocks to the targeting rule correspond closely to the typical interpretations of identified monetary policy shocks in the empirical literature on this topic (Christiano, Eichenbaum, and Evans 1996, 1999; Faust, Swanson, and Wright 2004; Romer and Romer 2004b; Bernanke, Boivin, and Eliasz 2005; Olivei and Tenreyro 2007; Gertler and Karadi 2015; Cloyne and Hürtgen 2016). That literature is able to identify a positively correlated response of inflation and the output gap to monetary policy shocks, in line with the following results.

Returning to optimal policy under discretion, we model implementation errors by including an AR(1) shock process e_t in the targeting rule (eq. [2]) to give

$$\pi_t = -\frac{\lambda}{\kappa} x_t - e_t, \tag{11}$$

where $e_t = \rho_e e_{t-1} + \zeta_t$ and ζ_t is zero mean and i.i.d. with variance σ_e^2.[15] We can show that equilibrium inflation and the output gap now both have an additional term proportional to e_t. Respectively, they are given by $\pi_t = s_1 \lambda u_t - s_2 \kappa e_t$ and $x_t = -s_1 \kappa u_t - s_2(1 - \beta \rho_e)e_t$, where $s_1 \equiv 1/(\lambda(1 - \beta\rho) + \kappa^2)$ and $s_2 \equiv \kappa/(\lambda(1 - \beta\rho_e) + \kappa^2)$.

With shocks to the targeting rule, neither equation is identified. The equilibrium values of inflation and the output gap both depend on a combination of both shocks. Consequently, if either equation is estimated by OLS, its regressor will be correlated with the regression error term and the resulting parameter estimate inconsistent. In particular, it follows from substituting the equilibrium values of π_t and x_t into the definition of the OLS estimator in the regression (eq. [4]) that

$$\text{plim}(\hat{\gamma}) = \frac{\text{plim}\left(\frac{1}{T}\sum_{t=1}^{T} x_t \pi_t\right)}{\text{plim}\left(\frac{1}{T}\sum_{t=1}^{T} x_t^2\right)} = \frac{\frac{-\lambda}{\kappa} \frac{s_1^2(1-\rho_e^2)}{s_2^2(1-\rho^2)} \frac{\sigma_u^2}{\sigma_u^2 + \sigma_e^2} + (1-\beta\rho_e)\kappa \frac{\sigma_e^2}{\sigma_u^2 + \sigma_e^2}}{\frac{s_1^2(1-\rho_e^2)}{s_2^2(1-\rho^2)} \frac{\sigma_u^2}{\sigma_u^2 + \sigma_e^2} + (1-\beta\rho_e)^2 \frac{\sigma_e^2}{\sigma_u^2 + \sigma_e^2}}. \tag{12}$$

The size of the simultaneity bias to each equation depends on the relative variances of the shocks.[16] Figure 5 plots simulated data for three cases. We set $\rho_e = 0.5$ and set the other parameters as before. First, the dark gray circles show the case where the cost-push shock has a variance 100 times larger than the targeting rule shock. These look almost identical to the case with only a cost-push shock: the circles trace out the targeting rule. Second, the black circles show the case when the shocks have equal variance. The slope is still negative, but flatter. The final case gives the cost-push shock a variance 100 times smaller than the targeting rule shock, and the data trace out a positively sloped line.

Looking at the regression coefficients in table 1, in the first two cases these are both strongly influenced by the endogenous policy response embodied in the optimal targeting rule. It also makes little difference whether or not the econometrician correctly controls for inflation expectations, which also enter the Phillips curve. In the third case, however,

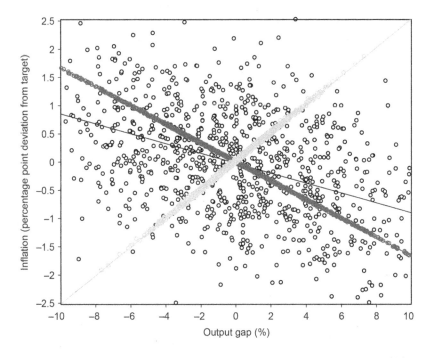

Fig. 5. Inflation/output gap correlation in model-simulated data: optimal discretion with shocks to the targeting rule. One thousand periods of data are simulated from the model described by equations (1) and (11). The black circles show the case when each ϵ_t and ζ_t is drawn from a standard normal distribution. The light gray circles show the case when each ϵ_t is instead drawn from an $N(0,10)$ distribution, and the dark gray circles each ζ_t is instead drawn from an $N(0,10)$ distribution.

Table 1
Ordinary Least Squares (OLS) Regressions of Inflation on the Output Gap in the Simulated Data

	Dependent Variable					
	π_t	$\pi_t - \beta E_t \pi_{t+1}$	π_t	$\pi_t - \beta E_t \pi_{t+1}$	π_t	$\pi_t - \beta E_t \pi_{t+1}$
	(i) $\sigma_u^2/\sigma_e^2 = 100$		(ii) $\sigma_u^2/\sigma_e^2 = 1$		(iii) $\sigma_u^2/\sigma_e^2 = 0.01$	
	(1)	(2)	(3)	(4)	(5)	(6)
x_t	−.1667	−.1805	−.0873	−.0792	.2523	.1275

Note: Table shows the OLS regression coefficients of OLS for the shock distributions described in figure 5. Specifications (2), (4), and (6) (perfectly) control for inflation expectations by subtracting from π_t the true value of $\beta E_t \pi_{t+1}$. The true slope of the Phillips curve is $\kappa = 0.1275$, and the true slope of the optimal targeting rule is $-\lambda/\kappa = -0.1667$.

the regression coefficient turns positive. The estimate is actually upward biased in specification 5, which omits inflation expectations. Once these are controlled for, the bias becomes very small. The regression correctly identifies the slope of the Phillips curve to four decimal places.

The reason the bias disappears is straightforward. When cost-push shocks have a relatively low variance, most of the variation in the simulated data arises from the shocks to the targeting rule. With the Phillips curve stable, these movements in the targeting rule now trace out the Phillips curve, as shown graphically in figure 6. This suggests that if we can successfully control for the cost-push shocks u_t in equation (1), then we may be able to limit the bias in estimates of the Phillips curve.

C. Regional Phillips Curves

Partly to avoid the difficulties associated with identifying the Phillips curve at the national level, a number of authors have estimated Phillips curves at a more disaggregated, regional, or sectoral level (Fitzgerald and Nicolini 2014; Kiley 2015; Babb and Detmeister 2017; Leduc and Wilson 2017; Tuckett 2018; Vlieghe 2018; Hooper et al. 2019). In this subsection, we show that in an extended version of the basic model, this may also help the econometrician to identify the aggregate Phillips curve.

The key to identification is that, at the regional level, the endogenous response of monetary policy to demand shocks is switched off, ameliorating the simultaneity bias in estimating aggregate Phillips curves. This point was made by Fitzgerald and Nicolini (2014) as motivation for their

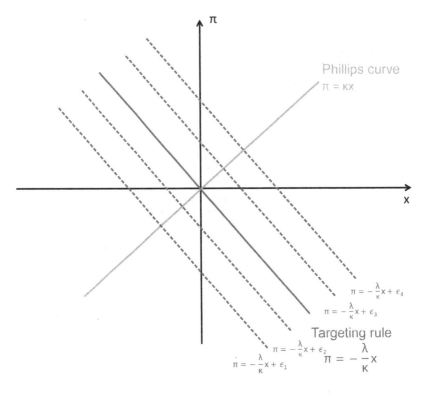

Fig. 6. Graphical illustration of optimal discretionary policy in response to targeting-rule shocks.

estimation of Phillips curves at a regional level. The same logic can explain why the Phillips curve may be more evident in countries within a monetary union such as the euro area.[17]

We assume that the aggregate Phillips curve (eq. [1]) continues to hold but that aggregate inflation and the aggregate output gap also depend on the weighted average of inflation and the output gap in each of n regions

$$\pi_t = \sum_{i=1}^{n} \alpha_i \pi_t^i,$$ (13)

$$x_t = \sum_{i=1}^{n} \alpha_i x_t^i,$$ (14)

where $\sum_{i=1}^{n} \alpha_i = 1$ and regional inflation is determined by a regional Phillips curve analogous to equation (1):

$$\pi_t^i = \beta E_t \pi_{t+1}^i + \kappa x_t^i + u_t^i,$$ (15)

with idiosyncratic cost-push shocks $u_t^i = \rho u_{t-1}^i + \epsilon_t^i$ and ϵ_t^i zero mean and i.i.d over time but potentially correlated across regions. We must also specify how idiosyncratic demand shocks and aggregate monetary policy affect the regional output gap with an equation analogous to the IS curve in the basic New Keynesian model, given by

$$x_t^i = E_t x_{t+1}^i - \sigma^{-1}(i_t - E_t \pi_{t+1}^i - r_t^i), \tag{16}$$

where the idiosyncratic demand shocks are given by $r_t^i = \rho_r r_{t-1}^i + e_r^i$, and e_r^i are zero mean and i.i.d. over time but potentially correlated across regions. The equations can be aggregated together to give the usual aggregate IS relation

$$x_t = E_t x_{t+1} - \sigma^{-1}(i_t - E_t \pi_{t+1} - r_t). \tag{17}$$

We therefore allow inflation and the output gap to be determined partly by idiosyncratic shocks to each region but restrict the monetary policy rate i_t to be the same across all n regions.

We next denote for any regional variable its (log) deviation from the aggregate as $\hat{z}_t^i = z_t^i - \Sigma_{i=1}^n \alpha_i z_t^i$. We can then subtract equation (1) from equation (15) to give a Phillips curve in terms of log deviations from aggregate inflation:

$$\hat{\pi}_t^i = \beta E_t \hat{\pi}_{t+1}^i + \kappa \hat{x}_t^i + \hat{u}_t^i. \tag{18}$$

Subtracting equation (17) from equation (16) gives an equivalent IS curve

$$\hat{x}_t^i = E_t \hat{x}_{t+1}^i + \sigma^{-1}(E_t \hat{\pi}_{t+1}^i + \hat{r}_t^i). \tag{19}$$

Monetary policy is set (under discretion) by minimizing the same aggregate period loss function as in Section II, subject to the aggregate Phillips curve (eq. [1]).[18] Policy therefore follows the same targeting rule (eq. [2]), depending solely on aggregate variables.[19]

The crucial difference to the identification problem at the regional level is that although monetary policy perfectly offsets the aggregate demand shocks, $r_t = \Sigma_{i=1}^n \alpha_i r_t^i$, it does not respond at all to the idiosyncratic regional deviations from that average, $\hat{r}_t^i$. The regressor in the Phillips curve equation $\hat{x}_t^i$ is now affected by exogenous demand shocks that do not influence the aggregate Phillips curve. As a result, the endogeneity problem is mitigated.

For each region, we can verify that one solution to the model described by equations (18) and (19) is

$$\hat{\pi}_t^i = c_1(1 - \rho)\hat{u}_t^i + c_2\kappa_i\hat{r}_t^i \tag{20}$$

and

$$\hat{x}_t^i = c_1\rho\sigma^{-1}\hat{u}_t^i + c_2(1 - \rho_r\beta)\hat{r}_t^i, \tag{21}$$

where $c_1 \equiv 1/((1 - \rho)(1 - \rho\beta) - \rho\kappa\sigma^{-1})$ and $c_2 \equiv \sigma^{-1}/((1 - \rho_r)(1 - \rho_r\beta) - \rho_r\kappa\sigma^{-1})$.[20] Unlike aggregate inflation, which evolves in line with the exogenous shocks to the Phillips curve, regional inflation also depends on idiosyncratic demand shocks. In the simplest case, when the shocks are independent and entirely transitory ($\rho = \rho_r = 0$), the equilibrium output gap deviation will be independent of the idiosyncratic cost-push shocks $\hat{u}_t^i$ and a simple regression of $\hat{\pi}_t^i$ on $\hat{x}_t^i$ will give a consistent estimate of κ.

Away from that special case, there remain challenges to identification. First, even if the idiosyncratic cost-push shocks $\hat{u}_t^i$ are uncorrelated with demand (absent any monetary policy response), they will inject additional noise in finite samples. Particularly if there is limited cross-sectional variation in the regional data, this will lead to imprecise estimates of κ. Moreover, in practice the shocks are unlikely to be independent of the forces driving aggregate demand, even absent changes in monetary policy. Many types of regional supply shocks are likely to simultaneously increase regional inflation and reduce regional output below its potential. If such shocks are large, this correlation may still impart a significant negative bias into estimates of κ.

Second, with $\rho > 0$ or $\rho_r > 0$, there will be omitted variable bias unless the econometrician can control for the effect of regional inflation expectations. Although possible in principle, reliable data are likely to be less readily available than at the national level. If cross-sectional variation in inflation expectations is important, there is perhaps likely to be more chance of success when estimating at the country level within a single multicountry monetary authority. Alternatively, if that variation is constant over time, it can be controlled for using region fixed effects.

D. The Wage Phillips Curve

Although identification of the price Phillips curve is complicated by the endogenous response of optimal monetary policy, the focus of the original Phillips study was the correlation between wage inflation and unemployment in the United Kingdom. In this subsection, we comment on how optimal monetary policy maps into the original wage Phillips curve relationship between wage inflation and unemployment. Intuitively, one might expect the wage Phillips curve to be less vulnerable to identification issues related to the endogeneity of monetary policy, because wage inflation is one step removed from the price inflation–targeting remit of most central banks.

As well as a different dependent variable (wage inflation rather than price inflation), the typical wage Phillips curve attempts to explain inflation using variation in unemployment or the unemployment gap rather than the output gap. Using unemployment in the equation is unlikely to solve the identification issues arising from the behavior of monetary policy for at least two reasons.

First, many central banks' remits explicitly specify unemployment or employment as one of their (secondary or dual) target variables. As such, they will optimally set policy to close any gap between unemployment and its natural rate, unless there is a trade-off between that goal and their inflation targets, in which case they will seek to balance the two goals, as was the case with the output gap in Section II. Monetary policy will therefore blur the structural relationship between inflation and the unemployment gap in a similar way. Second, even for central banks without an explicit mandate to minimize fluctuations in employment, when there is comovement between the output gap and the unemployment gap, policy will often implicitly seek to stabilize employment.[21]

There are, however, reasons to think that using wage inflation as the dependent variable might lessen some of the identification problems. Nominal wage rigidities can be incorporated into the basic model in an analogous way to price rigidities, as introduced by Erceg, Henderson, and Levin (2000). With both wage and price stickiness, some shocks, such as innovations to firms' desired price markups, will lead to a wedge between the rate of price inflation and the output gap, but not between the rate of wage inflation and the output gap. Because inflation-targeting central banks typically target price inflation, policy makers may respond by adjusting the output gap to achieve their desired trade-off with price inflation. But doing so would lead to variation in wage inflation operating via the wage Phillips curve. Put differently, if some shocks only directly affect the price Phillips curve and not the wage Phillips curve, then the output gap will be correlated with the error term in the former but not the latter, which will be consistently estimated.

The wage Phillips curve may not face quite as severe problems, but there remain limits to how easily it can be identified under optimal monetary policy. First, although there may be some shocks that only affect the price Phillips curve, there are likely to be several more that affect both curves (for a given output gap). Wage markup shocks will increase both price and wage inflation relative to the prevailing output gap. Erceg et al. (2000) show that shocks to household consumption or leisure preferences, or to total factor productivity, will conversely move price and wage inflation in opposite directions for a given output gap. Because the inflationary impact of these shocks will lead policy makers to attempt to lean against them via the output gap, this will induce a correlation between the output gap and the shocks affecting the wage Phillips curve (for a given output gap). The direction of the bias will differ according to the shock, but the equation will in general not be identified.

Second, even if price inflation shocks are particularly prevalent, many typical examples of such shocks, such as changes in oil prices, have relatively transitory effects on price inflation. Because monetary policy is typically thought to have its peak effect on inflation with some lag, attempting to offset very transitory shocks may not be possible. As a result, policy makers are perhaps less likely to respond to the very shocks that would otherwise have helped econometricians identify the wage Phillips curve. Conversely, when transitory shocks are affecting price inflation, wage inflation can sometimes give a better signal of underlying price pressures, which may lead policy makers to behave at times as if they were targeting wage inflation.[22]

E. Larger DSGE Models

In addition to nominal wage rigidities, larger macroeconomic models of the type used for policy analysis in central banks usually have a range of other frictions, additional factors of production, and a richer dynamic structure.[23] In this subsection, we study how the intuition underlying Phillips curve identification in the basic New Keynesian model translates to the aggregate supply relationship in larger models.

An overriding conceptual issue in larger DSGE models is that there typically is no single, stable Phillips curve relationship between inflation and the output gap. In the basic model, the output gap is proportional to firms' real marginal costs, but this is a special case that does not generalize to larger models. The reduced-form Phillips curve correlation therefore varies for different shocks. We illustrate this point in figure A1 (figs. A1–A3, table A1, and app. are available online; see https://www.nber.org/data-appendix/c14245/appendix.pdf), which shows the inflation-output gap relationship in a large-scale DSGE model conditional on each type of shock in the model. We use the COMPASS model, described in Burgess et al. (2013), which was designed for forecasting and policy analysis at the Bank of England. The model is in the tradition of well-known medium-scale DSGE models such as Christiano, Eichen-baum, and Evans (2005) and Smets and Wouters (2007), in which similar findings would emerge, as well as DSGE models used in other central banks. The simulated Phillips curve varies markedly depending on the shock. Conditional on demand-type shocks, such as to government spending or world demand, there is a positive relationship between in-flation and the output gap. Conditional on cost-push type shocks to wage or price markups, the correlation turns negative.

Even when we restrict our attention to those shocks we typically think of as demand, there are different reduced-form Phillips curves for differ-ent shocks: the investment adjustment cost shock has a slope more than twice as steep as a government spending shock, for example. These dif-ferent reduced-form slopes arise for several reasons. First, the shocks do not all have the same impact on the output gap relative to real marginal costs and inflation. Second, they each have different dynamic effects (e.g., some shock processes are estimated to be more persistent than oth-ers), which influences the contemporaneous Phillips curve correlations. And related to both points, the simulations incorporate an endogenous monetary policy response via the model's Taylor rule. Although the Tay-lor rule is not sufficient to hide the positive Phillips curve relationships completely, it will be exerting some influence, the scale of which will de-pend on the specific shock.[24]

Given these conceptual difficulties, how should we think of the Phil-lips curve in larger DSGE models? One interpretation, consistent with the Phillips curve's inception as an empirical regularity in the UK data, is that is simply the average reduced-form relationship, conditional on a demand shock having occurred. The slope of such an object would clearly change over time if some types of shock became more or less fre-quent. It would also be vulnerable to the Lucas critique. But if policy makers judged that such changes were relatively slow moving, they may still find such an empirical Phillips curve a useful input into their decisions.

Under that interpretation, the logic we have outlined for the basic model continues to complicate estimation of empirical Phillips curves in larger models. Figure 7a shows another DSGE simulation using Bur-gess et al. (2013), this time for all shocks in the model. Despite the pres-ence of supply shocks and an endogenous monetary policy response, a positively sloped Phillips curve emerges.

Figure 7b runs an otherwise identical simulation with the model's Taylor rule replaced by the optimal monetary policy under discretion. As in the examples from the basic model, the positively sloped Phillips

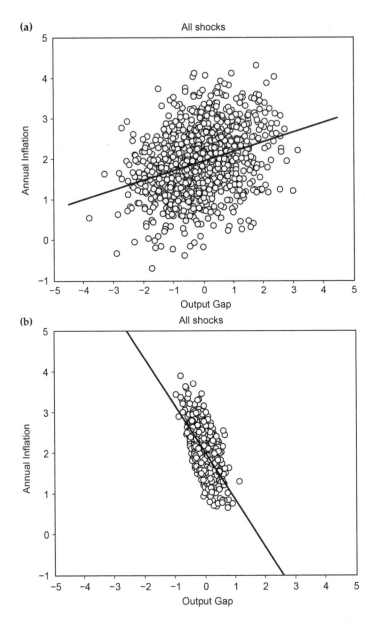

Fig. 7. Inflation/output gap correlation in simulated data from a large-scale dynamic stochastic general equilibrium model. One thousand periods of data are simulated from the model in Burgess et al. (2013) using the MAPS toolkit described in the same paper. Each period a set of unanticipated shocks are drawn independently from a standard normal distribution. The straight lines show the lines of best fit from an ordinary least squares regression of the simulated annual inflation data on the (contemporaneous) flexible price output gap. Panel *a* shows the results using the estimated Taylor rule in the model. Panel *b* replaces

curve disappears and its estimated sign turns negative. This is true irrespective of the shock.[25]

Even in larger models, we would argue one can still interpret the Phillips curve as a structural equation. Although they need not feature a simple structural relationship between inflation and the output gap, larger New Keynesian models will contain some kind of equivalent aggregate supply constraint. Typically this will contain measures of real marginal costs rather than the output gap.[26] It is also likely to have a richer dynamic structure. Given that structure and wider variety of shocks, if one is able to estimate the full structural model and there is enough variation in the data, then it may be possible to recover any structural aggregate supply relationship. But precisely because we do not know the true model of the economy, such an approach may be less robust to misspecification than the empirical Phillips curve described earlier.

Moreover, as long as the structural aggregate supply relationship can be specified as a relationship between inflation and some measure of slack, the identification issues we raise in the simple model may still apply. In Burgess et al. (2013), the Phillips curve for consumer price inflation is a function of past and future inflation, the marginal cost of final output production, and a markup shock. Figure A3 (available online) shows simulated data from the model under a specification of optimal discretionary policy where the policy maker targets inflation and, instead of the output gap, the marginal cost of final output production. Just as with the effect of demand shocks on the output gap in the basic model, the policy maker is able to perfectly offset the effect of all shocks on the marginal cost. In equilibrium, the only shock that has any effect on the policy maker's chosen target variables is the markup shock, which creates a trade-off between them.

These findings from a larger model designed for practical policy use in central banks suggest another source of variation to identify the structural Phillips curve or aggregate supply relationship. If the measure of slack targeted by the policy maker is different to the one that directly influences inflation, then the policy maker will not seek to offset all variation in the inflation-relevant measure. In the previous example, if the policy maker seeks to minimize fluctuations in the output gap, this will

---

the Taylor rule with the optimal discretionary monetary policy, where the policy maker minimizes, period by period, an ad hoc loss function containing the discounted sum of squared deviations of annual inflation from target (with a weight of 1) and the output gap (with a weight of 0.25). The solution is calculated using the algorithm of Dennis (2007).

not always minimize movements in real marginal costs, because the relationship between the two measures of slack will vary according to the mix of shocks. The reasoning is analogous to the discussion of the wage Phillips curve in the previous section. The policy maker's actions will only blur the structural Phillips curve in equilibrium to the extent the policy targets are correlated with the measures of inflation and slack in the aggregate supply relationship.

V. Solutions to the Estimation Challenge in Practice

In this section, we examine Phillips curve identification in practice using US data. The previous subsection suggested at least three ways econometricians could recover the structural Phillips curve:

1. Supply shocks: if we can control for these well enough, we should be able to recover the Phillips curve.

2. Instrumental variables: with good instruments for the output gap, uncorrelated with cost-push shocks, the structural Phillips curve can be recovered.

3. Regional data: monetary policy does not offset regional demand shocks, whereas time fixed effects can control for aggregate supply shocks.

In summary, the identification challenge arises from the presence of cost-push shocks to the Phillips curve and the partial accommodation of these by monetary policy makers. The size of the simultaneity bias is magnified because monetary policy seeks to offset any demand shocks that, in practice, might otherwise help identify the curve.

Each solution attempts to circumvent these issues by isolating the remaining demand-driven variation in inflation. The first two solutions use aggregate time-series data and the third turns to the regional cross section. Although a large number of papers have estimated Phillips curves without addressing the identification issue we raise here, many others over the years have followed one or more of these approaches, either implicitly or explicitly. Our discussion provides a framework that ties together these different solutions.

The econometric solutions to simultaneity in economics are well known. And econometricians will no doubt continue to come up with other innovative ways to successfully identify Phillips curves.[27] But there are reasons to think that, using aggregate data, the task is likely to become ever more difficult. Boivin and Giannoni (2006) showed that both the variance and the effect of monetary policy shocks had become smaller in the period since the early 1980s, and similar arguments have recently been made by Ramey (2016). Both suggest that in economies such as the United States, with established policy frameworks, policy is now largely conducted systematically. This limits the remaining exogenous variation in aggregate demand needed to recover the Phillips curve.

An alternative avenue, therefore, is to turn to cross-sectional data. As in Fitzgerald and Nicolini (2014), we next show that using regional data on inflation and unemployment by metropolitan area, a steeper Phillips curve reemerges.

A.   The Empirical Phillips Curve in the Aggregate Data

For our empirical exploration, we turn our attention to the United States, where Phillips' UK findings were translated by Samuelson and Solow (1960). Our inflation data are the (seasonally adjusted) quarterly annualized log change in core consumer price index (CPI) inflation. Although personal consumption expenditure inflation has been the Federal Open Market Committee's preferred measure since 2000, for most of our sample, monetary policy focused on CPI inflation (Board of Governors of the Federal Reserve System 2000). It also allows us to more readily compare with the US regional price data, which are a CPI measure. Using core inflation rather than headline is a straightforward mechanical way of stripping out a subset of the cost-push shocks affecting headline inflation, in line with our first solution detailed earlier.

Again for comparability with the regional data, we use the (seasonally adjusted) quarterly unemployment gap as our proxy for slack, measured as the civilian unemployment rate less the Congressional Budget Office (CBO) estimate of the long-term natural rate of unemployment. Using the unemployment gap, we would therefore expect to see a negative structural relationship with inflation. Figure 8 plots the two time series, alongside a simple scatter plot of the data over our sample period of 1957–2018. The reduced-form Phillips curve slope is flat and not significantly different from zero. But as is clear from the time series and has been well documented elsewhere, the full sample masks a great deal of time variation in the relationship.

Figure 9 shows how the correlation has varied over time. We split the time periods according to Fed chair over our sample period.[28] We split Paul Volcker's chairmanship into two periods, given the very different inflation and output dynamics at the start and end of his tenure.[29]

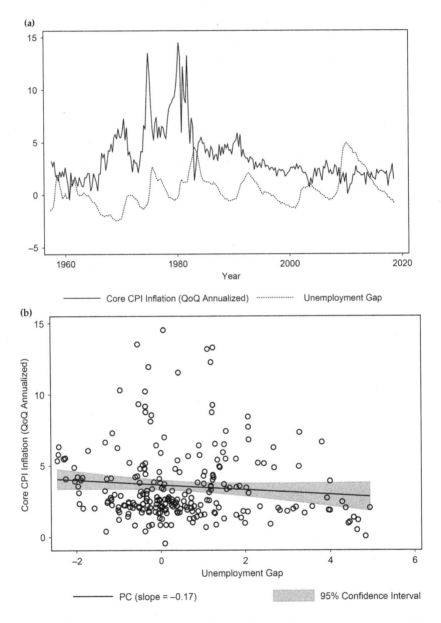

Fig. 8. US core consumer price index (CPI) inflation and the unemployment gap: 1957 Q1–2018 Q2. (*a*) Time series. (*b*) Scatter plot. Figures show plots of quarterly annualized core CPI inflation against the Congressional Budget Office estimate of the unemployment gap. Phillips curve (PC) slope and the confidence interval around it are estimated using ordinary least squares. QoQ = quarter on quarter.

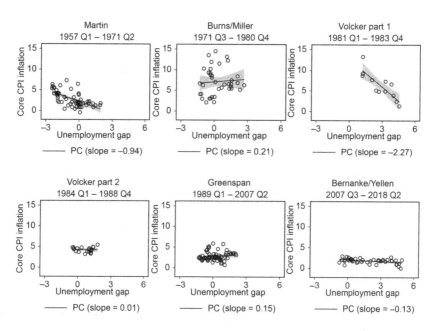

Fig. 9. Phillips correlation by Fed chair. Figure shows scatter plots of quarterly annualized core consumer price index (CPI) inflation against the Congressional Budget Office estimate of the unemployment gap, split by time period. We lag the tenure dates of each Fed chair by six quarters as a way of reflecting the lags between monetary policy actions and their effect on real activity and inflation. Phillips curve (PC) slopes and confidence intervals are estimated using ordinary least squares.

The data can be explained with the traditional narrative of the US Phillips curve over the second half of the twentieth century, as discussed in histories by King (2008) and Gordon (2011). In the later years of William McChesney Martin's 19-year term, with the Phillips curve viewed as an exploitable long-run trade-off, overly accommodative fiscal and monetary policies led to unemployment falling steadily below today's estimate of its natural rate (Romer and Romer 2004a). Inflation rose at the same time, resulting in a downward sloping Phillips curve visible in the data (driven by rises in x_t in eq. [1]).

During Arthur Burns's tenure in the 1970s, a combination of factors increased both inflation and unemployment, leading to a disappearance of any discernible Phillips curve correlation. Those factors were a series of large cost shocks (increases in u_t in eq. [1]) brought about by oil supply disruption (Gordon 1977; Blinder 1982) and the Federal Reserve's inability, unwillingness (DeLong 1997), or miscalculations (Orphanides 2002) in trying to lean against them (falls in e_t in eq. [11]) and their impact on inflation expectations (increases in $E_t \pi_{t+1}$ in eq. [1]; Barro and Gordon 1983; Chari, Christiano, and Eichenbaum 1998).

The beginning of Paul Volcker's tenure saw a reemergence of a steep negative Phillips curve slope, as tighter monetary policy induced rises in unemployment and a sustained fall in inflation (driven by falls in σ_e^2 or ρ_e in eq. [11], or equivalently a fall in λ and a related fall in $E_t \pi_{t+1}$ in eq. [1]: Clarida, Galí, and Gertler 2000).

For the subsequent two decades, the Great Moderation under Paul Volcker and then Alan Greenspan, the Phillips correlation all but disappeared. The causes of the Great Moderation are often divided into those relating to good policy, good luck (in the form of lower shock variance, particularly of supply shocks), and changes in the structure of the economy (Stock and Watson 2002).

Despite the Great Moderation coming to an end with the 2008 financial crisis and a large rise in unemployment, the Phillips curve correlation that reappeared under the tenures of Ben Bernanke and Janet Yellen has been at best weak. The lack of a large deflation following the crisis has sparked a burgeoning literature attempting to explain the "missing disinflation" by appealing to one or more of: a flatter structural Phillips curve slope, better anchored inflation expectations or increases in inflation expectations, the inflationary effects of financial frictions, or weaker potential supply growth (see Coibion and Gorodnichenko 2015 for a discussion).

The reduced-form evidence in figure 9 has led many commentators to conclude that the Phillips curve has flattened over time. It is also consistent with estimates using more sophisticated techniques. In an influential contribution, Ball and Mazumder (2011) estimate a time-varying Phillips curve using median inflation as a measure of core inflation. They report that the Phillips curve steepened from –0.23 in 1960–72 to –0.69 in 1973–84 and then flattened to –0.14 in 1985–2010. Blanchard et al. (2015) and Blanchard (2016), extending the nonlinear Kalman filter estimates of IMF (2013), find that the Phillips curve slope fell from around –0.7 in the 1970s to around –0.2 from the 1990s onward.

Over the period since 1990 (spanning the Great Moderation, then the financial crisis and its aftermath), a flat Phillips curve is common across a range of typical empirical specifications. Table 2 presents simple OLS estimates using data on quarterly annualized core CPI inflation and the unemployment gap/rate, over a sample from 1990 to 2018. The first column shows a simple bivariate regression of inflation on the CBO measure of the unemployment gap. The second estimates a typical New Keynesian Phillips curve by replacing the constant term with a survey-based

Table 2

Ordinary Least Squares (OLS) Phillips Curve Regressions Using Aggregate US Data: 1990–2018

	Phillips Curve					
	Bivariate	New Keynesian	Accelerationist	Hybrid $(U_t - U_t^*)$	Hybrid (U_t)	Hybrid $B(L)(U_t - U_t^*)$
	(1)	(2)	(3)	(4)	(5)	(6)
Unemployment rate					−.081** [.038]	
Unemployment gap:	−.204*** [.074]	−.170*** [.048]	−.010 [.042]	−.078** [.037]		.503* [.272]
First lag						−1.008** [.458]
Second lag						.291 [.437]
Third lag						.152 [.237]
Sum						−.062* [.037]
Constant	2.583*** [.179]				−.054 [.284]	
Inflation expectations		.943*** [.037]		.388*** [.105]	.641*** [.152]	.384*** [.103]
Core CPI inflation:						
First lag			.404*** [.091]	.252** [.103]	.223** [.096]	.278*** [.097]
Second lag			.475*** [.083]	.343*** [.098]	.312*** [.095]	.331*** [.107]
Third lag			.092 [.089]	−.013 [.083]	−.050 [.091]	−.029 [.079]
Observations	118	118	118	118	118	118
R^2	.100	.950	.957	.963	.745	.965

Note: The first five columns in the table show the estimated OLS coefficients and standard errors for regressions nested by the hybrid Phillips curve $\pi_t = \alpha + \gamma_1(U_t - U_t^*) + \gamma_2 E_t \pi_{t+1} + \Sigma_{i=1}^3 \gamma_{2+i}\pi_{t-i} + \varepsilon_t$. Specification (1) constrains $\gamma_2 = 0$, $\gamma_3 = 0$, $\gamma_4 = 0$, and $\gamma_5 = 0$. Specification (2) constrains $\alpha = 0$, $\gamma_3 = 0$, $\gamma_4 = 0$, $\gamma_5 = 0$. Specification (3) constrains $\alpha = 0$ and $\gamma_2 = 0$. Specification (4) constrains $\alpha = 0$, and specification (5) omits U_t^* and uses U_t as the measure of activity. Specification (6) constrains $\alpha = 0$ while also including 3 lags of $(U_t - U_t^*)$. $B(L)$ represents a third-order lag polynomial. Data are quarterly seasonally adjusted measures from 1990 Q1 to 2018 Q2. Newey-West standard errors are reported in brackets. CPI = consumer price index.

*$p < .10$.
**$p < .05$.
***$p < .01$.

measure of forward-looking inflation expectations from the Survey of Professional Forecasters.[30] The third estimates an accelerationist-style Phillips curve (Phelps 1967; Friedman 1968) by using (three) lags of inflation as a proxy for inflation expectations. The fourth, fifth, and sixth columns nest both models in a hybrid Phillips curve (Gali and Gertler 1999), which features both forward-looking expectations and lags of inflation (motivated either as an alternative proxy for inflation expectations or as an additional source of inflation dynamics). The three hybrid curves feature different specifications for unemployment: they use either the unemployment rate or else the unemployment gap, with or without additional lags.

Across the different specifications, the steepest Phillips curve slopes are only –0.20 (for the bivariate regression) and –0.17 (augmenting with survey-based inflation expectations). These are in line with the flattened Phillips curve slope found by Blanchard et al. (2015). In all of the specifications featuring lags of inflation the slope is flatter still and not always significant. The sum of the coefficients on the forward- and backward-looking inflation terms is close to 1 in each of the estimates (ranging from 0.9 to 1.1), in line with natural rate theories of unemployment, which predict stable long-run inflation if and only if $U = U^*$.

In all, the results from these "naive" Phillips curve estimates would suggest that the relationship still exists but that the slope is relatively flat. Because policy makers also pay close attention to similar estimates, the identification issue we highlight has the potential to provide misleading inferences for monetary policy. A flatter Phillips curve implies a higher "sacrifice ratio" associated with bringing inflation back to target, which could lead policy makers to place greater weight than optimal on avoiding volatility in output and employment relative to inflation (Blanchard et al. 2015). At worst, weaker evidence of a clear link between real activity and inflation could be interpreted as a sign that there is no short-run policy trade-off between the two goals, leading policy makers to abandon the natural rate hypothesis (Taylor 1998; Cogley and Sargent 2001). Given its importance for policy, we next discuss the different approaches to identifying the Phillips curve using aggregate data.

B. Identification Using Aggregate Data

In the extensive literature estimating Phillips curves, a number of papers have adopted approaches similar to those we suggest, implicitly or explicitly addressing the identification difficulties we highlight here.[31]

Encouragingly, even in the period since the first draft of this paper was circulated, several others have proposed new identification strategies to mitigate simultaneity bias in Phillips curve estimation. In this subsection, we discuss the findings from some of those contributions and categorize them according to our conceptual framework.

Controlling for Supply Shocks

In principle, if econometricians can perfectly control for the effect of any cost-push or other trade-off inducing shocks, then any remaining variation in the output gap and inflation must be due to movements in aggregate demand. As in our previous estimates, the many papers that estimate Phillips curves using core inflation are already implicitly controlling for cost-push shocks to some degree, by stripping out their direct effects on the price data.[32] Others include the change in the oil price as a regressor (e.g., Roberts 1995).

The idea of controlling for supply shocks was even present in the original Phillips (1958) article, which describes periods during which cost-push effects led to deviations from the fitted curve. More recently, it has been associated with the "triangle model" of Gordon (1982), originally developed to account for the shift in inflation dynamics in the 1970s.[33] As described in Gordon (2013), the model includes several variables to control for changes in aggregate supply: food and energy price inflation, relative import price inflation, changes in trend labor productivity, and dummies reflecting the start and end of the Nixon price controls in the 1970s.[34]

Despite including these variables to control for supply shocks, Gordon (2013) still finds a flattening in the Phillips curve slope coefficient on the long-term unemployment gap: from −0.50 to −0.31 when he extends his sample from 1962–96 to 1962–2013.[35] The smaller absolute coefficient could be due to a flattening in the structural Phillips curve slope, but it could also be due to increasing difficulties with the practical implementation of the approach in the recent data. The solution is arguably more suited to helping identify the Phillips curve in a period such as the 1970s, when there were large, easily identifiable cost-push shocks and a higher variance of monetary policy shocks than more recently.[36]

A related idea is that of Coibion and Gorodnichenko (2015), who argue that the supply shock imparted by higher oil prices also pushed up inflation between 2009 and 2011 by increasing firms' inflation expectations, which they proxy using household expectations (see also

Hasenzagl et al. 2019). Following Roberts (1995), they use the Michigan Survey of Consumers and find a stable Phillips curve slope of between −0.2 and −0.3 (using the unemployment gap) in both the 1981–2007 and 1981–2013 periods.

The large number of supply variables in Gordon's model point toward a general practical difficulty with this approach, which is that there are many trade-off inducing shocks that need to be controlled for, and which of these are most important may vary over time. As an example, the explanations in the DSGE models of Christiano, Eichenbaum, and Trabandt (2015) and Gilchrist et al. (2017) for the lack of disinflation during the financial crisis rely on financial frictions that simultaneously increased inflation and decreased real activity. That suggests one may also need to add a measure of financial frictions as an additional explanatory variable.

In some senses, the many papers that estimate the slope of a Phillips curve as part of a fully specified New Keynesian DSGE model are also adopting a variant of this approach. Schorfheide (2008) shows how full information maximum likelihood estimation of a simple New Keynesian model corrects for the simultaneity bias that markup shocks introduce into the slope of the Phillips curve. But he also reports evidence from the literature on how sensitive such estimates are to model specification, with estimates of the coefficient on the output gap varying from 0 to 4.

Instrumental Variable Estimation

An alternative solution is to use instrumental variable methods. The econometrician must find a valid instrument that correlates with the demand variation in the output gap and is uncorrelated with the cost-push shock. The fitted value from a first-stage regression will then purge the output gap measure of the endogenous response of monetary policy to the cost-push shock, meaning it can be used to recover the true Phillips curve slope.

Instrumental variable methods have been common in much of the literature estimating New Keynesian Phillips curves, including influential papers by Galí and Gertler (1999) and Galí, Gertler, and López-Salido (2001). These papers use only lagged variables as instruments. Although these should be orthogonal to the current period cost-push innovation, the exclusion restriction will not generally be satisfied if the cost-push shocks exhibit autocorrelation. As discussed in Mavroeidis et al. (2014) and more recently in Barnichon and Mesters (2019), the shocks will in this case still be correlated with the lagged variables. The instruments used must be of a greater lag length than the lag order of the cost-push shocks, but with highly autocorrelated cost-push shocks, such instruments are likely to have low relevance.

Alternatively, separately identified demand shocks can be used as a set of external instruments, as recently proposed by Barnichon and Mesters (2019). To satisfy the exclusion restriction, the candidate instruments should be uncorrelated with the cost-push shocks in equation (1). Monetary policy shocks, which are not usually thought to affect supply, are a natural candidate.

Essentially, this strategy applies the findings from the large literature on identifying monetary policy shocks to recover the Phillips curve (e.g., Christiano et al. 1996, 1999; Romer and Romer 2004b; Bernanke et al. 2005; Uhlig 2005; Olivei and Tenreyro 2007; Cloyne and Hürtgen 2016). Given the major focus of that literature has been to try to remove the systematic response of monetary policy to economic developments, it should be able to successfully distill the Phillips curve relationship.

Recent work by Barnichon and Mesters (2019) follows exactly this approach. Using the Romer and Romer (2004b) narrative measure of monetary policy shocks as instruments for the output gap, they find a much steeper Phillips curve slope than under OLS.

The approach faces the same challenges as outlined by Ramey (2016) for the monetary policy shock literature. She argues that in the period since 1990, monetary policy has been set more systematically, and as a result, there is only a limited amount of true exogenous variation in the data, leading to weak instrument issues.

Identification of monetary policy shocks using high-frequency data may offer one solution (Kuttner 2001; Faust et al. 2004; Gertler and Karadi 2015; Nakamura and Steinsson 2018). The short-time windows over which these shocks are identified help remove any traces of endogenous monetary policy (Nakamura and Steinsson 2018), which might otherwise be amplified if the shocks were weak instruments for the output gap. Barnichon and Mesters (2019) use the high-frequency identified shocks of Gertler and Karadi (2015) for the post-1990 period and find evidence of a flatter Phillips curve slope than in the earlier period.

Other demand shocks, such as fiscal shocks to government spending or taxes, could in principle also be used as external instruments. But for them to successfully capture sufficient variation in the output or unemployment gap, the shocks must not be offset by any endogenous monetary policy response. In the basic model presented in Section II, fiscal shocks do not help identify the Phillips curve, because they are completely offset by optimal monetary policy. Relative to monetary policy shocks, a second drawback is that some fiscal changes are more likely to affect aggregate supply, and so they may not satisfy the exclusion restriction.

Both drawbacks are evident in the large-scale DSGE model simulations we show in the appendix (available online). Figure A2 (available online) shows that under the loss-minimizing monetary policy, there is little remaining variation in inflation and the output gap following government spending shocks. And as the shock affects supply and therefore induces a small trade-off between these two policy goals, the variation that does remain results in a negative correlation between the two variables. These simulations also highlight that the Phillips curve may vary for different types of demand shock. If so, then the curve conditional on a monetary policy shock is arguably the more relevant one for monetary policy makers, because it relates directly to their policy instrument.

Related to these ideas, a recent paper by Galí and Gambetti (forthcoming) estimates Phillips curves conditional on identified demand shocks in a vector autoregression. They find that although endogeneity issues do lead to downward bias in estimates of the US wage Phillips curve, there has also been a structural flattening over time.

C. Identification Using Regional Data

Given some of the practical difficulties using aggregate data in the presence of systematic monetary policy, an alternative solution is to exploit cross-sectional variation. An interesting recent approach in this vein is Jordà and Nechio (forthcoming), who take advantage of the fact that economies with fixed exchange rates are unable to implement independent monetary policies.

To show the possibility of using regional data to identify the aggregate US Phillips curve, we use a panel of city-level price inflation and unemployment data as in Fitzgerald and Nicolini (2014). Hooper et al. (2019) also make use of US city-level (and state-level) data in their detailed study of the US wage and price Phillips curves. Our city-level data set, containing price data, is an extended and updated version of the one used by Kiley (2015) and Babb and Detmeister (2017).

Data Description

We use data from 28 US metropolitan areas published by the US Bureau of Labor Statistics (BLS).[37] Together these areas account for more than one-third of the US population (Babb and Detmeister 2017). There is significant size heterogeneity across the sample—weighted by average labor force, the largest 3 areas (New York, Los Angeles, and Chicago) account for 31% of the total, whereas the smallest 13 areas account for less than 2% each. Because six cities in our sample were discontinued after 2017, we opt to exclude the observations from first half (H1) of 2018 onward.[38] Our full sample runs from the H1 of 1990 to the second half (H2) of 2017,[39] with some gaps for metropolitan areas where the data were only published in the later part of the sample.[40]

The inflation series is the annualized log change in the semiannual CPI excluding food and energy. For the majority of metropolitan areas, data are also available at a higher frequency, but to maximize our cross-sectional sample, we opt to convert these to semiannual data.[41] The city-level CPI data are not seasonally adjusted by the BLS.

For unemployment, we take the BLS's metropolitan statistical area (MSA) measures of unemployed as a percentage of the share of civilian labor force.[42] The BLS publishes both seasonally adjusted and unadjusted labor force data at the metro area level—we use the unadjusted series, consistent with the CPI data. We take the average of the unemployment rate to convert the monthly published data to semiannual averages.

We also run specifications using survey-based measures of 12-month inflation expectations from the University of Michigan Consumer Survey. The Michigan survey includes data published for four broad geographical regions: the North East, North Central, South, and West. We assign each metropolitan area to its appropriate region (or the region containing most of the metropolitan area's population, for metro areas that span more than one region).

Regional Data Results

To motivate our regional empirical specification, first note that we only have data on the unemployment rate at the regional level rather than the unemployment gap to proxy for the output gap. Our strategy assumes that the regional Phillips curves are of a form similar to equation (15), transformed to include the regional unemployment gap $(U_t^i - U_t^{*i})$:

$$\pi_t^i = \beta E_t \pi_{t+1}^i - \kappa(U_t^i - U_t^{*i}) + u_t^i. \tag{22}$$

If, as is likely, the regional equilibrium unemployment rate, U_t^{*i}, is positively correlated with the actual unemployment rate, then in a pooled OLS regression such as

$$\pi_{it} = \alpha + \gamma_1 E_t \pi_{it+1} + \gamma_2 U_{it} + \varepsilon_{it}, \tag{23}$$

the omitted variable will bias the estimated coefficient $\hat{\gamma}_2$ toward zero. To partially address this, we run specifications including metropolitan area fixed effects (α_i):

$$\pi_{it} = \alpha_i + \gamma_1 E_t \pi_{it+1} + \gamma_2 U_{it} + \varepsilon_{it}, \tag{24}$$

which control for time-invariant regional differences in U^* (as well as time-invariant inflation expectations), although not for time variation in those regional differences.

However, as long as the regional unemployment rate is correlated with the aggregate unemployment rate, and regional inflation is affected by aggregate cost-push shocks, the slope estimate will still be biased by the endogenous response of monetary policy to aggregate cost-push shocks. To avoid this, note that our theoretical Phillips curve in terms of regional deviations from the aggregate equation (18) can be rearranged to give

$$\pi_t^i = \pi_t + \beta E_t(\pi_{t+1}^i - \pi_{t+1}) + \kappa(x_t^i - x_t) + \hat{u}_t^i$$
$$= \beta E_t \pi_{t+1}^i + \kappa x_t^i + (\pi_t - \beta E_t \pi_{t+1} - \kappa x_t) + \hat{u}_t^i, \tag{25}$$

where x_t^i are uncorrelated with $\hat{u}_t^i$ but are correlated with the aggregate cost-push shock $u_t = \pi_t - \beta E_t \pi_{t+1} - \kappa x_t$. We can therefore remove any monetary policy-induced correlation between the regressor and the error term by also including time fixed effects (δ_t):

$$\pi_{it} = \alpha_i + \gamma_1 E_t \pi_{it+1} + \gamma_2 U_{it} + \delta_t + \varepsilon_{it}, \tag{26}$$

which will also control for any time-varying changes in the aggregate equilibrium unemployment rate.

To compare across the different specifications, we estimate each of equations (23), (24), and (26). As additional controls, we include seasonal dummies and, given the data are semiannual, just a single lag of inflation. For completeness, we also show results including time fixed effects but not including metropolitan area fixed effects. The results are shown in table 3. All four estimates of the Phillips curve slope are statistically significant and with the correct sign. In the first column, the pooled OLS estimate of −0.15 suggests a flat Phillips curve. It is slightly larger than the estimates with lagged dependent variables using aggregate data in table 2, but no steeper than the estimates without lagged inflation.[43]

Figure 10a and 10b illustrates the slope coefficient. In figure 10a, the scatter plots core inflation against unemployment. Both variables are

Table 3
US Metro Area Phillips Curve: 1990–2017

	Regression			
	Pooled OLS (1)	Metro Area FE Only (2)	Year FE Only (3)	Year and Metro Area FE (4)
Unemployment rate	−.150***	−.162***	−.272***	−.379***
	[.016]	[.019]	[.036]	[.052]
Inflation expectations	.598***	.589***	.259*	.225
	[.058]	[.059]	[.147]	[.141]
Core CPI inflation:				
First lag	.362***	.371***	.122***	.105***
	[.035]	[.036]	[.035]	[.034]
Observations	1,525	1,525	1,525	1,525
R^2	.321	.350	.450	.487
Metro area FE	No	Yes	No	Yes
Year FE	No	No	Yes	Yes
Seasonal dummies	Yes	Yes	Yes	Yes

Note: The table shows coefficients and standard errors estimated from four regional Phillips curve specifications. Core consumer price index (CPI) inflation is the dependent variable in each case. Specification (1) estimates equation (23) (plus controls) by pooled ordinary least squares (OLS). Specification (2) estimates equation (24) (plus controls) using group (area) fixed effects (FE). Specification (3) is identical to specification (1) apart from the inclusion of a set of year dummy variables. Specification (4) is identical to specification (2) apart from the inclusion of a set of year dummy variables. The additional controls are one lag of core CPI inflation and a seasonal dummy variable for each metropolitan area that takes the value of 1 in second half (H2) and 0 in first half (H1). All specifications contain a constant. Data are semiannual nonseasonally adjusted measures from 1990 H1 to 2017 H2. Robust standard errors (clustered by metro area) are reported in brackets.
*$p < .10$.
***$p < .01$.

shown as the residuals following a regression on the other controls in the first column of table 3, such that the line of best fit shows the estimated Phillips curve slope. Figure 10b shows averages of the same data, where the unemployment and inflation data are averaged across 100 equal-sized bins according to the unemployment rate.

In the second column, we include area fixed effects and the point estimate of the slope is slightly larger, although not significantly so.

In the third column, we include year fixed effects but not area fixed effects, purging the data of any aggregate-level variation over time, including changes in monetary policy and in the natural rate of unemployment. The estimated Phillips curve slope steepens to −0.27, as shown in figure 11a and 11b.

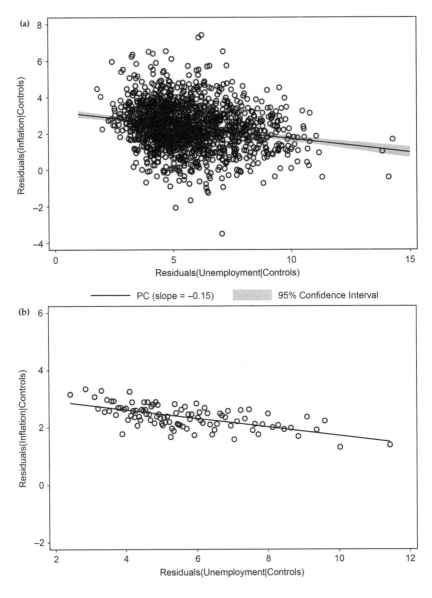

Fig. 10. Pooled ordinary least squares: metropolitan area core consumer price index (CPI) inflation versus unemployment (both regressed on controls). The figures are a graphical illustration of the Phillips curve (PC) slope estimated in specification (1) in table 3: (*a*) the residuals from a regression of core CPI inflation on all regressors other than the unemployment rate, against the residuals from a regression of the unemployment rate on all other regressors; (*b*) averages of the same data, where the unemployment and inflation data are averaged across 100 equal-sized bins according to the unemployment rate.

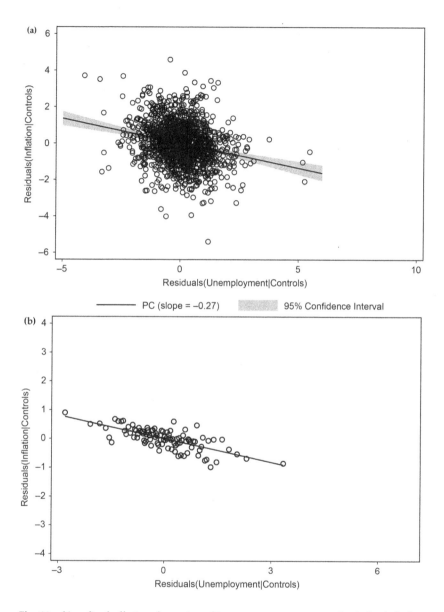

Fig. 11. Year fixed effects only: metropolitan area core consumer price index inflation versus unemployment (both regressed on controls). The figures are a graphical illustration of the Phillips curve (PC) slope estimated in specification (3) in table 3. See figure 10*a* and 10*b* for details.

In the fourth column, metro area fixed effects are also included, controlling for any time-invariant unobserved factors such as different average levels of U^* across regions. The resulting Phillips curve is -0.38, 2.5 times larger than the pooled OLS estimate.[44] The residuals and slopes including both sets of fixed effects are shown in figure 12a and 12b, as well as in figure 13, which plots the estimated Phillips curve by metropolitan area, with different intercept terms for each city.

These results provide evidence of a steeper US Phillips curve at the regional level. They are consistent with the idea that because monetary policy endogenously offsets changes in aggregate demand and leans against cost-push shocks, identification is blurred at the aggregate level.

Robustness

As discussed in Section IV.C, including time fixed effects in our regional Phillips curve estimates removes the bias from aggregate supply shocks and the endogenous monetary policy response to them. But regional inflation may still be affected by idiosyncratic regional cost-push or supply shocks. Although aggregate monetary policy should not respond to regional deviations in inflation, the shocks themselves may still be positively correlated with regional unemployment. If so, our estimates will still be biased against finding a steep negative slope. If regional supply shocks are important, our estimate of -0.38 should be interpreted as a lower bound (in absolute terms), with the true Phillips curve slope steeper still.

To examine the robustness of our results, we next explore two strategies that may help mitigate simultaneity bias from regional supply shocks. Each is analogous to one of our suggested solutions using aggregate data.

First, one option is to use a regional demand instrument to purge the unemployment data of regional supply shocks. We do this using a Bartik (1991)-type instrument for regional government spending. In doing so, we adapt the methods of Nekarda and Ramey (2011), who use a Bartik instrument to examine the effect of government spending at the industry level, and of Nakamura and Steinsson (2014), who compute the effect of military spending on different US states and regions.

Bartik-type instruments are formed by interacting a time-invariant, region-specific "exposure" variable, which we denote B_i, and a national (or industry) growth rate or shock.[45] In our setting, we construct a Bartik exposure variable, B_i, that aims to capture which cities are likely to be more affected by changes in national government spending. To do so, we take the inner product of each industry j share of nominal shipments

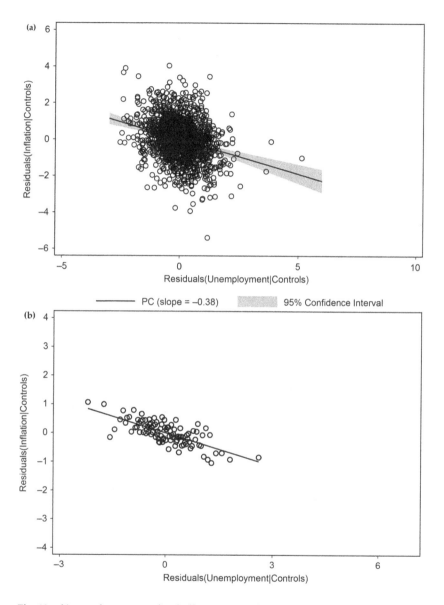

Fig. 12. Year and metro area fixed effects: metropolitan area core consumer price index inflation versus unemployment (both regressed on controls). The figures are a graphical illustration of the Phillips curve (PC) slope estimated in specification (4) in table 3. See figure 10a and 10b for details.

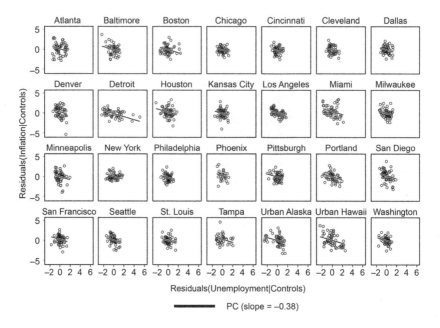

Fig. 13. Year and metro area fixed effects: metropolitan area core consumer price index (CPI) inflation versus unemployment by metro area (both regressed on controls). The figures are a graphical illustration of the Phillips curve (PC) slope estimated in specification (4) in table 3. For each metropolitan area, the figure plots the residuals from a fixed effects regression of core CPI inflation on all regressors other than the unemployment rate, with a different area fixed effect plotted for each city, against the residuals from a fixed effects regression of the unemployment rate on all other regressors.

to government (in 1992), θ_j, from the data set of manufacturing industries constructed by Nekarda and Ramey (2011), and the city's share of employment in that industry (in 1993), E_{ij}/E_i, from the Census Bureau's County Business Patterns:

$$B_i \equiv \sum_j \theta_j \frac{E_{ij}}{E_i}. \qquad (27)$$

We combine these data sources at the two-digit Standard Industrial Classification (SIC) level, which gives us 20 distinct industries.[46] We then interact our exposure variable with a measure of the growth rate of real aggregate federal government consumption, or federal government defense consumption, taken from the Bureau of Economic Analysis's National Income and Product Account tables. The intuition underlying the instrument is that increases in national government spending should increase demand more in more highly exposed cities. Highly exposed cities are those where employment is skewed toward industries that are more heavily involved in producing shipments to government, particularly defense-oriented industries.

Table 4 shows the results of the instrumental variable estimation. For convenience, the first column repeats the OLS results with year and metro

Table 4
US Metro Area Phillips Curve, Instrumental Variables Estimates: 1990–2017

		Regression			
		2SLS Instrument			
	OLS	$\Delta_{3y}\ln G_t^D \times B_i$	$\Delta_{3y}\ln G_t \times B_i$	$C(L)\Delta\ln G_t \times B_i$	$\Delta_{3y}\ln G_t^D \times \alpha_i$
	(1)	(2)	(3)	(4)	(5)
Unemployment rate	−.379***	−.454**	−.392*	−.252	−.508***
	[.052]	[.209]	[.207]	[.158]	[.105]
Inflation expectations	.225 ·	.219	.224	.201	.215
	[.141]	[.141]	[.139]	[.138]	[.139]
Core CPI inflation:					
First lag	.105***	.089	.103*	.119**	.077**
	[.034]	[.057]	[.056]	[.049]	[.034]
Observations	1,525	1,525	1,525	1,413	1,525
R^2	.487	.485	.487	.486	.482
		2SLS First-Stage Estimates[a]			
Gov. spending instrument		9.237***	11.027***		
		[2.104]	[2.434]		
Sum of leads/lags				5.642	
				[4.446]	
R^2		.828	.828	.836	.849
Instrument(s) F-stat		83.5	84.8	12.0	10.4
Cluster robust F-stat		19.3	20.5	11.5	n/a

Note: Specification for all regressions is the same as specification (4) in table 3. B_i is as defined in the text. G_t is the semiannual level of real federal government consumption. G_t^D is the semiannual level of real federal government defense consumption. $C(L)$ is the sum of a sixth-order lag and sixth-order lead polynomial. α_i is a metro area fixed effect. All regressions include year and metro area fixed effects and a set of seasonal dummies for each metro area. Regression (4) is estimated over a sample from 1990 first half (H1) to 2015 second half (H2). All other regressions are estimated over a sample from 1990 H1 to 2017 H2. All instruments are standardized to have a unit variance. Robust standard errors (clustered by metro area) are reported in brackets. OLS = ordinary least squares; 2SLS = two-stage least squares; CPI = consumer price index; n/a = not applicable.
[a]Dependent variable: unemployment rate.
*$p < .10$.
**$p < .05$.
***$p < .01$.

area fixed effects. The remaining columns show results with different variants of the instrument. The second column interacts the exposure variable with the 3-year log change in (real) federal government defense consumption; the third column uses the 3-year log change in total federal government consumption. The fourth column uses six leads and lags of the semiannual change in total federal government consumption. The final column uses a variant of the instrument used by Nakamura and Steinsson (2014) and interacts the 3-year log change in defense consumption with a metro area fixed effect rather than the Bartik exposure variable.

Examining the results, they raise questions about the usefulness of our government demand instrument at the city level, in contrast to the findings of Nakamura and Steinsson (2014) at the state level. The second-stage results give broadly similar point estimates of the Phillips curve slope, albeit with much higher standard errors. But the first-stage results consistently suggest that increases in national government spending lead to significant increases in unemployment in areas with higher exposure relative to areas with lower exposure, rather than decreases. If the instrument was successfully capturing variation in aggregate demand, we would expect these coefficients to be negative. It therefore seems highly unlikely that the instrument is successfully purging the data of any regional supply shocks.[47]

Second, we already control for regional cost-push shocks to some extent by excluding from our CPI measure some of the products that are most likely to be affected by them: food and energy. If some areas are more exposed to increases in food and energy inflation, then headline regional inflation will be subject to greater regional cost-push shocks in those areas. But if such shocks are important, we would expect them to exert a smaller direct influence on core CPI inflation, leading to a smaller negative bias.

In table A1 (available online), we compare our baseline results to Phillips curves estimated using alternative subsets of the CPI basket, and we find that the slopes are broadly similar across different measures. This provides some reassurance that regional supply shocks are not exerting a significant bias on our results.

VI. Conclusion

We use a standard analytical framework to explain why inflation follows a seemingly exogenous statistical process or, in other words, why the Phillips curve cannot be easily identified with macroeconomic data.

In the framework, a monetary authority minimizes welfare losses, measured as deviations of inflation and output from their targets, subject to a Phillips curve. This leads the authority to follow an optimal targeting rule in which it seeks to increase inflation when the output gap decreases. This imparts a negative relation between inflation and the output gap that blurs the identification of the positively sloped Phillips curve. In equilibrium, inflation inherits the statistical properties of any cost-push shocks affecting the Phillips curves (e.g., energy price shocks, exchange rate changes).

We show that shocks to the targeting rule are key for the identification of the Phillips curve. These targeting shocks can take the form of monetary policy shocks in a Taylor rule or, in a multiregion setting or a multicountry monetary union, idiosyncratic demand shocks affecting the various regions or countries in different ways. In a univariate regression analysis, if the relative variance of these shocks is sufficiently high, vis-à-vis the remaining variance of the cost-push shocks that cannot be controlled for, the slope of the Phillips curve can be identified. Similarly, identification of monetary policy or other demand shocks allows the positive relationship between inflation and output gap to be distilled.

We have also shown how the simple framework here can jointly rationalize several empirical findings on the Phillips curve. First, it should be weaker in periods when there are large cost shocks—such as the 1970s—and when monetary policy is relatively successful in achieving its targets—as in the inflation-targeting era. Second, wage Phillips curves should be more evident in the data that price Phillips curves. And third, the Phillips curve relationship should appear stronger in disaggregated panel data than in aggregate data.

To summarize, the paper explains the identification problem posited by the estimation of Phillips curves, rationalizes findings in the empirical literature, and discusses practical solutions to the identification problem, showing evidence of a steeper Phillips curve in US regional data. In doing so, the paper hopes to address a recent wave of work questioning the existence of a link between inflation and slack, a key building block of the prevalent monetary policy framework.

Endnotes

Author email addresses: McLeay (michael.mcleay@bankofengland.co.uk), Tenreyro (s.tenreyro@lse.ac.uk). This paper was motivated by a conversation with Ben Broadbent and Jan Vlieghe. We would like to thank participants at the 34th NBER Annual Conference on Macroeconomics; as well as Francesco Caselli, Martin Eichenbaum, Benjamin Friedman, Mark Gertler, Marc Giannoni, Andy Haldane, Richard Harrison, Michael

Klein, Per Krussell, John Leahy, Clare Macallan, Frederic Mishkin, Jonathan Parker, Valerie Ramey, Chris Redl, Ricardo Reis, Matthew Rognlie, Martin Seneca, Jan Vlieghe, Matt Waldron, and Iván Werning for helpful discussions, comments, and suggestions; and Oliver Ashtari Tafti for superb research assistance. Tenreyro acknowledges financial support from ERC grant MACROTRADE 681664. The views expressed herein are those of the authors and do not necessarily reflect the views of the Bank of England or the National Bureau of Economic Research. For acknowledgments, sources of research support, and disclosure of the authors' material financial relationships, if any, please see https:// www.nber.org/chapters/c14245.ack.

1. For a selection of the vast media comment on the issue, see articles in the *Financial Times*, the *Wall Street Journal*, and the *Economist* and opinion pieces by Alan Blinder, Paul Krugman, and Lawrence Summers linked in the working paper draft of this article (available online).

The output gap is defined as the deviation of output from its potential; in the original paper of Phillips (1958), the focus was the negative relationship between wage inflation and unemployment.

2. This result follows straightforwardly from the basic New Keynesian model as derived in Clarida et al. (1999), whereas similar results would obtain in the classic setting of Barro and Gordon (1983).

3. See also a series of blog posts by Nick Rowe (e.g., https://worthwhile.typepad.com /worthwhile_canadian_initi/2010/12/milton-friedmans-thermostat.html), who uses the analogy (credited to Milton Friedman) of the relationship between a room's temperature and its thermostat.

4. Relatedly, others have examined mechanisms through which changes in monetary policy behavior could change the underlying structural Phillips curve. For example, Ball, Mankiw, and Romer (1988) showed how increases in average inflation rates, by changing the frequency with which firms reset prices, could change the deep parameters that determine its slope.

5. Gordon (2013) terms it the "Fed view."

6. The effect of endogenous monetary policy on inflation expectations also features in some leading explanations of the "missing disinflation" following the financial crisis, such as Del Negro, Giannoni, and Schorfheide (2015).

7. In the full model derived in Galí (2008), this is the welfare-relevant gap between output and its efficient level.

8. Clarida et al. (1999) show how minimizing such a loss function is equivalent to maximizing the welfare of the representative agent in the model. But it can alternatively be motivated as a simple way to capture the preferences enshrined in the mandates of modern (flexible) inflation targeting central banks: see Carney (2017b), for example.

9. It is also consistent with the observation that in larger DSGE models such as Smets and Wouters (2007), inflation is largely explained by exogenous markup shocks (King and Watson 2012).

10. Stock and Watson (2009) raise the possibility that, despite its failure to forecast or explain the data, the Phillips curve is still useful for conditional forecasting. They pose the question, "suppose you are told that next quarter the economy would plunge into recession, with the unemployment rate jumping by 2 percentage points. Would you change your inflation forecast?" (100).

11. See Nason and Smith (2008), Mavroeidis, et al. (2014), and Krogh (2015) for discussions.

12. Using equation (3) to substitute out for π_t in equation (2) gives the equilibrium evolution of the output gap $x_t = -\kappa/(\kappa^2 + \lambda(1 - \beta\rho))u_t$, whereas the regression error term is equal to $\varepsilon_t = u_t + \beta E_t \pi_{t+1} = (1 + \rho\lambda/(\kappa^2 + \lambda(1 - \beta\rho)))u_t$.

13. This graphical illustration of optimal discretionary policy is from Seneca (2018): we are grateful to him for making it available to us. A similar graphical exposition appears in Carlin and Soskice (2005) as well as in papers at least as far back as Kareken and Miller (1976; with thanks to Marc Giannoni for alerting us to the latter reference).

14. Other than the fact that the slope of the Phillips curve happens to appear in the optimal targeting rule.

15. Clarida et al. (1999) and Svensson and Woodford (2004) show in the basic New Keynesian model that when there are policy control lags that mean all variables are

predetermined in advance, up to an unforecastable shock, the optimal targeting rule will take exactly this form, where e_t is the forecast error. We subtract it from the right-hand side of equation (11) to match the usual convention that a positive monetary policy shock involves a policy tightening.

16. Carlstrom et al. (2009) show a similar equation to illustrate the OLS estimate bias in their framework.

17. Nakamura and Steinsson (2014) present evidence that endogenous monetary and tax policies reduce national fiscal multipliers relative to local ones.

18. This differs from the monetary policy that would be welfare-optimal in the model, because welfare would also be lowered by dispersion in prices within a region, even if average inflation was zero. Clarida, Galí, and Gertler (2001) show in the context of an open economy model that the welfare-optimal policy would minimize a loss function that included the sum across countries of the squared deviations of inflation rather than the square of the sum of deviations.

19. Although to ensure determinacy, the policy maker's instrument rule will need to respond to idiosyncratic variables.

20. Although this is one solution, depending on how policy is implemented, there may be a multiplicity of equilbria. It is beyond the scope of this paper to study those, so we assume that the policy maker's instrument rule is able to rule them out. In practice, this will involve responding to deviations of regional inflation or regional output gaps from their equilibrium values, even when those deviations have no impact on aggregate inflation or the aggregate output gap.

21. Galí (2011) shows how the basic framework can be easily extended to include unemployment in a way that closely resembles the output gap in the basic model.

22. In addition, the welfare-optimal policy in models with sticky wages typically involves placing a positive weight on avoiding wage inflation (Erceg et al. 2000). But we are not aware of any central banks that officially target wage inflation in practice.

23. See, for example, Brubakk and Sveen (2009); Edge, Kiley, and Laforte (2010); Adolfson et al. (2013); Burgess et al. (2013) for descriptions of models used respectively at Norges Bank, the Federal Reserve Board, the Riksbank, and the Bank of England.

24. Estimated Taylor rules often find large coefficients on interest rate smoothing, which will limit the amount the policy maker in the model chooses to offset large movements in contemporaneous inflation.

25. Figure A2 (available online) shows the correlation under discretion conditional on each shock. In this more complex setting, the reduced-form slope does not represent any single optimal targeting rule. But the same intuition continues to hold: monetary policy will seek to minimize any variation in the output gap that would cause inflation to move in the same direction. Conversely, following a markup (or cost-push) shock, monetary policy will aim to reduce the output gap at times when inflation is above target.

26. In the model simulated before, there is a more stable positive relationship across different shocks between inflation and the relevant measure of real marginal costs than with the output gap.

27. See Barnichon and Mesters (2019), Galí and Gambetti (forthcoming), and Jordà and Nechio (forthcoming) for some recent examples, discussed further in the text.

28. We also lag the tenure dates by six quarters to reflect the lags between monetary policy actions and their effect on real activity and inflation. Christiano et al. (2005) and Boivin and Giannoni (2006) both find that monetary policy has its peak impact on output after around four quarters, and on quarterly inflation after eight quarters.

29. We split the sample at the end of 1983 in line with convention in dating the Volcker disinflation (Goodfriend and King 2005).

30. We use 10-year ahead inflation expectations, as suggested by Bernanke (2007) and Yellen (2015) as having a stronger empirical fit with the data. We also extend the time series back seven quarters to 1990 Q1 using the additional 10-year ahead CPI inflation expectations data series from other sources provided on the Survey of Professional Forecasters webpage (combined from the Philidelphia Fed's Livingston Survey and from the Blue Chip Economic Indicators); and by linearly interpolating two remaining missing datapoints for 1990 Q3 and 1991 Q3. See Coibion, Gorodnichenko, and Kamdar (2018) for an extensive review of the use of survey expectations in the Philllips curve.

31. See Mavroeidis et al. (2014) for a comprehensive summary.

32. See Hasenzagl et al. (2019) for evidence on the different channels through which cost-push shocks to energy prices affect inflation.

33. It was subsequently refined in a series of papers, most recently in Gordon (2013).

34. The model also includes a large number of lags of inflation (up to 6 years) to capture additional dynamic factors affecting inflation.

35. Gordon instead emphasizes the smaller flattening in the point estimate when using the short-term unemployment rate as the relevant concept of slack, although this measure correlates less closely with estimates of the overall output gap than the total unemployment rate—largely due to the large negative output gap during the financial crisis.

36. The standard deviation of the Romer and Romer (2004b) monetary policy shock series is 2.5 times smaller in the period from 1990 onward.

37. We list the full set of areas we use in the appendix (available online). The earlier conference draft of this paper used a smaller sample of only 23 areas. Moving to the full set yields almost identical results.

38. We use the terms "city" and "metropolitan area" interchangeably.

39. Metropolitan area unemployment is published from 1990. In the conference draft of this paper, we also used CPI price-level data only from 1990 onward. Here we make use of the pre-1990 CPI data to construct inflation (and lagged inflation) rates for 1990.

40. CPI data for Tampa are published only from 1997 H2; Phoenix from 2002 H1. Our results are robust to excluding both cities.

41. Where the semiannual CPI figure is published by the BLS, we use that. Where only monthly data are published, we take the semiannual average. Where the published data are published only in certain months, we follow BLS methodology and estimate the missing months via interpolation, before taking the semiannual average (see also Fitzgerald and Nicolini 2014).

42. The local unemployment data use the core-based statistical area (CBSA) delineations of metropolitan areas, which the CPI data have also used since 2018, having previously used sightly different MSA definitions. We match the unemployment data to the currently used definition, because the BLS treats this as continuous with the old one for CPI. For the subset of cities where CPI data were only ever published under the old definition, we sum unemployment and the labor force data for the matching CBSA metropolitan and micropolitan areas.

43. Note that the estimated coefficient on inflation expectations is not robust to changes in the sample. Estimating pooled OLS on a sample beginning in 1991 instead of 1990 reduces the point estimate from 0.60 to 0.36.

44. Because the pooled OLS results have a higher coefficient on lagged inflation, then taken literally, the estimates suggest that the medium-run Phillips curve slopes are more similar across specifications, a point made by our discussant Matthew Rognlie. But we are inclined to focus more on the instantaneous slope coefficient, because the coefficient on lagged inflation is likely to be picking up inflation persistence unrelated to changes in unemployment. Moreover, the Phillips curve slope coefficients we report are relatively robust to including different dynamic specifications (or no dynamics) or to estimating using annual or biannual data.

45. See Borusyak, Hull, and Jaravel (2018); Goldsmith-Pinkham, Sorkin, and Swift (2018); and Jaeger, Ruist, and Stuhler (2018) for recent critical discussions of the use of these instruments.

46. The County Business Patterns publish employment data at the MSA level from 1993 but only at the two-digit level of aggregation. We have also experimented with aggregating the underlying county data, which are published at the four-digit SIC code level. This has the drawback that for a large fraction of the industry-county pairs, the employment data are published only as a range. A smaller fraction of industry-MSA pairs is also published only as a range. Where this is the case, we take the midpoints of the range.

47. Instead, the instrument appears to be combining the fact that national government has been countercyclical over our sample with the fact that those cities with higher values of B_i also seem to be more cyclical. As evidence of the latter fact, a regression of the regional unemployment rate on our exposure variable interacted with the simple average of metro area unemployment rates also leads to a significant positive coefficient. This is in contrast to the finding reported by Nakamura and Steinsson (2014) when carrying out a similar test at the state level using their instrument.

References

Adolfson, Malin, Stefan Laséen, Lawrence Christiano, Mathias Trabandt, and Karl Walentin. 2013. "Ramses II—Model Description." Occasional Paper Series 12, Sveriges Riksbank, Stockholm.

Atkeson, Andrew, and Lee E. Ohanian. 2001. "Are Phillips Curves Useful for Forecasting Inflation?" *Federal Reserve Bank of Minneapolis Quarterly Review* 25 (1): 2–11.

Babb, Nathan R., and Alan K. Detmeister. 2017. "Nonlinearities in the Phillips Curve for the United States: Evidence Using Metropolitan Data." Finance and Economics Discussion Series 2017-070, Board of Governors of the Federal Reserve System, Washington, DC.

Ball, Laurence, N. Gregory Mankiw, and David Romer. 1988. "The New Keynesian Economics and the Output-Inflation Trade-off." *Brookings Papers on Economic Activity* 1:1–65.

Ball, Laurence, and Sandeep Mazumder. 2011. "Inflation Dynamics and the Great Recession." *Brookings Papers on Economic Activity* 42 (Spring): 337–81.

Barnichon, Regis, and Geert Mesters. 2019. "Identifying Modern Macro Equations with Old Shocks." Discussion Paper no. DP13765, Center for Economic and Policy Research, Washington, DC. https://docs.wixstatic.com/ugd/8ac201_48b1201ec4a74fddae04bcc5aadf9c89.pdf.

Barro, Robert J., and David B. Gordon. 1983. "A Positive Theory of Monetary Policy in a Natural Rate Model." *Journal of Political Economy* 91 (4): 589–610.

Bartik, Timothy J. 1991. *Who Benefits from State and Local Economic Development Policies?* Kalamazoo, MI: W. E. Upjohn Institute for Employment Research.

Bernanke, Ben S. 2007. "Inflation Expectations and Inflation Forecasting." Speech given at the Monetary Economics Workshop of the NBER Summer Institute, Cambridge, MA. https://www.federalreserve.gov/newsevents/speech/bernanke20070710a.htm.

———. 2010. "The Economic Outlook and Monetary Policy." Speech given at the Federal Reserve Bank of Kansas City Economic Symposium, Jackson Hole, WY. https://www.federalreserve.gov/newsevents/speech/files/bernanke20100827a.pdf.

Bernanke, Ben S., Jean Boivin, and Piotr Eliasz. 2005. "Measuring the Effects of Monetary Policy: A Factor-Augmented Vector Autoregressive (FAVAR) Approach." *Quarterly Journal of Economics* 120 (1): 387–422.

Blanchard, Olivier. 2016. "The Phillips Curve: Back to the '60s?" *American Economic Review* 106 (5): 31–34.

Blanchard, Olivier, Eugenio Cerutti, and Lawrence Summers. 2015. "Inflation and Activity—Two Explorations and Their Monetary Policy Implications." Working Paper no. 21726, NBER, Cambridge, MA.

Blinder, Alan S. 1982. "The Anatomy of Double-Digit Inflation in the 1970s." In *Inflation: Causes and Effects*, ed. Robert E. Hall, 261–82. Chicago: University of Chicago Press. https://www.nber.org/books/hall82-1.

Board of Governors of the Federal Reserve System. 2000. "Monetary Policy Report to the Congress." Board of Governors, February. https://www.federalreserve.gov/boarddocs/hh/2000/February/FullReport.pdf.

Boivin, Jean, and Marc P. Giannoni. 2006. "Has Monetary Policy Become More Effective?" *Review of Economics and Statistics* 88 (3): 445–62.

Borusyak, Kirill, Peter Hull, and Xavier Jaravel. 2018. "Quasi-Experimental Shift-Share Research Designs." Working Paper no. 24997, NBER, Cambridge, MA.

Brainard, William C., and James Tobin. 1968. "Pitfalls in Financial Model Building." *American Economic Review* 58 (2): 99–122.

Brubakk, Leif, and Tommy Sveen. 2009. *NEMO—A New Macro Model for Forecasting and Monetary Policy Analysis.* Norges Bank Economic Bulletin 1/2009. Oslo: Norges Bank.

Bullard, James. 2018. "The Case of the Disappearing Phillips Curve." Presentation at the 2018 ECB Forum on Central Banking on the Macroeconomics of Price- and Wage-Setting, Sintra, Portugal, June 19. https://www.stlouisfed.org/~/media/files/pdfs/bullard/remarks/2018/bullard_ecb_sintra_june_19_2018.pdf.

Burgess, Stephen, Emilio Fernandez-Corugedo, Charlotta Groth, Richard Harrison, Francesca Monti, Konstantinos Theodoridis, and Matt Waldron. 2013. "The Bank of England's Forecasting Platform: COMPASS, MAPS, EASE and the Suite of Models." Working Paper no. 471, Bank of England, London.

Carlin, Wendy, and David Soskice. 2005. "The 3-Equation New Keynesian Model—A Graphical Exposition." *B.E. Journal of Macroeconomics* 5 (1): 1–38.

Carlstrom, Charles T., Timothy S. Fuerst, and Matthias Paustian. 2009. "Inflation Persistence, Monetary Policy, and the Great Moderation." *Journal of Money, Credit and Banking* 41 (4): 767–86.

Carney, Mark. 2017a. "[De]Globalisation and Inflation." Speech delivered at the 2017 IMF Michel Camdessus Central Banking Lecture. https://www.bankofengland.co.uk/-/media/boe/files/speech/2017/de-globalisation-and-inflation.pdf.

———. 2017b. "Lambda." Speech given at the London School of Economics. https://www.bankofengland.co.uk/-/media/boe/files/speech/2017/lambda.pdf.

Cecchetti, Stephen G., Michael E. Feroli, Peter Hooper, Anil K. Kashyap, and Kermit L. Schoenholtz. 2017. "Deflating Inflation Expectations: The Implications of Inflation's Simple Dynamics." US Monetary Policy Forum. http://people.brandeis.edu/~cecchett/Polpdf/USMPF2017.pdf.

Chari, V. V., Lawrence J. Christiano, and Martin Eichenbaum. 1998. "Expectation Traps and Discretion." *Journal of Economic Theory* 81 (2): 462–92.

Christiano, Lawrence J., Martin Eichenbaum, and Charles L. Evans. 1996. "The Effects of Monetary Policy Shocks: Evidence from the Flow of Funds." *Review of Economics and Statistics* 78 (1): 16–34.

———. 1999. "Monetary Policy Shocks: What Have We Learned and to What End?" In *Handbook of Macroeconomics*, Vol. 1A, ed. John B. Taylor and Michael Woodford, 65–148. Amsterdam: Elsevier.

———. 2005. "Nominal Rigidities and the Dynamic Effects of a Shock to Monetary Policy." *Journal of Political Economy* 113 (1): 1–45.

Christiano, Lawrence J., Martin Eichenbaum, and Mathias Trabandt. 2015. "Understanding the Great Recession." *American Economic Journal: Macroeconomics* 7 (1): 110–67.

Clarida, Richard, Jordi Galí, and Mark Gertler. 1999. "The Science of Monetary Policy: A New Keynesian Perspective." *Journal of Economic Literature* 37 (4): 1661–707.

———. 2000. "Monetary Policy Rules and Macroeconomic Stability: Evidence and Some Theory." *Quarterly Journal of Economics* 115 (1): 147–80.

———. 2001. "Optimal Monetary Policy in Open versus Closed Economies: An Integrated Approach." *American Economic Review* 91 (2): 248–52.

Cloyne, James, and Patrick Hürtgen. 2016. "The Macroeconomic Effects of Monetary Policy: A New Measure for the United Kingdom." *American Economic Journal: Macroeconomics* 8 (4): 75–102.

Cochrane, John H. 1994. "Comment on 'What Ends Recessions?' by Christina D. Romer and David H. Romer." *NBER Macroeconomics Annual* 9:58–74.

Cogley, Timothy, and Thomas J. Sargent. 2001. "Evolving Post-World War II US Inflation Dynamics." *NBER Macroeconomics Annual* 16:331–73.

Coibion, Olivier, and Yuriy Gorodnichenko. 2015. "Is the Phillips Curve Alive and Well after All? Inflation Expectations and the Missing Disinflation." *American Economic Journal: Macroeconomics* 7 (1): 197–232.

Coibion, Olivier, Yuriy Gorodnichenko, and Rupal Kamdar. 2018. "The Formation of Expectations, Inflation, and the Phillips Curve." *Journal of Economic Literature* 56 (4): 1447–91.

Del Negro, Marco, Marc P. Giannoni, and Frank Schorfheide. 2015. "Inflation in the Great Recession and New Keynesian Models." *American Economic Journal: Macroeconomics* 7 (1): 168–96.

DeLong, J. Bradford. 1997. "America's Peacetime Inflation: The 1970s." In *Reducing Inflation: Motivation and Strategy*, ed. Christina D. Romer and David H. Romer, 247–80. Chicago: University of Chicago Press. http://www.nber.org/books/rome97-1.

Dennis, Richard. 2007. "Optimal Policy in Rational Expectations Models: New Solution Algorithms." *Macroeconomic Dynamics* 11 (1): 31–55.

Dotsey, Michael, Shigeru Fujita, and Tom Stark. 2018. "Do Phillips Curves Conditionally Help to Forecast Inflation?" *International Journal of Central Banking* 14 (4): 43–92.

Draghi, Mario. 2017. "Accompanying the Economic Recovery." Speech given at the ECB Forum on Central Banking, Sintra, Portugal, June 27. https://www.ecb.europa.eu/press/key/date/2017/html/ecb.sp170627.en.html.

Edge, Rochelle M., and Refet S. Gürkaynak. 2010. "How Useful Are Estimated DSGE Model Forecasts for Central Bankers?" *Brookings Papers on Economic Activity* 41 (2): 209–44.

Edge, Rochelle M., Michael T. Kiley, and Jean-Philippe Laforte. 2010. "A Comparison of Forecast Performance between Federal Reserve Staff Forecasts, Simple Reduced-Form Models, and a DSGE Model." *Journal of Applied Econometrics* 25 (4): 720–54.

Erceg, Christopher J., Dale W. Henderson, and Andrew T. Levin. 2000. "Optimal Monetary Policy with Staggered Wage and Price Contracts." *Journal of Monetary Economics* 46 (2): 281–313.

Faust, Jon, Eric T. Swanson, and Jonathan H. Wright. 2004. "Identifying VARS Based on High Frequency Futures Data." *Journal of Monetary Economics* 51 (6): 1107–31.

Fitzgerald, Terry J., and Juan Pablo Nicolini. 2014. "Is There a Stable Relationship between Unemployment and Future Inflation? Evidence from US Cities." Working Paper no. 713, Federal Reserve Bank of Minneapolis.

Forbes, Kristin, Lewis Kirkham, and Konstantinos Theodoridis. 2017. "A Trendy Approach to UK Inflation Dynamics." Discussion Paper no. 49, Bank of England External MPC Unit, London.

Friedman, Milton. 1968. "The Role of Monetary Policy." *American Economic Review* 58 (1): 1–17.

Gali, Jordi. 2008. *Monetary Policy, Inflation, and the Business Cycle: An Introduction to the New Keynesian Framework*. Princeton, NJ: Princeton University Press.

———. 2011. "The Return of the Wage Phillips Curve." *Journal of the European Economic Association* 9 (3): 436–61.

Gali, Jordi, and Luca Gambetti. Forthcoming. "Has the US Wage Phillips Curve Flattened? A Semi-Structural Exploration." In *Changing Inflation Dynamics, Evolving Monetary Policy*, ed. J. Gali and D. Saravia. Santiago: Central Bank of Chile.

Galí, Jordi, and Mark Gertler. 1999. "Inflation Dynamics: A Structural Econometric Analysis." *Journal of Monetary Economics* 44 (2): 195–222.

Galí, Jordi, Mark Gertler, and J. David López-Salido. 2001. "European Inflation Dynamics." *European Economic Review* 45 (7): 1237–70.

Gertler, Mark, and Peter Karadi. 2015. "Monetary Policy Surprises, Credit Costs, and Economic Activity." *American Economic Journal: Macroeconomics* 7 (1): 44–76.

Gilchrist, Simon, Raphael Schoenle, Jae Sim, and Egon Zakrajšek. 2017. "Inflation Dynamics during the Financial Crisis." *American Economic Review* 107 (3): 785–823.

Goldfeld, Stephen M., and Alan S. Blinder. 1972. "Some Implications of Endogenous Stabilization Policy." *Brookings Papers on Economic Activity* 1972 (3): 585–644.

Goldsmith-Pinkham, Paul, Isaac Sorkin, and Henry Swift. 2018. "Bartik Instruments: What, When, Why, and How." Working Paper no. 24088, NBER, Cambridge, MA.

Goodfriend, Marvin, and Robert G. King. 2005. "The Incredible Volcker Disinflation." *Journal of Monetary Economics* 52 (5): 981–1015.

Goodhart, C. A. E. 1984. "Problems of Monetary Management: The UK Experience." In *Monetary Theory and Practice*, 91–121. London: Palgrave. https://rd.springer.com/chapter/10.1007/978-1-349-17295-5_4.

———. 1989. *Money, Information and Uncertainty*. Basingstoke: Macmillan International Higher Education.

Gordon, Robert J. 1977. "The Theory of Domestic Inflation." *American Economic Review* 67 (1): 128–34.

———. 1982. "Inflation, Flexible Exchange Rates, and the Natural Rate of Unemployment." In *Workers, Jobs, and Inflation*, ed. Martin Neil Baily. Washington, DC: Brookings Institution.

———. 2011. "The History of the Phillips Curve: Consensus and Bifurcation." *Economica* 78 (309): 10–50.

———. 2013. "The Phillips Curve Is Alive and Well: Inflation and the NAIRU during the Slow Recovery." Working Paper no. 19390, NBER, Cambridge, MA.

Haldane, Andrew G. 1998. "On Inflation Targeting in the United Kingdom." *Scottish Journal of Political Economy* 45 (1): 1–32.

Haldane, Andrew G., and Danny Quah. 1999. "UK Phillips Curves and Monetary Policy." *Journal of Monetary Economics* 44 (2): 259–78.

Hall, Robert E. 2013. "The Routes Into and Out of the Zero Lower Bound." Paper presented at the Global Dimensions of Unconventional Monetary Policy Federal Reserve Bank of Kansas City Symposium, Jackson Hole, WY. https://www.kansascityfed.org/publicat/sympos/2013/2013hall.pdf.

Hasenzagl, Thomas, Filippo Pellegrino, Lucrezia Reichlin, and Giovanni Ricco. 2019. "A Model of the Fed's View on Inflation." Discussion Paper no. 12564, Center for Economic and Policy Research, Washington, DC.

Hooper, Peter, Frederic S. Mishkin, and Amir Sufi. 2019. "Prospects for Inflation in a High Pressure Economy: Is the Phillips Curve Dead or Is It Just Hibernating?" Working Paper no. 25792, NBER, Cambridge, MA.

IMF (International Monetary Fund). 2013. "The Dog That Didn't Bark: Has Inflation Been Muzzled or Was It Just Sleeping?" In *World Economic Outlook, April 2013: Hopes, Realities, Risks*, chapter 3. Washington, DC: IMF.

Jaeger, David A., Joakim Ruist, and Jan Stuhler. 2018. "Shift-Share Instruments and the Impact of Immigration." Working Paper no. 24285, NBER, Cambridge, MA.

Jordà, Òscar, and Fernanda Nechio. Forthcoming. "Inflation Globally." In *Changing Inflation Dynamics, Evolving Monetary Policy*, ed. J. Galí and D. Saravia. Santiago: Central Bank of Chile.

Kareken, John H., and Preston J. Miller. 1976. "The Policy Procedure of the FOMC: A Critique." In *A Prescription for Monetary Policy: Proceedings from a Seminar Series*. Minneapolis: Federal Reserve Bank of Minneapolis.

Kareken, John H., and Robert M. Solow. 1963. "Lags in Monetary Policy." In *Stabilization Policies*, ed. E. Cary Brown, 14–96. New York: Prentice Hall.

Kiley, Michael T. 2015. "An Evaluation of the Inflationary Pressure Associated with Short- and Long-Term Unemployment." *Economics Letters* 137:5–9.

King, Robert G. 2008. "The Phillips Curve and U.S. Macroeconomic Policy: Snapshots, 1958–1996." *Federal Reserve Bank of Richmond Economic Quarterly* 94 (4): 311–59.

King, Robert G., and Mark W. Watson. 2012. "Inflation and Unit Labor Cost." *Journal of Money, Credit and Banking* 44 (s2): 111–49.

Krogh, Tord S. 2015. "Macro Frictions and Theoretical Identification of the New Keynesian Phillips Curve." *Journal of Macroeconomics* 43:191–204.

Kuttner, Kenneth N. 2001. "Monetary Policy Surprises and Interest Rates: Evidence from the Fed Funds Futures Market." *Journal of Monetary Economics* 47 (3): 523–44.

Leduc, Sylvain, and Daniel J. Wilson. 2017. "Has the Wage Phillips Curve Gone Dormant?" FRBSF Economic Letter 2017-30, Federal Reserve Bank of San Francisco.

Lucas, Robert E., Jr. 1976. "Econometric Policy Evaluation: A Critique." *Carnegie-Rochester Conference Series on Public Policy* 1:19–46.

Mavroeidis, Sophocles, Mikkel Plagborg-Møller, and James H. Stock. 2014. "Empirical Evidence on Inflation Expectations in the New Keynesian Phillips Curve." *Journal of Economic Literature* 52 (1): 124–88.

Mishkin, Frederic S. 2007. "Inflation Dynamics." *International Finance* 10 (3): 317–34.

Nakamura, Emi, and Jón Steinsson. 2014. "Fiscal Stimulus in a Monetary Union: Evidence from US Regions." *American Economic Review* 104 (3): 753–92.

———. 2018. "High-Frequency Identification of Monetary NonNeutrality: The Information Effect." *Quarterly Journal of Economics* 133 (3): 1283–330.

Nason, James M., and Gregor W. Smith. 2008. "Identifying the New Keynesian Phillips Curve." *Journal of Applied Econometrics* 23 (5): 525–51.

Nekarda, Christopher J., and Valerie A. Ramey. 2011. "Industry Evidence on the Effects of Government Spending." *American Economic Journal: Macroeconomics* 3 (1): 36–59.

Olivei, Giovanni, and Silvana Tenreyro. 2007. "The Timing of Monetary Policy Shocks." *American Economic Review* 97 (3): 636–63.

Orphanides, Athanasios. 2002. "Monetary-Policy Rules and the Great Inflation." *American Economic Review* 92 (2): 115–20.

Peston, Maurice H. 1972. "The Correlation between Targets and Instruments." *Economica* 39 (156): 427–31.

Phelps, Edmund S. 1967. "Phillips Curves, Expectations of Inflation and Optimal Unemployment over Time." *Economica* 34:254–81.

Phillips, Alban W. 1958. "The Relation between Unemployment and the Rate of Change of Money Wage Rates in the United Kingdom, 1861–1957." *Economica* 25 (100): 283–99.

Powell, Jerome H. 2018. "Monetary Policy and Risk Management at a Time of Low Inflation and Low Unemployment." Speech given at the "Revolution or Evolution? Reexamining Economic Paradigms" 60th Annual Meeting of the National Association for Business Economics, Boston. https://www .federalreserve.gov/newsevents/speech/files/powell20181002a.pdf.

Primiceri, Giorgio E. 2006. "Why Inflation Rose and Fell: Policy-Makers' Beliefs and U.S. Postwar Stabilization Policy." *Quarterly Journal of Economics* 121 (3): 867–901.

Ramey, Valerie A. 2016. "Macroeconomic Shocks and Their Propagation." In *Handbook of Macroeconomics*, Vol. 2, ed. John B. Taylor and Harald Uhlig, Chapter 2, 71–162. Amsterdam: Elsevier.

Roberts, John M. 1995. "New Keynesian Economics and the Phillips Curve." *Journal of Money, Credit and Banking* 27 (4): 975–84.

———. 2006. "Monetary Policy and Inflation Dynamics." *International Journal of Central Banking* 2 (3): 193–230.

Romer, Christina D., and David H. Romer. 2004a. "Choosing the Federal Reserve Chair: Lessons from History." *Journal of Economic Perspectives* 18 (1): 129–62.

———. 2004b. "A New Measure of Monetary Shocks: Derivation and Implications." *American Economic Review* 94 (4): 1055–84.

Samuelson, Paul A., and Robert M. Solow. 1960. "Analytical Aspects of Anti-Inflation Policy." *American Economic Review* 50 (2): 177–94.

Sargent, Thomas, Noah Williams, and Tao Zha. 2006. "Shocks and Government Beliefs: The Rise and Fall of American Inflation." *American Economic Review* 96 (4): 1193–224.

Schorfheide, Frank. 2008. "DSGE Model-Based Estimation of the New Keynesian Phillips Curve." *Federal Reserve Bank of Richmond Economic Quarterly* 94 (4): 397–433.

Seneca, Martin. 2018. "A Graphical Illustration of Optimal Monetary Policy in the New Keynesian Framework." http://seneca.dk/Seneca_graphicalNK analysis.pdf.

Smets, Frank, and Rafael Wouters. 2007. "Shocks and Frictions in US Business Cycles: A Bayesian DSGE Approach." *American Economic Review* 97 (3): 586–606.

Stock, James H., and Mark W. Watson. 2002. "Has the Business Cycle Changed and Why?" *NBER Macroeconomics Annual* 17:159–218.

———. 2007. "Why Has U.S. Inflation Become Harder to Forecast?" *Journal of Money, Credit and Banking* 39 (s1): 3–33.

———. 2009. "Phillips Curve Inflation Forecasts." In *Understanding Inflation and the Implications for Monetary Policy*, ed. Jeff Fuhrer, Yolanda K. Kodrzycki, Jane Sneddon Little, and Giovanni P. Olivei, Chapter 3, 99–186. Cambridge, MA: MIT Press.

Svensson, Lars E. O. 1997. "Inflation Forecast Targeting: Implementing and Monitoring Inflation Targets." *European Economic Review* 41 (6): 1111–46.

Svensson, Lars E. O., and Michael Woodford. 2004. "Implementing Optimal Policy through Inflation-Forecast Targeting." In *The Inflation-Targeting Debate*, ed. Ben S. Bernanke and Michael Woodford, 19–92. Chicago: University of Chicago Press.

Taylor, John B. 1998. "Monetary Policy Guidelines for Unemployment and Inflation Stability." In *Inflation, Unemployment, and Monetary Policy*, ed. Benjamin M. Friedman, 29–54. Cambridge, MA: MIT Press.

Tuckett, Alex. 2018. "What Can Regional Data Tell Us about the UK Phillips Curve?" Bank of England Bank Underground. https://bankunderground.co .uk/2018/04/13/what-can-regional-data-tell-us-about-the-uk-phillips-curve.

Uhlig, Harald. 2005. "What Are the Effects of Monetary Policy on Output? Results from an Agnostic Identification Procedure." *Journal of Monetary Economics* 52 (2): 381–419.

Vlieghe, Gertjan. 2018. "From Asymmetry to Symmetry: Changing Risks to the Economic Outlook." Speech given at the Confederation of British Industry, Birmingham, UK. https://www.bankofengland.co.uk/-/media/boe/files/speech/2018/from-asymmetry-to-symmetry-changing-risks-to-the-economic-outlook-speech-by-gertjan-vlieghe.

Williams, John C. 2006. "Inflation Persistence in an Era of Well-Anchored Inflation Expectations." FRBSF Economic Letter 2006-27, Federal Reserve Bank of San Francisco.

Woodford, Michael. 1994. "Nonstandard Indicators for Monetary Policy: Can Their Usefulness Be Judged from Forecasting Regressions?" In *Monetary Policy*, ed. N. Gregory Mankiw, Chapter 3, 95–115. Chicago: University of Chicago Press. https://www.nber.org/books/greg94-1.

———. 2003. *Interest and Prices: Foundations of a Theory of Monetary Policy*. Princeton, NJ: Princeton University Press.

Worswick, G. D. N. 1969. "Fiscal Policy and Stabilization in Britain." *Journal of Money, Credit and Banking* 1 (3): 474–95.

Yellen, Janet L. 2015. "Inflation Dynamics and Monetary Policy." Speech given at the Philip Gamble Memorial Lecture, University of Massachusetts, Amherst, Amherst, MA. https://federalreserve.gov/newsevents/speech/yellen20150924a.pdf.

Comment

Marc P. Giannoni, *Federal Reserve Bank of Dallas*

I. Introduction

Since Phillips (1958), economists have sought to estimate a Phillips curve relationship or a positive relation between inflation, π_t, and a measure of the output gap, x_t. Although historically such a relationship could be easily detected, the Phillips curve appears to have flattened in the United States more recently. Some authors have suggested that inflation does not depend on slack, that it is largely exogenous. This raises the key question: What changed? The answer to that question is critical for much of macroeconomics and in particular for monetary policy. With most central banks around the world seeking to stabilize inflation around a target level (e.g., 2% in the United States), it is crucial to understand the determinants of inflation and to know whether monetary policy can still affect inflation.

Several potential explanations have been provided for the flattening of the Phillips curve. Some have suggested that structural changes in the economy in recent decades have played a significant role (e.g., Duca 2019). In many of models of sticky prices, more rigid prices than in the past or increases in market concentration and pricing power (De Loecker and Eeckhout 2017) could also result in a flattening of the Phillips curve. McLeay and Tenreyro argue instead that monetary policy itself is responsible for the flattening of the Phillips curve. The explanation is simple: If the central bank conducts optimal monetary policy, seeking to minimize deviations of inflation from target and output from potential output, then it should set its policy instruments to increase inflation when output is below potential and vice versa. It follows that optimal policy causes a negative correlation between inflation and the output gap. That negative correlation blurs in turn the positive correlation implied by the Phillips curve, so that in equilibrium, the correlation between inflation and the output gap may be positive, negative, or null, depending on the variability of shocks perturbing either the Phillips curve or the optimal policy relationship. The authors make the point very clearly through a sharp and elegant analysis, in the context of a simple New Keynesian model.

After exposing the identification problem in estimating the slope of a Phillips curve, McLeay and Tenreyro propose strategies to estimate the Phillips curve and present evidence of a robust Phillips curve in the United States. This is a very nice and transparent paper that should be read by all of those who are interested in understanding and estimating the Phillips curve.

In the remainder of this discussion, I will briefly review the authors' story in the historical context and will quibble in Section III with the authors' proposed identification of the Phillips curve, focusing in particular on the role of expectations.

II. The Story

A key point of the paper is that one should distinguish between (i) a reduced-form Phillips curve, that is, an *empirical* relationship between inflation and a measure of the output gap, and (ii) a structural Phillips curve, that is, the underlying relationship between inflation, the output gap, inflation expectations, and possibly other factors, resulting from the firms' optimal setting of their prices. In the debate about the flattening of the Phillips curve, the two concepts are often mixed, as the structural Phillips curve may be difficult to identify. As the authors make clear, optimal policy can lead to a flattening or even a negative relationship between inflation and the output gap in the reduced-form Phillips curve, even though there is a well-defined positively sloped underlying structural Phillips curve. The authors' result does not rely on assuming that the policy maker conducts optimal policy under discretion and that it has a quadratic objective function. Consider the standard (structural) New Keynesian Phillips curve (eq. [1] in the paper) that characterizes the trade-off between inflation, π_t, and the output gap, x_t, faced by the central bank:

$$\pi_t = \beta E_t \pi_{t+1} + \kappa x_t + u_t, \tag{1}$$

with a slope κ that is positive by assumption. In the face of "cost-push shocks," u_t, it is generally not possible to stabilize both inflation and the output gap. Suppose that the central bank can control the output gap, for example, via a short-term policy rate; that it observes u_t and that it seeks to stabilize inflation at its target ($\pi_t = 0$) as in the case of a pure inflation-targeting regime. Optimal policy would then imply that the output gap respond negatively to the cost-push shock

$$x_t = -\kappa^{-1} u_t$$

so that, in equilibrium, inflation and hence inflation expectations are completely stabilized around the inflation target:

$$\pi_t = 0, \ E_t \pi_{t+1} = 0,$$

as illustrated by the x-axis in figure 1 (which is adapted from figure 3 in the paper). The implication of this policy is that inflation would be uncorrelated swith the output gap. In other words, even though the underlying structural Phillips curve implies a positive relationship between inflation and the output gap, inflation targeting gives rise to a flat reduced-form

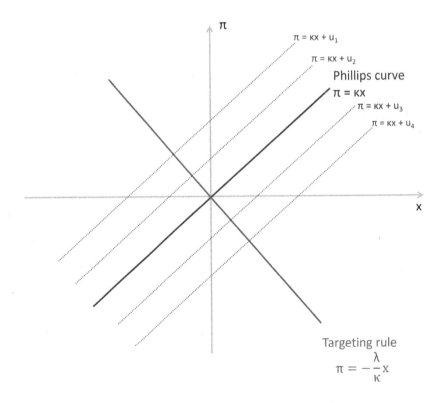

Fig. 1.   Structural Phillips curve and optimal policy

Phillips curve relationship, with inflation apparently unrelated to the output gap.

In the case that the central bank cares both about inflation and output gap deviations from target, as the authors point out, optimal policy under discretion gives rise to a negative relationship between inflation and the output gap. Indeed, when the central bank seeks to minimize the loss function:

$$E_0 \sum_{t=0}^{\infty} \beta^t \left[\pi_t^2 + \lambda x_t^2 \right], \tag{2}$$

subject to the behavior of the private sector represented by the structural Phillips curve (eq. [1]), optimal policy under discretion, that is, taking private sector expectations $E_t \pi_{t+j}$, $E_t x_{t+j}$ as given, results in the optimal targeting rule:

$$\pi_t = -\frac{\lambda}{\kappa} x_t, \tag{3}$$

which states that the central bank seeks to increase inflation when output is below potential and vice versa, as illustrated by the downward-sloping gray line in figure 1. As exogenous shocks u_t shift the Phillips curve but not the optimal policy relation (eq. [2]), equilibrium realizations of inflation and the output gap draw not the Phillips curve but rather the optimal target criterion (eq. [2]). In equilibrium, π_t, x_t depend only on u_t

$$\pi_t = \frac{\lambda}{\kappa^2 + \lambda(1 - \beta\rho)} u_t, \quad x_t = -\frac{\kappa}{\kappa^2 + \lambda(1 - \beta\rho)} u_t,$$

where ρ is the degree of serial correlation in u_t so that the covariance between inflation and the output gap

$$\text{cov}(\pi_t, x_t) = \frac{-\lambda\kappa}{(\kappa^2 + \lambda(1 - \beta\rho))^2} \text{var}(u_t) < 0$$

is necessarily, and the correlation $\text{corr}(\pi_t, x_t) = -1$.

A. Targeting Rule versus Taylor Rule

Some readers may find a target criterion of the form (eq. [3]) to be unrealistic. We should however note that its characterization of monetary policy is not too different from that under a conventional Taylor rule.

Indeed, the optimal target criterion (eq. [3]) implies that the policy rate i_t is set so as to satisfy $\pi_t + (\lambda/\kappa)x_t = 0$. The policy rate can thus be related to inflation and the output gap according to a conventional Taylor-type rule:

$$i_t = \phi \left(\pi_t + \frac{\lambda}{\kappa} x_t \right)$$

with a large coefficient $\phi(\rightarrow \infty)$. If, in addition, policy makers care to also stabilize other variables such as the interest rate, then the optimal policy response to inflation and the output gap would likely be of a similar form but with a smaller coefficient $0 < \phi < \infty$, and the optimal interest rate would in addition respond to these other variables (e.g., the lagged interest rate).

B. Historical Context

As the authors recognize, the flattening or disappearance of an empirical relationship such as the reduced-form Phillips curve as a consequence of a successful monetary policy is an old idea that goes back at least to Kareken and Solow (1963), who emphasized that if monetary policy succeeds at offsetting all shocks that affect income, then we would observe fluctuations in money growth and a perfectly steady path for income. Similar ideas have been reinforced and generalized by many authors since then, most prominently with Goodhart's "law" (1981)[1] and the Lucas (1976) critique,[2] and it is still mentioned in recent work (e.g., Hooper, Mishkin, and Sufi 2019). Unfortunately, it appears that much of the profession is quick to forget these powerful lessons when the empirical relationship between two key macroeconomic variables appears to have weakened, and so it is important that McLeay and Tenreyro remind us of this. As we learned from Lucas (1976), these lessons do not apply merely to relationships between two macroeconomic variables; they can be more pervasive. For instance, when Boivin and Giannoni (2006) documented the fact that impulse response functions of inflation and output to an unexpected 25 basis points change in the federal funds rate had become more muted in the post-1980 period, compared with the 1960–80 period, they asked whether this was due to a structural change in the economy (such as a flattening of the structural Phillips curve or a diminished sensitivity of economic activity to interest rate changes) or to a change in policy itself; they found that a more aggressive stance of policy toward inflation stabilization in the post-1980 period could explain most if not all of the change in estimated impulse response functions.

III. Identifying the Structural Phillips Curve

Aside from making it very clear that one should not conclude that the Phillips curve has disappeared based on correlations between inflation and the output gap, or simple regressions, McLeay and Tenreyro describe in simple terms the identification problem, propose ways to address it, and provide evidence that there is a structural Phillips curve with positive slope between inflation and the output gap. As figure 1 illustrates, cost-push shocks u_t help trace the policy rule, not the Phillips curve. If the policy rule is itself subject to disturbances e_t so that it becomes

$$\pi_t = -\frac{\lambda}{\kappa} x_t - e_t, \qquad (4)$$

then fluctuations in e_t may help trace the structural Phillips curve. The identification problem arises when we face shocks to both the policy (targeting) rule and the Phillips curve.

Focusing on equations (1) and (4) provides a transparent way of characterizing the identification problem, in a near-static environment (for given inflation expectations), in which the Phillips curve implies a positive contemporaneous relation between π_t and x_t, whereas policy implies a negative contemporaneous relation between these two variables. If only we could control for the cost-push shocks u_t, then shocks to the policy rule (represented by the downward-sloping gray line in fig. 1) would trace out the structural Phillips curve. Similarly, the identification problem can be partly addressed in the case of regional Phillips curve subject to region-specific cost-push shocks, but with monetary policy responding to aggregate economic conditions, as McLeay and Tenreyro as well as other recent studies have proposed (Hooper et al. 2019).

A. Difficulties with Identification via Disturbances to the Optimal Target Criterion

Although the authors make a strong case for identifying the Phillips curve using equations (1) and (4), I am concerned that it may not be as easy to identify the Phillips curve in more complicated setups, in particular when the policy rule disturbances e_t are not exogenous and depend on other variables, including variables affecting the residuals u_t themselves, or if the residuals u_t capture more than exogenous cost-push shocks, indeed if they depend on variables that also shift the policy rule.

To illustrate this point, I consider a few examples:

• Take again the simple Phillips curve (eq. [1]) and the objective function (eq. [2]), but assume that optimal policy is conducted under commitment. Then, as pointed out by McLeay and Tenreyro, optimal policy can be represented by an optimal target criterion of the form (eq. [4]) with $e_t = -(\lambda/\kappa)x_{t-1}$. If the cost-push shock is serially correlated, then e_t and u_t are correlated. A suitable instrument is thus needed.

• Assume instead that inflation involves some inertia as modeled, for example, in Christiano, Eichenbaum, and Evans (2005), and as appears realistic in the data. Then, as shown in Giannoni and Woodford (2004, eq. [12]), lagged inflation appears both in the Phillips curve (eq. [1]) and in the optimal target criterion (eq. [4]), so that e_t and u_t would both be functions of lagged inflation.

• When the representative household faces habit persistence in expenditures, then again, as shown in Giannoni and Woodford (2004, eq. [47] and eq. [53]), both the Phillips curve and the optimal target criterion involve the lagged output gap, so that u_t and e_t in equations (1) and (4) would be both functions of x_{t-1} and hence would be correlated.

• Suppose, alternatively, that the policy maker faces a Phillips curve of the form (eq. [1]) but cares about interest rate variability in addition to the two other terms entering the objective function (eq. [2]). Then, the optimal target criterion involves a relationship between current and forecasts of inflation, output gaps, as well as lags of the output gap and interest rates (see Giannoni and Woodford 2004; eq. [22]). Again, that would imply that the terms u_t and e_t in equations (1) and (4) would be correlated.

Similar concerns arise when the model involves both price and wage stickiness, so that a Phillips curve arises for price and for wage inflation; when monetary policy actions have delayed effects on macroeconomic variables, so that optimal policy depends on expectations of future inflation and output gaps; and so on.

B. Identifying the Phillips Curve: Static versus Dynamic

Although McLeay and Tenreyro make an important conceptual point and provide a very intuitive way of characterizing the difficulty in identifying the Phillips curve in a near-static framework, I am skeptical that one can fully recover the Phillips curve without taking a stronger stance on dynamic relationships linking the key macroeconomic variables. The simple New Keynesian Phillips curve considered is an invaluable tool to develop intuition, but much of the empirical literature suggests that inflation responds to measures of slack in a more inertial fashion. Similarly, whereas the simple model considered assumes that policy makers can instantaneously affect economic activity and the output gap, empirical evidence suggests the effects are more sluggish. (If not, it would be difficult to explain why inflation has been below its target and economic activity has been below estimates of its potential for so many years following the Great Recession.) This implies that the dynamic relationship between inflation and the output gap is more complex than described by the simple New Keynesian model and that it is important to properly model these dynamics to identify a Phillips curve.

Estimated dynamic stochastic general equilibrium (DSGE) models are a valuable tool to characterize the joint dynamics of key macroeconomic variables and thus of the complex interactions between the Phillips curve and policy. In such dynamic models, inflation expectations play a key role, and a monetary policy aimed at stabilizing inflation and hence inflation expectations does also imply a flattening of the reduced-form Phillips curve. A potential downside of such fully specified models is that they are necessarily misspecified. A key question, then, is whether such models can explain important recent episodes. In particular, Del Negro, Giannoni, and Schorfheide (2015) study whether a standard DSGE model along the lines of Christiano et al. (2005) and Smets and Wouters (2007) augmented with financial frictions and estimated with data up to 2008Q3 can explain the US macroeconomic behavior during and after the Great Recession. They find that as soon as credit spreads jump in the fall of 2008, the model successfully predicts the sharp contraction in activity and the modest and protracted decline in inflation, as shown in figure 2. They also find that data on credit spreads and inflation expectations, in addition to the standard data series used by, for example, Smets and Wouters (2007), are important in properly characterizing the state of the economy.

To understand why inflation does not collapse given the sharp drop in output, it is useful to consider a simplified version of the forward-looking Phillips curve considered in the model. That simplified Phillips curve, which is similar to equation (1)—except that x_t is replaced with

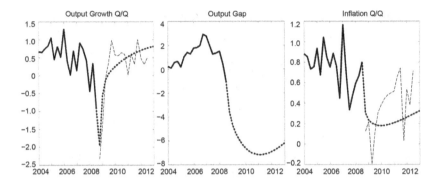

Fig. 2. Dynamic stochastic general equilibrium (DSGE) model forecast of gross domestic product (GDP) growth, the output gap, and GDP deflator inflation, based on the model in Del Negro et al. (2015). Out-of-sample forecast starting in 2008Q4 (dotted lines); data used in estimation (solid lines); and ex post realization of the data (dashed lines).

real marginal costs—implies that inflation does not depend only on the current gap (or marginal cost), but on the entire path of future gaps:

$$\pi_t = \sum_{j=0}^{\infty} \beta^j E_t \left[\underbrace{\kappa\, x_{t+j}}_{\text{gaps}} + \underbrace{u_{t+j}}_{\text{mark-up shocks}} \right].$$

It follows that inflation and inflation expectations in the model remain well anchored, despite the sharp collapse in output, because monetary policy is expected to be aggressive enough to close the gaps in the future.

Similarly to McLeay and Tenreyro, although the model includes a structural Phillips curve that involves a positive relationship between inflation and the output gap, inflation was predicted to move relatively little in the face of the output collapse. However, in contrast to McLeay and Tenreyro, according to the DSGE model, it was not the contemporaneous monetary stimulus (at the end of 2008 and in early 2009) that helped stabilize inflation; indeed, short-term nominal rates were constrained by the zero lower bound at that time. Instead, the expectation of future stimulus induced expectations of closing output gaps in the future and hence helped keep inflation near its target.

IV. Conclusion

McLeay and Tenreyro have written a very nice paper that clearly and elegantly exposes the identification problem in estimating the slope of a Phillips curve when policy makers seek to stabilize inflation and/or the output gap. They propose interesting strategies to estimate the Phillips curve and present evidence of a robust Phillips curve in the United States. The simplicity of the framework considered allows the authors to provide numerous insights. I have expressed some reservations about the ability to generalize the results beyond the current framework, in particular when one faces more complex dynamic interactions between inflation, inflation expectations, activity, and policy. In more complicated environments, I suspect that DSGE model estimation remains necessary to better characterize the joint dynamics of macro variables, and the role of expectations.

Endnotes

Author email address: Giannoni (marc.giannoni@dal.frb.org). The views expressed in this discussion are those of the author and do not necessarily represent those of the Federal Reserve Bank of Dallas or the Federal Reserve System. For acknowledgments, sources of research support, and disclosure of the author's material financial relationships, if any, please see https://www.nber.org/chapters/c14246.ack.
1. Goodhart (1981, 116): "Any observed statistical regularity will tend to collapse once pressure is placed upon it for control purposes."
2. Lucas (1976, 40–41): "A change in policy [parameters] affects the behavior of the system in two ways: first by altering the time series behavior of [policy variables]; second by leading to modification of the behavioral parameters . . . governing the rest of the system. . . . It follows that any change in policy will systematically alter the structure of econometric models."

References

Boivin, J., and M. P. Giannoni. 2006. "Has Monetary Policy Become More Effective?" *Review of Economics and Statistics* 88 (3): 445–62.
Christiano, L. J., M. Eichenbaum, and C. Evans. 2005. "Nominal Rigidities and the Dynamic Effect of a Shock to Monetary Policy." *Journal of Political Economy* 113 (1): 1–45.
De Loecker, J., and J. Eeckhout. 2017. "The Rise of Market Power and the Macroeconomic Implications." Working Paper no. 23687, NBER, Cambridge, MA.
Del Negro, M., M. P. Giannoni, and F. Schorfheide. 2015. "Inflation in the Great Recession and New Keynesian Models." *American Economic Journal: Macroeconomics* 7 (1): 168–96. https://doi.org/10.1257/mac.20140097.
Duca, J. V. 2019. "Inflation and the Gig Economy: Have the Rise of Online Retailing and Self-Employment Disrupted the Phillips Curve?" Dallas Fed Working Paper no. 1814. https://doi.org/10.24149/wp1814.
Giannoni, M. P., and M. Woodford. 2004. "Optimal Inflation Targeting Rules." In *The Inflation-Targeting Debate*, ed. B. Bernanke and M. Woodford, 93–162. Chicago: University of Chicago Press.
Goodhart, C. 1981. "Problems of Monetary Management: The U.K. Experience." In *Inflation, Depression, and Economic Policy in the West*, ed. Anthony S. Courakis, 111–46. Totowa, NJ: Barnes & Noble.

Hooper, P., F. S. Mishkin, and A. Sufi. 2019. "Prospects for Inflation in a High Pressure Economy: Is the Phillips Curve Dead or Is It Just Hibernating?" Working Paper no. 25792, NBER, Cambridge, MA.

Kareken, John H., and Robert M. Solow. 1963. "Lags in Monetary Policy." In *Stabilization Policies*, ed. E. Cary Brown, 14–96. New York: Prentice Hall.

Lucas, R. E., Jr. 1976. "Econometric Policy Evaluation: A Critique." *Carnegie-Rochester Conference Series on Public Policy* 1:19–46.

Phillips, A. W. 1958. "The Relation between Unemployment and the Rate of Change of Money Wage Rates in the United Kingdom, 1861–1957." *Economica* 25 (100): 283–99. https://doi.org/10.2307/2550759.

Smets, F., and R. Wouters. 2007. "Shocks and Frictions in US Business Cycles: A Bayesian DSGE Approach." *American Economic Review* 97 (3): 586–606. https://doi.org/10.1257/aer.97.3.586.

Comment

Matthew Rognlie, *Northwestern University and NBER*

Recently, I had a dream where I was trying to explain supply and demand to an audience of intransigent economists. How could I say that demand curves sloped downward, they asked, when for so many goods, a simple plot of quantity demanded against price showed the opposite? How could these curves be useful concepts when, even by the most generous account, their parameters shifted from year to year?

I knew the answers. The incorrect slope of demand was no surprise; a plot of quantities against prices would reveal the demand curve only if the variation was caused by supply shocks. And yes, supply and demand did move around from year to year, but this did not invalidate the concepts. If I am selling oil, I can predict that a sudden decline in supply (embargo) will increase the price, I can predict that a new source of supply (fracking) will decrease the price, and I can predict that a decline in demand (fuel efficiency) will decrease the price. All of this is useful information.

The dream audience was unmoved. But upon waking up, I was relieved to find myself in a world where economists are not so silly. We understand that supply and demand is a useful framework, even if there is an identification problem and even if there is no consensus on the parameters for a particular market. In fact, we persist even in the face of more profound theoretical complications, like imperfect competition or increasing returns.

Then I started reading commentary on the Phillips curve and economists started seeming awfully silly again. Somehow, a weak reduced-form relationship in the aggregate data has led many people to deny the Phillips curve as a structural relationship. In the face of this criticism, McLeay and Tenreyro's paper is a vitally important rejoinder.

I.   McLeay and Tenreyro's Argument: The Identification Problem

The Phillips curve is a supply curve. It embeds the supply side of the economy, and it captures how in the aggregate, when greater pressure is put on the most important factor of production (labor), firms will want to set higher prices.

As with any supply curve, we need demand shocks for identification. A naive look at the data—if it does not take the source of variation into account—may find that the curve slopes in the wrong direction or fail to detect any pattern at all.

In fact, it is worse than this: the "divine coincidence" in the basic New Keynesian model implies that, when feasible, monetary policy should target zero output gap and zero inflation.[1] The only shocks that break this result are those that shift the relationship between the output gap and inflation—in other words, those that shift the Phillips curve itself. But the optimal response to a "cost-push shock" to the Phillips curve that pushes up inflation is to engineer a negative output gap. As McLeay and Tenreyro powerfully point out, such shocks imply a negative relationship between the output gap and inflation in the data.

Effectively, under optimal monetary policy, there are only supply shocks, not demand shocks. This is the worst possible situation for identifying a supply curve.

One can illustrate the situation with an analogy. Suppose that a driver is on a long, hilly highway, and we want to study the relationship between the gas pedal and acceleration. If the driver is trying to maintain a constant speed, she will only press harder on the pedal when trying to climb a hill. The raw data would indicate a clear negative relationship between the pedal and acceleration—the opposite of the causal relationship. And adding hills as a control variable would not help: without hills, there would be no variation at all.

Solving the Identification Puzzle: Aggregate Data

To get a better result, we want drivers to make mistakes, ideally random ones: pushing down or letting up on the pedal for no good reason, so that the pedal-acceleration relationship is not caused by hills alone. This is related to an idea often used to study monetary policy: to look at an identified monetary shock. The response to these shocks can tell us about the Phillips curve and indeed many other macro relationships of interest—see, for instance, Christiano, Eichenbaum, and Evans (2005) or Barnichon and Mesters (2019).

The problem is that these shocks only exist if monetary policy makes random mistakes. Monetary policy in the most recent few decades, even if it has made plenty of mistakes, may have made these mistakes in a systematic enough fashion that true shocks are few and far between. This is the critique of Ramey (2016), and as McLeay and Tenreyro point out, it makes identifying the Phillips curve increasingly difficult.

One ideal situation for the econometrician would be a new, aggressive driver experimenting with radical new driving policies. And indeed, McLeay and Tenreyro find that the first part of Volcker's term has by far the most negative unemployment-inflation relationship of all periods grouped by Fed chair, with a slope of −2.27.

Another possibility would be a driver struggling with a broken pedal, who is not equipped to maintain a constant speed. Yet in the Bernanke-Yellen era of the zero lower bound, McLeay and Tenreyro find a much weaker unemployment-inflation relationship, at just −0.13. Does this mean that the Phillips curve is weakening? Or is "broken pedal" not an accurate depiction of life at the zero lower bound, where the Fed was able to respond to shocks at the margin with forward guidance and quantitative easing, even if it could not eradicate the output gap entirely?

Solving the Identification Puzzle: Disaggregation

The difficulty of answering this question has led many researchers to try their luck with an alternative strategy: using disaggregated data.[2] Because different states or metro areas in the United States do not have their own monetary policies, they cannot adjust nominal interest rates in response to supply shocks. This avoids the bias that is created by monetary policy at the aggregate level.

Of course, real interest rates and relative prices can still adjust, so this approach is not free from bias, as McLeay and Tenreyro readily acknowledge. For instance, if a metro area experiences an adverse supply shock that decreases productivity in both the tradable and nontradable sectors, then by making tradables less competitive this may increase unemployment while simultaneously raising the price of nontradable goods that enter into the local consumer price index.

Still, this is a very useful source of evidence. Because the bias from cost-push shocks is downward, the results from this strategy provide a lower bound for the steepness of the Phillips curve, which may be tighter than the lower bound from aggregate data. In addition, I suspect that due to tradable goods and factors, the slope of regional Phillips curves should in theory be less steep than the slope of aggregate curves—so that, even more so, the regional data should understate the strength of the true relation.

In this light, McLeay and Tenreyro's results are encouraging: with year and metro area fixed effects, they find an instantaneous slope coefficient of –0.379 over the period 1990–2017, as compared with –0.150 from pooled ordinary least squares. My only caution is that in the fixed effects specification they also find much smaller coefficients on expectations and lags, so that if we interpret the results literally as a Phillips curve, then the slope of the medium-run Phillips relation—which accumulates many instantaneous responses through leads and lags—is not so steep in relative terms after all. I am not too worried by this, however: again, the regional Phillips curve is likely to understate the aggregate relationship.

Two Additional Directions

In the remaining discussion, I want to look in two directions that McLeay and Tenreyro—who understandably focus on the conventional form of the price Phillips curve—de-emphasize. First, I will show that the wage Phillips curve is alive and well in the US time series, even if transmission to prices is not immediately visible. Second, I will argue that the theory underlying the standard Phillips curve relies on extreme assumptions about rational expectations and common knowledge, and that although some form of Phillips curve is quite likely to exist, it need not resemble the Phillips curves derived in the conventional New Keynesian model.

II. The Remarkable Wage Phillips Curve

In the aftermath of the Great Inflation and Volcker disinflation, the Phillips curve hit rock bottom in professional credibility. Summers (1991)—hardly a neoclassical—asked "Should Keynesian Economics Dispense with the Phillips Curve?" The answer was yes. He commented that "the textbook Keynesian view of aggregate supply possesses many of the attributes that Thomas Kuhn has ascribed to dying scientific paradigms."

But a funny thing has happened in the post-Volcker era: The original Phillips curve, the negative correlation between unemployment and wage growth, has returned in plain sight.

Figure 1a shows the two time series: wage growth for private industry, measured in a centered one-year window around each quarter using the Employment Cost Index, and average unemployment within

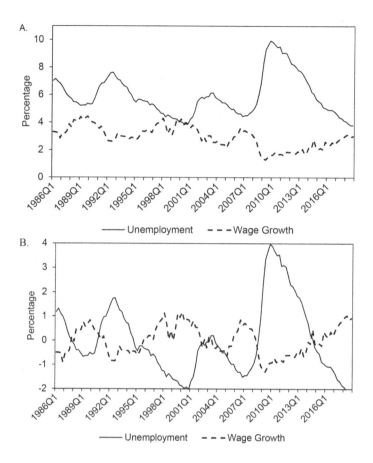

Fig. 1. Wage inflation (centered one-year Employment Cost Index for private industry wages growth) versus unemployment, 1986–present. (*a*) Raw series. (*b*) Detrended series.

the quarter. The negative co-movement is visually obvious: when unemployment spikes during recessions, wage growth plummets, and as unemployment creeps back down during the expansion, wage growth reasserts itself. This does not necessarily prove causality or that the unemployment rate is the best measure of labor market slack for the Phillips curve, but as a correlation, the wage-unemployment Phillips curve appears as healthy as ever.

Figure 1*b* detrends the data, removing secular declines in both the unemployment rate and wage growth. The correlation becomes even more apparent: every swing in unemployment has an effect on wage growth as its mirror image. A scatterplot of these observations, in figure 2*a*, reveals a remarkably healthy Phillips curve. For most of the domain, the slope is

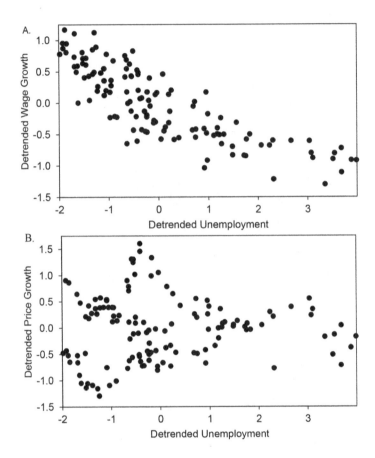

Fig. 2. Detrended wage and price growth versus unemployment, 1986–present. (*a*) Wages (centered one-year Employment Cost Index growth). (*b*) Prices (centered one-year core personal consumption expenditure inflation).

roughly −1/2, with an increase in unemployment of 2 percentage points corresponding to annual wage growth that is 1% smaller. But it appears to flatten when unemployment reaches more than 2 percentage points above trend. The observations in this region are all from the worst period of the Great Recession, where wage growth did not fall nearly as much as a linear extrapolation of the Phillips curve would suggest.

All this is consistent with a traditional view of the wage Phillips curve: The curve is convex, and secular trends in the natural rate of unemployment (and possibly inflation expectations) imply that the detrended data have a better fit. But does this have a causal interpretation? And what does it say about price inflation?

Transmission to Price Inflation

If labor market tightness causes nominal wage inflation, then transmission to price inflation is not guaranteed in the short run: although wages are an important component of overall costs, they are not 100% of costs, and markups can absorb year-to-year variation. Figure 2*b*, constructed analogously to figure 2*a* but for core personal consumption expenditure price inflation rather than wage inflation, reveals just how weak this short-run transmission can be: the modern price "Phillips curve" is a cloud of points with no obvious interpretation, and at best a slight negative correlation.

In the longer run, however, one-for-one transmission to price inflation seems almost inevitable. Figure 3, which plots the net labor share of corporate factor income in the United States, shows why. Although there is plenty of short- to medium-term variation in the labor share, most of this is mean-reverting and the long-run variation appears to be bounded.

A fairly large movement in the labor share would be, for instance, from 75% to 80%. If this corresponded to a decline in markups, it would imply excess wage growth over price growth of 80% /75% = 1.067. Annualized over 5 years, this would be a big deal: about 1.3% per year. But over

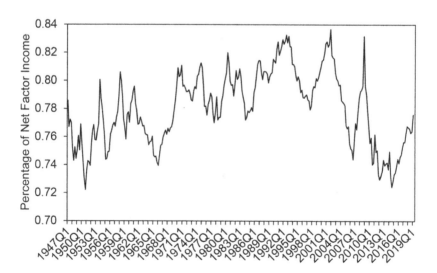

Fig. 3. Net labor share of corporate factor income (National Income and Product Accounts).

50 years, it would only be 0.13% per year—not a major influence on long-run price inflation. There is simply no realistic level change in markups that can matter much, over the span of decades, for the rate of price inflation versus wage inflation.

Are Other Interpretations Possible?

If this story is right, then the medium- to long-term price Phillips curve should be robust and the conventional central bankers' view of inflation is correct—over a long enough time horizon.

Is there any alternative? Because the wage Phillips curve in figure 2a is just a correlation, the case is not quite settled. I find it difficult, however, to think of a different story that matches both the data and our own understanding of the labor market. By and large, firms set wages in nominal terms, and in response to tighter hiring conditions and the threat of turnover, they allow nominal wages to grow a little more. If this wage growth causes markups to shrink but tight labor market conditions persist, these firms are likely to restore their markups by raising prices, not trimming wages (which would be suicidal in a tight labor market).

Perhaps reduced markups exert some downward pressure on wages—so that more wage growth this year, by reducing markups, means less growth next year, as firms adjust wages to bring markups back into line. If this effect was strong enough, in principle it could stop transmission to price inflation entirely: firms would keep prices constant and allow markups to absorb wage growth fluctuations in the short run, then eventually reverse course to avoid any long-term change in markups. But in this case, I would imagine that the unemployment-wage relationship would be disrupted, to the point where figure 2a would be far less clean.

Why Is the Wage Phillips Curve So Much Clearer than the Price Phillips Curve?

I have suggested a story for why figure 2a is so much nicer than figure 2b: the link between labor market tightness and wage growth is much more immediate than the link with price growth. First, markups provide a short-run buffer between wages and prices. In addition, several other shocks may affect prices more than nominal wages—for instance, energy shocks, or even some productivity shocks—further muddying the price Phillips curve.

McLeay and Tenreyro offer a distinct and complementary story: because central banks target price rather than wage inflation, we should expect the identification problem to be worse for the price Phillips curve. This is a nice corollary to their main argument, and I think it is almost certainly part of the explanation for why the wage curve performs so much better. One can even interpret the Great Recession in this light: one reason why central banks were not more aggressive to combat unemployment in the early 2010s was that they were looking at price inflation (which, thanks in part to energy prices, was surprisingly high) rather than wage inflation (which was not).

More generally, McLeay and Tenreyro's identification argument is compelling enough that it is hard to imagine figure 2a could exist in a world where central banks systematically targeted wage inflation.

III.   The Subtle Theory of Phillips Curves

Most of us remember the standard formulation of the New Keynesian Phillips curve for price inflation. McLeay and Tenreyro use this formulation in their theoretical discussion—understandably, because the point of their paper is to address the mainstream New Keynesian literature.

But where does this equation come from? I will argue that the usual specification is surprisingly subtle and assumption-contingent. Some form of Phillips curve likely exists, but it is probably not the one in the textbooks.

To start, consider the most basic log-linearized Calvo model as in Galí (2015), with no firm-specific cost shocks. This implies that firm i setting its price in period t chooses an optimal price:

$$p_{it}^* = (1 - \beta\theta)\mathbb{E}_{it}\sum_{s=0}^{\infty}(\beta\theta)^s(\Theta\widehat{mc}_{t+s} + p_{t+s}), \qquad (1)$$

where p_{t+s} is the aggregate price level at time s, $\widehat{mc}_{t+s}$ is the deviation of aggregate real marginal cost from steady state, β is the discount rate, $1 - \theta$ is the likelihood of price adjustment, and $\Theta \in [0, 1]$ is closer to zero when there is more strategic complementarity.

Equation (1) is straightforward and not hard to derive from the basic firm problem. In the case $\Theta = 1$ with no strategic complementarity, it simply states that the firm wants to move its price in proportion to the discounted average of expected nominal marginal cost, over the lifetime of that price. The discount rate β and price survival probability θ combine into the factor $\beta\theta$ in equation (1) that discounts future costs.

Applying the law of iterated expectations, we can consolidate equation (1) to the simpler-looking expression:

$$p_{it}^* = \mathbb{E}_{it}[(1 - \beta\theta)(\Theta\widehat{mc}_t + p_t) + \beta\theta p_{it+1}^*], \qquad (2)$$

which replaces terms from $t + 1$ onward with firm i's expectation of its own optimal reset price at $t + 1$. This is possible because of the geometric discounting in equation (1), under which tomorrow's expected choice enters today as a sufficient statistic for the future.

I would argue that equations (1) and (2) are somewhat robust, in the sense that many different formulations of a forward-looking price-setting problem will lead to similar expressions. In the absence of exact geometric discounting (like that produced by Calvo or Rotemberg pricing), we would not be able to consolidate to the form (eq. [2]), but it might not be too far off. Perhaps the biggest weakness is the implicit invocation of rational expectations when applying the law of iterated expectations between equations (1) and (2).

The much more doubtful features of the New Keynesian Phillips curve emerge after equation (2). How, indeed, do we go from discounting by $\beta\theta$ in equations (1) and (2) to discounting by just β in the traditional New Keynesian Phillips curve? The answer is a near miracle of common knowledge and rational expectations.

To see this, we can rewrite equation (2) as

$$\pi_{it}^* = (1 - \beta\theta)\Theta\mathbb{E}_{it}\widehat{mc}_t + \beta\theta\mathbb{E}_{it}\pi_{it+1}^* + \mathbb{E}_{it}\pi_t, \qquad (3)$$

where $\pi_t \equiv p_t - p_{t-1}$ and $\pi_{it}^* \equiv p_{it}^* - p_{t-1}$.

Now, if we impose common knowledge, we can—because there are no firm-specific cost shocks—drop the i subscripts and also drop the expectations operator for date-t outcomes. Then, if we multiply by $(1 - \theta)$ and use the log-linearized aggregate price law of motion $\pi_t = (1 - \theta)\pi_t^*$, we can rewrite this as

$$(1 - \theta)\pi_t^* = (1 - \beta\theta)(1 - \theta)\Theta\widehat{mc}_t + \beta\theta\mathbb{E}_t(1 - \theta)\pi_{t+1}^* + (1 - \theta)\pi_t \qquad (4)$$

$$\pi_t = (1 - \beta\theta)(1 - \theta)\Theta\widehat{mc}_t + \beta\theta\mathbb{E}_t\pi_{t+1} + (1 - \theta)\pi_t.$$

The final step is to subtract the $(1 - \theta)\pi_t$ on the far right of equation (4) from both sides and divide by θ, giving the standard form of the marginal cost New Keynesian Phillips curve:

$$\pi_t = \frac{(1 - \beta\theta)(1 - \theta)}{\theta}\Theta\widehat{mc}_t + \beta\mathbb{E}_t\pi_{t+1}. \qquad (5)$$

Now we know how the discount factor of $\beta\theta$ in equation (2) becomes just β in equation (5): the term $(1 - \theta)\pi_t$ on the right of equation (4) added an extra factor of θ^{-1}. But we should also be suspicious: originally we had $\mathbb{E}_{it}\pi_t$ in equation (3), and we were able to replace by π_t to get the term on the right only by imposing common knowledge. Away from common knowledge, we will generally have $\mathbb{E}_{it}\pi_t \neq \pi_t$; and if variation in higher-order expectations is muted, this will result in much more equilibrium discounting than in equation (5). If expectations are formed adaptively, or higher-order expectations coalesce around recent events or historical averages, then the true Phillips curve will have lags as well.[3]

And, of course, it is an even greater leap to write a Phillips curve in terms of the output gap or unemployment directly rather than with marginal cost as in equation (1). If the relationship between the output gap and marginal cost is more complex than in the simplest New Keynesian model—as it surely is—then swapping the two without further modifying the New Keynesian Phillips curve is incorrect.[4]

Lessons from the Theory

At a conceptual level, the existence of some kind of Phillips curve seems quite robust. Prices are set in response to costs, and if there are nominal rigidities impeding immediate adjustment, then the rate of price change will respond to costs. Costs, in turn, are affected by demand pressure. The same is true for wages and the labor market.

But to go from a result like equation (3)—which requires "only" firm optimality and rational expectations—to the specific, standard form of the New Keynesian Phillips curve requires extraordinary assumptions, assumptions that are sure to be false. We should not expect such a curve to appear robustly in the data. If we try to estimate it, the numbers we will get back are at best reduced-form correlations, which need not carry over between different policy regimes or the impulses to different shocks. For instance, if inflation targeting has been successful at anchoring expectations—especially higher-order expectations—at a certain level, then the Phillips curve (eq. [5]) is likely to be shallower and feature much more discounting.[5]

Both McLeay and Tenreyro, and the applied literature more broadly, are sophisticated about this. They contemplate specifications with, for instance, different mixes of leads and lags (and also none at all). They run analyses separately by subperiod to account for the possibility that inflation targeting or other changes in policy have altered the curve.

I worry, however, that as a profession we have not fully acknowledged just how hard it should be to estimate Phillips curves, especially price Phillips curves, even if we understand the identification conundrum posed by McLeay and Tenreyro.[6] Economists love nothing better than a single, tractable equation—officially blessed by microfoundations—that can be taken to the data. The New Keynesian Phillips curve is exactly this. Most card-carrying macroeconomists can recite it, but I suspect that very few could explain exactly how it is derived or what assumptions are required.[7]

This has led to some unfortunate polarization of the debate. We must either, it sometimes seems, accept the Phillips curve as a quantitative relationship that should be estimated in some form or else deny the existence of a Phillips curve altogether. Yet a much better answer is in the middle. Like supply and demand, the Phillips curve is a conceptual building block that is indispensable to thinking about the world. It can also offer rough guidance to supplement our very limited information—for instance, by telling us in 2010 or 2011 that sustained inflation was highly unlikely. The standard is not, and should not be, a stable curve that holds up in regression after regression.

This is not to deny the importance of empirical work on the relationship between slack and inflation. But these efforts should aim to be indicative, not authoritative. A goal of estimating "the" Phillips curve is almost certainly too ambitious, and the best work may have more of a micro flavor, building up our knowledge of price and wage setting along whatever dimensions we can. Empirical success is more likely when there are fewer steps in the causal chain (unemployment to wage inflation) and less likely when there are more (output gap to price inflation).

Before we can do any of this, however, we need to throw out bad arguments against Phillips curves and understand why estimating them poses such a challenge. This makes McLeay and Tenreyro's paper an essential foundation for future work.

Endnote

Author email address: Rognlie (matthew.rognlie@northwestern.edu). For acknowledgments, sources of research support, and disclosure of the author's material financial relationships, if any, please see https://www.nber.org/chapters/c14247.ack.

1. I remember the fury of my first-year graduate macro class, when—after tediously deriving the New Keynesian Phillips curve—I showed that inflation under optimal policy was zero anyway for all the shocks we had considered thus far.

2. Some examples of papers in this emerging literature are Fitzgerald and Nicolini (2014) and Beraja, Hurst, and Ospina (2019).

3. None of this ground is new to me: it is covered, for instance, by Angeletos and Lian (2018) and Angeletos and Huo (2018).

4. Applying this reasoning, Sbordone (2002) estimated a price Phillips curve directly using evidence on marginal cost.

5. This raises the unpleasant possibility that inflation targeting may be a self-defeating approach to stabilization because by weakening the Phillips curve, it cannibalizes its own signal. This would be an extreme version of the paper's mechanism: beyond just limiting the visibility of the Phillips curve to the econometrician, the central bank's behavior might drastically weaken the relationship itself.

6. On top of the theoretical issues I emphasize, Mavroeidis, Plagborg-Møller, and Stock (2014) convincingly demonstrate the formidable econometric difficulties of estimating Phillips curves.

7. One piece of evidence for this statement: although substituting nonrational or heterogeneous expectations of π_{t+1} directly into equation (5) is incoherent—given that the derivation requires rational expectations and common knowledge, and relaxing these assumptions changes other parts of the equation—many prominent papers do exactly that.

References

Angeletos, George-Marios, and Zhen Huo. 2018. "Myopia and Anchoring." Working Paper no. 24545, NBER, Cambridge, MA.

Angeletos, George-Marios, and Chen Lian. 2018. "Forward Guidance without Common Knowledge." *American Economic Review* 108 (9): 2477–512.

Barnichon, Regis, and Geert Mesters. 2019. "Identifying Modern Macro Equations with Old Shocks." Discussion Paper no. DP13765, Center for Economic and Policy Research, Washington, DC.

Beraja, Martin, Erik Hurst, and Juan Ospina. 2019. "The Aggregate Implications of Regional Business Cycles." *Econometrica* 87 (6): 1789–833.

Christiano, Lawrence J., Martin Eichenbaum, and Charles L. Evans. 2005. "Nominal Rigidities and the Dynamic Effects of a Shock to Monetary Policy." *Journal of Political Economy* 113 (1): 1–45.

Fitzgerald, Terry J., and Juan Pablo Nicolini. 2014. "Is There a Stable Relationship Between Unemployment and Future Inflation? Evidence from US Cities." Working Paper no. 713, Federal Reserve Bank of Minneapolis.

Gali, Jordi. 2015. *Monetary Policy, Inflation, and the Business Cycle: An Introduction to the New Keynesian Framework and Its Applications.* Princeton, NJ: Princeton University Press.

Mavroeidis, Sophocles, Mikkel Plagborg-Møller, and James H. Stock. 2014. "Empirical Evidence on Inflation Expectations in the New Keynesian Phillips Curve." *Journal of Economic Literature* 52 (1): 124–88.

Ramey, Valerie A. 2016. "Macroeconomic Shocks and Their Propagation." In *Handbook of Macroeconomics*, Vol. 2, ed. John B. Taylor and Harald Uhlig, 71–162. Amsterdam: Elsevier.

Sbordone, Argia M. 2002. "Prices and Unit Labor Costs: A New Test of Price Stickiness." *Journal of Monetary Economics* 49 (2): 265–92.

Summers, Lawrence H. 1991. "Should Keynesian Economics Dispense with the Phillips Curve?" In *Issues in Contemporary Economics*, Vol. 2, *Macroeconomics and Econometrics*, ed. Mark Nerlove, 3–20. London: Springer.

Discussion

Valerie Ramey opened the general discussion by praising the paper as a good illustration of how theory and empiricism can inform each other. In particular, identification strategies rooted in theory are essential to good empirical work, she argued. Ramey discussed two identification issues when it comes to estimating Phillips curves. First, cost-push shocks are correlated with the explanatory variable, that is, output. Second, monetary policy is endogenous. The paper carefully addresses the second issue by exploiting variations at the regional level, according to Ramey. However, the first issue persists and the paper's estimates should be interpreted as lower bounds on the slope of the Phillips curve, she argued. Ramey encouraged the authors to use existing state-level data sets on demand shocks, as in Emi Nakamura and Jón Steinsson ("Fiscal Stimulus in a Monetary Union: Evidence from US Regions," *American Economic Review* 104, no. 3 [2014]: 753–92), to address the first issue. The authors were very much in agreement with Ramey's comment.

Frederic Mishkin seconded the authors' conclusions by referring to recent work of his. Peter Hooper, Frederic S. Mishkin, and Amir Sufi ("Prospects for Inflation in a High Pressure Economy: Is the Phillips Curve Dead or Is It Just Hibernating?" [Working Paper no. 25792, NBER, Cambridge, MA, May 2019]) found that the Phillips curve is flatter for periods during which monetary policy is more effective at stabilizing inflation. Indeed, the objective and the control variable should be uncorrelated when monetary policy is set optimally, he argued. Hooper et al. ("Prospects for Inflation in a High Pressure Economy") exploit regional variations—as in the authors' paper—to identify the relationship between unemployment and inflation. The identification assumption is that monetary policy is exogenous to regional shocks. Regional variations have also been exploited in the context of fiscal policy, Mishkin noted, citing again the work of Nakamura and Steinsson ("Fiscal Stimulus in a

Monetary Union"). Furthermore, Mishkin and coauthors document the presence of important nonlinearities in the Phillips curve. These nonlin-earities point toward a more responsive monetary policy when labor markets are tight, he suggested. Mishkin emphasized that identifying these nonlinearities requires a longer sample than the one used by the authors. Finally, Hooper et al. ("Prospects for Inflation in a High Pressure Economy") inspect both the price and wage Phillips curves. Their findings are in line with those presented by one of the discussants, Matthew Rognlie: there is no evidence of a disappearing Phillips curve when using wage data. Mishkin concluded with advice for policy makers. Central bankers should not interpret the apparent flattening of the Phillips curve as evidence that inflation will remain low in the future. In particular, anchoring inflation expectations is crucial for achieving price stability, Mishkin argued.

Iván Werning offered two comments. The first one was related to the paper's framing. Werning noted that the authors raise an identification issue and propose a strategy to address it. At the same time, they partly motivate their exercise using existing evidence on the flattening of the Phillips curve. However, he wondered whether these estimates are sensitive to using (or not) Hodrick-Prescott-filtered inflation data (see James H. Stock and Mark W. Watson ["Business Cycle Fluctuations in US Macroeconomic Time Series," in *Handbook of Macroeconomics*, vol. 1, ed. John B. Taylor and Michael Woodford, 3–64 (Amsterdam: Elsevier, 1999)]). The second comment was related to the implementation of optimal policy. Optimal policy requires knowledge of parameters that are impossible to identify in the first place when policy is set optimally, he noted. Werning asked how monetary authorities resolve this tension in practice. James Stock followed up on Werning's first comment. Filtering data affects the estimates of price and wage Phillips curves differently, he argued. In particular, the price Phillips curve is still flattening over time, despite filtering, whereas the wage Phillips curve is not, confirming a point made earlier by Frederic Mishkin. The authors confirmed that the paper's motivation lies in the identification issue itself rather than on existing evidence on the flattening of the aggregate Phillips curve. On the second comment, the authors agreed that setting monetary policy optimally supposes that policy makers know the exact shape of the Phillips curve, which might be difficult in practice.

Kristin Forbes praised the paper for providing a very intuitive explanation for the flattening of the Phillips curve. She viewed this explanation as very complementary to the ones already put forth in the literature, including the role of mismeasurement of the output gap and inflation. Forbes offered a suggestion based on existing work of hers. Using UK data, Kristin J. Forbes, Lewis Kirkham, and Konstantinos Theodoridis ("A Trendy Approach to UK Inflation Dynamics" [Research Paper no. 5268-18, MIT Sloan, Cambridge, MA, January 2018]) found that inflation is more responsive to changes in the exchange rate than in the output gap or unemployment. She argued that extending the paper's analysis to allow for asymmetric responses to changes in unemployment and exchange rate would be an interesting avenue. The authors were very sympathetic to Forbes's suggestion. Exchange rate movements act as large cost-push shocks in a small open economy like the United Kingdom, they pointed out. This explains in part why the slope of the price Phillips curve is not significant in the United Kingdom, whereas the slope of the wage Phillips curve is.

James Stock followed up on Forbes's comment. He saluted the authors' effort to provide a unifying exposition of the issues inherent to the identification of the aggregate Phillips curve, from weak identification to the robustness of the wage Phillips curve. Stock also suggested using locally determined prices—instead of core consumer price index, as in the paper—when exploiting regional variations. The authors thanked Stock for his suggestion and referred to an ongoing project of theirs, which uses disaggregated price data in the United Kingdom.

Jordi Galí commented on the difference between Phillips curves at the regional and national levels. He pointed out that the elasticity of labor supply is an important determinant of the slope of the Phillips curve. Labor is mobile across regions, he noted, whereas it is mostly immobile across countries. As a consequence, the slopes of regional and national Phillips curves are predicted to be different, he suggested. Galí also asked the authors whether they had found evidence of a flattening of Phillips curves at the regional level. Erik Hurst and Michael Klein added that regional mobility has declined over time, referring in particular to recent work by Benjamin A. Austin, Edward L. Glaeser, and Lawrence H. Summers ("Jobs for the Heartland: Place-Based Policies in 21st Century America" [Working Paper no. 24548, NBER, Cambridge, MA, April 2018]). Klein also asked whether there is evidence of a flattening Phillips curve in Europe. The authors observed that a higher elasticity of labor supply at the regional level would bias their estimates downward so that they provide a lower bound on the slope of the aggregate Phillips curve.

Regarding a potential flattening of regional Phillips curves, they mentioned that their sample—which begins in 1990—is too short to investigate time trends. The same issue applies to the European monetary union, they argued.

The authors concluded the general discussion by thanking the two discussants, Marc Giannoni and Matthew Rognlie, for their comments.

5

Trading Up and the Skill Premium

Nir Jaimovich, *University of Zurich and CEPR*
Sergio Rebelo, *Northwestern University, NBER, and CEPR*
Arlene Wong, *Princeton University and NBER*
Miao Ben Zhang, *University of Southern California*

I. Introduction

US income inequality has greatly increased in the last four decades. This increase has motivated a plethora of policy proposals aimed at narrowing the gap between rich and poor. These proposals include making income taxes more progressive (Diamond and Saez 2011; Landais, Picketty, and Saez 2011), introducing wealth taxes (Saez and Zucman 2019), subsidizing college tuition for students from low-income households (Chetty et al. 2017), and investing in neighborhoods to promote upward mobility (Chetty and Hendren 2018).

In evaluating these and other policy proposals, it is useful to understand the dynamics of income inequality: Are there stabilizing forces that naturally narrow the gap between rich and poor? One such force is the likely increase in the relative supply of high-skill workers. In the canonical model used by Katz and Murphy (1992) and many others, this increase lowers the skill premium, naturally reducing income inequality.

In this paper, we argue that this stabilizing force is likely to be weaker than suggested by the canonical model. This weakness stems from the fact that as income rises, households "trade up." That is, they increase the quality of the goods and services they consume. Trading up fosters inequality in labor earnings because, as we show in this paper, high-quality goods are more intensive in skilled labor than low-quality goods. So, as households improve the quality of what they consume, they increase the demand for skilled labor, contributing to a rise in the skill premium.

This paper has an empirical and a theoretical component. In our empirical work, we show that skill intensity rises with quality and that the quality of household consumption rises with income.

To study the relation between quality and skill intensity, we proceed as follows. We use the price of a good or service as a proxy for its quality.

The idea underlying this approach is that consumers are willing to pay more for an item if they perceive it to be of higher quality. Our price measures come from two sources: Nielsen Homescan and Yelp!, a website where consumers post review information about different goods and services.

We match each establishment in the Yelp! data and each manufacturing firm in the Nielsen Homescan data with the microdata of Occupational Employment Statistics (OES) from the Bureau of Labor Statistics (BLS). We combine these data with the US Department of Commerce Current Population Survey (CPS) to construct measures of skill intensity for each establishment and manufacturing firm in our data.

To document the relation between quality and income, we use data from Nielsen Homescan as well as data on durable expenditures from the Consumer Expenditure Survey (CEX).

In our theoretical work, we propose a simple model consistent with our two facts. The model is designed to be as similar as possible to the canonical model used by Katz and Murphy (1992) to study the dynamics of the skill premium. In our model, both skill-biased technical change (SBTC) and Hicks-neutral technical change (HNTC) increase real income, thus expanding the demand for quality. Because quality is intensive in high-skill workers, the demand for these workers rises, leading to an endogenous rise in the skill premium and a widening of the income distribution.

Our model has implications for how we interpret the past dynamics of the skill premium. Using Fernald's (2014) estimates of the rate of HNTC, we compute the rate of SBTC consistent with the rate of change in the quality of goods consumed estimated by Bils and Klenow (2001).[1] We find that our model accounts for the observed rise in the skill premium in the last 4 decades with an annual rate of SBTC of 1.05% per year. In contrast, the canonical model used by Katz and Murphy (1992) requires a rate of SBTC of 5.5% per year.

Our model also has implications for the future dynamics of the skill premium. To explore these implications, we forecast the increase in the supply of skilled workers. To isolate the effect of this supply increase, we abstract from HNTC and SBTC. The canonical model implies a 21% fall in the skill premium. In contrast, our model predicts a 15% fall in the skill premium. This smaller decline in the skill premium occurs because the preponderance of high-skill workers in the labor force is associated with higher household income that boosts the demand for quality, increasing the demand for skilled labor.

To explore these results and study the robustness of our conclusions, we consider two variants of the benchmark model. The first variant has two types of households, one composed by high-skill workers and the other by low-skill workers. These households consume different levels of quality, so there are two quality levels produced in equilibrium. We find that the results are similar to those of the benchmark model. The reason for this similarity is that in our basic calibration the price-quality schedule is not far from linear, so producing two levels of quality instead of one does not affect substantively the properties of the equilibrium.

In the second variant of the benchmark model, the household consumes two types of goods, a basic good with a constant level of quality and a quality good, whose quality can vary on a continuum. The level of SBTC required to explain the rise in the skill premium in this model is in between that implied by our benchmark model and the canonical model, but closer to the benchmark model. These properties result from the presence of two effects. First, a rise in income is spent in part on the basic good, weakening the degree of trading up. Second, because the quality good is superior, its share in spending rises with income. This effect increases the impact of income rises on the degree of trading up and on the skill premium.

Our work is related to five strands of literature. The first strand is the large body of work on SBTC surveyed by Acemoglu and Autor (2011). The second strand is the literature on the role of capital deepening in explaining the evolution of the skill premium (e.g., Krusell et al. 2000; Polgreen and Silos 2008; Burstein and Vogel 2017). We show in the appendix that incorporating the trading-up phenomenon in these models reduces the resulting estimates of the elasticity of substitution between unskilled labor and capital. The third strand is work on skill-biased structural change (e.g., Acemoglu and Guerrieri 2008; Buera and Kaboski 2012; Boppart 2015; Buera, Kaboski, and Rogerson 2015; Alon 2018). This work emphasizes how rises in income shift demand toward sectors that are more intensive in skilled work. In contrast, we emphasize that, as income rises, the demand for quality increases, raising the demand for skilled labor within a given sector. One important difference between these two mechanisms is that the process of upgrading quality within a sector is presumably unbounded, whereas sectoral reallocation is likely to be bounded. The fourth strand is work on the importance of quality choice in growth models (e.g., Grossman and Helpman 1991a, 1991b; Stokey 1991; Zweimüller 2000; Foellmi and Zweimüller 2006), trade models (e.g., Verhoogen 2008; Fieler, Eslava, and Xu 2018), and macro models (e.g., Jaimovich, Rebelo, and Wong 2019). The fifth strand is the industrial organization literature on product differentiation (e.g., Shaked and Sutton 1982; Berry 1994).

This paper is organized as follows. Sections II and III contain our empirical work. In Section IV, we present our benchmark model and discuss its implications for the rate of SBTC required to explain the rise in the skill premium. We also consider an extension of the model with two heterogeneous households. In Section V, we analyze the model with two goods, one with constant quality and the other with variable quality. Section VI concludes.

II. Quality and Skill Intensity

In this section, we measure the intensity of skilled labor in establishments that are in the same sector but produce products of different quality. To accomplish this goal, we first construct measures of both the quality of goods produced and skill intensity by establishment. We then study the relation between quality and skill intensity.

There are three approaches used in the literature to measure quality. The first approach, which we adopt in this paper, is to use relative prices as proxies for quality. The idea underlying this approach is that consumers are willing to pay more for an item if they perceive it to be of higher quality.[2] The second approach is to infer quality from the materials and labor costs used in production (e.g., Verhoogen 2008). The third approach is to structurally estimate quality using data on prices and quantities combined with functional form assumptions about household utility (e.g., Verhoogen 2008; Hottman, Redding, and Weinstein 2016). We focus on relative prices as measures of quality because doing so allows us to use a broader sample of goods and of firms included in the OES data set.[3]

There is strong evidence that relative prices are positively correlated with the quality measures produced by the other two approaches. For example, Verhoogen (2008) finds that higher-quality items, which have higher costs of production, also have higher prices. Hottman et al. (2016) and Khandelwal (2010) find that quality is strongly positively correlated with relative prices within product groups.

Before we dive into our empirical analysis, it is useful to illustrate our results with data for the restaurant sector. According to OES data, the key occupations in restaurants are managers and executives, chefs and head cooks, first-line supervisors of food preparation, cooks and food preparation workers, waiters and waitresses, serving workers, and marketing and sales staff. Chefs, a high-skill occupation, represent on average 20% of the workforce in a full-service restaurant but only 2% in a limited-service restaurant.[4] As income rises and consumers trade up in the quality of the restaurants they patronize, the demand for chefs expands, contributing to a rise in the skill premium.

A. Measuring Skill Intensity

Our measure of the intensity of skilled labor is based on two data sets. The first is the OES data collected by the BLS, which cover 1.1 million establishments, representing 62% of total employment and spanning all sectors of the North American Industry Classification System (NAICS) at a six-digit level. Unfortunately, the OES does not contain information on worker education attainment. For this reason, we calculate the distribution of employees across 12 wage bins for each occupation and establishment from the OES and relate this wage distribution to the wages of skilled workers estimated using the CPS. We use the information regarding wages, education, and industry in the CPS as follows. For every industry in the CPS, we compute the average wage of college graduates. We classify workers in the OES as skilled if their wage exceeds the average wage of college graduates for their industry. We then compute for each establishment in the OES data the fraction of employment and of the wage bill accounted for by skilled workers.

We proceed similarly to construct two other measures of the share of skilled workers. For our second measure, we classify workers as skilled if their wage exceeds the average wage of workers with "some college or more" for the workers' industry. For our third measure, we classify workers as skilled if their wage exceeds the average wage for all workers in the respective industry.

Table 1 displays our results for different sectors. Consider, for example, the sector of manufacturing. Using the first measure of skill, we find that the fraction of manufacturing workers who are skilled is 13.9% and that these workers earn 43.1% of the wage bill. Using the second and broader classification of skill, we find that the fraction of manufacturing workers who are skilled is 20.9% and that the share of the wage bill earned by these workers is 49.4%. Using the third and broadest classification of skill, we find that the fraction of manufacturing workers who are skilled is 29.8% and that the share of the wage bill earned by these workers is 59.6%.

Table 1
Establishments' Share of Skilled Workers

	Number of Establishments	Skilled 1		Skilled 2		Skilled 3	
Sample	(1)	Emp (2)	Wage (3)	Emp (4)	Wage (5)	Emp (6)	Wage (7)
All sectors	1,131,170	16.7	36.9	23.7	45.6	27.7	49.9
NAICS sector:							
Management	13,997	50.3	53.6	63.5	59.5	61.0	63.0
Educational	39,385	33.6	25.4	38.0	38.2	40.9	48.0
Information	33,176	29.3	45.4	34.8	58.2	40.0	64.3
Utilities	6,217	29.8	30.3	35.9	31.1	55.9	31.6
Professional	106,407	28.9	29.1	34.3	38.1	37.6	48.6
Transportation	43,934	28.3	25.7	40.5	37.1	46.6	42.0
Construction	82,188	23.8	44.2	29.4	51.7	38.7	71.7
Finance	56,599	23.6	53.8	30.1	59.6	31.9	64.9
Wholesale	86,176	19.8	31.3	26.8	41.6	30.9	51.6
Health care	124,463	16.4	55.1	27.1	59.8	29.7	63.0
Other services	73,062	15.4	10.4	24.4	22.7	27.8	24.7
Manufacturing	107,826	13.9	43.1	20.9	49.4	29.8	59.6
Entertainment	26,549	12.0	38.9	20.0	53.2	19.7	55.5
Real estate rental	37,750	10.3	49.9	16.1	56.8	24.8	58.7
Retail	121,065	9.6	42.7	17.8	52.1	21.7	56.1
Administrative	77,873	8.8	74.6	17.2	84.1	25.6	82.3
Accommodation	50,700	3.2	31.7	10.4	43.4	11.5	43.3

Note: This table shows the average share of skilled workers per establishment by sector computed using Occupational Employment Statistics surveys of establishments from May 2004 to November 2007. We consider three definitions of skilled workers. In "Skilled 1, 2, and 3," workers are skilled if their wage exceeds the average wage of college graduates in the industry, the average wage of workers with some college education in the industry, and the average wage of workers in the industry, respectively. The three average wages for each industry are estimated with Current Population Survey data. Columns 2, 4, and 6 (labeled "Emp") refer to the average employment share of skilled workers per establishment. Columns 3, 5, and 7 (labeled "Wage") refer to the average share of wages received by skilled workers per establishment. See text for more details.

B. *Quality Measures*

We use prices of goods as a proxy for their quality. Our price measures come from two sources. The first is data from Yelp!, a website where consumers post review information about different goods and services. The second is Nielsen Homescan data.

Yelp!-based Quality Measures

For each store and location pair, Yelp! asks users to classify the price of the goods and services they purchased into one of the following four

categories: $ (low), $$ (middle), $$$ (high), and $$$$ (very high). Be-
cause there are few observations in the very high category, we merge
the last two categories into a single high-price category.

We match Yelp! establishments to the OES establishments in three
steps. First, we match the contact phone numbers of Yelp! establish-
ments to the contact phone numbers of the OES establishments. When-
ever this method does not work, we base the match on name, industry
(NAICS three digit), and zip code.[5] When multiple OES establishments
are matched to one (or multiple) Yelp! establishment(s), we average the
skill measures of all the OES establishments that are matched to each
Yelp! establishment and assign that average skill measure to the Yelp!
establishment.[6] Third, because zip codes are not available for every es-
tablishment in the OES database, we conduct a matching procedure sim-
ilar to that used in our second step based on name, industry (NAICS three
digit), and county. With these three steps, we obtain the share of skilled
labor for 9,908 Yelp! establishments. These data cover the retail, accom-
modation, entertainment, and information services sectors.

Nielsen-based Quality Measures

To extend our analysis to the manufacturing sector, we use the Nielsen
Homescan data. This data set contains prices paid and quantities of gro-
ceries purchased at a barcode (Universal Product Code [UPC]) level for
113 thousand households over the period 2004–10. Nielsen organizes
barcodes into 613 product modules according to where they would likely
be stocked in a store.

To construct a measure of quality for each manufacturing firm, we
proceed as follows. First, we link each item k (defined at a UPC level)
in Nielsen with the manufacturing firm f that produced the UPC using
information obtained from GS1 US.[7] We focus on the 2006 data set to
match the sample period of the OES data.

Second, we compute the sales-weighted average price across all trans-
actions made during the month t, p_{kft}, for each item k produced by firm f.
Similarly, for each product module $m(k)$ that item k belongs to, we cal-
culate $p_{m(k)t}$, the sales-weighted average price within the product mod-
ule. For each item k, we then calculate the price p_{kft} in month t relative
to the average price in the product module, $p_{m(k)t}$:

$$R_{kft} = \frac{p_{kft}}{p_{m(k)t}}.$$

By dividing prices by the average price in the product module, we can
compare the relative prices of items across different categories of goods.

For single-product firms, our measure of quality is the average relative price for each given item produced by the firm in 2006. For multiproduct firms, we compute the firm f's relative price as a weighted average of the relative price of different products, weighted by sales in 2006 (w_{kf}):

$$R_{f,2006} = \sum_{k \in \Omega} w_{k,f,2006} R_{k,f,2006},$$

where Ω denotes the set of all products in the Nielsen data.

Third, we link each manufacturing firm f in the Nielsen-GS1 database to the OES firms. To do so, we perform a fuzzy merge of the first component of the firm names from the Nielsen-GS1 firm with the first component of the OES legal or trade names. We take a conservative approach in classifying a successful fuzzy merge. A merge between Nielsen-GS1 and the OES is defined as successful if one of the following three situations occur: (i) the similarity score is above 95%, (ii) the similarity score, computed using the Levenshtein distance, is above 90% and two names share the same first two words, or (iii) the similarity score is above 85% and one name contains the other name. This approach yields about 1,600 firms, which include over 29,000 OES establishments.

C. Quality and Skill Intensity

Table 2 documents our first fact using the Yelp! data set: the share of high-skill workers employed increases with the quality of the goods produced by the firm. Consider, for example, the results we obtain using our measure of skilled workers based on the average wage of college graduates in the industry. The fraction of high-skill workers is 3.54, 6.38, and 9.49 in our low-, middle-, and high-quality tiers, respectively. Our estimates of skill intensity naturally vary with the breadth of the definition of skill. But, as table 2 shows, our three alternative definitions of high skill generate similar estimates of the differences in skill intensity of high- versus low-quality goods.

Table 3 provides results analogous to those in table 2 obtained using Nielsen's Homescan data. Here, too, the share of high-skill workers employed is an increasing function of the quality of the goods produced by the firm. Consider, for example, the results we obtain using our measure of skilled workers based on the average wage of college graduates in the industry. The fraction of high-skill workers is 1.2–1.5 times higher in

Table 2
Quality and Share of High-skill Workers in Retail

Sample	Number of Establishments (1)	Skilled 1		Skilled 2		Skilled 3	
		Emp (2)	Wage (3)	Emp (4)	Wage (5)	Emp (6)	Wage (7)
Yelp! sample	9,908	6.01	16.9	13.94	29.02	15.40	31.14
By quality:							
Low	2,316	3.54	11.15	9.60	21.32	11.48	23.81
Middle	6,089	6.38	17.28	14.94	30.19	16.01	31.80
High	1,503	9.49	23.72	19.40	36.97	21.53	40.24

Note: This table shows the average share of skilled workers per establishment per Yelp! quality tier. Low quality refers to the $ Yelp! category. Middle quality refers to the $$ Yelp! category. High quality refers to the $$$ and $$$$ Yelp! categories. The statistics are based on the Occupational Employment Statistics survey of establishments from May 2004 to November 2007. We consider three definitions of skilled workers. In "Skilled 1, 2, and 3," workers are skilled if their wage exceeds the average wage of college graduates in the industry, the average wage of workers with some college education in the industry, and the average wage of workers in the industry, respectively. The three average wages for each industry are estimated with Current Population Survey data. Columns 2, 4, and 6 (labeled "Emp") refer to the average employment share of skilled workers per establishment. Columns 3, 5, and 7 (labeled "Wage") refer to the average share of wages received by skilled workers per establishment. See text for more details.

the high-quality tier when compared with the low-quality tier. The difference between the skill intensity of high- and low-quality products is lower than in the Yelp! data. This property is likely to reflect smaller differences in the quality of groceries, which are the most important category of goods in Nielsen Homescan, than in other categories such as durables.

D. Quality and Routine Work

Acemoglu and Autor (2011) argue that the distinction between skilled and unskilled workers may be less relevant to study new forms of automation. These forms of automation, such as artificial intelligence, might replace routine tasks that are performed by high-skill workers (e.g., radiologists).

In table 4, we study the relation between quality and the intensity of routine and nonroutine work. Two patterns emerge from our data. First, the share of routine workers is lower in the production of high-quality goods when compared with that of low-quality goods. So quality is

Table 3
Quality and Share of High-skill Workers

	Number of Firms	Skilled 1		Skilled 2		Skilled 3	
		Emp	Wage	Emp	Wage	Emp	Wage
Sample	(1)	(2)	(3)	(4)	(5)	(6)	(7)
Nielsen sample	1,097	12.64	30.76	22.04	42.43	28.04	48.30
By quality:							
Low	384	10.46	25.89	20.47	38.67	26.03	44.04
Middle	339	11.63	29.30	21.14	41.25	26.55	46.82
High	374	15.79	37.08	24.48	47.38	31.45	54.02

Note: This table shows the average share of skilled workers per establishment for each quality tier for the food manufacturing sector. The low-, middle-, and high-quality tiers are based on the firms in the bottom third, middle third, and top third of relative prices (within each product category) of firms in Nielsen Homescan data, respectively. The statistics are based on the Occupational Employment Statistics survey of establishments from May 2004 to November 2007. We consider three definitions of skilled workers. In "Skilled 1, 2, and 3," workers are skilled if their wage exceeds the average wage of college graduates in the industry, the average wage of workers with some college education in the industry, and the average wage of workers in the industry, respectively. The three average wages for each industry are estimated with Current Population Survey data. Columns 2, 4, and 6 (labeled "Emp") refer to the average employment share of skilled workers per establishment. Columns 3, 5, and 7 (labeled "Wage") refer to the average share of wages received by skilled workers per establishment. See text for more details.

intensive in nonroutine work. Second, the part of nonroutine work that rises with quality is abstract work, not manual work.

III. Quality and Income

Our second empirical fact is that the quality of the goods and services consumed by households rises with income. We document this fact using data from the CEX and the Nielsen Homescan data. Our findings corroborate previous results in the literature. Bils and Klenow (2001) show that for a wide range of durable goods in the CEX, households with higher total expenditures consume higher-quality goods. Similarly, Faber and Fally (2019), Jaravel (2019), and Argente and Lee (2016) show that higher-income households consume higher-quality goods. There is also a large trade literature that shows that as countries get richer, they increase the quality of what they consume (see, e.g., Verhoogen 2008; Fieler et al. 2018).

Table 4
Quality and Share of Workers Performing Different Tasks

				Nonroutine			
		Routine		Manual		Abstract	
	Number						
	of Firms	Emp	Wage	Emp	Wage	Emp	Wage
Sample	(1)	(2)	(3)	(4)	(5)	(6)	(7)
By quality:							
Low	384	76.66	62.78	5.24	3.36	18.10	33.87
Middle	339	80.62	62.77	2.35	1.57	17.03	35.66
High	374	69.16	51.44	7.60	3.95	23.24	44.60

Note: This table shows the average share of workers per establishment performing each of the three following tasks: routine, nonroutine manual, and nonroutine abstract. We stratify the summary statistics by quality tier for establishments in the food-manufacturing sector. The low-, middle-, and high-quality tiers are based on firms in the bottom third, middle third, and top third of relative prices of firms in Nielsen Homescan data, respectively. The statistics are based on the Occupational Employment Statistics survey of establishments from May 2004 to November 2007. Columns 2, 4, and 6 (labeled "Emp") refer to the average employment share of routine, nonroutine manual, and nonroutine abstract per establishment, respectively. Columns 3, 5, and 7 (labeled "Wage") refer to the average share of wages received by of routine, nonroutine manual, and nonroutine abstract per establishment, respectively. See text for more details.

A.   Consumer Expenditure Survey

Our first data set includes durable expenditures from the CEX. Our data cover 73,000 households over the period 1980–2013. Durables are defined as categories whose items have a life that exceeds 2 years. These categories include home furnishing (e.g., carpeting, curtains, mattresses, and sofas), appliances (e.g., dryers, microwaves, stoves, and radios), electronics, and vehicles. The advantage of using durables expenditures is that, given that households are unlikely to buy more than one item at a time, we can, as in Bils and Klenow (2001), use expenditures as a measure of the price paid for each item.

We estimate the quality Engel curve as follows. As in Bils and Klenow (2001), we express the unit price of an item paid by household h at time t as $x_{ht} = z_{ht} q_{ht}$, where z_{ht} is the quality-adjusted price and q_{ht} is the quality of the item. We estimate θ, the elasticity of quality with respect to income, using the following specification:

$$\ln(q_{ht}) = \beta_0 + \theta \ln(y_{ht}) + \epsilon_{ht},$$

where y denotes the income of household h in period t, and ϵ_{ht} denotes the residual.

We can rewrite this specification as

$$\ln(x_{ht}) = \beta_0 + \theta \ln(y_{ht}) + \ln(z_{ht}) + \epsilon_{ht}. \tag{1}$$

The logarithm of quality-adjusted price, $\ln(z_{ht})$, is an unobservable variable that reflects differences in prices across time and across households that are not related to the choice of quality. It can, for instance, be due to differences in shopping intensity across households, which affects the prices paid for the same item. It may also be due to differences in the discounts available in different locations. As in Bils and Klenow (2001), we include demographic controls to account for these unobservable factors that may affect prices paid. These controls include the age of the households, family size, household fixed effects, and time fixed effects.

Table 5 reports our regression results using five income quintile dummies, so that θ is a vector. This table shows that high-income households pay on average 80% more than low-income households for items of a given category. In our view, these differences are too large to be

Table 5
Prices and Income: Consumer Expenditure Survey (CEX)

CEX Survey Durables	Regression 1	Regression 2
Relative to income quintile 1:		
Income quintile 2	.205	.197
	(.010)	(.010)
Income quintile 3	.368	.353
	(.010)	(.010)
Income quintile 4	.533	.513
	(.010)	(.009)
Income quintile 5 (top)	.834	.82
	(.010)	(.010)
Time fixed effects	Yes	Yes
Category fixed effects	Yes	Yes
Demographic controls	Yes	No
Number of observations	824,851	824,851

Note: This table shows the θ estimates implied by regression 1 and reports the log-difference in price paid by each income quintile relative to the lowest income quintile. We used CEX data for the period 1980–2013. Column 1 includes demographic controls for age, family size, and number of income earners in the household. Column 2 does not include demographic controls. Estimates in both columns 1 and 2 are clustered by household. See text for more details.

explained by price discrimination or different search intensities. For example, Aguiar and Hurst (2007) estimate that doubling the shopping frequency lowers the price paid for a given good by only 7% to 10%.

B. Nielsen Homescan

We supplement the empirical evidence on the relation between income and quality for durable goods with a second data set, the Nielsen Homescan data, which focuses on nondurable goods such as grocery products.

We compute an average price across households, $\bar{P}_{imt}$, for every item i in product module m and time t. By using this average price, we ensure that differences in overall prices paid by households reflect differences in choice of item-store rather than shopping intensity (i.e., using coupons and taking advantage of promotions). For each household, we compute the price of module m at time t as

$$\log (P_{hmt}) = \sum_i w_{iht} \log (\bar{P}_{imt}).$$

We then estimate the following regression:

$$\log (P_{hmt}) = \beta_0 + \sum_k \beta_k 1(y_{ht} \in k) + \gamma X_{ht} + \lambda_t + \lambda_m + \varepsilon_{hmt}, \qquad (2)$$

where $1(y_{ht} \in k)$ is a dummy variable equal to 1 if the household income is in quintile k, X_{ht} denotes demographic controls (age group, employment status, size of family, and ethnicity), λ_t denotes time fixed effects, λ_m denotes product-module fixed effects, and is the error term.

Table 6 reports our estimates. Columns 1 and 2 report results without and with demographic controls, respectively. The results are similar. Households in the top quintile choose items that are 22.7% more expensive than households in the bottom quintile. This difference is economically large given that most of the products included in Nielsen's Homescan data are groceries. This is an expenditure category in which price differentials are relatively small when compared with categories such as durable goods.

IV. A Simple Model

In this section, we consider a simple model that is consistent with our two empirical facts. First, firms that produce higher-quality goods employ a higher share of high-skill workers. In other words, quality is skill

Table 6
Prices and Income: Nielsen Homescan Data

Nielsen Homescan	Regression 1	Regression 2
Relative to income quintile 1:		
Income quintile 2	.0399	.0398
	(.0004)	(.0004)
Income quintile 3	.0911	.0908
	(.0004)	(.0004)
Income quintile 4	.151	.150
	(.0004)	(.0004)
Income quintile 5 (top)	.227	.224
	(.0004)	(.0004)

Note: This table shows the coefficients for β_k implied by regression 2 and reports the log-difference in price paid by each income quintile relative to the lowest income quintile. We used Nielsen Homescan data for the period 2004–10. Column 1 includes demographic controls for age, family size, and number of income earners in the household. Column 2 does not include demographic controls. Estimates in both columns 1 and 2 are clustered by household. See text for more details.

intensive. Second, the quality of the goods a household consumes rises with income. In other words, quality is a normal attribute. We then consider the implications of our model for the measurement of SBTC.

Before we delve into the details of our model, we review the key features of the canonical model used to explain the rise in the skill premium. In this model, output, Y, is produced according to the following production function:

$$Y = A[\alpha(SH)^\rho + (1 - \alpha)L^\rho]^{\frac{1}{\rho}}, \qquad (3)$$

where S denotes the level of SBTC, A denotes the level of HNTC, H is the supply of skilled work, and L is the supply of unskilled work.

Output is produced by firms that are competitive in product and factor markets. The optimization conditions for these firms imply that the skill premium, defined as the ratio of the wage rate of skilled, W_H, and unskilled, W_L, workers, is given by

$$\frac{W_H}{W_L} = \frac{\alpha}{1 - \alpha} S_t^\rho \left(\frac{H}{L}\right)^{\rho-1}. \qquad (4)$$

This expression implies that changes in A have no impact on the skill premium. Computing logarithmic growth rates of the two sides of equation (4), we obtain

$$\Delta \log \left(\frac{W_H}{W_L} \right) = \rho \Delta \log (S) + (\rho - 1)\Delta \log \left(\frac{H}{L} \right). \qquad (5)$$

According to the estimates in Acemoglu and Autor (2011), the relative supply of effective labor of skilled workers H/L increased by about 110% and the skill premium increased 22% between 1970 and 2008. As in Acemoglu and Autor (2011), we assume that ρ equals 0.41.[8] Equation (5) implies that $\Delta \log(S) = 210.8\%$, which corresponds to an average annual rate of SBTC of 5.5%.

A. Homogeneous Households

We make some simplifying assumptions so that our model is as similar as possible to the canonical model used in the SBTC literature. These assumptions are (i) no capital in production, (ii) a single production sector, and (iii) households consume a single unit of the consumption good, so changes in expenditures translate fully into changes in the quality of the goods consumed. These assumptions allow us to derive results without taking a stand on the form of the utility function.

Household

We consider a representative household composed by the same fraction of skilled and unskilled workers present in the population. The household pools its resources and buys a single unit of a consumption good of quality q at a price $P(q)$. The household budget constraint is given by

$$P(q) = W_H H + W_L L,$$

where H and L denote high- and low-skill workers, respectively. We treat the supply of high- and low-skill workers as exogenous and assume that workers are identical within each skill group. Household utility is given by

$$U = V(q),$$

where $V'(q) > 0$, $V''(q) \leq 0$.

Production

Final goods are produced by competitive firms using skilled and unskilled labor according to the production function:

$$Y = A[\alpha(SH)^\rho + q^{-\gamma\rho}(1-\alpha)(L)^\rho]^{\frac{1}{\rho}}, \tag{6}$$

where $\rho > 0$, $\gamma \geq 0$, and q denotes the quality of the good produced. When $\gamma = 0$, this production function is identical to the one used in the canonical model (eq. [3]). Firms only produce the level or levels of quality demanded by households.

The equilibrium price of a good of quality q is given by

$$P(q) = \frac{1}{A}\left[\alpha^{\frac{1}{1-\rho}}(S)^{\frac{\rho}{1-\rho}}W_H^{\frac{\rho}{\rho-1}} + (1-\alpha)^{\frac{1}{1-\rho}}(q)^{\frac{\gamma\rho}{\rho-1}}W_L^{\frac{\rho}{\rho-1}}\right]^{\frac{\rho-1}{\rho}}.$$

The production function (eq. [6]) with $\gamma > 0$ together with the perfect-competition assumption implies two key properties. First, $P'(q) > 0$; that is, the price of a final good is increasing in its quality. Second, quality is intensive in high-skill labor; that is, the labor share of high-skill labor, $W_HH/(W_HH + W_LL)$, is increasing in q.

Skill Premium

The firms' optimization conditions imply that the skill premium is given by

$$\frac{W_H}{W_L} = \frac{\alpha q^{\gamma\rho}(S)^\rho}{(1-\alpha)}\left(\frac{H}{L}\right)^{\rho-1}. \tag{7}$$

Computing growth rates, we see that the change in the skill premium is the one obtained in the canonical model (eq. [5]) plus the effect of trading up on the skill premium, which is given by the term $\gamma\rho\Delta\log(q)$ in the following expression:

$$\Delta\log\left(\frac{W_H}{W_L}\right) = \rho\Delta\log(S) + (\rho-1)\Delta\log\left(\frac{H}{L}\right) + \gamma\rho\Delta\log(q). \tag{8}$$

Equations (7) and (8) show that quality plays a role that is similar to that of SBTC. Other things equal, a rise in quality increases the demand for skilled labor raising the skill premium.

Skill-Biased Technical Change and Hicks-Neutral Technical Change

When we combine the household budget constraint and the firms' first-order condition, we obtain the following equation:

$$A \times S = \frac{\left(\frac{W_H}{W_L}\right)^{\frac{1}{\rho}} \left(\frac{H}{L}\right)^{\frac{1-\rho}{\rho}}}{\alpha^{\frac{1}{\rho}} L \left[\frac{W_H}{W_L} \frac{H}{L} + 1\right]^{\frac{1}{\rho}}}. \tag{9}$$

Equation (9) implies that, holding constant H and L, a change in A has the same impact on the skill premium as a change in S. This equivalence holds because in our model a change in A triggers a change in q:

$$q = \left[A(1-\alpha)^{\frac{1}{\rho}} \left(\frac{W_H}{W_L} H + L\right) \left(\frac{W_H H}{W_L L} + 1\right)^{\frac{1-\rho}{\rho}}\right]^{\frac{1}{\gamma}}, \tag{10}$$

and this change in q has an effect on the skill premium that is similar to that of a rise in S (see eq. [7]).

Quantitative Results

The estimates in Acemoglu and Autor (2011) suggest that between 1970 and 2008 the skill premium increased by 25 percentage points, whereas the effective ratio of high-skill labor to low-skill labor increased by 110 percentage points. In what follows, we use our model to characterize the combinations of SBTC and HNTC that are consistent with these observed changes in W_H/W_L, H, and L.

Using equation (9) to compute logarithmic growth rates, we obtain

$$\Delta A + \Delta S = \frac{1}{\rho}(\Delta W_H - \Delta W_L) + \frac{1-\rho}{\rho}(\Delta H - \Delta L) - \Delta L + \frac{1}{\rho}\Delta \left(1 + \frac{W_H H}{W_L L}\right). \tag{11}$$

Following Acemoglu and Autor (2011), we set $\rho = 0.41$. Given this value of ρ, we can compute the right-hand side of equation (11), which is equal to 1.92% on an annual basis. The left-hand side of the equation gives us the combinations of ΔA and ΔS that match the right-hand side.

Table 7 reports results for both our model and the canonical model for different combinations of HNTC and SBTC. We choose γ equal to 1.15 so that for our benchmark calibration (row 3) our model is consistent with the Bils and Klenow (2001) estimates for Δq (3.8% per year).

Row 1 corresponds to the case where there is no HNTC or SBTC. In the canonical model, the skill premium falls by 65%. In our model, this fall is only 46%. The reason for this result is that in our sample more workers became skilled over time, creating a rise in income that induces

Table 7
Trading-up and Canonical Model

		Cumulative $\Delta(W_H/W_L)$ (%)	
	ΔS	Trading-up Model	Canonical Model
ΔA	(1)	(2)	(3)
(1) .00	.00	−46	−65
(2) .87	.00	−25	−65
(3) .87	1.05	25	−48

Note: All numbers in percentages. ΔA and ΔS are reported on an annual basis. $\Delta(W_H/W_L)$ is the value for the entire sample.

households to trade up, expanding the demand for high-skill labor and increasing the skill premium.

In row 3, we set the rate of SBTC to 0 and choose the annual rate of HNTC to match Fernald's (2014) estimates for total factor productivity growth for the period 1970–2008 (0.87% per year). Our model predicts a 25% fall in the skill premium because the rise in the demand for skilled workers is not strong enough to overcome the increase in the relative supply of skilled workers. In this calibration, HNTC accounts for 30% of the rise in the skill premium, whereas in the canonical model it accounts for 0% of this rise.[9]

Row 3 reports results for our benchmark specification. We set the annual rate of HNTC to match Fernald's (2014) estimates and choose the annual growth rate of SBTC so that our model is consistent with the observed rise in the skill premium. The required annual rate of SBTC is 1.05%, a much more plausible number than the 5.5% required by the canonical model to match the observed rise in the skill premium. In the canonical model, the configuration of HNTC and SBTC considered in row 3 results in a 48% fall in the skill premium. Comparing rows 2 and 3, we see that even though in our benchmark calibration the rate of SBTC is only 1.05% per year, the presence of SBTC is essential to produce a rise in the skill premium.

The Future of the Skill Premium

Our model can shed some light on the future evolution of the skill premium. We start by forecasting the fraction of high-skill workers in 2026 using data from the US Department of Education. To simplify, we treat this fraction as exogenous. High-skill workers are defined as those with educational attainment equal to some college or associate degree, bachelor's degree, and advanced degree. A linear regression fits well the data from 1992 to 2016, so we base our projections on this regression. We forecast a rise in the fraction of high-skill workers from 62% in 2008 to 71% in 2026.

To isolate the impact of this increase in the supply of skilled workers, we first abstract from technical progress. We calibrate our model with the same value of γ used in the benchmark case (1.15). Our results are reported in row 1 of table 8. The canonical model implies a moderation in income inequality with the skill premium falling by 21%. In contrast, our model predicts a decline of only 15% in the skill premium. This smaller decline in the skill premium occurs because the preponderance of high-skill workers in the labor force means higher household income, which boosts the demand for quality, increasing the demand for skilled labor.

B. Heterogeneous Households

In the model described earlier, we make several simplifying assumptions to derive analytical results about the impact of trading up on the skill premium. In particular, there is only one quality level produced in equilibrium. So the model cannot, by construction, match the cross-sectional relation between quality and the share of high-skill workers used in production.

Table 8
Forecasting the Skill Premium: Trading-up and Canonical Model

		Cumulative $\Delta(W_H/W_L)$ (%)	
ΔA	ΔS	Trading-up Model	Canonical Model
(1) .0	.0	−14	−21
(2) .8	.0	25	−21

Note: Next, we use the forecast of the rate of change in Hicks-neutral technical change produced by Fernald (2016), which is 0.8% per year. Our results are reported in row 2. Our model implies that the skill premium will increase by 25% between 2008 and 2026, the same as occurred between 1970 and 2008. These results reflect the fact that, according to our projections, the fraction of high-skill workers will increase by less in the future than in the 1970–2008 period.

In this subsection, we extend the model by considering an economy where there is more than one consumption good produced in equilibrium. This version of our model has two types of households. The first type has only low-skill workers and the second type only high-skill workers. These households receive different income levels and, as a result, they consume goods of different quality.

Production

Household type $j \in \{L, H\}$ consumes goods of quality q_j, which are produced according to

$$Y_{q_j} = A\left[\alpha(SH_j)^\rho + q_j^{-\gamma\rho}\left(1 - \alpha\right)L_j^\rho\right]^{\frac{1}{\rho}}.$$

The price of a good of quality q_j is

$$P_{q_j} = \frac{1}{A}\left[\alpha^{\frac{1}{1-\rho}}S^{\frac{\rho}{1-\rho}}W_H^{\frac{\rho}{1-\rho}} + q_j^{\frac{\gamma\rho}{\rho-1}}(1 - \alpha)^{\frac{1}{1-\rho}}W_L^{\frac{\rho}{1-\rho}}\right]^{\frac{\rho-1}{\rho}}. \tag{12}$$

We assume perfect labor mobility, which implies that the skill premium is identical in both the high- and low-quality production sectors. The first-order conditions for competitive output producers imply that the skill premium in each sector j is given by

$$\frac{W_H}{W_L} = \frac{\alpha}{1 - \alpha}(q_j^\gamma \times S)^\rho \left(\frac{H_j}{L_j}\right)^{\rho-1}.$$

For future reference, we note that using the expression for the skill premium implies that total expenditure in each of the goods produced is given by

$$P_{q,j}Y_{q,j} = W_L L_{q,j}\left[1 + \frac{W_H}{W_L}\left(\frac{H_{q,j}}{L_{q,j}}\right)\right].$$

Households

There is a measure $\Gamma(H)$ of skilled workers and $\Gamma(L) = 1 - \Gamma(H)$ of unskilled workers. The supply of skilled work measured in efficiency units is $H = H_{q,L} + H_{q,H}$. Similarly, the supply of unskilled workers in efficiency units is $L = L_{q,L} + L_{q,H}$.

The maximization problem of high-skill households is

$$\max U = V(q_H),$$

subject to

$$P(q_H) = W_H H.$$

Similarly, the maximization problem of low-skill households is

$$\max U = V(q_L),$$

subject to

$$P(q_L) = W_L L.$$

Equilibrium

Using the budget constraints of low- and high-skill workers, we obtain

$$L_{q,L} \left[1 + \frac{W_H}{W_L} \left(\frac{H_{q,L}}{L_{q,L}} \right) \right] = L,$$

$$L_{q,H} \left[1 + \frac{W_H}{W_L} \left(\frac{H_{q,H}}{L_{q,H}} \right) \right] = \frac{W_H}{W_L} H.$$

As in the previous section, we look for combinations of SBTC and HNTC that are consistent with the observed changes in the skill premium and aggregate changes in L and H.

To solve this two-sector model, we proceed as follows. We guess $H_{q,L}/L_{q,L}$. The budget constraint of low-skill workers implies a value for $L_{q,L}$. Using this value, we can compute $H_{q,L}$ and $H_{q,H}$. We can then compute the ratio of the two qualities produced:

$$\frac{q_H^\gamma \left(\frac{W_H}{W_L} \frac{H_H}{L_H} + 1 \right)^{\frac{\rho-1}{\rho}} \Gamma_H}{q_L^\gamma \left(\frac{W_H}{W_L} \frac{H_L}{L_L} + 1 \right)^{\frac{\rho-1}{\rho}} \Gamma_L} = \frac{W_H}{W_L} \frac{H}{L}.$$

Given the observed skill premium, the overall measures of high- and low-skill workers, and the equilibrium sectoral allocation, these identify the ratio of qualities, q_H/q_L. With this ratio, we then verify that the skill premium is identical in both sectors.

Before commenting on the implications for the measurement of the SBTC, we note that we can compute the share of high-skill workers in labor income ($W_H H/(W_L H + W_H L)$) in the production of the high- and low-quality goods. Importantly, the model has no free parameters that allow us to target these ratios, so it is of interest to see whether the model comes close to the observed numbers in the data. The ratio of these shares is 2.4 in the beginning of the sample and 2.5 in the end of the sample. We also compare the share of high-skill labor ($H/(H + L)$) used in the production of the high- and the low-quality goods. The ratio of these shares is 2.8 in the beginning of the sample and 3.6 in the end of the sample. These values are somewhat higher than those reported in table 2 for the ratio of highest quality ($$$) and the lowest quality ($).

Once we find the equilibrium sectoral allocation, we use the fact that each consumer purchases one unit of the good and, thus, $Y_{q,j} = \Gamma(j)$ from which it follows that for each sector the following equation holds:

$$\Delta A - \gamma \Delta q_H = \frac{\rho - 1}{\rho} \Delta \left(1 + \frac{W_H}{W_L} \frac{H_H}{L_H}\right) + \Delta \Gamma_H - \Delta \left(\frac{W_H}{W_L} H\right).$$

The right-hand side is a given number (given the data and the equilibrium sectoral allocation). Hence, given different values of ΔA, we can recover Δq for each of the two sectors. Then from the skill premium equation,

$$\frac{W_H}{W_L} = \frac{\alpha}{1 - \alpha} (q_j^\gamma \times S)^\rho \left(\frac{H_j}{L_j}\right)^{\rho-1},$$

we can recover the consistent value of ΔS.

We redo the analysis for the same configurations of γ, ΔA, and ΔS used in table 7. The results are almost identical, showing that our results are robust to introducing the form of income heterogeneity embodied into this model. The reason for this robustness is that in our calibration the price-quality schedule is close to linear, so that producing two levels of quality instead of one does not affect substantively the properties of the equilibrium. The linearity of the price-quality schedule comes from two sources. First, the value of $\rho(0.41)$ is close to 0.5, which makes the exponent $(\rho - 1)/\rho$ in equation (12) close to 1. Second, the value of γ (1.15) is also close to 1.

It is interesting to ask how real wages of low- and high-skill workers evolve over time in our benchmark calibration. We deflate wages with the price level evaluated at a constant quality level, the one consumed in the beginning of the sample. These quality levels are denoted by q_{0H} and q_{0L} for high- and low-skill households, respectively. The real wages for high- and low-skill workers are $W_H/P(q_{0H})$ and $W_L/P(q_{0L})$, respectively. The prices $P(q_{0H})$ and $P(q_{0L})$ change between the beginning and end of the sample as a result of endogenous changes in wages and the two types of technical progress, SBTC and HNTC. The annual rate of change in prices is as follows: $\Delta P(q_{0L}) = -1.3\%$ and $\Delta P(q_{0H}) = -4.7\%$. Because W_L is the *numeraire*, the rate of change in the real wage of the low-skill household is the symmetric of the price change: $\Delta W_L / P(q_{0L}) = -1.3\%$. The rate of change in the real wage of the high-skill household is $\Delta W_H / P(q_{0H}) = 5.3\%$. Because the price of quality falls more for the high-skill workers than for the low-skill workers, the ratio of the real wages of high- and low-skill workers grows by more than the skill premium. In other words, the divergence in real wages across skill groups exceeds the rise in the skill premium.

V. Quantity and Quality

In our benchmark model, whenever a household receives additional income it devotes it fully to increasing the quality of the good it consumes. In this section, we explore how the impact of trading up changes when the household buys both one unit of a quality good, available in a continuum of different qualities, and a basic good (C) with a fixed level of quality.

We assume that the utility function takes the form used by Bils and Klenow (2001):

$$U = \frac{C^{1-\frac{1}{\sigma}}}{1 - \frac{1}{\sigma}} + \nu \frac{q^{1-\frac{1}{\sigma_q}}}{1 - \frac{1}{\sigma_q}}. \tag{13}$$

The budget constraint of the representative household is

$$P(q) \times 1 + C = HW_H + LW_L.$$

The basic good is produced according to the following production function:

$$Y_c = A \left[\alpha (SH_c)^\rho + (1 - \alpha)(L_c)^\rho \right]^{\frac{1}{\rho}}.$$

The quality good is produced according to

$$Y_q = A \left[\alpha (SH_q)^\rho + q^{-\gamma\rho}(1 - \alpha)(L_q)^\rho \right]^{\frac{1}{\rho}}.$$

The labor market clearing conditions are

$$H = H_c + H_q,$$
$$L = L_c + L_q.$$

The goods market clearing conditions are

$$Y_q = 1,$$
$$Y_c = C.$$

We calculate the annual rate of change in SBTC that rationalizes the rise in the skill premium over the period 1970–2008. We use the same annual rate of HNTC (0.83) and the same value of ρ (0.41) used in the benchmark model. The value of σ is set to 1, and the ratio σ_q/σ is chosen to match the estimates of Bils and Klenow (2001), which is 0.76.

We search for combinations of α, ν, and γ that allow us to match three targets. The first is the annual growth rate for q_t estimated by Bils and Klenow (2001) (3.8%). The second is the average share of quality goods in expenditure (41%). The third is the ratio of the share of skilled labor in income in high- versus low-quality goods from table 3:

$$\frac{\frac{W_H H_q}{W_H H_q + W_L L_q}}{\frac{W_H H_c}{W_H H_c + W_L L_c}} = 1.6.$$

Here we are using the basic good as the low-quality good and the quality good as the high-quality good.

We find that the level of SBTC necessary to rationalize the skill premium is 1.4%. This value is in between the value obtained for the benchmark model (1.05%) and the canonical model (5.5%) but closer to the value implied by the benchmark model.

The intuition for these results is as follows. A rise in income produces less trading up because some of the additional income is spent on the basic good. As a result, the effect of a rise in income on the skill premium is weaker than in the benchmark model. There is, however, another effect. The utility function (eq. [13]) implies that the quality good is a superior good, so its share in spending rises as income rises, expanding the demand for skilled workers and contributing to increasing the skill premium. This effect is absent in our benchmark model. In that model, the share of income spent on the high-quality good cannot rise because it is already 100%.

VI. Conclusions

In this paper, we show empirically that as income rises, households trade up to higher-quality goods and that these goods are intensive in skilled labor. As a result, the demand for high-skill labor rises, increasing the skill premium. This trading-up phenomenon amplifies the effect of SBTC by creating an endogenous rise in the demand for skilled workers.

In the canonical model, technical change has to be skill biased to produce a rise in the skill premium. In our model, any factor that raises income increases the skill premium. This idea has important implications for the future evolution of the skill premium. Growth in income that is not accompanied by an increase in the supply of skilled workers is likely to increase the skill premium even in the absence of skill-biased technological change.

Acemoglu and Autor (2011) argue that the distinction between skilled and unskilled workers may be less relevant to study forms of automation such as artificial intelligence, which may replace routine tasks performed by high-skill workers. Motivated by this argument, we study the relation between quality and the intensity of routine and nonroutine works. We find that low-quality goods are intensive in routine work and that high-quality goods are intensive in nonroutine, abstract work. So, as households trade up, we expect to see a rise in the relative wages of nonroutine, abstract workers.

The choice of the quality of goods and services consumed by households has implications not just for the skill premium but also for changes in the overall wage distribution. We find that quality increases lead to a relative decline in the demand for routine workers. According to the estimates of Autor and Dorn (2013), workers in the 10th to 50th percentiles of the 1980 wage distribution have jobs with a high share of routine tasks. So the wages of these workers are likely to decline relative to the wages of workers on the bottom and top of the wage distribution.

Taken as a whole, our evidence suggests that considering endogenous changes in the quality of consumption is an important avenue for future work on the dynamics of income inequality.

Appendix

Capital Deepening and the Skill Premium

Krusell et al. (2000) argue that capital deepening associated with investment-specific technical progress explains much of the rise in the skill premium. To reexamine their analysis, we adopt their functional form for the production function. Output with quality q is produced according to the following nested Constant Elasticity of Substitution (CES) function,

$$Y_q = K_S^\gamma \left[\alpha (\lambda K_E^\sigma + (1-\lambda)H^\sigma)^{\frac{\varrho}{\sigma}} + q^{-\gamma\rho}(1-\alpha)(L)^\rho \right]^{\frac{1-\gamma}{\rho}}, \qquad (14)$$

where K_S is the stock of structures and K_E is the stock of equipment.

To retain the one-sector character of the model, we assume that investing I_{qt} units of output with quality q_t yields $P(q_t)$ units of installed capital. The capital accumulation equation takes the form

$$K_{St+1} = P_{qt}I_{qSt} + (1-\delta)K_{St},$$

$$K_{Et+1} = P_{qt}I_{qEt} + (1-\delta)K_{Et},$$

where I_{qSt} and I_{qEt} denote the investment in structures and equipment, respectively.

The market clearing condition for output is

$$Y_{qt} = 1 + I_{qSt} + \frac{I_{qEt}}{z_t},$$

where $1/z_t$ is the relative price of equipment. Recall that the representative household buys one unit of a good with quality q_t.

We use the wage of low-skill workers as the *numeraire*,

$$W_L = 1,$$

but for clarity we retain the symbol W_L in the derivations that follow.

Output producers are competitive in goods and factors markets. Profit maximization implies the following first-order conditions:

$$P_q \gamma K_S^{\gamma-1} \left[\alpha (\lambda K_E^\sigma + (1-\lambda)H^\sigma)^{\frac{\varrho}{\sigma}} + q^{-\gamma\rho}(1-\alpha)(L)^\rho \right]^{\frac{1-\gamma}{\rho}} = R_S,$$

$$P_q (1-\gamma) K_S^\gamma \left[\alpha (\lambda K_E^\sigma + (1-\lambda)H^\sigma)^{\frac{\varrho}{\sigma}} + q^{-\gamma\rho}(1-\alpha)(L)^\rho \right]^{\frac{1-\gamma-\rho}{\rho}}$$

$$\times \; \alpha (\lambda K_E^\sigma + (1-\lambda)H^\sigma)^{\frac{\varrho-\sigma}{\sigma}} \frac{\lambda K_E^\sigma}{K_E} = R_E, \qquad (15)$$

$$P_q (1-\gamma) K_S^\gamma \left[\alpha (\lambda K_E^\sigma + (1-\lambda)H^\sigma)^{\frac{\varrho}{\sigma}} + q^{-\gamma\rho}(1-\alpha)(L)^\rho \right]^{\frac{1-\gamma-\rho}{\rho}}$$

$$\times \; \alpha (1-\lambda)(\lambda K_E^\sigma + (1-\lambda)H^\sigma)^{\frac{\varrho-\sigma}{\sigma}} \frac{H^\sigma}{H} = W_H, \qquad (16)$$

$$P_q (1-\gamma) K_S^\gamma \left[\alpha (\lambda K_E^\sigma + (1-\lambda)H^\sigma)^{\frac{\varrho}{\sigma}} + q^{-\gamma\rho}(1-\alpha)(L)^\rho \right]^{\frac{1-\gamma-\rho}{\rho}}$$

$$\times \; q^{-\gamma\rho}(1-\alpha)(L)^{\rho-1} = W_L, \qquad (17)$$

where R_S and R_E are the rental rates on structures and equipment, respectively.

These first-order conditions imply that the price of a good with quality q is

$$P_q = \frac{R_S^{\gamma}\left[\alpha^{\frac{1}{1-\rho}}\left(\lambda^{\frac{1}{1-\sigma}}R_E^{\frac{\sigma}{\sigma-1}} + (1-\lambda)^{\frac{1}{1-\sigma}}W_H^{\frac{\sigma}{\sigma-1}}\right)^{\left(\frac{\sigma-1}{\sigma}\right)\left(\frac{\rho}{\rho-1}\right)} + (1-\alpha)^{\frac{1}{1-\rho}}q^{\left(\frac{\gamma\rho}{\rho-1}\right)}(W_L)^{\frac{\rho}{\rho-1}}\right]^{\left(\frac{\rho-1}{\rho}\right)(1-\gamma)}}{\gamma^{\gamma}(1-\gamma)^{1-\gamma}}.$$

(18)

Equations (16) and (17) imply that the skill premium is given by

$$\frac{\alpha(1-\lambda)(\lambda K_E^{\sigma} + (1-\lambda)H^{\sigma})^{\frac{\rho-\sigma}{\sigma}}H^{\sigma-1}}{(1-\alpha)q^{-\gamma\rho}L^{\rho-1}} = \frac{W_H}{W_L}.$$

(19)

Combining equations (15) and (16), we obtain

$$\left(\frac{1-\lambda}{\lambda}\right)\left(\frac{K_E}{H}\right)^{-\sigma}R_E K_E = W_H H.$$

(20)

Combining equations (19) and (20), the skill premium can be written as

$$\frac{\alpha(1-\lambda)^{\frac{\rho}{\sigma}}}{(1-\alpha)} \times \frac{\left[1 + \frac{R_E K_E}{W_H H}\right]^{\frac{\rho-\sigma}{\sigma}}}{q^{-\gamma\rho}}\left(\frac{H}{L}\right)^{\rho-1} = \frac{W_H}{W_L}.$$

(21)

If we abstract from the impact of quality by assuming that q is constant and equal to 1, we obtain the same expression for the skill premium equation used in Krusell et al. (2000).

Some Analytics

Recall that σ is the parameter that governs the elasticity of substitution between capital and high-skill workers. To see the effects of the presence of quality on the point estimates for σ, it is useful to log-linearize equation (21),

$$(\rho - \sigma)\frac{1}{1 + \frac{W_H H}{R_E K_E}}(\hat{K}_E - \hat{H}) + (\rho - 1)(\hat{H} - \hat{L}) + \gamma\rho\hat{q} = \widehat{W_H} - \widehat{W_L},$$

(22)

where $\hat{x}$ denotes the logarithmic growth rate of x. Solving equation (22) for σ, we obtain

$$\sigma = \frac{1 + \frac{W_H H}{R_E K_E}}{\hat{K}_E - \hat{H}}$$

$$\times \left[\frac{\rho(\hat{K}_E - \hat{H})}{1 + \frac{W_H H}{R_E K_E}} + (\rho - 1)(\hat{H} - \hat{L}) - \widehat{W_H} + \widehat{W_L} + \gamma \rho \hat{q} \right]. \tag{23}$$

Capital-skill complementarity requires $\sigma \leq \rho$. How are these estimates affected by trading up? The answer to this question depends on the value of $\gamma \rho \hat{q}[1 + W_H H/(R_E K_E)]/(\hat{K}_E - \hat{H})$. In the Krusell et al. (2000) data, $\hat{K}_E - \hat{H} > 0$. Because $\rho > 0$, an increase in $\hat{q}$ implies that the right-hand side is overall a higher number. Because $\sigma < 0$, the degree of capital-skill complementarity required to match the same empirical facts is reduced.

Trading up also affects the point estimates of ρ, the parameter that governs the degree of substitutability between unskilled workers and the composite good of equipment capital and skilled workers. To see this effect, note that the value of ρ as a function of a given value of σ can be expressed as

$$\rho = \frac{\frac{\sigma(\hat{K}_E - \hat{H})}{1 + \frac{W_H H}{R_E K_E}} + \left(\widehat{W_{II}} + \hat{H} - \widehat{W_L} - \hat{I} \right)}{\frac{\hat{K}_E - \hat{H}}{1 + \frac{W_H H}{R_E K_E}} + \left(\hat{H} - \hat{L} \right)}{1 + \frac{\gamma q}{\frac{\hat{K}_E - \hat{H}}{1 + \frac{W_H H}{R_E K_E}} + \left(\hat{H} - \hat{L} \right)}}. \tag{24}$$

The change in the level of quality affects only the denominator, reducing the value of ρ. As a result, the degree of substitutability of unskilled labor and the composite good of equipment and skilled worker $(1/(1 - \rho))$ will fall.

In this analysis, we are holding constant the value of σ when analyzing the effects of quality on the measurement of ρ and vice versa when analyzing the effects of quality for the measurement of σ. Naturally, both of these estimates can change as a result of quality. We thus proceed by jointly estimating these two parameters.

Estimation

In this section, we estimate the production function using the approach proposed by Polgreen and Silos (2008).[10] In this approach, the posterior distribution is obtained by combining a prior distribution for the vector of parameters with a measurement-error-based likelihood function for the data.

The estimation is based on three conditions. The first is the equation for the labor share in income:

$$\frac{W_L L}{P_q Y_q} + \frac{W_H H}{P_q Y_q} = (1 - \gamma) Y_q^{\frac{-\rho}{1-\gamma}} \left[\alpha(1 - \lambda)(\lambda K_E^\sigma + (1 - \lambda)H^\sigma)^{\frac{\rho-\sigma}{\sigma}} H^\sigma + q^{-\gamma\rho}(1 - \alpha)L^\rho \right].$$

The second condition is the equation for the ratio of labor income of skilled and unskilled agents:

$$\frac{W_H H}{W_L L} = \frac{\alpha(1 - \lambda)(\lambda K_E^\sigma + (1 - \lambda)H_q^\sigma)^{\frac{\rho-\sigma}{\sigma}} H^\sigma}{q^{-\gamma\rho}(1 - \alpha)L_q^\rho}.$$

The third condition equates the rate of return to investing in structures and equipment:

$$\gamma K_S^{\gamma-1} \left[\alpha(\lambda K_E^\sigma + (1 - \lambda)H^\sigma)^{\frac{\rho}{\sigma}} + q^{-\gamma\rho}(1 - \alpha)(L)^\rho \right]^{\frac{1-\gamma}{\rho}} + (1 - \delta)$$

$$= (1 - \gamma)K_S^\gamma \left[\alpha(\lambda K_E^\sigma + (1 - \lambda)H^\sigma)^{\frac{\rho}{\sigma}} + q^{-\gamma\rho}(1 - \alpha)(L)^\rho \right]^{\frac{1-\gamma-\rho}{\rho}}$$

$$\times \alpha(\lambda K_E^\sigma + (1 - \lambda)H^\sigma)^{\frac{\rho-\sigma}{\sigma}} \lambda K_E^{\sigma-1} + \frac{(1 - \delta)z_{t-1}}{z_t}.$$

Estimating ρ and σ

We begin by replicating the analysis of Polgreen and Silos (2008) and estimate ρ and σ in a model without quality choice. The resulting estimates are $\rho = 0.4470$ and $\sigma = -0.3871$.

We now estimate ρ and σ in a model with quality choice. As we do not have a time series for Δq, we consider a constant trend in quality at the annual growth rate estimated by Bils and Klenow (2001). We obtain the following estimates: $\rho = 0.2485$ and $\sigma = -0.3730$. As suggested by our analytical results, incorporating quality choice into the model implies a fall in the degree of substitutability of unskilled labor and the composite good of equipment and skilled worker ($1/(1 - \rho)$). This elasticity of substitution between unskilled labor and capital falls from $1/(1 - 0.4470) = 1.81$ to $1/(1 - 0.2485) = 1.33$.

Endnotes

Author email addresses: Jaimovich (nir.jaimovich@uzh.ch), Rebelo (s-rebelo@north western.edu), Wong (arlenewong@princeton.edu), Zhang (miao.zhang@marshall.usc .edu). We thank Daron Acemoglu, Gadi Barlevy, Carlos Burga, Martin Eichenbaum, Berthold Herrendorf, Eric Hurst, Ben Moll, Jonathan Vogel, and Carlo Zanella for their comments. For acknowledgments, sources of research support, and disclosure of the authors' material financial relationships, if any, please see https://www.nber.org/chapters /c14253.ack.

1. These estimates are obtained by regressing the BLS's inflation measure on the growth rate of expenditures instrumented with the slope of the quality Engel curve.

2. See Jaimovich et al. (2019) for evidence that supports this assumption.

3. Structural estimation generally requires price shifters to instrument for price changes. A commonly used price shifter for an item sold in a particular county is the average price of the item in other counties. Using this shifter restricts the analysis to items sold in many counties, which results in a substantial reduction in sample size.

4. At Alinea, a high-end restaurant in Chicago, chefs represent 30% of the workforce.

5. A major challenge is that the phone number in the OES database can be either the phone number of the establishment or the phone number of the contact person for the establishment, such as the person's mobile phone number. We obtain industry codes of Yelp! establishments by matching them to the ReferenceUSA database, which covers the near universe of establishments in the United States. Establishments from the two data sets with the same industry, zip code, and similar names based on bigram are also matched. This fuzzy name matching increases the match rate of the two data sets.

6. For instance, two Starbucks coffee shops may locate in the same zip code. In this case, our approach assumes that the two coffee shops share the same skill measure.

7. We thank David Argente, Munseob Lee, and Sara Moreira for sharing their code to link UPCs to firms with us. These links between items and firms are also used in Hottman et al. (2016) and in Argente, Lee, and Moreira (2019).

8. Estimates for ρ generally range from 0.16 (Card and Lemieux 2001) to 0.5 (Angrist 1996).

9. In the absence of HNTC and SBTC, the skill premium falls by 46% (table 7, row 1 of col. 2). HNTC and SBTC together raise the change in the skill premium from −46% to +25%. With HNTC and no SBTC, the skill premium falls by 25%. So the fraction of the rise in the skill premium accounted for by HNTC is $[-25 - (-46)] = (25 - (-46)) = 30\%$.

10. We are extremely grateful to Pedro Silos for kindly sharing with us his code and for various consultations.

References

Acemoglu, D., and D. Autor. 2011. "Skills, Tasks and Technologies: Implications for Employment and Earnings." In *Handbook of Labor Economics*, Vol. 4, 1043–171. Amsterdam: Elsevier.

Acemoglu, D., and V. Guerrieri. 2008. "Capital Deepening and Nonbalanced Economic Growth." *Journal of Political Economy* 116:467–98.

Aguiar, Mark, and Erik Hurst. 2007. "Lifecycle Production and Prices." *American Economic Review* 97 (5): 1533–59.

Alon, Titan. 2018. "Earning More by Doing Less: Human Capital Specialization and the College Wage Premium." Manuscript, University of California at San Diego.

Angrist, J. D. 1996. "Short-run Demand for Palestinian Labor." *Journal of Labor Economics* 14 (3): 425–53.

Argente, David, and Munseob Lee. 2016. "Cost of Living Inequality during the Great Recession." Manuscript, Penn State University, Pennsylvania.

Argente, David, Munseob Lee, and Sara Moreira. 2019. "How Do Firms Grow? The Life Cycle of Products Matters." Manuscript, Kellogg School of Management, Northwestern University.

Autor, David H., and David Dorn. 2013. "The Growth of Low-Skill Service Jobs and the Polarization of the US Labor Market." *American Economic Review* 103 (5): 1553–97.

Berry, S. T. 1994. "Estimating Discrete-Choice Models of Product Differentiation." *RAND Journal of Economics* 25 (2): 242–62.

Bils, Mark, and Peter J. Klenow. 2001. "Quantifying Quality Growth." *American Economic Review* 91 (4): 1006–30.

Boppart, Timo. 2015. "To Which Extent Is the Rise in the Skill Premium Explained by an Income Effect?" Working paper, IIES Stockholm University.

Buera, F. J., J. P. Kaboski, and R. Rogerson. 2015. "Skill Biased Structural Change." Working Paper no. w21165, NBER, Cambridge, MA.

Buera, Francisco J., and Joseph P. Kaboski. 2012. "The Rise of the Service Economy." *American Economic Review* 102 (6): 2540–69.

Burstein, Ariel, and Jonathan Vogel. 2017. "International Trade, Technology, and the Skill Premium." *Journal of Political Economy* 125 (5): 1356–412.

Card, D., and T. Lemieux. 2001. "Can Falling Supply Explain the Rising Return to College for Younger Men? A Cohort-Based Analysis." *Quarterly Journal of Economics* 116 (2): 705–46.

Chetty, R., and N. Hendren. 2018. "The Impacts of Neighborhoods on Intergenerational Mobility II: County-Level Estimates." *Quarterly Journal of Economics* 133 (3): 1163–228.

Chetty, Raj, John N. Friedman, Emmanuel Saez, Nicholas Turner, and Danny Yagan. 2017. "Mobility Report Cards: The Role of Colleges in Intergenerational Mobility." Working Paper no. w23618, NBER, Cambridge, MA.

Diamond, Peter, and Emmanuel Saez. 2011. "The Case for a Progressive Tax: From Basic Research to Policy Recommendations." *Journal of Economic Perspectives* 25 (4): 165–90.

Faber, Benjamin, and Thibault Fally. 2019. "Firm Heterogeneity in Consumption Baskets: Evidence from Home and Store Scanner Data." *Review of Economic Studies*, Manuscript, University of California, Berkeley.

Fernald, John. 2014. "A Quarterly, Utilization-adjusted Series on Total Factor Productivity." FRBSF Working Paper 2012–19, Federal Reserve Bank of San Francisco.

Fernald, John G. 2016. "Longer-Run U.S. Growth: How Low?" Manuscript, Federal Reserve Bank of San Francisco.

Fieler, A. C., M. Eslava, and D. Y. Xu. 2018. "Trade, Quality Upgrading, and Input Linkages: Theory and Evidence from Colombia." *American Economic Review* 108 (1): 109–46.

Foellmi, Reto, and Josef Zweimüller. 2006. "Income Distribution and Demand-Induced Innovations." *Review of Economic Studies* 73 (4): 941–60.

Grossman, Gene M., and Elhanan Helpman. 1991a. "Quality Ladders in the Theory of Growth." *Review of Economic Studies* 58 (1): 43–61.

———. 1991b. "Quality Ladders and Product Cycles." *Quarterly Journal of Economics* 106 (2): 557–86.

Hottman, Colin, Stephen J. Redding, and David Wenstein. 2016. "Quantifying the Sources of Firm Heterogeneity." *Quarterly Journal of Economics* 131 (3): 1291–364.

Jaimovich, Nir, Sergio Rebelo, and Arlene Wong. 2019. "Trading Down and the Business Cycle." *Journal of Monetary Economics* 102:96–121.

Jaravel, Xavier. 2019. "The Unequal Gains from Product Innovations: Evidence from the U.S. Retail Sector." *Quarterly Journal of Economics* 134 (2): 715–83.

Katz, L. F., and K. M. Murphy. 1992. "Changes in Relative Wages, 1963–1987: Supply and Demand Factors." *Quarterly Journal of Economics* 107 (1): 35–78.

Khandelwal, Amit. 2010. "The Long and Short (of) Quality Ladders." *Review of Economic Studies* 77 (4): 1450–76.

Krusell, P., L. E. Ohanian, J. V. Ríos-Rull, and G. L. Violante. 2000. "Capital-skill Complementarity and Inequality: A Macroeconomic Analysis" *Econometrica* 68 (5): 1029–53.

Landais, Camille, Thomas Piketty, and Emmanuel Saez. 2011. *Pour une révolution fiscale: Un impôt sur le revenu pour le XXIème siècle*. Seuil: La Republique des Idees.

Polgreen, L., and P. Silos. 2008. "Capital-skill Complementarity and Inequality: A Sensitivity Analysis." *Review of Economic Dynamics* 11 (2): 302–13.

Saez, Emmanuel, and Gabriel Zucman. 2019. "How Would a Progressive Wealth Tax Work? Evidence from the Economics Literature." Manuscript, University of California Berkeley (February).

Shaked, A., and J. Sutton. 1982. "Relaxing Price Competition through Product Differentiation." *Review of Economic Studies* 49:3–13.

Stokey, Nancy L. 1991. "Capital, Product Quality, and Growth." *Quarterly Journal of Economics* 106 (2): 587–616.

Verhoogen, E. A. 2008. "Trade, Quality Upgrading, and Wage Inequality in the Mexican Manufacturing Sector." *Quarterly Journal of Economics* 123 (2): 489–530.

Zweimüller, J. 2000. "Schumpeterian Entrepreneurs Meet Engel's Law: The Impact of Inequality on Innovation-Driven Growth." *Journal of Economic Growth* 5 (2): 185–206.

Comment

Daron Acemoglu, *Massachusetts Institute of Technology and NBER*

There is by now a huge literature on the increase in the college premium and other dimensions of inequality in the United States and many other Western nations (see Acemoglu and Autor [2011] for an overview of this literature). As I discuss in the following text, the focal explanation in this literature is that technological changes of the last 4 decades have increased the demand for skills and have pushed up premia to different kinds of skills, college education among them (though other factors including globalization and changes in labor market institutions have also contributed to these trends).

The paper by Jaimovich, Rebelo, Wong, and Zhang tackles an important topic and develops a relatively underresearched line of inquiry within this broad literature. The main idea is that a major contributor to the increase in the demand for skills has been "trading up" (the authors' term) by households to higher-quality products as they have become richer. Higher-quality products are argued to be more intensive in skilled labor. As a result, this process has naturally brought a higher demand for skills as a by-product of economic growth.

This is an important idea, and one I sympathize with a lot. The paper also has a noteworthy original contribution in providing compelling motivating evidence. It estimates product quality from a variety of sources, links these to establishment-level demand for skills from the microdata of the Occupational Employment Statistics (OES) data set of the Bureau of Labor Statistics, and verifies that higher-quality products are more skill intensive than products of lower quality. This empirical work alone is worth more than the price of admission.

But the paper does not fully deliver on this very promising research agenda. The reason why it fails to do that is interesting and instructive. It is because it follows a methodology I call quantitative Friedmanite modeling. This approach combines Friedman's (1953/2008) famous methodological dictum that realism of assumptions does not matter (sometimes called the "as if" hypothesis) with an emphasis on developing quantitative evaluations of macro models calibrated with some plausible choice of parameters. This methodology has some obvious shortcomings at the best of times (replicating some moments in the data based on microeconomic parameter choices does not reject alternative hypotheses nor does it provide clear support for the proposed mechanisms). In the current context, however, it is even more problematic because it pushes the authors away from engaging with the key economic forces their own hypothesis and evidence bring to the table.

I use the rest of this short essay to briefly discuss the paper's contribution, what I mean by quantitative Friedmanite modeling, why this methodology fails to shed light on the issues at hand, and the different approaches that might have been more fruitful.

The Contribution

Most analyses of the demand for skills in labor and macro literatures do not distinguish between quality differences across goods and assume that the demand for the different types of goods (with different skill intensities) have the same income elasticity, so that changes in the income level (or even income distribution) of households do not directly change the demand for skills.

The current paper starts by relaxing these assumptions. First, it allows for quality differences between different goods. For example, Dunkin' Donuts coffee and handcrafted artisanal coffee are not perfect substitutes, and the latter has a higher income elasticity so that as consumers become richer, their demand will shift away from Dunkin' Donuts toward the specialized coffee shops (see, e.g., Shaked and Sutton 1982). Second, it posits that the production functions for lower- and higher-quality goods are different and producing higher-quality goods requires more skills. In the context of the coffee example, Dunkin' Donuts is assumed to need less skilled workers than the specialized coffee shop.

Put these two pieces together, and we can conclude that as (some) households in the economy become richer, they will change the composition of their demand and in particular they will start demanding higher-quality vintages—namely, more of the handcrafted coffee and less of the Dunkin' Donuts fare. All else equal, this will increase the demand for skills and put upward pressure on the skill premium.

This is a very plausible mechanism, but of course the devil is in the details. How important is it? Why is it that higher-quality vintages require more skilled workers?

Moreover, the mechanism, though underresearched and probably underappreciated, has featured in other papers already. Two lines of work are particularly noteworthy. The first is a series of papers by Marco Leonardi (2003, 2015), which argues for the same type of differential income elasticity and investigates how much of the increase in the demand for skills this mechanism can account for. In Leonardi's work, for example, higher-skilled workers demand more of the goods produced by other higher-skilled workers, whereas lower-skilled workers consume less skill-intensive goods. The second line comprises a number of theoretical investigations of the inequality implications of nonhomothetic preferences, including Zweimuller (2000), Foellmi and Zweimuller (2006), and Foellmi, Wuergler, and Zweimuller (2014), as well as related work by Matsuyama (2002).

Despite this earlier literature, it is fair to say that there has been no fully convincing evidence that the production of higher-quality products is more skill intensive. The most important contribution of the current paper is to establish this fact.

The authors first estimate the quality of different products using data from Yelp! and the Nielsen Homescan data. For example, from Yelp!, they use the information on the price categories (low, middle, high, and very high) provided by users. They then match the Yelp! establishments to the OES establishments, where they can measure various proxies for skill intensity. They focus on measures of skills based on wages (rather than education), so skilled workers are those with relatively high wages (either on average or compared to other workers in the same industry). This raises a nontrivial concern—that is, rent-sharing will show up as greater demand for skills.

Setting aside this concern that should be investigated more systematically, the results are fairly consistent and very interesting: establishments selling higher-quality products employ a greater share of high-skill workers. Another result, which is even more telling (as I argue in the following), is that using data on occupations from OES, they demonstrate that a smaller fraction of workers in high-quality establishments perform routine tasks. So on the basis of this correlation, it appears that high-quality production necessitates more nonroutine tasks to be completed.[1]

These results are an important contribution to the literature and are telling about the relationship between quality upgrading and the nature of work. Notably, this relationship probably goes beyond the demand for skills; as the authors' own findings illustrate, there is an important change in the types of tasks that are being performed (e.g., the shift from routine to nonroutine tasks).

Even if it needs to be probed and investigated at greater length, and especially separated from rent-sharing effects, this intriguing empirical pattern suggests the need to understand how the production process of higher-quality products differs from that of lower-quality products, what dimensions of skills are more important for producing high-quality products, and how this interacts with technology. The types of models and approaches that would permit such an investigation are available in the economic growth and labor economics literatures. However, the current paper takes another path, not uncommon in modern macro but, as I argue, ultimately unsatisfactory for analyzing the issues at hand.

The Quantitative Friedmanite Modeling Methodology

Milton Friedman's famous (1953/2008) essay applied a (simplified) version of Karl Popper's approach to economics and proposed a simple economic methodology. It can be summarized by stating that a theory should be judged solely on the basis of its "predictions," with no regard to whether its assumptions are accurate or descriptively realistic. Friedman boldly stated: "Viewed as a body of substantive hypotheses, theory is to be judged by its predictive power for the class of phenomena which it is intended to 'explain.' Only factual evidence can show whether it is 'right' or 'wrong' or, better tentatively 'accepted' as valid or 'rejected'" (149).

Friedman had a harsh assessment of efforts to judge a theory by its descriptive realism, calling such attempts "fundamentally wrong and productive of much mischief. Far from providing an easy means of sifting valid from invalid hypotheses, it only confuses the issue, promotes misunderstanding about the significance of empirical evidence for economic theory, produces a misdirection of much intellectual effort devoted to the development of positive economics, and impedes the attainment of consensus on tentative hypotheses in positive economics" (153).

When describing the behavior of expert billiards players, we can make much progress by modeling their behavior as if they are undertaking the full mathematical calculations of the trajectory of the ball once it is hit by the cue. We can, Friedman argued, make progress in economics by similarly imposing various "as if" assumptions, even if these are patently false. All that matters is that our theory, building on these assumptions, provides valid predictions for the problem at hand. Applying this reasoning, for example, he concluded that much of the work on monopolistic competition was misguided because it was motivated by the desire to provide a better approximation to markets in which firms were neither pure monopolists nor one of many perfectly competitive businesses (Friedman 1953/2008, 153). So far as Friedman's methodology was concerned, perfect competition was just fine because its predictions about the effect of changes in demand were not falsified, and hence the theory could be "tentatively accepted."

Although many philosophers and economists have raised myriad valid concerns about Friedman's economic methodology, it has had a curiously enduring influence on economic research. As the philosopher Daniel Hausman (1992/2008, 183) remarked, "Methodologists have had few kind words for Milton Friedman's [methodology], yet its influence persists." Hausman instead advocated "looking under the hood," that is, studying how different components of the theory generate the relevant predictions and whether they are realistic and receive empirical support. As such, he identified the most fundamental weakness of Friedman's approach: reliability of empirical predictions has to be evaluated recognizing that any model, particularly in social sciences, is useful primarily as an aid to better understand the problem being studied. The wrong mechanisms, even if they lead to the right empirical predictions within some context, are worse than useless because they propagate the wrong kind of understanding. Looking under the hood and striving for some sort of congruence between features of what we include in our models and the reality we are studying are some of the ways in which we can attempt to achieve this. Looking under the hood does not mean shying away from simplifying assumptions. But it does require that we are clear about the core mechanisms for the phenomena we are studying, and we judiciously use simplifying assumptions for abstracting from other aspects, while striving to represent and systematically investigate these core mechanisms.

Friedman's methodology has influenced modern macroeconomics too. The ideal espoused by Friedman was to subject economic hypotheses derived from various "as if" assumptions (and preferably in Friedman's assessment starting with perfect competition and similar settings where the market worked well) to a battery of rigorous empirical tests. One branch of modern macro has combined Friedman's methodology with quantitative evaluation/calibration. In standard statistical theory, a null hypothesis is compared to an alternative. In its modern versions, there is an effort to undertake "causal inference," for example, using randomized control trials, regression discontinuity type strategies, or instrumental variables estimation (e.g., Angrist and Pischke 2008). What I call the quantitative Friedmanite modeling methodology instead starts with similar "as if" assumptions and then compares the magnitudes implied by the model under some parametric assumptions (sometimes chosen on the basis of standard parameter choices in the literature and sometimes on the basis of estimates from micro data) to some selected moments in the macro data.

This methodology can be a powerful approach for evaluating whether a particular mechanism can be "quantitatively important." One of its most celebrated applications was to argue that productivity-shock-driven business cycles could account for the magnitude of fluctuations in the US data (Kydland and Prescott 1982). But this methodology may sometimes discourage efforts to look "under the hood." This, I argue, is what has held back the current paper.

Jaimovich et al.'s Model of Higher-Quality Production

Jaimovich et al. make two major simplifying assumptions. First, they assume (in their main model) that households are homogenous, and thus the demand for quality is uniform across the entire economy. Second, they model the production of higher-quality goods with a small variation on the canonical approach to the demand for skills in labor economics, which builds on Katz and Murphy's (1992) specification derived from a constant elasticity of substitution aggregate production function with factor-augmenting technologies (see also Tinbergen 1974; Goldin and Katz 2007). Let me start with the latter choice.

The aggregate production function the authors specify takes the form

$$Y = A[\alpha(S^H H)^\rho + q^{-\gamma\rho}(1 - \alpha)(S^L L)^\rho]^{1/\rho}. \tag{1}$$

Here, L denotes the supply of unskilled labor and H is the supply of skilled labor, whereas $1/(1 - \rho)$ is the elasticity of substitution between skilled and unskilled labor (and is taken to be greater than 1), α is a distribution parameter designating the importance of skilled labor relative to unskilled labor, and S^H represents any technology that increases the relative (physical) productivity of skilled labor (which is equivalent to generic skill-biased technological change under the assumption that $\rho > 0$). I have also added a symmetric term S^L to their specification for later discussion. Crucially, all technological change takes a factor-augmenting form as in the canonical approach. The new term is $q^{-\gamma \rho}$ and captures the effects of quality. Higher quality, corresponding to higher q, directly reduces the productivity of lower-skilled workers. (The model is equivalent to Katz and Murphy's formulation when $\gamma = 0$.)

The authors then choose some parameter values motivated by the previous literature and their own descriptive work and derive the quantitative implications of their model. They conclude that when the trading-up mechanism is included the implications are much more plausible. Comparing their model to the baseline without q (or with $\gamma = 0$), where S^H would need to increase by about 5.5% annually to account for the rise of the college premium, they report that with the trading-up mechanism an annual increase of only 1.05% in S^H is necessary to account for the data.

Jaimovich et al.'s production function (eq. [1]) is a strange one. Higher quality directly makes lower-skilled workers less productive (recall that $\gamma > 0$). Implicitly drawing on the quantitative Friedmanite methodology, the authors do not defend the realism of this production function. The predictions (or the quantitative implications) are derived as if there is such an aggregate production function, as this matches their own empirical work that higher-quality goods are more skill intensive. The lack of descriptive realism is not viewed as a roadblock.

Yet this assumption is problematic, and its lack of realism is a telltale sign of these problems. To understand these issues, let us first review some of the recent developments in the labor economics literature on the demand for skills (with the full admission that this is my own take on these developments, partly based on my own work).

Problems with the Canonical Approach to the Demand for Skills

Acemoglu and Autor (2011, 2012) point out three problems with the canonical approach on which Jaimovich et al. build. First, the empirical fit of Katz and Murphy's (1992) approach deteriorates considerably after their sample ends. Second, in contrast to the prediction of a model in which the demand for more skilled activities is growing, the US data paint a picture in which firms are expanding employment more in lower-skill occupations than in higher-skill occupations. In fact, there is a notable pattern of employment polarization, where middle-skill occupations are disappearing and being replaced mostly by lower-skill occupations (see also Acemoglu 1999; Autor and Dorn 2013).

Third and most important, in the standard model, skill-biased technological change increases the demand for skills and skill premia, but unless there is technological regress and new technologies reduce the productivity of some types of workers, the model cannot generate declines in real wages. Mathematically, in equation (1), any combination of increases in S^H and S^L will always raise the real wage of low-skill workers (see Acemoglu 2002). To generate a decline in the real wages of low-skill workers, it is not sufficient to have skill-biased technological change—that is, we need a decline in S^L, meaning technological regress. Secular deteriorations in technology are implausible to say the least. But in the data, the real wages of low-skill workers have declined precipitously since the late 1970s, especially when we focus on men.

Acemoglu and Autor (2011, 2012) interpret these as fundamental failures of the canonical approach and propose an alternative based on tasks. In this approach, production requires the performance of a range of tasks. Technology and factor prices determine the allocation of tasks to factors. Technology is no longer just factor augmenting. Technological changes that reduce the range of tasks allocated to a factor can lead to a decline in the real wage of that factor—even if these technological changes have nothing to do with technological regress. These papers, as well as Autor, Levy, and Murnane (2003) and Acemoglu and Restrepo (2018, 2019, forthcoming), propose models of automation where new technologies embedded in machines, such as computerized control or robots, enable the substitution of capital for tasks previously performed by labor, especially low-skilled labor (see also Zeira 1998). Such automation will increase the demand for skills but, more importantly, may also reduce the real wages of low-skilled workers. The evidence in Acemoglu and Restrepo (forthcoming), for example, shows that the introduction of industrial robots is associated with significant wage declines for workers with less than college education.

Let me give a brief overview of how this would work, drawing on the model from Acemoglu and Restrepo (2019), which assumes there is a single type of labor (introducing workers with different levels of skills is straightforward).[2] Suppose that the unique final good in the economy, Y, is produced by combining a set of tasks, with measure normalized 1, with production function given by

$$Y = \left(\int_0^1 Y(z)^{\frac{\sigma-1}{\sigma}} dz \right)^{\frac{\sigma}{\sigma-1}}, \tag{2}$$

where $Y(z)$ denotes the output of task z for $z \in [0, 1]$, and $\sigma \geq 0$ is the elasticity of substitution between tasks.

Tasks can be produced using capital or labor according to the production function

$$Y(z) = \begin{pmatrix} A^L \gamma^L(z)l(z) + A^K \gamma^K(z)k(z) & \text{if } z \in [0, I] \\ A^L \gamma^L(z)l(z) & \text{for all } z \end{pmatrix}.$$

Tasks $z \leq I$ are (technologically) automated and can be produced with capital, whereas tasks $z > I$ are not automated and can only be produced with labor. In addition, $l(z)$ and $k(z)$ denote the total labor and capital allocated to producing task z. The framework also allows for standard factor-augmenting technology terms, A^L and A^K. The terms $\gamma^L(z)$ and $\gamma^K(z)$ represent the productivity of labor and capital in different tasks. Let us assume that $\gamma^L(z)/\gamma^K(z)$ is increasing in z so that labor has a comparative advantage in higher-indexed tasks. In this framework, an increase in I corresponds to automation, expanding the set of tasks that can be produced with capital. Under the assumption that capital is cheap so that firms are happy to produce (technologically) automated tasks with capital, the equilibrium of this model can be equivalently represented as the equilibrium of an economy with an aggregate production function but in this instance derived from the micro structure of the model at the task level. In particular, this derived aggregate production function takes the form

$$Y = \left(\left(\int_0^I \gamma^K(z)^{\sigma-1} dz \right)^{\frac{1}{\sigma}} (A^K K)^{\frac{\sigma-1}{\sigma}} + \left(\int_I^1 \gamma^L(z)^{\sigma-1} dz \right)^{\frac{1}{\sigma}} (A^L L)^{\frac{\sigma-1}{\sigma}} \right)^{\frac{\sigma}{\sigma-1}}. \tag{3}$$

Holding the level of automation, I, constant, the results from this framework are identical to those from the canonical approach (the elasticity of substitution between capital and labor is now given by the elasticity of substitution between tasks, σ). But critically, automation (an increase in I) changes things. Most notably, an increase in I allocates tasks from labor to capital and always reduces the term in front of labor $((\int_I^1 \gamma^L(z)^{\sigma-1} dz)^{1/\sigma})$ and increases the term in front of capital $((\int_0^I \gamma^K(z)^{\sigma-1} dz)^{1/\sigma})$. Because of this reallocation of tasks from labor to capital, automation may reduce the value of the marginal product of labor and real wages. This happens despite the fact that there is no technological regress (Acemoglu and Restrepo 2018, 2019).

Here we come full circle to the quantitative Friedmanite methodology. Suppose the task-based approach described in the previous paragraph is on target; it is indeed the case that new technologies enable automation and as a result reduce real wages (even though they increase productivity). The Friedmanite methodology might try to capture the same phenomenon by imposing a reduced-form aggregate production function (like the one in eq. [1]) and then forcing this production function and its implications on the data, it would conclude that this is happening because A^L is decreasing (technological regress). If the prediction we care about is matching the decline in real wages, this fix works. But it would lack complete descriptive realism for at least two reasons. First, the idea that there is actual technological regress, though imposed in this approach, would make no empirical sense. Second, the Friedmanite approach would also eschew any engagement with the key economic mechanisms at work, in this instance, the reallocation of tasks across factors (which is in fact responsible for the phenomenon we are trying to understand, the decline in real wages).

The situation is actually worse than this because once we approach the problem at the right level (in this instance, at the level of the allocation of tasks to factors), we understand that automation does not always reduce real wages. As Acemoglu and Restrepo (2018, 2019) show, the impact of automation on real wages depends on the balance between a displacement effect (what I have emphasized so far) and a productivity effect (resulting from the fact that the substitution of cheaper capital for labor increases effective productivity and thus may increase the demand for labor).[3] This implies that the effects of different waves of automation could be quite different. One wave of automation may have a smaller productivity effect, reducing real wages. Yet another wave with a more substantive productivity effect may raise real wages.[4] In consequence, the Friedmanite approach would be forced to maintain that in the case of the first wave there is significant technological regress but not so in the second wave. In short, it would have to get into lots of twists and turns to try to "get the right predictions," and at the root of these problems is exactly its insistence on not calibrating its assumptions to the micro structure of the problem being studied.

The parallel of the Friedmanite solution to this problem and Jaimovich et al.'s modeling approach are evident. Instead of assuming that there is a decline in A^L (or in S^L in eq. [1]), the authors introduce another parameter, q, which does the same and effectively reduces the productivity of low-skill workers. They are not deterred by their assumptions not matching the micro structure. In particular, despite their own very interesting empirical finding that quality upgrading is associated with a change in the task structure of establishments, they prefer the reduced-form modeling approach that ignores what is happening at the task level.

On the basis of this, it is not far-fetched to conjecture that their modeling would be subject to similar problems. For example, it may well be that different waves of quality upgrading are associated with different ways of reorganizing tasks and differently sized productivity effects. Hence, directly assuming that the production of higher-quality goods reduces the productivity of low-skill workers may fit the facts for one wave and be a terrible approximation for another.

None of this increases our confidence in the quantitative exercise the authors perform. Even if the parameter values they use for this may be justified, the quantitative estimates they generate still depend heavily on the specific model imposed on the data (in the form of their eq. [1]), so unless we have confidence in this model, we cannot place much stock in its quantitative findings.

This reasoning underpins my conclusion that the descriptive work they present is intriguing and in fact supports the idea that there are systematic differences in the skill intensity of the production process of low- and high-quality goods, but their model does not further enlighten the mechanisms at work, and the quantitative exercise does not generate numbers we can really trust.

An Alternative Approach

On the basis of what I have discussed so far, my preferred approach to this problem should be evident. This approach would start by specifying how the set of tasks that needs to be performed for the production of a high-quality product is different from the set of tasks for a low-quality product. For example, perhaps customers paying more for a handcrafted artisanal coffee also want the barista to talk to them about movies or politics, so the set of tasks associated with the production of such a cup of coffee is different than the production of a cup of Dunkin' Donuts coffee. It is this change in the set of tasks that then necessitates the establishment to have a different composition of skills.

The data the authors use can start giving us some clues. For example, in addition to the change in the composition of routine and nonroutine occupations in the aggregate, the authors could look at how this differs depending on the nature of the product the establishment is supplying. Is it more pronounced for establishments that are more service intensive? For those that directly interact with customers more? For those that are more technology intensive? For products that are more customized?

Another interesting question concerns whether greater skill intensity of the production of higher-quality products is a consequence of prevailing factor prices. For example, if college graduates earned twice as much, would specialized coffee shops still hire them as baristas? Put differently, the attributes of higher-quality products themselves may be endogenous, and when skill premia are sufficiently high, the attributes that require these skills may be cut back.

We could also investigate whether the composition of occupations changes significantly and whether the occupations added as goods become higher quality (Acemoglu and Restrepo [2019] show that the diversity of occupations in an industry is associated with the introduction of new tasks).

Modeling Demand for Quality

The modeling of the demand for quality is secondary for the approach of the paper, and this is the reason the authors start with a representative agent model and then consider heterogeneity only in the appendix. However, the secondary nature of this aspect of the model is itself a consequence of another "as if" assumption—this time eschewing the competition between products of different qualities.

It is natural to presume, once again from the micro structure of the problem, that different quality variants of the same good are going to be much closer substitutes than two distinct products. If so, the location of different variants on the quality ladder will affect the market power of producers. This was the starting point of Shaked and Sutton's classic (1982) paper I mentioned above, showing how the distribution of income determines both the quality levels of products and markups. The linkage between quality distributions and markups emerges through a related but distinct channel in other growth and industrial organization models (e.g., Aghion et al. 2001; Acemoglu and Akcigit 2012).

These micro interactions may matter as well when it comes to the demand for skills, as a high level of markup for an establishment reduces the demand for the type of labor it employs, and via this channel, may have an impact on the skill premium. This too is an important and interesting area for future research.

Conclusion

In sum, this paper is on an important and exciting topic and starts by documenting a novel and fascinating fact—namely, establishments producing higher-quality products use more highly skilled workers. The paper is most likely correct that quality upgrading (what the authors call trading up) contributes to the demand for skills. But how important is this effect? And even more critically, what are the micro mechanisms by which it operates?

The modeling approach the paper takes, which assumes that quality enters as a shifter of an otherwise canonical constant elasticity of a substitution production function for a unique final good, does not ultimately help us appreciate these mechanisms any better and, partly as a result of this, is not a good basis for answering questions related to the quantitative importance of this channel.

All the same, this paper has taken an important step in drawing our attention to the role of quality upgrading and its labor market implications. We have every reason to expect that others will follow and will build on the interesting facts that this paper has already started documenting.

Endnotes

Author email address: Acemoglu (daron@mit.edu). For acknowledgments, sources of research support, and disclosure of the author's material financial relationships, if any, please see https://www.nber.org/chapters/c14254.ack.
1. See Acemoglu and Autor (2011) and Autor and Dorn (2013) on routine and nonroutine tasks and their relationship to the organization of production.
2. Models with different types of labor and automation are considered in Acemoglu and Autor (2011) and Acemoglu and Restrepo (2018, forthcoming).
3. It also depends on the simultaneous creation of new tasks, which I suppress here because this is not central to the methodological issue at hand.
4. However, regardless of the elasticity of substitution, automation always reduces the labor share in value added (see Acemoglu and Restrepo 2018, 2019).

References

Acemoglu, Daron. 1999. "Changes in Unemployment and Wage Inequality: An Alternative Theory and Some Evidence." *American Economic Review* 89 (5): 1259–78.
Acemoglu, Daron. 2002. "Technical Change, Inequality, and the Labor Market." *Journal of Economic Literature* 40 (1): 7–72.
Acemoglu, Daron, and Ufuk Akcigit. 2012. "Intellectual Property Rights Policy, Competition and Innovation." *Journal of the European Economic Association* 10 (1): 1–42.
Acemoglu, Daron, and David Autor. 2011. "Skills, Tasks and Technologies: Implications for Employment and Earnings." *Handbook of Labor Economics* 4:1043–171.
———. 2012. "What Does Human Capital Do? A Review of Goldin and Katz's the Race between Education and Technology." *Journal of Economic Literature* 50 (2): 426–63.
Acemoglu, Daron, and Pascual Restrepo. 2018. "The Race between Machine and Man: Implications of Technology for Growth, Factor Shares and Employment." *American Economic Review* 108 (6): 1488–542.

———. 2019. "Automation and New Tasks: How Technology Displaces and Reinstates Labor." *Journal of Economic Perspectives* 33 (2): 3–30.

———. Forthcoming. "Robots and Jobs: Evidence from US Labor Markets." *Journal of Political Economy.*

Aghion, Philippe, Christopher Harris, Peter Howitt, and John Vickers. 2001. "Competition, Imitation and Growth with Step-by-Step Innovation." *Review of Economic Studies* 68 (3): 467–92.

Angrist, Joshua D., and Jörn-Steffen Pischke. 2008. *Mostly Harmless Econometrics: An Empiricist's Companion.* Princeton, NJ: Princeton University Press.

Autor, David H., and David Dorn. 2013. "The Growth of Low-Skill Service Jobs and the Polarization of the U.S. Labor Market." *American Economic Review* 103 (5): 1553–97.

Autor, David H., Frank Levy, and Richard Murnane. 2003. "The Skill Content of Recent Technological Change: An Empirical Exploration." *Quarterly Journal of Economics* 118 (4): 1279–333.

Foellmi, Reto, Tobias Wuergler, and Josef Zweimuller. 2014. "The Macroeconomics of Model T." *Journal of Economic Theory* 153 (3): 617–47.

Foellmi, Reto, and Josef Zweimuller. 2006. "Income Distribution and Demand-Induced Innovations." *Review of Economic Studies* 73 (4): 941–60.

Friedman, Milton. (1953) 2008. "Methodology of Positive Economics." Reprinted in *The Philosophy of Economics: An Anthology*, 3rd ed., ed. Daniel M. Hausman, 145–78. Cambridge: Cambridge University Press.

Goldin, Claudia, and Lawrence Katz. 2007. The Race between Education and Technology. Cambridge, MA: Belknap.

Graetz, Georg, and Guy Michaels. Forthcoming. "Robots at Work." *Review of Economics and Statistics.*

Hausman, Daniel M. (1992) 2008. "Why Look under the Hood?" Reprinted in *The Philosophy of Economics: An Anthology*, 3rd ed., ed. Daniel M. Hausman, 183–87. Cambridge: Cambridge University Press.

Katz, Lawrence F., and Kevin M. Murphy. 1992. "Changes in Relative Wages, 1963–1987: Supply and Demand Factors." *Quarterly Journal of Economics* 107 (1): 35–78.

Kydland, Finn E., and Edward C. Prescott. 1982. "Time to Build and Aggregate Fluctuations." *Econometrica* 50:1345–70.

Leonardi, Marco. 2003. "Product Demand Shifts and Wage Inequality." Discussion Paper no. 908, IZA Institute of Labor Economics, Bonn, Germany.

———. 2015. "The Effect of Product Demand on Inequality: Evidence from the United States and the United Kingdom." *American Economic Journal: Applied Economics* 7 (3): 221–47.

Matsuyama, Kiminori. 2002. "The Rise of Mass Consumption Societies." *Journal of Political Economy* 110 (5): 1035–70.

Shaked, Avner, and John Sutton. 1982. "Relaxing Price Competition through Product Differentiation." *Review of Economic Studies* 49 (1): 3–13.

Tinbergen, Jan. 1974. "Substitution of Graduate by Other Labour." *Kyklos* 27 (2): 217–26.

Zeira, Joseph. 1998. "Workers, Machines, and Economic Growth." *Quarterly Journal of Economics* 113 (4): 1091–117.

Zweimuller, Josef. 2000. "Schumpeterian Entrepreneurs Meet Engel's Law: The Impact of Inequality on Innovation-Driven Growth." *Journal of Economic Growth* 5 (2): 185–206.

Comment

Jonathan Vogel, *University of California, Los Angeles*

The skill premium and inequality, more generally, have increased dramatically in the United States since 1980; see the top panel of figure 1. This rise has coincided with a substantial increase in the relative supply of skilled workers; see the bottom panel of figure 1. To the extent that relative supply and demand shape relative prices, these patterns reveal a sizable skill-biased shift in relative demand. A large literature across a range of subfields within economics investigates the roles of various economic forces in generating such a shift. This literature emphasizes in particular two broad categories of observable shocks: a fall in the quality-adjusted cost of capital equipment that is relatively more substitutable for less skilled labor (including computers, software, industrial robots, etc.) and demand shocks biased toward jobs that are relatively intensive in skilled labor (induced by international trade, offshoring, structural transformation, etc.). One central goal of this broad literature is to quantify how important each shock is in explaining the evolution of the skill premium and how much remains unexplained (often referred to as "skill-biased technological change").

"Trading Up and the Skill Premium" does a good job of empirically motivating the potential importance of a particular channel that has not featured prominently (or at all) in this literature: a within-industry version of the link between structural transformation and inequality. The authors provide evidence that higher-income consumers disproportionately purchase higher-quality varieties within industries and that higher-quality varieties within industries are skill intensive. This evidence suggests that an increase in income will generate a skill-biased demand shock (i.e., an increase in relative expenditure on skill-intensive varieties at fixed prices) within industries.[1]

The main point of our discussion is that this first pass at quantification is missing two key elements. First, the connection between the model

A. Evolution of the Skill Premium

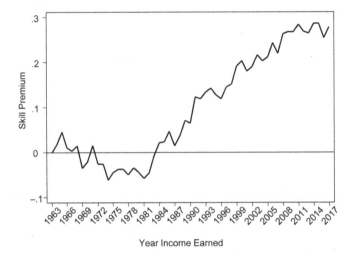

Year Income Earned

B. Evolution of Relative Skill Supply

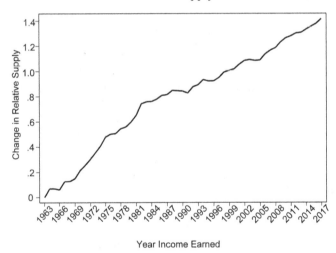

Year Income Earned

Fig. 1. The evolution of the composition-adjusted skill premium and the composition-adjusted relative supply of skilled hours.

and the data can be strengthened: the baseline model can be taken to the data analogously to the "canonical model" (described in the paper) with the same data used to estimate the canonical model and an almost identical identification assumption. And when it is, the resulting parameter values differ substantially from those to which the authors calibrate their model. Second, the baseline model lacks sufficient theoretical flexibility in a particular sense that we clarify in the following.

Solving the Model

The baseline "Trading Up" (TU) model links changes in the skill premium, denoted by $\omega_t \equiv w_{Ht}/w_{Lt}$, to four primitive shocks: changes in the supply of skilled labor (H_t), changes in the supply of unskilled labor (L_t), Hicks-neutral technical change (A_t), and skill-biased technical change (S_t). How important are changes in each of these shocks for generating the observed evolution of the skill premium?

Two equations are sufficient to characterize the impact of all primitive shocks on the skill premium in the TU model. The first equation links changes in the skill premium ($d\ln\omega_t$) to changes in the relative supply of skilled labor ($d\ln H_t/L_t$), skill-biased technical change ($d\ln S_t$), and endogenous changes in quality ($d\ln q_t$),

$$d \ln \omega_t = \rho d \ln S_t + (\rho - 1)d \ln \left(\frac{H_t}{L_t}\right) + \gamma\rho d \ln q_t.$$

This equation is a simple extension of the canonical model, incorporating one additional term associated with the impact of changes in endogenous quality ($d\ln q_t$). The second equation links changes in quality to changes in Hicks-neutral productivity ($d\ln A_t$), factor supplies ($d\ln H_t$ and $d\ln L_t$), and the skill premium ($d\ln\omega_t$) for any $\gamma > 0$,

$$\gamma\rho d \ln q_t = \rho d \ln A_t + \nu_t d \ln H_t + (\rho - \nu_t)d \ln L_t + \nu_t d \ln \omega_t,$$

where $\nu_t \equiv H_t w_{Ht}/(H_t w_{Ht} + L_t w_{Lt})$ is the share of labor payments accruing to skilled labor. Combining these two equations and solving for the change in the skill premium yields

$$d \ln \omega_t = \frac{\rho - 1 + \nu_t}{1 - \nu_t}d \ln H_t + d \ln L_t + \frac{\rho}{1 - \nu_t}(d \ln S_t + d \ln A_t). \quad (1)$$

Equation (1) connects changes in the skill premium to the underlying shocks and clarifies two points. First, the value of the parameter γ plays no role in the response of the skill premium to the underlying shocks (as long as $\gamma \neq 0$) for given values of ρ, ν_t, and shocks; we return to this below.[2] Second, as noted in the paper, only the sum of $d\ln S_t$ and $d\ln A_t$ matters rather than either directly.

Equation (1) also provides a more direct link between the model and the data than taken in the paper, a point to which we now turn.

Estimation

We can approximate the level of the skill premium as

$$\ln \omega_t \approx c_1 + \frac{\rho - 1 + \nu_t}{1 - \nu_t} \ln H_t + \ln L_t + \frac{\rho}{1 - \nu_t}(\ln A_t + \ln S_t),$$

where c_1 is the constant of integration and then reexpress this as

$$y_t \approx c_2 + (\rho - 1) \ln H_t + \rho(\ln A_t + \ln S_t),$$

where $y_t \equiv (1 - \nu_t)(\ln \omega_t - \ln L_t) - \nu_t \ln H_t$ is observable (because ν_t is observable), and $c_2 \equiv (1 - \nu_t)c_1$. Exactly as in the canonical model, we can express

$$\ln A_t + \ln S_t \equiv c_3 + gt + \tilde{\varepsilon}_t$$

without loss of generality, where g is trend growth in the combination of Hicks-neutral and skill-biased productivities. Combining the previous two expressions, we obtain

$$y_t = \alpha + \beta \ln H_t + \gamma t + \varepsilon_t, \tag{2}$$

where $\alpha \equiv c_2 + \rho c_3$, $\beta \equiv \rho - 1$, $\gamma \equiv g\rho$, and ε_t contains both $\rho\tilde{\varepsilon}_t$ and approximation error.

Equation (2) resembles the estimating equation in the canonical model—which we replicate in the following—except the independent variable $\ln(H_t/L_t)$ in the canonical model is replaced with $\ln(H_t)$ here and the dependent variable $\ln \omega_t$ in the canonical model is replaced by y_t here. We estimate equation (2) using annual data from the March Current Population Survey (CPS) covering working years from 1963 through 2017, composition adjusting the skill premium and factor supplies, and instrumenting for H_t—which depends on hours worked—using the population of those with college education. We obtain estimates of $\beta = -0.345$ (with standard error 0.044) and $\gamma = 0.016$ (with standard error 0.0017). These coefficients imply parameter values $\rho = 0.655$ and $g = 0.025$.

To understand the extent to which the mapping from data to parameters differs between the TU model and the canonical model, which the authors use to calibrate their model, we estimate the canonical model

$$\ln \omega_t = \alpha' + \beta' \ln \left(\frac{H_t}{L_t}\right) + \gamma' t + \varepsilon_t'$$

on our data and using our approach to composition adjusting. We obtain estimates of $\beta' = -0.522$ (with standard error 0.053) and $\gamma' = 0.020$ (with standard error 0.001). The mapping from coefficients to parameters in the canonical model is $\rho = 1 + \beta'$ and $g = \gamma'/\rho$ so that we infer parameter values $\rho = 0.478$ and $g = 0.041$.

Implications

There are four implications that we can reach at this point. First, taking a value of ρ that is estimated from the canonical model, which has a different mapping from primitive shocks to the skill premium, is inconsistent with the TU model. Second, it is also unnecessary. The TU model can be estimated directly under an identification assumption that is analogous to that in the canonical model.

Third, when estimated in an internally consistent manner, the TU model continues to dramatically reduce the required strength of the time trend relative to the canonical model, from $g = 4.1\%$ per year in the canonical model to $g = 2.5\%$. Indeed, for any value of $d \ln A_t > 0$, the required growth rate of skill-biased technology is strictly less than 2.5% per year, as the time trend in the TU model—unlike in the canonical model—is generated by the sum of the growth rates of $d\ln A_t$ and $d\ln S_t$. This is the key point of the quantitative model, and we find that it is robust.

Fourth, the TU model is not sufficiently flexible in two respects. The parameter that appears to control the importance of quality upgrading, γ, plays no role (for any value $\gamma \neq 0$). It does not shape the elasticity of the skill premium to any shock, which depends only on ρ and v_t.[3] It does not shape the measurement of these elasticities, as v_t is data and ρ is estimated as shown above. Finally, γ does not shape the measurement of the underlying primitive shocks, as H_t and L_t are data and A_t and S_t are not measured.

In addition, the fact that γ plays no role in shaping the impact of shocks on the skill premium implies that a single parameter, ρ, shapes the response of the skill premium to skill supply, whereas there is no flexibility whatsoever regarding the impact of unskilled labor supply. Because of these restrictions, the TU model appears inconsistent with the data. The following estimating equation is structural in both the TU and canonical models:[4]

$$\ln \omega_t = \alpha'' + \beta_H \ln H_t + \beta_L \ln L_t + \gamma''t + \varepsilon_t''. \tag{3}$$

The canonical model predicts that $\beta_H = -\beta_L$. The TU model predicts that $\beta_L = 1$ and that $\beta_{Ht} = (\rho - 1 + v_t)/(1 - v_t)$ so that the average treatment effect estimated by the equation above is approximately $\beta_H = 0.02$ (evaluating β_{Ht} at the average value across time of v_t) or $\beta_H = 0.05$ (evaluating the average value across time of β_{Ht}).[5] Estimating equation (3) using the same data as previously described, we obtain estimates $\beta_H = -0.53$ (standard error 0.057) and $\beta_L = 0.54$ (standard error 0.094). These estimates are consistent with the prediction of the canonical model but inconsistent with either prediction of the TU model.

In summary, we find the empirical motivation compelling. The authors provide the first empirical evidence of which we are aware that higher-income consumers disproportionately purchase higher-quality varieties within industries and that higher-quality varieties within industries are skill intensive. This evidence suggests that an increase in income will generate a skill-biased demand shock within industries, raising the relative demand for skilled workers within industries and, therefore, raising the skill premium. We look forward to the next generation of quantification.

Endnotes

Author email address: Vogel (jonathan.e.vogel@gmail.com). For acknowledgments, sources of research support, and disclosure of the author's material financial relationships, if any, please see https://www.nber.org/chapters/c14255.ack.
1. This is a within-industry version of the mechanism emphasized in Buera, Kaboski, and Rogerson (2015); Caron, Fally, and Markusen (2017); and He (2018), each of which focuses on reallocation across industries.
2. Note that given the value of ρ, the evolution of ν_t is pinned down by the evolution of the shocks.
3. In equation (9), the authors demonstrate a related result that the value of γ is irrelevant for shaping the value of $A_t S_t$ conditional on the skill premium.
4. The estimate of β_H in the TU model is the average treatment effect, as the impact of changes in H_t is heterogeneous across time given changes in ν_t.
5. The TU model features an increasing relationship between H_t and the skill premium, like models of directed technical change, for sufficiently high ρ or ν_t; this is satisfied for later years in the sample when ν_t has risen sufficiently.

References

Buera, F. J., J. P. Kaboski, and R. Rogerson. 2015. "Skill Biased Structural Change." Working Papers no. 21165, NBER, Cambridge, MA.
Caron, J., T. Fally, and J. Markusen. 2017. "Per Capita Income and the Demand for Skills." Working Papers no. 23482, NBER, Cambridge, MA.
He, Z. 2018. "Trade and Real Wages of the Rich and Poor: Cross-Region Evidence." Mimeo, University of Pennsylvania.

Discussion

Chang-Tai Hsieh opened the general discussion with a question on measurement. The authors' model can be used to back out a measure of skill-biased technical change (SBTC), he noted. However, this measure is model dependent and its units vary with the parametrization, he argued. Hsieh asked the authors about a possible empirical counterpart to this measure. The authors agreed that their measure of quality or SBTC is model dependent. However, they argued that there is a formal equivalence between their model with SBTC and existing models with capital and skill complementarities (but no SBTC), such as Per Krusell, Lee E. Ohanian, José-Víctor Ríos-Rull, and Giovanni L. Violante ("Capital-Skill Complementarity and Inequality: A Macroeconomic Analysis," *Econometrica* 68, no. 5 [2000]: 1029–53), for which units are somewhat more interpretable. In those models, changes in the price of capital increase the complementarity between capital and high-skill labor. This mechanism amplifies the response to shocks, they noted, just like the "trading up" phenomenon in their model.

Richard Blundell argued that the market for childcare constitutes a good case study of trading up. Childcare is a nontradable, low-skill good, he noted. However, the demand for this service has increased over time as women's incomes improved. In appearance, this runs counter to the authors' premise. But in reality, the composition of the demand for childcare changed, Blundell said. As incomes grew, so did the demand for skilled childcare. Blundell noted that the literature on the subject typically allows for variable quality in the production of care, much like in the authors' paper. The authors agreed with Blundell's comment. They added that childcare is a particularly interesting service in that it could be produced at home as well. Allowing for choices at the extensive margin would be an interesting extension, they said.

Erik Hurst inquired about the response of real wages to SBTC in the authors' model. The nominal wage of high-skill workers increases relative to that of low-skill workers. However, high-skill workers also consume the high-quality good, whose price also increases, in larger proportion. Hurst wondered whether the authors' model had a clear prediction in terms of consumption inequality. They agreed that the response of real wages could in theory be ambiguous. This is an interesting moment to look at in the data, they argued, and it could discipline their calibration.

Jonathan Parker noted that the authors' model is static. Allowing for lead or lag dynamics could be instructive, he noted. The authors were very sympathetic to Parker's suggestion. In particular, rich dynamics could emerge from lags in the adoption of new technologies for the production of high-quality goods or from slow training or skill reallocation, they mentioned.

Three topics dominated the rest of the discussion: further dimensions of heterogencity, redistributive policies, and the effect of SBTC on real wages across skill groups.

On the first topic, Mark Gertler discussed a testable implication of the authors' amplification mechanism. He noted that high-skill workers employed by firms producing high-quality goods should benefit more from SBTC compared with those employed by firms producing low-quality goods. Gertler wondered whether the authors could confirm this prediction empirically. The authors were very receptive to Gertler's suggestion. They could indeed study inequality within skill groups, they mentioned, either across industries or across tasks, echoing a point raised by one of the discussants, Daron Acemoglu.

Chad Syverson emphasized another dimension of heterogeneity: geographic location. High-skill, wealthy individuals tend to cluster in metropolitan areas and crowd out lower-skill individuals, he suggested. Syverson argued that the corresponding decrease in the demand for low-quality, nontradable services could have contributed to the erosion of the city premium for low-skill workers, alluding to the work of David Autor ("Work of the Past, Work of the Future" [NBER Working Paper no. 25588, February, National Bureau of Economic Research, Cambridge, MA, 2019]). The authors were in agreement with Syverson's comment.

Turning to the second topic, Richard Blundell referred to recent evidence on the effect of redistributive policies. In particular, the literature has found that an increase in the minimum wage tends to increase demand for goods produced by minimum wage workers, Blundell noted. Similarly, he suggested that the expansion of the earned income tax credit in the United States increased demand for low-quality care offered by female, low-wage workers. Acemoglu cited complementary evidence by Marco Leonardi, Michele Pellizzari, and Domenico Tabasso ("Wage Compression within the Firm: Evidence From an Indexation Scheme," *Economic Journal* 129, no. 624 [2019]: 3256–91). The authors were very receptive to Blundell's comment. Changing the minimum wage or increasing the progressivity of taxation should affect the composition of consumption and the corresponding demand for skills, they added. Exploring these effects is a promising avenue for future research, they argued.

On the third topic, Jonathan Parker and Martin Eichenbaum noted that the two discussants, Daron Acemoglu and Jonathan Vogel, seemed to disagree on the nature of SBTC and its implications for real wages across skill groups. Parker noted that both discussants assumed a linear time trend in SBTC in their models. Economic growth is more chaotic in reality, Parker argued, and so might be SBTC. Eichenbaum drew a parallel with Greg Kaplan's discussion of the paper by Margherita Borella, Mariacristina De Nardi, and Fang Yang ("The Lost Ones: The Opportunities and Outcomes of Non-College Educated Americans Born in the 1960s" [NBER Working Paper no. 25661, March, National Bureau of Economic Research, Cambridge, MA, 2019]) earlier that day. Kaplan had emphasized the importance of measuring price indices correctly when comparing welfare across cohorts. In the context of the authors' paper, Eichenbaum wondered whether accounting for differences in the consumption bundles across skill groups could help reconcile the discussants' views. Acemoglu argued that accounting for heterogeneous consumption bundles would not overturn the decline in real wages observed in the data for the bottom 10% of the earnings distribution. Kaplan seconded Acemoglu on that point. This empirical observation was part of the motivation for Acemoglu's framework.

6

Special Deals with Chinese Characteristics

Chong-en Bai, *Tsinghua University*
Chang-Tai Hsieh, *University of Chicago and NBER*
Zheng Song, *Chinese University of Hong Kong*

I. Introduction

A standard explanation for the extraordinary economic growth in China over the last 4 decades is that this growth was driven by the gradual improvement of formal economic institutions. Advocates of this explanation point to reforms such as the restoration of incentives to farmers and opening to foreign investment in the 1980s, the centralization of the banking system that started in the mid-1990s, the restructuring of state-owned firms and cleanup of the bad debts in the late 1990s and early 2000s, accession to the World Trade Organization (WTO) in 2001, and the gradual removal of internal migration barriers.[1]

Although these policy reforms are undeniably important, this narrative sits uneasily with other pieces of evidence. Huang (2008) documents that many of the pro-market reforms of the 1980s were later reversed. It is still the case that there is no clear formal legal protection for private property in China, nor is there an independent judiciary that enforces contracts and adjudicates commercial disputes. Acemoglu and Robinson (2012), drawing on the account in McGregor (2010), discuss the case of an entrepreneur who was arrested in 2003, allegedly for competing with a state-owned firm, and jailed for 5 years without a trial or charges being filed. Formal rules and laws facing private business are still opaque and onerous. Many foreign companies find their access to the Chinese market blocked for reasons that are not immediately transparent. The World Bank's *Doing Business* indicators has for many years ranked China near the bottom of the world in terms of the "ease of starting a business," roughly at the same level of countries such as Iraq and the Congo.

But how can economy with such poor institutions grow at the rate and for as long as China has? The answer, we suggest, lies in the set of *informal* institutions that emerged in China in the early 1990s. The key feature of these informal institutions is that special deals are readily available to private firms. As suggested by Acemoglu and Robinson (2012) and the World Bank's *Doing Business* indicators, formal institutions for private firms are poor in China. Chinese private firms succeed, in part, by obtaining a special deal from a local political leader, which enables them to either break the formal rules or obtain favorable access to resources. The prevalence of special deals is common in countries with poor formal institutions, and China is no different.[2]

The essence of special deals is that they are only available to some firms, and there is abundant evidence in many settings that the benefits of firms with special deals are outweighed by the costs borne by firms that are left out. In the case of China, however, there are three reasons why the benefits of special deals may exceed the cost. First, Chinese local governments have enormous administrative capacity and use it to provide a "helping hand" to favored firms. This helping hand ranges from providing exemptions to regulations to lobbying the central government for the right to break rules, improving local infrastructure, providing land (and to a lesser extent credit) at below market prices, and blocking entry of other firms that threaten the profits of the favored firms. Some of this help, such as blocking competitors, lowers welfare; however, much of it, such as exemptions to inefficient regulations, is probably growth enhancing.

Second, local political leaders have high-powered incentives to provide special deals. For example, the largest car company in China is a joint venture between General Motors and the City of Shanghai. Dunne (2011, 11), a longtime observer of China's automobile market, describes Shanghai's support for General Motors in the following way: "The commercial goal of selling more GM Buicks and Chevrolets in China becomes a political and economic campaign to enhance the power and might of the City of Shanghai. Think of it as Shanghai Inc. with the Mayor as the Chairman and CEO." Local leaders may support private firms simply out of a sense of duty or because local leaders who show competence in supporting private business are recognized and promoted. The benefits can also be entirely monetary, ranging from tuition payments for their child to (hidden) equity stakes in favored private firms held by family members. Because of the high-powered incentives to support private firms, a large and increasing number of Chinese firms benefit from the special deals. So the Chinese system is best described not simply as a regime of special deals but one where there is almost "free entry" into special deals.

Third, a large number of local governments actively support private firms. Moreover, they compete ferociously with other local governments to attract and support their businesses. As described by McGregor (2010, 175–76), "What is obvious for anyone who travels around the country is how much of the economy is driven by another factor altogether, a kind of Darwinian internal competition that pits localities against each other . . . each Chinese province, city, county, and village furiously compete to gulp down any economic advantage they can lure their way." Competition between local governments is crucial in limiting the predatory power of protected firms. A local government can block competitors of favored firms in its locality but has no ability to do so in other cities. Competition also gives firms options when faced with incompetent or predatory local governments.

In summary, China has "extractive economic institutions" to borrow Acemoglu and Robinson's (2012, 439) pithy term, where political elites extract rents from the rest of society. But extractive economic institutions in China come with unique "Chinese characteristics" that have made all the difference. First, local political elites extract rents by enabling favored firms to generate more profits in the first place. They can do this because of the enormous administrative capacity of local governments, and the resulting growth of local businesses enables local elites to extract even more rents. Second, local elites get personal benefits from these rents and, thus, the local administrative apparatus is laser-focused on supporting favored firms. Third, thousands of local governments compete ferociously to attract and support firms, thus limiting the ability of an individual local government to harm other businesses.

Understanding the Chinese system as a regime of special deals also clarifies the risks that China faces. First, special deals rely on the discretion of local officials and their incentives to provide special deals. And here a central fact is the anti-corruption campaign that has been in place since 2014. Although there is limited information on the crackdown, if local officials are motivated by private economic benefits, the crackdown on corruption will dampen their incentive to use their authority to grease the wheel for private firms. If special deals as practiced in China have been growth enhancing, as we suggest they have, the crackdown on corruption will result in lower growth. Second, special deals are at the root of the tension between China and its trading partners. Companies based in countries that do not have access to special deals find themselves disadvantaged when they compete with Chinese companies that do. Foreign companies in the Chinese market either have to make their own special deal or, as is the case with Chinese firms that do not have a special deal, find that their intellectual property and contracts are not well respected. An important and still unresolved question is how the world trading system can accommodate countries based on rules as well as those based on access to special deals.

Our narrative of special deals with Chinese characteristics is closely related to Huang's (2008) account of "capitalism with Chinese characteristics" and Xu's (2011) description of China as "regionally decentralized authoritarianism." Huang (2008) documents the emergence of special deals in China in the early 1990s and argues that such deals are harmful to economic growth. Xu (2011) argues that powerful local governments are behind the growth of private firms but is silent on the key fact that local support for private firms almost always takes the form of special deals. Our hypothesis is that it is precisely the combination of special deals and powerful local governments that has underpinned China's economic success over the last 30 or so years and, at the same time, has created risks for the future.

The paper proceeds as follows. We first describe how special deals in China work. We then lay out a model of special deals to examine how the Chinese characteristics, such as high administrative capacity, ability to obtain private benefits, and local competition, determine the magnitude of special deals and their effect on economic growth. The next section uses data from multiple sources, including the Chinese Annual Survey of Industrial Firms (ASIF), the Economic Censuses, firm registries from the State Administration of Industry and Commerce (SAIC), microdata on land sales, and a survey of politically connected firms, to provide suggestive evidence on the nature of special deals that firms grow when they have access to special deals and that local governments support their favored local firms. The last section discusses the risks inherent in an economic institution based on access to special deals.

II. How Do Special Deals Work in China?

We begin by describing how a specific local government supports private business. We visited a city in southern China in 2013 where we had extensive discussions with local officials and private businesses.[3] It was abundantly clear that the central focus of the local government was to attract and support private businesses. There were seven vice-mayors in the city and most of their time was spent prospecting for new businesses to set up in the city and solving the problems for a subset of local private firms already in the city. We estimate that each vice-mayor was the point person for about 30 private firms. The vice-mayors spent most of their time on business development, even if their official portfolio had nothing to do with it. Figure 1 replicates a document handed to us by the city's vice-mayor who oversees the local department of Education and Civil Affairs, as the vice-mayor proudly explained how the document describes his main job. The city's Department of Education and Civil Affairs is in charge of local schools, but what the vice-mayor of education actually spends his time on is actively looking for quality prospects and arranging special deals for these businesses. We witnessed a monthly meeting organized by the party-secretary and mayor with the seven vice-mayors to coordinate their activities supporting private business. We estimate that about 200 private businesses in this city, most of them the city's largest employers, have special deals negotiated by the vice-mayors, the mayor, or even the local Communist Party secretary.

What we witnessed in this city is also evident to anyone who has done business in China that a central priority of Chinese local governments is to attract and support private businesses. We illustrate the consequences by looking at how local governments affected the implementation of China's formal industrial policy in the last 2 decades. In the late 1990s, the central government designated nine "strategic and pillar" industries that were restricted to a handful of state-owned firms.[4] In 2015, the central government made explicit an additional list, the so-called negative list, of

Fig. 1. Work program of a vice-mayor of education. The flowchart in Chinese was given to us by the vice-mayor of education and civil affairs of a Chinese city. The translation in the right column is ours.

12 industries in which foreign firms were prohibited.[5] Of the 12 negative list industries, 7 were also on the list of strategic and pillar industries, so a total of 14 industries were off-limits for private and/or foreign
firms.

The goal of these policies was to create powerful state-owned firms in
these sectors by restricting entry.[6] However, despite the official rules
that restricted entry by private firms, new private firms established between 1998 and 2007 accounted for 62% of all firms in the "strategic" and
negative list sectors in 2007. This number is only slightly lower than the
share of new private firms in 2007 (67%) in industries where there were
no restrictions on private entry.[7]

The reason private firms were able to enter the strategic industries, despite the official rules that their presence was illegal, was because local
governments helped certain private firms circumvent the formal rules.
We illustrate how this happened with case studies of two strategic industries: the aluminum and automobile industries.

We begin with the aluminum market in China. In the early 2000s, this
market was dominated by the China Aluminum Corporation (Chinalco).
As one of the hundred or so state-owned companies directly controlled by
the Chinese central government, Chinalco had a 98% share of the aluminum market in China in the early 2000s. Chinalco had two main assets.
First, the central government passed a law that gave the company exclusive rights to purchase all bauxite deposits in China when the company
became a publicly listed company in 2001. Second, no other company
was legally allowed to produce aluminum. Yet, by 2008, the market share
of Chinalco dropped to less than 50% due to the entry of large private
firms in the aluminum market. One of these companies is the East Hope
(Sanmenxia) Aluminum Company, a subsidiary of the East Hope Group.
The East Hope Group was created in 1995 in Sichuan as one of the four
companies resulting from the breakup of the Hope Group. At the time,
the East Hope Group's main business was as a processor and distributor
of animal feed.

The East Hope Group decided to expand into aluminum (and heavy
metals more generally) in the early 2000s. McGregor (2010) tells the story
of how East Hope saw that Chinalco's Achilles' heel was that its exclusive right to purchase Chinese bauxite had been granted by the Chinese central government and not by the local governments with the
bauxite mines. East Hope Group was able to make a deal to purchase
bauxite with the local government of Sanmenxia, a small city in western Henan Province with large deposits of bauxite. Chinalco fought the

East Hope Group but the local government of Sanmenxia had enough political clout to make the deal stick. With the support of the local government of Sanmenxia, the East Hope Group started to produce aluminum in 2005. Many other private companies in Henan followed a similar path and had taken half of Chinalco's market share by 2008. When asked about the key to his success in the aluminum industry, East Hope's owner said, "Forgive me for being frank, but local officials, even corrupt ones, need to have political achievements" (McGregor 2010, 226).

The automobile industry was also dominated by state-owned firms in the early 2000s with similar restrictions as the aluminum industry on entry by private firms. In the mid-2000s, the largest car producer in China was Shanghai-GM, a joint venture between GM and the Shanghai Automobile Industrial Company (SAIC). SAIC is a publicly traded firm with a majority stake held by the Shanghai local government. SAIC also operates a joint venture with Volkswagen (Shanghai-Volkswagen) as well as a standalone car company. GM's strategy in China was to use the political power of its partner SAIC to obtain exclusive rights to sell "large" sedans (with engines larger than 2500cc), and the local government of Shanghai worked hard to protect GM's monopoly power. As Dunne (2011, 15) put it, "Car-building Chinese cities act almost like sovereign countries, building a fortress around their home markets, while working very hard to 'export' their cars to other Chinese cities," and Shanghai was no exception to this behavior.

However, GM's strategy of exploiting its monopoly power ran into resistance. The third car it wanted to sell in China was a replica of a small car made by GM's Korean subsidiary, the Daewoo Matiz. Another Chinese company, Chery, based in the small city of Wuhu, started to sell exactly the same car a full 6 months before GM was ready to sell the rebranded Daewoo Matiz. Chery had managed to get hold of the blueprints of the Daewoo Matiz and beat GM-Shanghai to market. As a local state-owned firm controlled by the Wuhu government, Chery was started in 1996 by the Wuhu vice-mayor at the time, Zhan Xialai, and an engineer, Yin Tongyao, from FAW in northern China, another large state-owned firm directly controlled by the central government. Dunne (2011) tells the story of the proposed division of labor between Mr. Zhan and Mr. Yin. The vice-mayor reportedly told the engineer: "You let me take care of the licenses; you just focus on getting some cars built here" (Dunne 2011, 129). With the political support of the Wuhu local government, Chery obtained the land, capital, and infrastructure it needed. But getting access to the license from central government to make cars took longer and was less straightforward. Initially the vice-mayor was only able to get a license to make car engines for Chery. A car engine permit was readily available because car engines were not one of the strategic sectors. Chery then used this license to buy a shuttered Ford engine factory in the United Kingdom and reassembled the engine assembly line in Wuhu. The vice-mayor then lobbied the central government for a license to make cars, which the central government agreed to but only under the condition that the cars were only to be sold in Wuhu. According to the vice-mayor, his next step was to enlist the support of his political patron in the central government, and they decided to pressure Shanghai Automobile (GM's partner in Shanghai) to take a 20% equity stake in Chery. SAIC resisted the move but succumbed to the political pressure from Wuhu's vice-mayor's political patron. So in 2000 SAIC took a 20% equity share in Chery, which the vice-mayor, who was then promoted to the party secretary and mayor of Wuhu, used to lobby the central government for the license to sell cars throughout China. This time they were successful, and one of the initial products of Chery was the replica of GM's Korean car.

Despite Chery's license to sell cars throughout China, however, it has found it very difficult to sell in the Shanghai market and in other Chinese cities where there is a local car company. In 2007, about one-third of Chery's sales were outside of China, where presumably it does not have to compete with companies that have special deals with the local government.[8] GM-Shanghai is formally registered as a foreign firm in China and is the largest car manufacturer in China. It has been successful financially primarily because it has used the political power of the Shanghai local government to protect its local market. Chery's local market—namely, the city of Wuhu—is simply too small for a similar strategy to be viable; thus, Chery's success is largely built on its sales outside of China. Shanghai-GM, despite being the largest car producer in China, only serves the domestic Chinese market.

Finally, we return to the case of the entrepreneur discussed by Acemoglu and Robinson (2012) who was jailed for 5 years for competing with a state-owned firm. The entrepreneur Dai Guofang had established a large steel company called Jiangsu Tieben in Changzhou City in 2002. However, as was the case with the aluminum and automobile industries, the steel industry was also one of the strategic industries where entry by large private firms was forbidden. Dai Guofang had gotten around this restriction by "breaking up" Jiangsu Tieben into 22 different companies, each of which fell below the official size threshold, and obtained a separate license for each of the 22 companies. Jiangsu Tieben was shuttered in 2003 on the orders of the central government and Mr. Guofang was arrested and remained in jail for 4 years without a sentence. Acemoglu and Robinson (2012) use this episode to illustrate the effect of Chinese extractive institutions, but there is an interesting epilogue to the story. After Mr. Guofang was released from prison in 2008 he created the Jiangsu Delong Nickel Company, this time with the support of a different local government in Jiangsu.[9] Mr. Guofang's new company is currently China's largest producer of nickel-iron alloys.[10]

We take away the following points. First, formal institutions for growth are poor in China. For example, there was an effort by the central government to protect favored firms in the aluminum and automobile industries. Second, support of local governments, such as the one in southern China we visited, is crucial to the success of the East Hope Group and Chery. Support of the local government was critical for both companies to circumvent the rules imposed by the central government to protect the incumbent firms (e.g., Chinalco in the aluminum industry and Shanghai-GM in the car industry). Third, the story of Chery illustrates how competition between local governments limited the ability of Shanghai-GM to exploit its monopoly power. And the story of Mr. Guofang illustrates the importance of competition in giving options to entrepreneurs whose deals fall through in other cities. Fourth, the allusion to corrupt local officials by East Hope's CEO hints that private benefits may be important in providing local officials with an incentive to support local firms.

III.   A Model of Special Deals

This section sketches a model of special deals in an environment with "bad" formal institutions. The key idea is that a subset of firms benefits from special deals to which other firms do not have access. We examine the determinants of the benefits that favored firms obtain, how many firms get access to deals, and the effect of special deals on the real wage.

Preferences are given by

$$U = \left(\int_0^1 C_z^{\frac{\sigma-1}{\sigma}} dz \right)^{\frac{\sigma}{\sigma-1}},$$

where $z \in [0, 1]$ indexes the product. There are two potential technologies for each product given by $(1 - \delta)e^{A(1-z)}$ ("A" technology) and $(1 - \delta)e^{Bz}$ ("B" technology), where $0 < \delta < 1$ represents the Total Factor Productivity

(TFP) loss from bad institutions. We view δ as a reduced-form representation of the productivity loss due to the thicket of official rules and regulations behind China's poor ranking in the World Bank's *Doing Business* indicators. Output is the product of the chosen technology and labor.[11] Given preferences and the production function, the profit-maximizing price is the standard markup over marginal cost.

Consider first a benchmark where the chosen technology is the product of $1 - \delta$ and $\max\{e^{A(1-z)}, e^{Bz}\}$. Define $\tilde{z}$ as the cutoff, where the A technology is chosen for $z < \tilde{z}$ and B is chosen for $z > \tilde{z}$. This cutoff is given by

$$\tilde{z} = \frac{A}{A + B}.$$

After imposing profit maximization and labor market clearing, the real wage ω is then

$$\omega = \frac{\sigma - 1}{\sigma}(1 - \delta)\left(\int_0^{\tilde{z}} e^{A(1-z)(\sigma-1)}dz + \int_{\tilde{z}}^1 e^{Bz(\sigma-1)}dz\right)^{\frac{1}{\sigma-1}},$$

where the cutoff product $\tilde{z}$ is defined earlier.[12]

Now consider a special deal regime where some firms get benefits and other firms do not. The political leader provides two types of benefits to a subset of the A firms. First, local political leaders in China help favored firms circumvent burdensome rules. These can take the form of firm-specific exemptions to official rules and the implicit sanctioning of violations of regulations (such as the East Hope Group's foray into the aluminum industry). We model this benefit as an increase in firm TFP from $(1 - \delta)e^{A(1-z)}$ to $(1 - \delta + \gamma)e^{A(1-z)}$ where $0 < \gamma < \delta$. We interpret γ as capturing the ability of the local government to alleviate the effect of poor overall institutions for specific firms. For example, γ would be low in places where the local bureaucracy is incompetent or where the local political leader has other priorities.

A second benefit is that potential competitors of the favored firms are blocked from the market. Chery found it very difficult to sell in Shanghai because the three dominant local automobile manufacturers are supported by the City of Shanghai.[13] The only taxis in Beijing are the Hyundai Elantra made by Hyundai's joint venture with the City of Beijing. The only taxis in Shanghai are the Volkswagen Santana made by Shanghai-Volkswagen. There is no formal law or regulation that Beijing taxi companies have to use Hyundai cars or Shanghai cab companies have to buy Volkswagen cars, but taxi companies fully understand the incentives of the local taxi regulator.

To capture this idea, suppose all A firms $z \in [0, z_c]$ are favored by the political leader (we will endogenize z_c shortly). If $z_c < \tilde{z}$, then the TFP of all A firms $z \in [0, z_c]$ exceeds the TFP of the corresponding B firms. So blocking has no effect and as long as $\gamma > 0$, the special deal regime raises the real wage. However, if $z_c > \tilde{z}$, then consumers get access to worse technologies for products $z \in [\tilde{z}, z_c]$. In this case, the effect of special deals on the real wage is ambiguous, as it depends on the benefit of $\gamma > 0$ for firms $z \in [0, z_c]$ relative to the loss from blocking better B technologies for $z \in [\tilde{z}, z_c]$.

A third institutional feature of special deals in China is that they are provided by local governments that compete ferociously with each other. Suppose that firms with the A technologies are in city A and firms with B technologies in city B. Further, assume that workers freely move between the two cities, implying that in equilibrium the real wage is the same in the two cities. There are two effects of local competition. First, we now have two cities supporting local firms instead of only one. So some B firms also get supported by their local government. Second, a local government can only protect firms in its locality but has no power in the other locality. Going back to the example of the automobile industry, GM was the favored firm in Shanghai but it did not have any preferences in Wuhu (or in any Chinese city outside of Shanghai).

To isolate this third effect, suppose the political leader in A supports local firms, but the one in B does nothing to support local firms (we can easily relax this assumption). We assume $z_c > \tilde{z}$ and that workers can freely move between the two cities. The key difference is that the political boss in A can only block competitors in his or her jurisdiction but has no power in B. These two assumptions limit the loss due to blocking. Intuitively, when city A blocks better technologies produced in city B, this raises the cost of living in city A and thus lowers the real wage in city A relative to B (for a given relative nominal wage). Workers then reallocate from A to B and the share of products made by A falls until the real wage is equalized in the two cities.[14]

Why would a political leader choose to provide special deals to some firms instead of reducing δ, which benefits all firms? One answer is that the political leader can extract rents from providing special deals, whereas he or she has limited ability to do so if all firms are treated equally. To capture this idea, we assume firms with special preferences pay a share $\beta^{\sigma-1}$ of their profits to the political leader (and nonfavored firms do not pay). This assumption implies that, all else equal, the political leader prefers to help more profitable (and presumably larger) firms.

If the political leader can get a share of the firm's profits if he or she provides the firm with a special deal, why does not the local leader make the deal available to all firms? One reason is the nature of a special deal regime in which the deals have to be individually negotiated. Each firm that has a special deal comes with a cost to the political leaders, either in the form of political capital or in the time their bureaucracy spends. This is one way to view the fact that the vice-mayors in the city we described work long hours negotiating deals and solving problems for the favored firms.

We capture this last idea by assuming each special deal entails a fixed cost given by $(Fe^A/w)^{\sigma-1}$. The political leader will therefore provide favors to firms when the return exceeds the fixed cost. Profits of the marginal firm z_c are proportional to $(((1 - \delta + \gamma)e^{A(1-z_c)})/w)^{\sigma-1}$. After equating the political leader's return from helping the marginal firm to the fixed cost, we get the following expression for z_c:

$$z_c = \ln\left(\frac{\beta(1 - \delta + \gamma)}{F}\right).$$

So the political leader provides deals to the most productive firms $z \in [0, z_c]$. The number of firms with special deals z_c is larger when the political leader gets more private benefits (β is larger), the local government has more capacity (γ is larger) and can thus provide more assistance, and the fixed cost F is low.

The key variables that determine the number of firms with access to special deals and their effect on the real wage are β ("private benefits"), γ ("state capacity"), and local competition. Figure 2 illustrates the effect on the real wage for different values of these parameters. It is useful to distinguish the following cases:

• **No private benefits:** This is simply the baseline economy. Here the degree of local competition and state capacity does not matter. Even when the local government has high capacity, this is not used because the political leader has no incentive to help.

• **Low capacity and large private benefits:** The *top panel* in figure 2 illustrates the effect of special deals on the real wage when $\gamma = 0$ for different values of β. Here the only effect of more private benefits (higher β) is to increase the number of firms that are protected from competitors. This effect is attenuated with local competition (this is the case labeled "two cities") because workers move from city A to B in response to higher

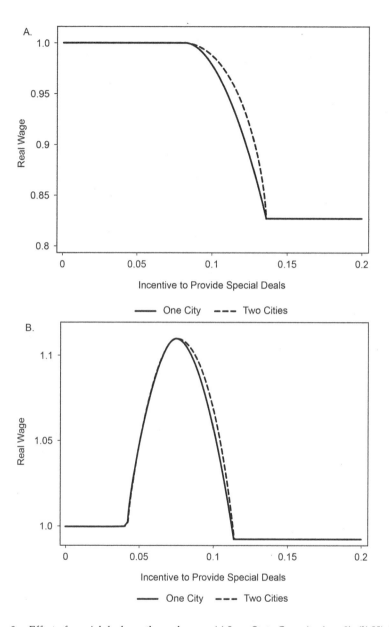

Fig. 2. Effect of special deals on the real wage. (*a*) Low State Capacity ($\gamma = 0$). (*b*) High State Capacity ($\gamma = 0.1$). Figures present the real wage when firms with "A" technology have access to special deals relative to the benchmark where $\beta = 0$ and $\gamma = 0$. "One-city" assumes "A" firms with special deals block competitors in cities A and B. Two cities assumes "A" firms with special deals only block competitors in city A. $\beta^{\sigma-1}$ is the political leader's share of firm profits. γ is the increase in TFP in the "favored" firms. The *bottom panel* assumes $\gamma = 0.1$.

costs in A. Still, the effect of special deals on the real wage is either nothing (for low levels of β) or negative (for high levels of β).

• **High capacity and large private benefits:** The *bottom panel* of figure 2
presents the case when local governments also alleviate bad institutions
for favored firms.[15] Favored firms get two benefits: a boost in TFP and
protection from competitors. Here, starting from low levels of β, more
private benefits increase the real wage. Intuitively for low levels of private benefits, an increase in β increases the number of favored firms.
These firms benefit from higher TFP, and these are already the firms
with the best technology so there is no negative effect from blocking better
competitors. Beyond the "optimal" level of private benefits (in the figure
around $\beta = 0.08$), further increases in β lower the real wage. The negative
effect of blocking more competitors outweighs the TFP boost of the marginal favored firms. And here, as in the "low capacity" case, the negative
effect is attenuated with competition between cities.

The model is highly stylized and can be extended in many directions.
Here we mention three. First, we assume perfect allocation of labor
within a city. We can extend the model to allow for other resources such
as land and capital, and a benefit the local leader can provide is access to
local resources. The aggregate effect depends on whether preferential
access to resources improves or worsens the allocation of resources. In
the next section, we examine the extent to which favored firms also obtain preferential access to land and capital.

Second, another benefit of local competition is that it gives options to
firms that find themselves in cities where the local leader is incompetent
or more generally where entrepreneurs do not get the support they
need. The story of Dai Guofang, who after trying several times was able
to find support for his heavy metals company in a different city, illustrates this. It would be easy to extend the model to allow firms to move
between cities and locate in the city that gives them the best deal.[16]

Third, the only cost of private benefits of political leaders in the model
is the potential loss of better products.[17] The model can be extended to
consider other losses. For example, the model is static, but if firms also
make a dynamic investment decision, their incentive to invest is lower
because a share of their profits goes to the political leader. In contrast,
if the political leader indirectly owns some of the equity (and we will
provide some evidence later in the paper that this might be the case),
then the political leader has the incentive to maximize the present discounted value of the flow of profits of the firm.

IV. Growth with Chinese Characteristics

The period between the early 1990s and 2008 before the onset of the global financial crisis was the highest growth episode in recent Chinese history, with gross domestic product (GDP) growth averaging 11% per year. We suggest that this growth was driven by the emergence of a special deal regime best characterized as a "high capacity and private benefits" regime. We present four types of evidence consistent with this interpretation. First, we present aggregate evidence of the growing importance of large firms, particularly of large conglomerates. Second, we show employment growth rates are higher in cities where returns to special deals are higher. Third, we present direct evidence of political ties and preferences of successful firms. Fourth, we provide evidence that localities block better firms from selling in their markets.

A. Growth of Large Firms and Conglomerates

The model described earlier assumes the incentive to provide special deals is that the local leader gets a share of the firm's profits. This assumption implies that, all else equal, political leaders prefer to provide deals to larger firms. Furthermore, if part of the special deal is that these firms are exempt from inefficient formal rules, then large firms will gain relative to other firms as a consequence of the availability of special deals.

We begin by showing the change in the importance of large firms in China. Table 1 shows the output share of firms in the top 1% of firms in the employment size distribution. The left columns present this information for above-scale firms in the industrial sector in 1998, 2002, and 2007. The right columns show this statistic for all industrial firms in 1995, 2004, and 2008.[18] The sales share of the top 1% above-scale industrial

Table 1
Sales Share of Top 1% Firms

Above-Scale Industrial Firms		All Industrial Firms	
1998	25.2%	1995	31.6%
2002	28.9%	2004	37.5%
2007	33.3%	2008	45.1%

Source: Above-scale industrial firms from the Annual Survey of Industrial Firms. All industrial firms from Economic Census.

firms increased from 25% to 33% between 1998 and 2007. For all industrial firms, the sales share of the top 1% firms increased from 31% to 45% between 1995 and 2008.

The largest firms in the Industrial Survey and Economic Census do not fully capture the extent to which large firms increasingly dominate the Chinese economy. Take the East Hope Group. East Hope is one of the four companies created in 1995 by the breakup of the Hope Group. The original business of the East Hope Group was animal feed processing and distribution, but East Hope is now one of the largest aluminum producers in China. By 2015, there were 213 firms in the East Hope Group, one of which is the East Hope (Sanmenxia) Aluminum Company. The majority of these firms are in the animal feed or heavy metal industries.[19] The Anbang Group is another example. The original company, Anbang Insurance, was founded in 2004. By 2015, Anbang Insurance had controlling stake in 94 companies.

The largest subsidiaries of the East Hope Group and Anbang Group are almost always joint ventures with other companies. The joint ventures of the East Hope Group have three distinctive features. First, they are all located outside of Sichuan Province, the home province of the East Hope Group. Second, almost all are joint ventures with state-owned firms. Third, they are typically the first firm the group established in the province and in a sector that is new to the group. For example, East Hope's initial companies in the coal, nonferrous metals, and chemicals industries were joint ventures with state-owned firms outside of Sichuan Province. These facts suggest that East Hope uses joint ventures with state-owned firms to buy access to special deals. The average equity share of state-owned firms in the joint ventures with East Hope in the animal feed sector is 28.6%. The equity share of state-owned enterprises of the joint ventures in heavy metals is 53.2%. We interpret this number as a rough estimate of the share of profits that East Hope has to give up—β in the model—in exchange for special deals outside of its core locality and business.

Anbang's subsidiaries follow a similar pattern. For example, one of Anbang's subsidiaries is the Chengdu Rural Commercial Bank. Anbang Insurance is the controlling shareholder of this bank. The other shareholders of Chengdu Bank are 10 local state-owned firms (from Chengdu) and 11 holding companies. Chengdu Bank itself owns 40 subsidiaries, all of them financial institutions located in other cities in Sichuan Province and all of them jointly owned by other local state-owned firms and holding companies.

Table 2
Average Number of Firms of Chinese Conglomerates

	1995	2015
Top 100	509	15,322
Top 500	115	5,979
Top 1,000	61	3,120

Source: Firm Registry of State Administration for Industry and Commerce. Entries are average number of firms per conglomerate among the 100, 500, and 1,000 largest conglomerates in 1995 and 2015.

We use the firm registration records from China's SAIC to document systematically the emergence of conglomerates such as the East Hope Group and Anbang Group. These data are a universe of all registered firms in China, and the data are unique in providing information on the owners. The owners can be another firm, a holding shell, or a private individual. Importantly, as long as the shell company is registered in China, the SAIC data identify the owners of the holding shells, and these owners can be individuals or (as is frequently the case) other holding shells.[20] But there is very limited economic information; the only information available is the firm's registered capital. Following Bai et al. (2019), we identify conglomerates as groups of firms with common owners. Table 2 presents the average number of firms in the largest Chinese conglomerates in 1995 and 2015. The average number of firms of the largest 100 conglomerates increased from 509 to more than 15,000 from 1995 to 2015. Among the 1,000 largest conglomerates, the average number of firms rose from 61 to more than 3,000 over the same time period.

Table 3 shows that not only has the size of the largest conglomerates increased but the ownership structure of the conglomerates has also changed. The table shows the share of the subsidiaries (i.e., all firms outside of the original core company of the conglomerate) of the conglomerates

Table 3
Jointly Owned Subsidiaries of Chinese Conglomerates

	1995 (%)	2005 (%)
Top 100	39	82
Top 500	25	85
Top 1,000	30	81

Source: Firm Registry of State Administration for Industry and Commerce. Entries are the weighted percentages of subsidiaries of the 100, 500, and 1,000 largest conglomerates that are jointly owned with other companies. Weights are the firm's registered capital.

that are joint ventures with other firms. Among the top 1,000 conglomerates in 1995, about 30% of the conglomerates' subsidiaries were joint ventures. By 2015, the share of joint ventures was more than 80%.

The evidence indicates that the largest Chinese conglomerates have grown by creating joint ventures with other companies. We interpret this pattern as an increase in β or γ that makes possible the entry of these firms. East Hope entered into joint ventures with state-owned firms outside of Sichuan to "buy" access to the political ties of these firms. Anbang entered into joint ventures with state-owned firms in Chengdu when it created the Chengdu Rural Commercial Bank, again presumably to obtain access to that market.

Ownership of the conglomerate's core firm also becomes shared with other parties. Let us go back to the original company of the Anbang Group (i.e., Anbang Insurance). The company was created in 2004 with eight investors, two of which are state-owned firms and six are holding shells.[21] By 2015, the equity share of the eight original investors had dropped to 19% and the new owners are a complex web of holding companies.

Figure 3 illustrates the ownership structure of Anbang Insurance in 2015. Anbang Insurance is the dark circle in the middle and the circles with other colors represent the owners. We further identify different types of owners by the color: gray for holding shells, white for state-owned firms, and open circles for individual owners. The circles immediately connected with the black circle represent the immediate owners of Anbang Insurance. In 2015, Anbang Insurance had 39 owners, two of which were state-owned firms (white circles) and 37 of which were holding shells (gray circles). And every holding shell in turn was owned by other holding shells, most of which in turn were owned by other holding shells, and so on.

It is clear is that the current owners (the individuals represented by the open circles in fig. 3) have worked really hard to hide their ownership of Anbang behind a series of holding companies. This pattern suggests that Anbang's original shareholders may have grown the company by sharing equity of its core companies in exchange for favorable treatment. We would need to know the price at which the original investors sold their equity stake to know for sure whether this was the case, but what seems clear is that Anbang's new owners have gone to great lengths to hide their ownership of the company.

B. Heterogeneity across Cities in Impact of Special Deals

In the previous section, we showed that large private firms, particularly mixed-ownership conglomerates, increasingly dominate the Chinese

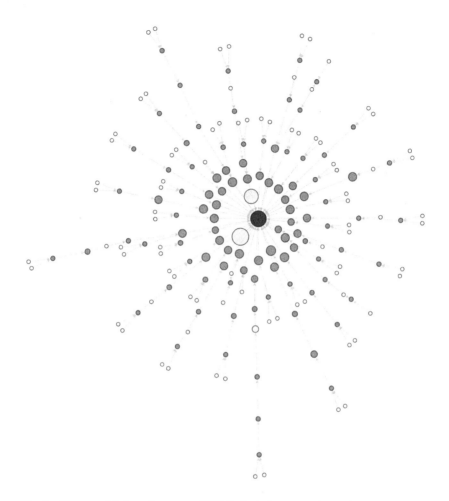

Fig. 3. Owners of Anbang Insurance, 2015. Each circle represents a unique company or individual. Arrows denote ownership links. Black circle is Anbang Insurance (the original company). Grey circles are holding shells. White circles are state-owned firms. Empty circles are individual persons. Subsidiaries of the Anbang Group are not included. Data are from SAIC ownership records.

economy. In the model we laid out in the previous section, favored firms benefit from a proportional increase in their TFP, so the return to a special deal is an increase in firm TFP. We now examine the cross-sectional implication of the same force. Specifically, if high-TFP firms benefit more from special deals, the effect of a city providing special deals on aggregate TFP in the city will be larger in cities where the right tail of the firm TFP distribution is thicker.

Figure 4 examines this hypothesis by showing the scatter plot of the employment growth rate of a city (y-axis) on the initial employment

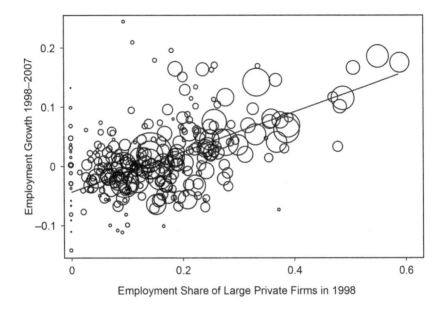

Fig. 4. Employment growth and initial share of large private firms. Each circle represents a city (size of circle represents the size of the city). The *y*-axis is the annualized employment growth rate of the city from 1998 to 2007. The *x*-axis is the employment share of private firms with more than 1,000 workers in 1998. The center, sloping line denotes ordinary least squares regression line. Data are from microdata of Annual Survey of Industrial Firms.

share of private firms with more than 500 employees (*x*-axis). The data are from the ASIF, so only above-scale industrial firms are included. The employment growth rate of a city is from 1998 to 2007 and is a proxy for aggregate TFP growth of the city.[22] The employment share of large private firms is from 1998 and is a proxy for the share of privately owned firms with high TFP. As can be seen, the relationship is clear: cities with a greater number of high-TFP firms initially also grow faster over time. After controlling for the city's initial level of employment, province fixed effects, and distance to the nearest port, the ordinary least squares regression of the city's employment growth rate from 1998 to 2007 on the city's employment share of large private firms yields a precisely estimated coefficient of 0.196 (SE = .029).

C. Political Ties and Preferential Treatment

We now turn to more direct evidence of links of ties between political leaders and firms. We begin by using the microdata of a survey of private firms that are members of the Chinese National Association of Industry and Commerce.[23] The survey identifies whether the firm's owner is a member of the local People's Congress or Political Consultative Committee (PC/ PCC), so we use this information to measure the relationship between PC/PCC membership and firm characteristics. About 30%–40% of the firms in the survey are owned by PC/PCC members, and this ratio is roughly constant over the years of the survey (1997 to 2012).[24]

What has changed over time is the advantage of firms owned by PC/ PCC members. The survey distinguishes between members of the PC/ PCC at the level of the provinces or above, prefectures, or counties or below. Table 4 shows the sales of firms owned by PC/PCC members (at each level of government) relative to sales of firms whose owners are not in the PC/PCC. Two facts stand out. First, not surprisingly, firms owned by PC/PCC members are larger. Second, the sales gap has increased over time. For owners in county-level PC/PCC, the sales gap increased by 1 log point between 1997 and 2012. And for owners in top-tier provincial-level PC/PCC, the sales gap increased by almost 3 log points over this period.

Table 5 examines whether politically connected firms had better access to capital.[25] The table reports results from a regression of log bank loans on indicator variables for PC/PCC membership (at the three levels), log sales, and indicator variables for industry. Controlling for industry and firm sales, firms owned by PC/PCC members have better access to bank loans. But there is no clear evidence that the preferential access increased between 2002 and 2012.

Table 4
Firm Sales and PC/PCC Membership

	1997	2006	2012
(1) Provincial PC/PCC	1.25	2.09	4.18
	(.22)	(.19)	(.27)
(2) Prefectural PC/PCC	1.02	1.63	2.51
	(.12)	(.10)	(.11)
(3) County PCC/PCC	.70	.99	1.72
	(.09)	(.07)	(.08)
N	1,946	3,836	4,616

Note: PC/PCC refers to People's Congress or Political Consultative Committee. Entries are coefficients (and standard errors) of a regression of log sales on indicator variables for whether the firm's owner is a member of a provincial-level or above PC/PCC (row 1), prefectural-level PC/PCC (row 2), or county-level or below PC/PCC (row 3). Omitted firms are those whose owners are not PC/PCC members. All regressions include indicator variables for two-digit industries.

Table 5
Access to Bank Loans and PC/PCC Membership

	2002	2006	2012
(1) Provincial PC/PCC	1.62	1.45	1.59
	(.31)	(.28)	(.40)
(2) Prefectural PC/PCC	.77	.86	1.04
	(.14)	(.14)	(.16)
(3) County PCC/PCC	.71	.62	.63
	(.11)	(.11)	(.12)
N	2,602	3,836	3,566

Note: Entries are coefficients (and standard errors) of a regression of log bank loans on indicator variables for whether the firm's owner is a member of a provincial-level or above PC/PCC (row 1), prefectural-level PC/PCC (row 2), or county-level or below PC/PCC (row 3). Omitted firms are those whose owners are not PC/PCC members. All regressions also include log sales and indicator variables for two-digit industries.

Figure 5 presents the evidence on capital productivity by firm size for a broader sample of firms.[26] The figure shows average capital productivity for the balanced panel of privately owned firms in 1998–2007 (*top panel*) and 2007–13 (*bottom panel*) in the Annual Survey of Industrial Production. The x-axis shows percentiles of the firm's initial size (in 1998 and 2007), and the y-axis shows the firm's capital productivity in the beginning and end years of each panel. Two points seem clear. First, in all time periods, capital productivity is decreasing in firm size. And if capital productivity is proportional to the marginal product of capital, then this suggests that, consistent with evidence shown in table 5, larger firms have preferential access to capital. Second, the advantage of large firms does not seem to change in the 1997–2007 period (the two lines in the *top panel* lie on top of each other). There is some evidence from the 2007–13 period that the relative advantage of large firms is growing, but the magnitude is quantitatively small.

In Bai, Hsieh, and Song (2016), we suggest that the patterns in the 1998–2007 panel can be explained as a consequence of the centralization of the financial system that took place in 1998. This reform removed the control of local governments over appointments to local branches of the state-owned banks. As a consequence, special deals provided by local governments did not include better access to capital. After 2008 these controls were lifted, with the initial purpose of financing the 4 trillion yuan fiscal stimulus in 2009–10, and local governments began to have access to capital through local financial vehicles. To the extent that some of these funds ended up in the hands of large favored private firms, this

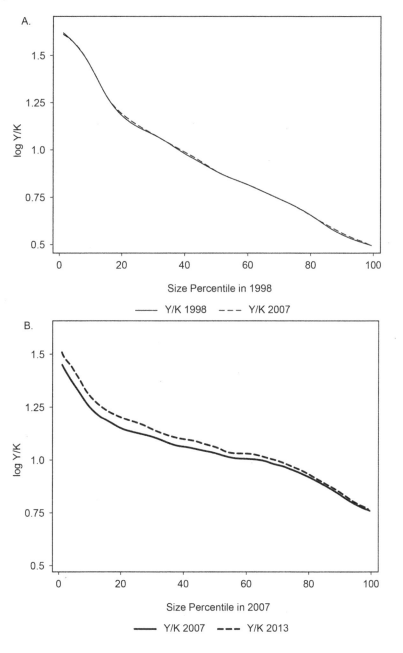

Fig. 5. Return to capital by firm size, (*a*) Y/K 1998 versus 2007 and (*b*) Y/K 2007 versus 2013. Firm-level data from Annual Survey of Industrial Firms. *Top panel* presents log Y/K of balanced panel of firms in 1997 and 2007 in the 2 years. *Bottom panel* shows log Y/K of balanced panel of firms in 2007 and 2013 in the initial and ending years. The *x*-axis is the size (measured by employment) percentile of the firm in 1998 (*top panel*) and 2007 (*bottom panel*).

could explain the pattern seen in the 2008–13 panel. But at least as of 2013, the effect is still quantitatively small.[27]

Local governments also provide land at below market costs to favored firms. Using the power of eminent domain, local governments obtain land from farmers, urban residents, and other channels, and resell the land to developers and firms. This is the main mechanism through which land use has been transformed in China in recent decades. We obtained transaction-level records of these sales from 2000 to 2014 from China's Ministry of Land Resources. For each transaction, we have information on the size of the parcel (in hectares), geographic location, sales price, and indicator variables for whether the land is to be used for housing, commercial real estate, or industrial real estate.

The *top panel* in figure 6 plots the allocation of this land between commercial, industrial, and residential use. Specifically, it shows the share of land (in hectares) sold to three types of end users. Roughly 50%–60% of new land was dedicated for industrial use. The *bottom panel* of figure 6 shows the log price per hectare of land sold for industrial use and commercial use relative to land destined for housing. Industrial land is sold at a substantial discount to residential land. In 2014, for example, the price of industrial land was more than 2 log points lower than that of residential land. In contrast, the price of commercial land is roughly the same as that of residential land.

The obvious problem with interpreting figure 6 as evidence that local governments subsidize favored firms with cheap land is that industrial land may be very different from residential land. Residential land may be mostly located in higher-priced urban locations, whereas industrial land is concentrated in cheaper, more remote locations. Table 6 shows the price gap after we introduce a succession of controls for location. Column 1 replicates the mean gap in prices shown in figure 6. On average, industrial land is 1.7 log points cheaper compared to residential land. Column 2 shows that the price gap drops to 1.5 log points after we introduce indicator variables for counties. So counties with cheaper land allocate more land to industrial use, but within the same county, industrial land is still cheaper than residential land. Column 3 keeps the indicator variables for county and adds controls for the distance of the land from the county center. There is little effect on the price gap. Finally, column 4 looks within narrowly defined neighborhoods and compares the price of land destined for different uses within the same neighborhood.[28] There is little change in the implied subsidy for recipients of industrial land.

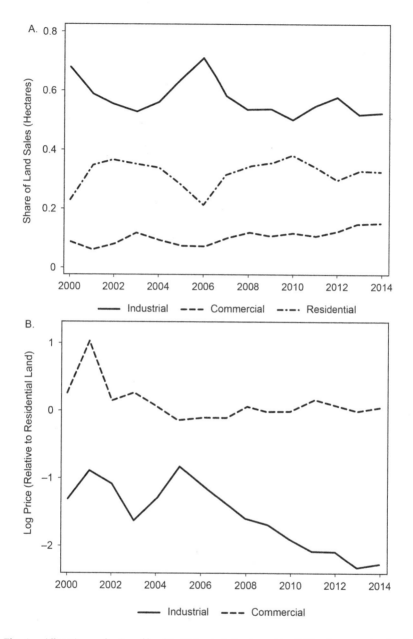

Fig. 6. Allocation and price of land in China (relative to residential land; transaction-level records from Ministry of Land Resources [N = 979,206]). (*a*) Share (in hectares) of land sales by type of user. (*b*) Average log price per hectare of commercial and industrial land (both relative to the price of residential land).

Table 6
Price of Industrial and Commercial Relative to Residential Land

	1	2	3	4
Commercial land	−.37	−.25	−.24	−.20
	(.00)	(.00)	(.00)	(.00)
Industrial land	−1.72	−1.51	−1.47	−1.46
	(.00)	(.00)	(.00)	(.00)
Controls:				
County	No	Yes	Yes	No
Distance from county center	No	No	Yes	No
Neighborhood	No	No	No	Yes

Note: Unit of observation is a land sale by a local government from the transaction-level records of the Ministry of Land Resources (N = 979,206). Entries are coefficients (and standard errors) of a regression of log price per hectare of the sale on indicator variables for commercial land and industrial land (omitted category is residential land). All regressions include indicator variables for year.

The ultimate question is whether the subsidies in land prices to industrial firms improve efficiency relative to the allocation before local governments started to sell the land. Most of this land comes from farmers, so the question is whether the land is now used more productively by industrial firms compared to its use as farmland. We do not have the data to answer this question, but here we point to evidence that the average labor productivity in the industrial sector is larger than in the agricultural sector.[29]

D. Local Protection and Exports

We argue that special deals in China are provided by local governments, and part of the deal is that competitors of the favored firms are blocked from the local market. For example, Shanghai-GM is one of the favored car companies in Shanghai and supposedly the Shanghai municipal government blocks nonlocal car companies (such as Chery) from the market. But if Chery produces better cars, it would outcompete Shanghai-GM in markets where Shanghai-GM is not protected. For example, as the largest car manufacturer in China in 2007, Shanghai-GM's export was negligible. In contrast, although Chery only accounted for 5% of domestic car sales, 20% of cars exported from China were produced by Chery. The idea then is that local protection breaks the relationship between productivity and local sales because some productive firms are blocked.

To examine how special deals affect the relationship between domestic sales and export sales, we recast utility as

$$U = \left(\int_0^1 C_z^{\frac{\sigma-1}{\sigma}} dz \right)^{\alpha \frac{\sigma}{\sigma-1}} M^{1-\alpha},$$

where M denotes imports of a homogeneous product made outside of China. The utility of consumers in the foreign country is the same. We assume the foreign country owns a limitless supply of the homogeneous good sold at a fixed price and buys differentiated varieties from China (city A or B). The rest of the model stays the same.[30]

We can now consider the effect of special deals on exports. Revert back to the case where city A supports firms $z \in [0, z_c]$, where $z_c > \tilde{z}$, and can only block competitors in the local market. Figure 7 summarizes the products sold in each market. Remember that productivity of A's firms falls as z increases. Figure 7 (*top panel*) shows that city A's most productive firms export to all markets (the foreign market and city B), but the least productive firms $z \in [\tilde{z}, z_c]$ only sell in the local market where they are protected from competition. The *bottom panel* in figure 7 shows that this is not true in city B. Remember that B is less productive as z decreases. All firms in B export to the foreign market but only the most productive firms $z \in [z_c, 1]$ sell to the other domestic market (city A). The least productive firms in B sell in the foreign market but are blocked in the domestic market in city A.

The *top panel* in figure 8 summarizes the prediction of the model on the relationship between exporting (to the foreign market) and the firm's domestic sales. In the model, firms with the smallest domestic sales export.

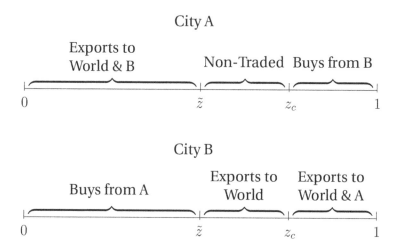

Fig. 7. Product specialization in two-city model of special deals

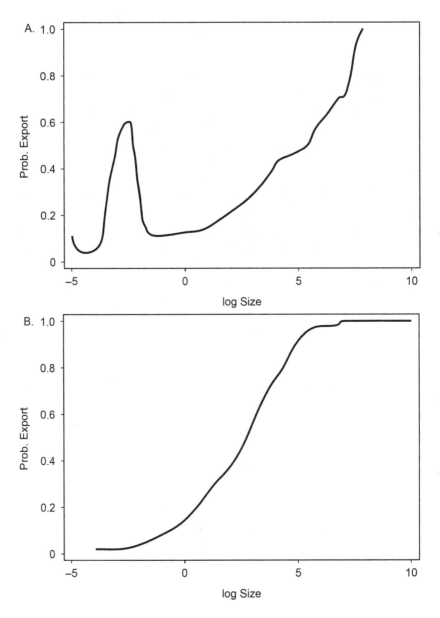

Fig. 8. Probability of exporting by firm size: (*a*) China versus (*b*) United States. Figures present probability of export versus log firm size (relative to the mean) in the Chinese (*top panel*) and US (*bottom panel*) data. Chinese data are from 1998 Annual Survey of Industrial Production. US data are from 1987 Manufacturing Census.

These are the firms in B that find their access to other domestic markets blocked. Moving up the size distribution, A's firms $z \in [\tilde{z}, z_c]$ are less productive than their counterparts in B but have larger domestic sales because market A is larger than market B. These firms do not export. We think of these firms as reflecting the case of Shanghai-GM having large domestic sales because of their privileged position in a large domestic market but do not export because they are not competitive without the protection. Lastly, the most productive firms in the two cities sell to all markets (foreign and all domestic markets).

The *top panel* in figure 8 shows the relationship between exporting and domestic sales in the cross section of the Chinese manufacturing data.[31] As can be seen, a remarkable feature of the Chinese data is that there is a cluster of firms with low domestic sales that also export. For comparison, the *bottom panel* in figure 8 shows the same relationship in the cross section of the US manufacturing data.[32] As can be seen, there is no such pattern in the US data.

The model also makes a strong prediction about the elasticity of domestic sales with respect to exports. For the most productive firms in the two cities, the elasticity of the share of the export market with respect to the share of the domestic market should be close to 1. But for the firms in B that find their access to city A blocked, the elasticity will be significantly lower than 1. Intuitively, higher productivity has a larger effect on their sales in the market where they face no barriers compared to their sales in the domestic Chinese market where they are blocked.

The *top panel* in figure 9 illustrates this prediction of the model (the thin line is the 45° line). The elasticity of domestic sales to exports predicted by the model is lower at low levels of exports. The *bottom panel* in figure 9 shows the elasticity in the Chinese data.[33] The elasticity of domestic sales to exports is essentially 0 for small firms and almost 1 for firms with above-mean export sales.

The idea that Chinese local governments protect local firms has a long history. Young (2000) argues that the decentralization of tax revenues in the 1980s coupled with price wedges prompted local governments to protect local industries to retain the revenues implied by the price wedge. The price wedges disappeared by the late 1980s and the 1994 tax reform that centralized tax revenues presumably removed the incentive of local governments to protect firms that generate large tax revenues.

Our argument is that the growth of the special deal regime increasingly became the main incentive for local governments to protect local firms but this time only for the favored firms. Our evidence suggests that many

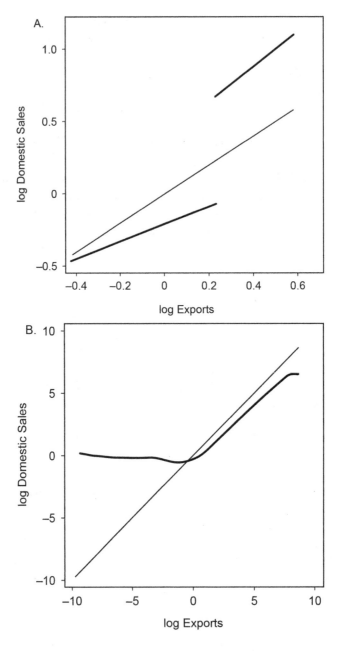

Fig. 9. Domestic sales versus exports: model versus data. (*a*) Model simulation. (*b*) Data: China. The relationship between log domestic sales (*y*-axis) and log exports (*x*-axis) is shown for exporting firms (firms that only sell to domestic market are excluded). *Top panel* is the model simulation. *Bottom panel* shows the Chinese data from 1998 Annual Survey of Industrial Production. The center, sloping line in both panels is the 45 degree line.

Chinese firms find large segments of the Chinese domestic market closed to them.[34] Local protection is welfare reducing, of course, but we argue that this effect is attenuated by the fact that local governments can only protect firms in their cities. In addition, the case of the East Hope Group suggests that many large firms have been able to strike deals with multiple local governments, which in principle can also attenuate the effect of local protection. A more important point though is that local protection is only one of the many effects of special deals, so it is imperative to take all these effects into account. And we argue that the productivity gains among the favored firms may well be significantly larger than the negative effects of local protection.

V.   Risks

This paper puts forward the hypothesis that China's growth, particularly since the early 1990s, is due to the increased availability of special deals by competing local governments. We do not provide a formal empirical test of this hypothesis, but we believe that the totality of the evidence we present is consistent with this interpretation.

If our hypothesis is correct, then it suggests that Chinese growth is a high-wire act. The effectiveness of the Chinese special deal system depends on the discretion of local officials and on minimizing the damage borne by firms that do not get special deals. A key question is, What exactly are the incentives of local party officials to support local companies? One possibility is that local party officials provide special deals for local companies because of their devotion to the job. For example, a local party official indicated to us that he values the ability to develop the local economy according to "his likes and dislikes." If so, then the question is the extent to which the selection of intrinsically motivated officials is effective and sustainable.

Another possibility is that local officials provide special deals because local party leaders who generate more "profits for the party" are promoted by the Communist Party's Organization Department. In the absence of access to the personnel files of the Communist Party, we do not know whether this is the case. It is possible, as some authors have done, to examine the correlation of promotion probability and local GDP growth, but the evidence from this work is inconclusive.[35]

A third possibility is that local party officials work very hard to support favored private firms because they are able to obtain private rents from these firms. If this is the case, the danger is that constraints on the ability of local officials to obtain private benefits will lower growth. Since 2014, there has been an unprecedented crackdown on corruption. Figure 10 presents the annual flow of new corruption cases of local party officials. The *top panel* shows the number of new corruption cases each year for party officials at the county level (*top panel*), city or prefecture level (*middle panel*), and provincial level (*bottom panel*). There was almost a doubling in the number of corruption cases of officials at the county level in 2014 and 2015. At the city level and provincial level, the number of anti-corruption cases more than quadrupled. The evidence for 2016 and 2017 show that the anti-corruption campaign, at least as seen by the number of arrests, has declined relative to 2014 and 2015.

The corruption crackdown was widely supported in China and has been effective by many accounts. Yet a concern implied by our theory is that the corruption crackdown has diminished the willingness of local officials to help local businesses. This could be because their main incentive was the monetary payoff, or it could be the fear of being accused of receiving a payoff or the resistance of intrinsically motivated officials. All these forces will diminish the extent to which firms get special deals. Figure 11 shows that Chinese growth has slowed down significantly since the onset of the 2008 global financial crisis. We do not know whether the anti-corruption campaign was the main driver of the growth slowdown, as there are other possibilities. Bai et al. (2016), for instance, documents that growing financial distortions due to the growth of local financing vehicles could also be important. At this point, the data we have at our disposal do not allow us to precisely quantify the importance of these forces.

Chinese authorities have made multiple efforts in recent years to move away from a regime of special deals. The Third Plenary Session of the 18th CPC Central Committee in November 2013 issued a resolution to "let the market play the decisive role in the allocation of resources." The State Council later issued a follow-up document that acknowledged special deals as a double-edged sword, which "promoted the investment growth and industry concentration to some extent" but "have disturbed the market order." Then it laid out specific policies to stop local leaders from providing special deals. On the government revenue side, local governments are not allowed to provide preferential tax policies, to reduce administrative fees or government funds from firms, or to assign land at a preferential or zero price. On the government expenditure side, local governments are prohibited from developing preferential policies for firms, including those by means of remitting taxes or granting subsidies.[36]

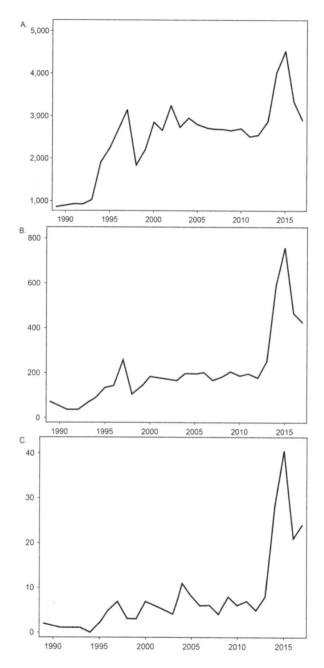

Fig. 10. Corruption cases by level of government. (*a*) County level, (*b*) city level, and (*c*) provincial level (annual reports of the Supreme People's Procuratorate of China).

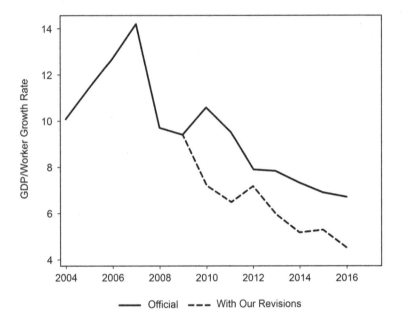

Fig. 11. Growth rate of GDP/worker (official numbers from China's National Bureau of Statistics. GDP growth labeled "with our revisions" from Bai, Hsieh, and Song 2019). GDP = gross domestic product.

Perhaps in reflection of these policy changes, China's ranking in the World Bank's *Doing Business* indicators has improved dramatically since 2013 from about the 80th percentile to about the 20th percentile in the world distribution of ease of starting of starting a business (see fig. 12).[37] However, the attempt to roll back the use of special deals appears to have been short-lived. The State Council essentially reversed its earlier decision on the use of preferential policies in 2015.[38] In 2015, the State Council issued a new document that recognizes the legitimacy of all the existing preferential policies and authorizes local governments to issue new preferential policies.

The Chinese special deal regime has been enormously successful in moving the Chinese economy to where it is today. We suggest that it has enabled the growth of the large number of Chinese firms that now dominate many world markets. We see, however, three dangers of the current system. First, a special deal system creates powerful entrenched interests that make reforms very difficult.[39] After all, a special deal regime, even with the Chinese characteristics that have underpinned high

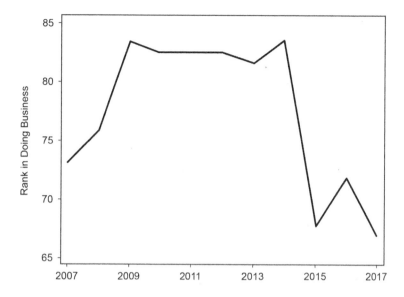

Fig. 12. China's rank in *Doing Business* indicators. Figure reports China's percentile rank in "ease of starting a business" from the World Bank's *Doing Business* project. We scale China's score by the number of countries in the data in each year to convert the score into a percentile rank.

growth for 3 decades, is a second-best solution. In terms of our model, the first best is to reduce δ to 0 with no special deals. But the difficulty is that once a special deal system is in place, local officials and large businesses benefit from these deals, and their interests are threatened with any reform that reduces δ and the extent of the special deals.

Second, some of the characteristics that made the system work in the past, such as unfettered ability to provide special deals, may no longer be present today. At the same time, other features of the special deal regime, such as the presence of powerful vested interest groups, are clearly still present and have a strong interest in blocking precisely the reforms that China may want to undertake in the future.

A third danger of the system is that companies based in other countries find themselves disadvantaged when they compete with Chinese companies with access to special deals that export into their market. At the same time, foreign companies in the Chinese market either have to make their own special deal or, as is the case with any Chinese firm that does not have a special deal, find that their intellectual property and contracts are not well respected. This tension between countries based on rules and one based on special deals is at the root of the conflict that China currently faces with its trading partners with no clear resolution in sight.

Endnotes

Author email addresses: Bai (baichn@sem.tsinghua.edu.cn), Hsieh (chsieh@chicagobooth .edu), Song (zheng.michael.song@gmail.com). We thank Yasheng Huang, Ruixue Jia, Santiago Levy, Jonathan Parker, Maurice Obstfeld, Raghuram Rajan, Meg Rithmire, Antoinette Schoar, Yingyi Qian, Yong Wang, and Xiaodong Zhu for helpful discussions. We are grateful to Xin Wang for his assistance with the State Administration of Industry and Commerce data. Feng Lin, Kazuatsu Shimizu, and Jihoon Sung provided extraordinary research assistance. The data from the US Census have been reviewed by the US Census Bureau to ensure no confidential information is disclosed. For acknowledgments, sources of research support, and disclosure of the authors' material financial relationships, if any, please see https:// www.nber.org/chapters/c14233.ack.

1. See Hsieh and Song (2015) on the quasi-privatization of the state-owned firms, Song, Storesletten, and Zilibotti (2011) on resource reallocation between state-owned and private firms, Brandt et al. (2017) on China's accession to the WTO, Lin (1992) on the agricultural reforms in the early 1980s, Kashyap and Dobson (2006) for an assessment of the 1998 reforms of the banking sector, and Tombe and Zhu (forthcoming) on the reduction in internal migration costs.

2. Hallward-Driemeir and Pritchett (2015) document the widespread use of special deals in countries with poor formal institutions.

3. We agreed to not identify the city to have frank discussions.

4. See http://www.gov.cn/jrzg/2006-12/18/content_472256.htm.

5. See "Notice of the General Office of the State Council on Printing and Distributing the Special Management Measures for the Market Entry of Foreign Investment in Pilot Free Trade Zones," State Council, 2015.

6. Brandt, Kambourov, and Storesletten (2018) show that entry barriers are negative related to the size of the state sector across Chinese cities.

7. We calculate these two numbers from the microdata of the Annual Survey of Industrial Production described later in the paper.

8. Chery accounted for 5% of total domestic sales of cars and 20% of Chinese exports of passenger cars in 2007.

9. Jiangsu Delong is located in Yangcheng City. See http://www.dlnis.com/About-Us /Profile.asp, accessed on January 29, 2019.

10. Jiangsu Delong also operates several nickel-iron alloy plants in Indonesia.

11. The chosen technology for product z is either $(1 - \delta)e^{A(1-z)}$ or $(1 - \delta)e^{Bz}$.

12. Many readers will recognize the model as Dornbusch, Fischer, and Samuelson (1977) with free labor mobility between two countries.

13. The three dominant local car companies in Shanghai are SAIC, Shanghai-GM, and Shanghai-Volkswagen.

14. The appendix (available online; see https://www.nber.org/data-appendix/c14233 /appendix.pdf) lays out the details of the model with two cities.

15. Figure 2 assumes $\gamma = 0.1$.

16. We also assume that a firm that is offered a special deal accepts the deal. We can also relax this assumption.

17. It also redistributes profits from the firm's owner to the politician, but this has no effect on the real wage.

18. The data from the industrial sector are the microdata of the Chinese Survey of Industrial Firms. These data are a census of above-scale industrial firms. The sales threshold was 5 million RMB and changed to 20 million RMB in 2011. We do not use the microdata from the Survey of Industrial Firms after 2007 because of the change in the sampling frame. (We do not have the microdata for 2008–10). The data for all industrial firms are from the microdata of the 1995, 2004, and 2008 Economic Censuses.

19. A small number of firms in the East Hope Group are real estate and finance companies. The numbers in this and the following paragraphs are based on the ownership records from the SAIC. We provide more details on these data later in this section.

20. We have no information on shell companies in the SAIC data that are registered outside of China.

21. The state-owned firms are Shangai Automobile (15%) and Sinopec (7%). Shanghai Automobile is owned by the city of Shanghai and GM's joint venture partner discussed earlier. Sinopec is one of the three centrally owned oil companies created by the breakup of the Ministry of Petroleum.

22. The logic is that with labor mobility aggregate growth in a city shows up on the extensive margin. See Brandt et al. (2018) for cross-city evidence on the size of the state sector, entry, and TFP from the economic census data.

23. The members of this association are generally large and politically connected firms. For example, average sales in 2008 in the survey are about nine times larger than in the 2008 Economic Census.

24. An average 24.4% of the firms in the survey are owned by members of the county or below PC/PCC, 12.6% by prefectural level PC/PCC, and 2.7% by provincial or above PC/PCC.

25. The survey only provides information on bank loans starting in 2002.

26. Firm capital productivity is scaled by the median value in the industry.

27. See also Cong et al. (2018) and Huang, Pagano, and Panizza (2019) for evidence of capital misallocation after 2008.

28. Neighborhoods are defined as square blocks of 9 square kilometers. We also tried squared blocks of 1 and 26 square kilometers and the results are essentially identical.

29. See, for example, Figure 17.1 in Brandt, Hsieh, and Zhu (2008).

30. We provide the details of the model with international trade in the appendix (available online).

31. Figure 8 plots the data for the 2007 cross section of the Chinese Annual Industrial Survey. The pattern is identical in all years of the data. We dropped export-processing plants from the sample.

32. The data are from the 1987 cross section of the US manufacturing census.

33. The data are from the 2007 cross section of the industrial survey.

34. Barwick, Cao, and Li (2017) document strong home (city-level) bias of car purchases using car registration data.

35. Li and Zhou (2005) find evidence from promotion of provincial-level officials that GDP growth is positively correlated with promotion. Shih, Adolph, and Liu's (2012) evidence suggests that personal connections are the primary determinant of promotion. Jia, Kudamatsu, and Seim (2015) find that political connections and economic performance are complements in terms of promotion in the party hierarchy.

36. "Reviewing and Regulating Preferential Policies for Taxation and Other Aspects," State Council Document No. 62, 2014.

37. It is difficult to know whether the improvement shown in figure 12 reflects real improvement or simply changes in methodology by the World Bank. The World Bank's *Doing Business* project revised its methodology in response to issues raised by the Chinese government. See "China Seeks to Water Down Key World Bank Report," *Financial Times*, May 6, 2013 for more details.

38. Document No. 25, State Council, 2015.

39. Song and Xiong (2018) review China's economic and financial risks. Many of them have roots in the vested interests created by special deals.

References

Acemoglu, Daron, and James Robinson. 2012. *Why Nations Fail: The Origins of Power, Prosperity, and Poverty.* New York: Crown.

Bai, Chong-En, Chang-Tai Hsieh, and Zheng Michael Song. 2016. "The Long Shadow of China's Fiscal Expansion." *Brookings Papers on Economic Activity* 47 (2): 129–81.

———. 2019. "A Forensic Examination of China's National Accounts." *Brookings Papers on Economic Activity* 2019:77–127.

Bai, Chong-En, Chang-Tai Hsieh, Zheng Michael Song, and Xin Wang. 2019. "Conglomerate Formation in China." *Brookings Papers in Economic Activity* 2019:77–127.

Barwick, Panle Jia, Shengmao Cao, and Shanghun Li. 2017. "Local Protectionism, Market Structure, and Social Welfare: China's Automobile Market." Unpublished manuscript.

Brandt, Loren, Chang-Tai Hsieh, and Xiaodong Zhu. 2008. "Growth and Structural Transformation in China." In *China's Great Economic Transformation*, ed. Loren Brandt and Thomas Rawski, 683–728. Cambridge: Cambridge University Press.

Brandt, Loren, Gueorgui Kambourov, and Kjetil Storesletten. 2018. "Barriers to Entry and Regional Economic Growth in China." Unpublished manuscript.

Brandt, Loren, Johannes Van Biesebroeck, Luhang Wang, and Yifan Zhang. 2017. "WTO Accession and Performance of Chinese Manufacturing Firms." *American Economic Review* 107 (9): 2784–820.

Cong, Lin William, Haoyu Gao, Jacopo Ponticelli, and Xiaoguang Yang. 2018. "Credit Allocation under Economic Stimulus: Evidence from China." Unpublished manuscript.

Dornbusch, Rudiger, Stanley Fischer, and Paul Samuelson. 1977. "Comparative Advantage, Trade, and Payments in a Ricardian Model with a Continuum of Goods." *American Economic Review* 67 (5): 823–29.

Dunne, Michael. 2011. *American Wheels, Chinese Roads: The Story of General Motors in China*. Singapore: Wiley.

Hallward-Driemeir, Mary, and Lant Pritchett. 2015. "How Business Is Done in the Developing World: Deals versus Rules." *Journal of Economic Perspective* 29 (3): 121–40.

Hsieh, Chang-Tai, and Zheng Michael Song. 2015. "Grasp the Large, Let Go of the Small: The Transformation of the State Sector in China." *Brookings Papers on Economic Activity* 2015 (1): 295–366.

Huang, Yasheng. 2008. *Capitalism with Chinese Characteristics*. Cambridge: Cambridge University Press.

Huang, Yi, Marco Pagano, and Ugo Panizza. 2019. "Local Crowding Out in China." Unpublished manuscript.

Jia, Ruixue, Masayuki Kudamatsu, and David Seim. 2015. "Political Selection in China: The Complementary Roles of Connections and Performance." *Journal of the European Economic Association* 13 (4): 631–68.

Kashyap, Anil, and Wendy Dobson. 2006. "The Contradiction in China's Gradualist Banking Reforms." *Brookings Papers in Economic Activity* 2006 (2): 103–48.

Li, Hongbin, and Li-An Zhou. 2005. "Political Turnover and Economic Performance: The Incentive Role of Personnel Control in China." *Journal of Public Economics* 89 (9–10): 1743–62.

Lin, Justin. 1992. "Rural Reform and Agricultural Growth in China." *American Economic Review* 82 (1): 34–51.

McGregor, Richard. 2010. *The Party: The Secret World of China's Communist Leaders*. New York: Harper Collins.

Shih, Victor, Christopher Adolph, and Mingxing Liu. 2012. "Getting Ahead in the Communist Party: Explaining the Advancement of Central Committee Members in China." *American Political Science Review* 106:166–87.

Song, Zheng, Kjetil Storesletten, and Fabrizio Zilibotti. 2011. "Growing Like China." *American Economic Review* 101 (1): 196–233.

Song, Zheng, and Wei Xiong. 2018. "Risks in China's Financial System." *Annual Review of Financial Economics* 10:261–86.

Tombe, Trevor, and Xiaodong Zhu. Forthcoming. "Trade, Migration and Productivity: A Quantitative Analysis of China." *American Economic Review.*

Xu, Chenggang. 2011. "The Fundamental Institutions of China's Reforms and Development." *Journal of Economic Literature* 49 (4): 1076–151.

Young, Alwyn. 2000. "The Razor's Edge: Distortions and Incremental Reform in the People's Republic of China." *Quarterly Journal of Economics* 115 (4): 1091–145.

Comment

Maurice Obstfeld, *University of California, Berkeley, Peterson Institute for International Economics, NBER, and CEPR*

December 18, 2018, marked the fortieth anniversary of the Third Plenary Session of the Eleventh Central Committee of the Chinese Communist Party (CCP), at which Deng Xiaoping launched China on its remarkable recent trajectory of economic growth. By giving greater play over time to market forces, Deng's reform and opening initiative spurred rapid income convergence. But it did so while preserving the CCP's political monopoly.

As figure 1 shows, China's real gross domestic product (GDP) growth (insofar as the official data are accurate) has been high on average although anything but smooth. Moreover, it has declined markedly since the last year of double-digit growth in 2010 and even more so since the heady precrisis peak.

China's politics have not evolved monotonically either. The year 2019 marked the thirtieth anniversary of the Tiananmen protests, sparked by the (vain) hope that China's economic evolution would encourage a commensurate political evolution. Chinese politics—and, I argue, economics— have only regressed under the more authoritarian rule of President Xiaoping Xi. In this paper, Chong-en Bai, Chang-Tai Hsieh, and Zheng Song likewise link China's falling growth rate over the past decade to political factors, but I emphasize a set of factors different from the one that they highlight.

What mechanism linking politics to growth do the authors emphasize? In his speech commemorating the fortieth anniversary of Deng's reforms, President Xi stated that "we will resolutely reform what should and can be reformed, and make no change where there should not and cannot be any reform."[1] An alternative title for this paper could have been "Chinese Cronyism: Can It Be Changed? Should It Be Changed?" The authors' main message is that cronyism is deeply ingrained in China's mode

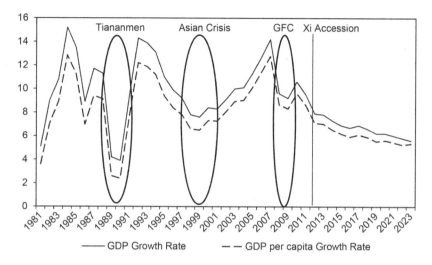

Fig. 1. China's growth and its deceleration since 2007 (percentage per year). GDP = gross domestic product; GFC = global financial crisis.

of doing business, but it has had beneficial growth effects that Xi's drive to consolidate power is stunting.

What the Paper Does

This paper assembles a fascinating body of evidence on how business is done in China. It makes the overarching claim that, since the early 1990s, China's primary growth driver has been an increasing availability of "special deals" that competing local governments offer to private firms. To support this account, the paper offers three lines of argument.

• Explanation of the special deal regime and anecdotes on how it can work to drive growth.
• A Dornbusch-Fischer-Samuelson (1977) model (DFS) of deals' allocation effects, for both (1) a two-city economy with labor mobility and (2) two cities with export markets. The underlying DFS model is essentially the two-country version of Eaton and Kortum (2002), parameterized as in the dynamic extension by Ken Rogoff and me (Obstfeld and Rogoff 1996).
• Four categories of supportive empirical argumentation:
  1. Data on the growth of large firms and conglomerates.
  2. Evidence that bigger firms generate faster employment growth.
  3. Evidence that firms that are more successful also are better connected politically.
  4. Evidence that the system encourages smaller firms to export.

Stepping Back before Diving In

Even before reviewing the latter categories of evidence, I want to lay out some reasons I am skeptical of the paper's basic thesis.

The paper lays out convincing evidence of the prevalence of cronyism—for example, the webs of hidden ownership and the preferential access to credit of firms owned by CCP-connected officials. Where it is much less convincing is in establishing that cronyism spurred growth. I did not see anything in the paper that one could construe as direct evidence.

The paper's DFS model establishes, at most, that special deals can have a level effect on productivity, not an effect on steady-state growth. Of course, given an increase in cronyism, the model might predict a transitional growth increase as the economy attains a new, higher level of total factor productivity (TFP). However, the paper leaves open if such effects can explain China's growth experience.

One would think a regime of special deals would soon hit diminishing returns at the national level. In particular, as competing subnational governments promote duplicative capacity bolstered by protective trade restrictions, distortions rise and the gains from specialization (including possible increasing returns) rapidly erode. True, exporting is an option, but export capacity has limits.

Even at the local level, I wonder if the multitudinous officials hustling noncooperatively for local deals, without necessarily internalizing the possibility of driving workers away through lower real wages, might push a city far past the optimum in their figure 2.

One avenue for cronyism to result in an (eventually) growth-limiting coordination failure is through excessive credit expansion. Indeed, the authors (Bai, Hsieh, and Song 2016) argued in an earlier paper that, starting with the 2008 crisis, uncoordinated local government credit extension for favored industries, through the mechanism of off-balance-sheet vehicles, "potentially worsens the overall efficiency of capital allocation. The long-run effect of off-balance-sheet spending by local governments may be a permanent decline in the growth rate of aggregate productivity and GDP" (129). I am not sure how to reconcile that finding with the claims in the present paper: according to the authors' evidence, firms controlled by CCP members had preferential access to bank loans even in the early 2000s, and they find no evidence that access had increased by 2012.

China's authorities have (belatedly) recognized the perils of unfettered credit growth, as indicated by their recent attempt to slow it down (fig. 2), which is an important reason for the recent decline in GDP growth.

As a general observation, I find it counterintuitive to argue that simply by easing preexisting distortions, cronyism unleashed growth rates

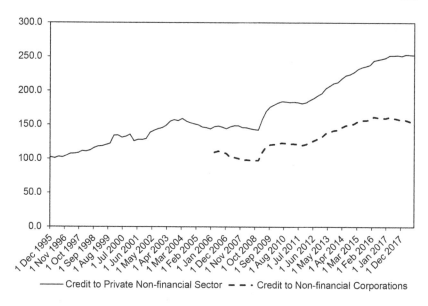

Fig. 2. Reining in China's credit growth (percentage of gross domestic product). Source for data is Bank for International Settlements.

as exceptional as those China has shown in recent decades, up until very recently. Distortions indeed were severe, but as the authors acknowledge, other forces were at play. A partial list would include trade reforms prior to World Trade Organization entry, the movement of labor from agriculture into the industrial sector with its higher average labor productivity, enhanced infrastructure and connectivity, and possibly even an easing of the urban housing constraints stressed by Hsieh and Moretti (2019) as a barrier to growth in the United States.

Are the Empirical Arguments Convincing?

As noted, Bai, Hsieh, and Song present four main empirical arguments for their thesis. They assert that although each one, alone, might not be convincing, the four taken together make a compelling case. I did not come away convinced that the whole exceeds the sum of its parts.

Section IV.A looks at the growth of firms and argues that sponsored firms will grow relative to others due to the relaxation of constraining regulations, often through joint ventures with dispersed and nontransparent ownership. I wonder about the extent to which the duplicative efforts in localities could actually mitigate concentration at the national level. More importantly, I do not see why greater concentration should necessarily spur growth; for market economies, the theory and evidence on this are certainly mixed, and different effects might be obtained for different concentration levels and at different phases of a firm or conglomerate's life cycle.

Section IV.B documents a city's employment growth tended to be higher over the period 1998–2007 when it contained a greater number of large firms. Again, the link to output growth is indirect, and it is unclear that the authors' favored mechanism is at work. Even if larger firms are favored and therefore hiring more workers, the productivity implications are unclear. Indeed, the paper's figure 5 indicates that, for a sample of privately owned firms, "capital productivity is decreasing in firm size." This seems to run counter to the idea that bigger necessarily implies greater productivity.

The suggested positive relationship between cronyism and city growth runs counter to other evidence. For example, Rodríguez-Pose and Zhang (2019) present evidence that better city institutions and measures to limit corruption promote urban growth. It would be helpful to know if the paper's figure 4 displays a pattern peculiar to China or if it would also characterize major market economies. The figure suggests that small cities tend to host smaller firms on average, and we also know that smaller cities may grow more slowly on average (see, e.g., reasons given in Hsieh and Moretti 2019). The discussion calls out for a more thorough, multivariate analysis.

Section IV.C explores firms' political ties. From the analysis in Section IV.A, however, we know it may be hard to determine beneficial ownership. Thus, I would not view this evidence as dispositive either. Indeed, even if political connections contribute to firm growth, the authors also show in this section that bigger, privately owned firms tend to have lower capital productivity. To my mind, this finding makes the link from political connections to overall GDP growth more questionable.

Finally, Section IV.D's evidence on firm size and exporting status is fascinating and does present a pattern different from what we see in market economies. It is not clear, however, that the specific model the authors present implies the distinctive spike of smaller exporting firms that their figure 8 shows (as opposed to the general point that a greater number of smaller firms will be induced to sell abroad owing to restrictions on sales in other localities). This pattern could be a product of the trade diversion their model implies, but why it takes this particular form remains a mystery, and I would guess that additional factors are in play.

Other Questions

Precisely because the ownership of firms is hard to determine, I would like to know more about the interactions between local private champions and state-owned enterprises (SOEs). Local governments also run many inefficient SOEs; they can support them in various ways, including through credit diversion, and it is hard to believe that there is a clear line between the large private firms and conglomerates that local governments have supported and the SOEs that they also support. Much of that interaction seems unlikely to benefit the efficiency of the private partners.

Clearly local governments have several incentives to support inefficient SOEs, including maintaining employment, maintaining influence, and maintaining tax revenues. These incentives differ across regions.

Figure 3 documents the relative profitability of three categories of firm. Industrial SOEs are more profitable than other SOEs, but all SOEs are far less profitable than private industrial enterprises. Reference to figure 3 in my comment on Bai, Hsieh, and Song (2016) shows similar trends for the postcrisis period but, in addition, that locally operated SOEs have been the least profitable among SOEs, generating even lower returns than those that are centrally controlled. Although private enterprise remains far more profitable in China, its profitability has declined since the crisis, in line with the authors' narrative, and more sharply than the relatively gentle decline in profitability of SOEs.

That profitability decline has coincided with a decline in overall GDP growth. The question is, Why is this happening?

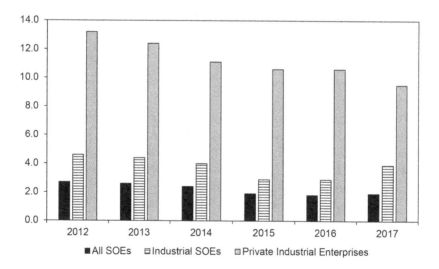

Fig. 3. Relative profitability of Chinese private enterprises and state-owned enterprises (SOEs; rate of return on assets, percent per year; IMF 2018).

Forces behind China's Growth Slowdown

Many factors are contributing to China's falling rate of growth. Among these are population aging, the rebalancing of the economy toward consumption and services, and a diminished scope to move labor from agriculture to manufacturing. China's antipollution drive is also biting, due to a growing middle class demanding cleaner air and water. As Pritchett and Summers (2014) have argued, none of this is inconsistent with the historical tendency for growth rates to fall as poorer countries converge.

More specific to the Chinese case, one could argue, as does Jin (2019), that China's exceptional growth is owed to a government-directed model of forced saving and export intensity that was unsustainable and has become counterproductive. The authors also hint that a special deal regime could ultimately be counterproductive by creating strong vested interests inimical to necessary reforms.

Bai, Hsieh, and Song argue that President Xi's anticorruption campaign has slowed China's growth by curtailing the scope for special deals. I agree that the anticorruption campaign has been a factor, though not primarily for the reason the authors suggest. The Xi crackdown has certainly had a chilling effect on initiative and entrepreneurship. Some of this effect, no doubt, is to discourage special deals. However, the negative growth effects likely extend beyond that specific mechanism.

More importantly, the anticorruption campaign has been a tool in President Xi's drive to consolidate political power in his own hands. Another facet of this drive, as Lardy (2019) documents, has been diversion of economic resources away from the private sector into the comparatively less productive state-owned sector (recall fig. 3). For example, China's credit clampdown may be disproportionately affecting private firms. Lardy argues that this reallocation is robbing China of substantially higher potential growth.

Rough indicators of the centralizing trends in credit allocation come from firms' debt-to-equity ratios. Figure 4 shows that over the Xi era through 2017, central SOEs accumulated debt relative to equity, whereas local SOEs did not. Industrial SOEs as a group have seen a mild decline in debt-to-equity, but within private industry (where debt ratios are lower) the decline has been sharper in both percentage points and proportional terms.

A more recent factor slowing China's growth has been trade tensions with the United States—tensions that escalated sharply after the conference at which the authors presented this paper. Because China has moved

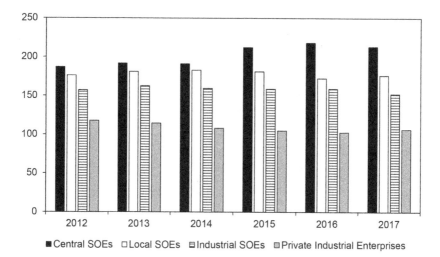

Fig. 4. Debt-to-equity ratios for state-owned enterprises (SOEs) and private enterprises (percentage; IMF 2018).

promptly to deploy offsetting macroeconomic stimulus, the effect of trade conflict on China's growth was not immediately dramatic in data on aggregate GDP. But the underlying effects have worsened the trade-offs that Chinese policy makers face.

Bai, Hsieh, and Song rightly question whether China's opaque economic arrangements are compatible with a rules-based global trading system. Indeed, some reformers within China welcome the external pressure on trade as a possible catalyst for economic liberalization and a turn back from Xi's increased support of the state-owned sector of the economy.

It may be overly optimistic to expect such a favorable resolution of current trade tensions. In his December 2018 speech commemorating Deng's reforms, President Xi also declared, "No one is in a position to dictate to the Chinese people what should or should not be done." At the same time, US devotion to a rules-based global trading system (as opposed to choosing its own rules to suit the moment) is not obvious. The two countries are on a collision course that goes far beyond economics. How this conflict is resolved will be a prime factor in Chinese growth—and global growth—in coming years.

Endnotes

Author email address: Obstfeld (obstfeld@econ.berkeley.edu). For acknowledgments, sources of research support, and disclosure of the author's material financial relationships, if any, please see https://www.nber.org/chapters/c14234.ack.

1. Speech transcript at Transcend Media Service, December 24, 2018, https://www.transcend.org/tms/2018/12/xi-jinpings-speech-on-40th-anniversary-of-chinas-reforms-opening-up-full-text, accessed June 6, 2019.

References

Bai, Chong-En, Chang-Tai Hsieh, and Zheng (Michael) Song. 2016. "The Long Shadow of China's Fiscal Expansion." *Brookings Papers on Economic Activity* 2:129–65.

Dornbusch, Rudiger, Stanley Fischer, and Paul A. Samuelson. 1977. "Comparative Advantage, Trade, and Payments in a Ricardian Model with a Continuum of Goods." *American Economic Review* 67:823–39.

Eaton, Jonathan, and Samuel Kortum. 2002. "Technology, Geography, and Trade." *Econometrica* 70:1741–79.

Hsieh, Chang-Tai, and Enrico Moretti. 2019. "Housing Constraints and Spatial Misallocation." *American Economic Journal: Macroeconomics* 11:1–39.

IMF (International Monetary Fund). 2018. "People's Republic of China: Staff Report for the 2018 Article IV Consultation." June 28. https://www.imf.org/en/Publications/CR/Issues/2018/07/25/Peoples-Republic-of-China-2018-Article-IV-Consultation-Press-Release-Staff-Report-Staff-46121.

Jin, Keyu. 2019. "China's Steroids Model of Growth." In *Meeting Globalization's Challenges*, ed. Luís A. V. Catão and Maurice Obstfeld. Princeton, NJ: Princeton University Press.

Lardy, Nicholas R. 2019. *The State Strikes Back: The End of Economic Reform in China?* Washington, DC: Peterson Institute for International Economics.

Obstfeld, Maurice, and Kenneth Rogoff. 1996. *Foundations of International Macroeconomics.* Cambridge, MA: MIT Press.

Pritchett, Lant, and Lawrence Summers. 2014. "Asiaphoria Meets Regression to the Mean." In *Prospects for Asia and the Global Economy*, ed. Reuven Glick and Mark M. Spiegel. Asia Economic Policy Conference 2013 Proceedings. San Francisco: Federal Reserve Bank of San Francisco.

Rodríguez-Pose, Andrés, and Min Zhang. 2019. "Government Institutions and the Dynamics of Urban Growth in China." Discussion Paper no. 13505 (February), Centre for Economic Policy Research, London.

Comment

Antoinette Schoar, Massachusetts Institute of Technology and NBER

The paper puts forward a provocative thesis. The proposition is that informal arrangements between bureaucrats and the private sector, so-called "special deals," have allowed the Chinese bureaucracy to overcome poor formal institutions, and these special deals are an important driver of the country's growth miracle. The argument is that Chinese local governments have well-developed administrative capacity and use it to provide these deals to favored firms to allow socially beneficial business transactions to go forward and spur economic development. The paper proposes that local political officials behave as if they have high-powered incentives to assist favored private firms because they are in competition with other local governments to attract businesses and show economic growth. Of course, many economists have argued that special deals or side payments can be a second-best solution for bureaucratic gridlock. For example, Fisman (2001) and McMillan and Woodruff (2002) have suggested that deals can "grease the wheels" in a system with high regulatory burdens, and De Soto (1989) famously emphasized the importance of the informal economy for growth in countries with overbearing regulation. The novel hypothesis put forward in the current paper is that special deals are the reason for growth, not a second-best solution.

Although the paper does not provide evidence on the causal nature of special deals for economic growth in China, of course, China is not the only country that promotes bureaucratic influence in economic decisions. The literature in other countries has typically found that a reliance on these special deals is a detriment to growth. Overall the cross-country evidence suggests that more corrupt countries also grow more slowly (Mauro 1995; Rodrik, Subramanian, and Trebbi 2004). These cross-country correlations are supported by micro studies, which show that reliance on these deals leads to distortions in resource allocation. In France, for example, a country that promotes national champion firms, a number of papers have shown that politically connected firms grow more slowly and have lower productivity (Kramarz and Thesmar 2013). In fact, the banking reform in the mid-1980s, which led to a reduction in government-directed credit to connected firms, reduced growth of connected firms but promoted the entry of more efficient new firms and overall improved net job creation and productivity (Bertrand, Schoar, and Thesmar 2007). Similarly, studies in other countries (La Porta, Lopez-de-Silanes, and Zamarripa 2003; Rajan and Zingales 2004; Khwaja and Mian 2005) have shown that subsidized loans go to connected firms that have low productivity. A growing set of experimental studies points to severe misallocation of resources from corruption. For example, professional and other licenses to ensure minimum skill level (such as driver's licenses) are awarded to unqualified people (Bertrand et al. 2007); perceived corruption leads to underprovision of public goods (Olken 2007, 2009) or distortion in talent allocation (Ferraz, Finan, and Moreira 2012).

Against the backdrop of the large literature on corruption, we have to ask if special deals in China are truly special. In other words, did the Chinese Communist Party figure out a way to set up its bureaucracy to solve the old problem of misalignment of incentives? In an interview with the *Financial Times*, Bhagwati (2014) suggests that the Communist Party has an advantage over a messy democracy because Chinese politicians have longer horizons and do not need to face reelection threats. As a result, they may see themselves as the residual claimants on the country's growth and are not distracted by short-term voting cycles. This is an intriguing idea and deserves serious consideration in light of China's unique development experience. Of course, in the spirit of Shleifer and Vishny (1993), one might ask why the central government did not design better rules from the start so that special deals would not be needed to fix problems of formal institutions if the party is trying to maximize the long-run welfare of the country. But one cannot dismiss out of hand that a complicated political economy between the legislature and the bureaucracy might make it difficult to change laws and regulations even if the bureaucracy has the best interest of the country at heart.

At its core, bureaucratic corruption is like a principal-agent problem, where bureaucrats trade off their career concerns and status in their government position against the income from corruption and the likelihood of being caught. The former is often long term and uncertain whereas the payoffs from special deals are often much more immediate and certain. Thus, the challenge is how to design incentives for bureaucrats to mitigate these corrupt impulses or even turn them into a force for beneficial decision-making as proposed in the current paper. A number of possible solutions have been proposed, notably going back to Weber (1922) who suggested creating a culture of elite bureaucrats, basically sidestepping the central problem and hoping for better humans. More recently, Becker and Stigler (1974) argue that providing efficiency wages for officials and monitoring their actions would be optimal. Di Tella and Weinschelbaum (2008) point out when agents are poor it is easier to monitor their bribe-taking via consumption because any large and unusual consumption patterns would not be explained by their legitimate income. But at the same time, incentives to engage in special deals are higher for poorer bureaucrats who have less to lose. Similarly, papers by Holmstrom (1982); Maskin, Qian, and Xu (2000); and Xiong (2018) stress the career tournaments of bureaucrats.

In the Chinese context, the problem of lower-level officials is how to keep them focused on the long term. This means that the benefits from being promoted or staying in the job have to be stronger than the benefits of diversion in the interim, which means that the center or the politburo has to have vast resources to provide such incentives. Similarly, there has to be the belief throughout the bureaucratic hierarchy that evaluation is fair and people get promoted based on performance, not on connections or political whims. If local officials feared that those who work on promoting long-run growth will not be rewarded in the end, it would undermine their willingness to abstain from extracting short-term rents. Finally, these local politicians must have a very strong belief in the efficacy of the tools they have at their disposal to promote growth.

A set of recent papers documents that the alignment of incentives along the hierarchy chain of the Chinese bureaucracy might not be as meritocratic as one might hope for the political tournament story to work. Persson and Zhuravskaya (2016) show some of the limitations to the idea that career concerns of local politicians are uniformly focused on the common goal. The authors show that local politicians use government resources to cater to demands of low-level provincial elites, who helped them rise to power. This suggests that local incentives create competing allegiances. In addition, Goh, Ru, and Zou (2019) show that personal connections to high-ranking officials reduce the punishment of lower-level officials in the case of corruption. Even in the wake of the anti-corruption program in China, connections to high-ranking politicians make local officials less likely to be investigated and receive lighter sentences. In contrast, the investigations of Central Committee members lead to more investigations of their connected city officials. This type of evidence suggests that local officials should worry that the career concerns are not stacked as clearly toward providing efficient economic outcomes. But, instead, many players are willing to further their own goals.

On a more macro level, the recent paper by Ru (2018) tracks the impact of a large set of special deals on the local economy. Local mayors in China are selected and promoted every 5 years in line with the Communist Party Congress. Those mayors who show significant growth during their time in office can be promoted to higher positions or larger cities. The paper looks at the type of deals mayors facilitate when they come into office. The paper supports the idea that there are career concerns for mayors, but it also shows that many of the projects or deals that the local governments undertake have mixed results on growth at best. Projects that support infrastructure building do indeed help to spur growth of private firms and state-owned enterprises (SOEs). However, projects and credit lines that support the expansion of SOEs, which is a large fraction of special deals, lead to significant crowding out of efficient private firms.

Finally, Lin et al. (2016) provide evidence from the effect of the anti-corruption campaign on the Chinese stock market. The paper uses the anti-corruption campaign as an event study in the Chinese public markets. On December 4, 2012, Xi Jinping announced a new "Eight-point Policy" to stop government officials and top executives in SOEs from demanding or accepting extravagant perks. Chinese market index increased significantly (15% over a 30-day window) after the announcement of the Eight-point Policy. Again, this evidence suggests that at least stock market participants do not see the ability to engage in special deals as a benefit to publicly traded firms.

In sum, my reading of the existing literature suggests that there is no evidence that special deals and corruption were a positive factor for growth in China. But it is remarkable nevertheless that the Chinese government managed to restrain corruption to a level that allowed for significant growth over the last 2 decades despite the massive opportunities to extract rents. Learning from the Chinese example of how it managed to set up institutions that contain corruption to allow rapid economic development to occur can be a powerful laboratory. And framing the analysis in this way seems more in line with a large prior literature on corruption. Going forward, it will be interesting to see if this system can provide sustained economic growth. Governance by one-party rule might be easier when an economy is closed and poor. Detection of excess consumption and spending by bureaucrats might have been easier in these early years, and shipping profits from corruption overseas was also more difficult. At the same time, the economic policies that were needed to create growth might be less ambiguous, for example, building roads and allowing some private enterprise. It might be less adept in a middle-income country where there is more uncertainty about which economic policies will foster innovation and inclusive growth.

Endnote

Author email address: Schoar (aschoar@mit.edu). For acknowledgments, sources of research support, and disclosure of the author's material financial relationships, if any, please see https://www.nber.org/chapters/c14235.ack.

References

Becker, G. S., and G. J. Stigler. 1974. "Law Enforcement, Malfeasance, and Compensation of Enforcers." *Journal of Legal Studies* 3 (1): 1–18.
Bertrand, M., S. Djankov, R. Hanna, and S. Mullainathan. 2007. "Obtaining a Driver's License in India: An Experimental Approach to Studying Corruption." *Quarterly Journal of Economics* 122 (4): 1639–76.
Bertrand, M., A. Schoar, and D. Thesmar. 2007. "Banking Deregulation and Industry Structure: Evidence from the French Banking Reforms of 1985." *Journal of Finance* 62 (2): 597–628.
Bhagwati, J. 2014. "Lunch with the FT: Jagdish Bhagwati." *Financial Times* (April 17). https://www.ft.com/content/f3a22bc8-c3db-11e3-a8e0-00144feabdc0.
De Soto, H. 1989. *The Other Path*. New York: Harper & Row.
Ferraz, C., F. Finan, and D. B. Moreira. 2012. "Corrupting Learning: Evidence from Missing Federal Education Funds in Brazil." *Journal of Public Economics* 96 (9–10): 712–26.
Fisman, R. 2001. "Estimating the Value of Political Connections." *American Economic Review* 91 (4): 1095–102.
Goh, J. R., H. Ru, and K. Zou. 2019. "Force behind Anti-Corruption: Evidence from China." https://ssrn.com/abstract=3227368.
Holmstrom, B. 1982. "Moral Hazard in Teams." *Bell Journal of Economics* 13 (2): 324–40.
Khwaja, A. I., and A. Mian. 2005. "Do Lenders Favor Politically Connected Firms? Rent Provision in an Emerging Financial Market." *Quarterly Journal of Economics* 120 (4): 1371–411.
Kramarz, F., and D. Thesmar. 2013. "Social Networks in the Boardroom." *Journal of the European Economic Association* 11 (4): 780–807.
La Porta, R., F. Lopez-de-Silanes, and G. Zamarripa. 2003. "Related Lending." *Quarterly Journal of Economics* 118 (1): 231–68.
Lin, C., R. Morck, B. Yeung, and X. Zhao. 2016. "Anti-Corruption Reforms and Shareholder Valuations: Event Study Evidence from China." Working Paper no. 22001, NBER, Cambridge, MA.
Maskin, E., Y. Qian, and C. Xu. 2000. "Incentives, Information, and Organizational Form." *Review of Economic Studies* 67 (2): 359–78.
Mauro, P. 1995. "Corruption and Growth." *Quarterly Journal of Economics* 110 (3): 681–712.

McMillan, J., and C. Woodruff. 2002. "The Central Role of Entrepreneurs in Transition Economies." *Journal of Economic Perspectives* 16 (3): 153–70.

Olken, B. A. 2007. "Monitoring Corruption: Evidence from a Field Experiment in Indonesia." *Journal of Political Economy* 115 (2): 200–249.

———. 2009. "Corruption Perceptions vs. Corruption Reality." *Journal of Public Economics* 93 (7–8): 950–64.

Persson, P., and E. Zhuravskaya. 2016. "The Limits of Career Concerns in Federalism: Evidence from China." *Journal of the European Economic Association* 14 (2): 338–74.

Rajan, R. G., and L. Zingales. 2004. *Saving Capitalism from the Capitalists: Unleashing the Power of Financial Markets to Create Wealth and Spread Opportunity.* Princeton, NJ: Princeton University Press.

Rodrik, D., A. Subramanian, and F. Trebbi. 2004. "Institutions Rule: The Primacy of Institutions over Geography and Integration in Economic Development." *Journal of Economic Growth* 9 (2): 131–65.

Ru, H. 2018. "How Do Individual Politicians Affect Privatization? Evidence from China." September 18. https://ssrn.com/abstract=3251361.

Shleifer, A., and R. W. Vishny. 1993. "Corruption." *Quarterly Journal of Economics* 108 (3): 599–617.

Tella, R. D., and F. Weinschelbaum. 2008. "Choosing Agents and Monitoring Consumption: A Note on Wealth as a Corruption-controlling Device." *Economic Journal* 118 (532): 1552–71.

Weber, M. 1922. *Economy and Society.* Berkeley, CA: University of California Press.

Xiong, W. 2018. "The Mandarin Model of Growth." Working Paper no. 25296, NBER, Cambridge, MA.

Discussion

Thomas Philippon opened the general discussion by commenting on the benefits of competition among localities in China. He referred to the findings of Joel Mokyr (*A Culture of Growth: The Origins of the Modern Economy* [Princeton, NJ: Princeton University Press, 2018]) on the link between political fragmentation and growth in Europe. Philippon recalled that, focusing on the period from 1500 to 1700, Mokyr found that political fragmentation prevented monarchs from impeding innovation. He pointed out that political fragmentation is particularly beneficial when combined with cultural unity, free trade, and absence of war. Philippon noted that China shares these three characteristics and that competition among localities seems to foster innovation, just like political fragmentation did in Europe a few centuries ago.

Frederic Mishkin spoke next. He noted that China experienced an important rural exodus. This reallocation of labor potentially increased productivity, he argued, by reassigning it from unproductive activities in the countryside to productive, capital-intensive ones in cities. Mishkin asked the authors to which extent reallocation could explain China's growth over the past decades. The authors argued that the evidence suggests that labor reallocation played a minor role, at least over the past two decades. In particular, they pointed out that real wages grew 6% to 7% on average over an extended period of time, which does not fit the labor reallocation narrative. The authors emphasized the role of capital misallocation instead, referring to existing work of theirs. In Chong-En Bai, Chang-Tai Hsieh, and Zheng Michael Song ("The Long Shadow of China's Fiscal Expansion," *Brookings Papers on Economic Activity* 47, no. 2 [2016]: 129–81), they found that capital misallocation has increased over the past 10 years. Part of this misallocation is imputed to the response to the Great Recession, they argued. Local governments circumvented institutional constraints on borrowing by setting up special-purpose vehicles. These entities proved hard to wind down, the authors explained, and ended up offering special deals to local firms, which contributed to credit misallocations. However, they pointed out, the evidence on the subject is not definitive.

Daron Acemoglu placed the question of special deals in a broader conceptual framework. Special deals can fuel two types of growth, he argued. They can foster investment, facilitate the adoption of technology at the world frontier, and encourage innovation, which is the type of growth emphasized by Alexander Gerschenkron (*Economic Backwardness in Historic Perspective* [Cambridge, MA: Harvard University Press, 1962]). Or they can encourage insider deals and channel credit to connected but inefficient firms. China's growth falls into the first category, he argued. The success of special deals in China stands in sharp contrast with the experience of other developing countries. This raises two questions, according to Acemoglu. What factors provide discipline on special deals? And what are the limits of special deals to generate long-term growth? Acemoglu provided tentative answers. On the first question, he emphasized the role of state capacity and export orientation. He noted that industrial policies that proved successful in China, South Korea, and Taiwan failed in some African countries. Part of the reason lies in the fact that these countries could not control local officials and lacked the bureaucratic capacity to implement these policies, he argued. Export orientation also provides some discipline on special deals, Acemoglu argued. He contrasted the case of China with that of Turkey: the two countries experienced similar growth since 2009, but the former is much more export oriented than the latter. Inefficiency built up much faster in Turkey due to the lack of an export discipline, according to Acemoglu. In particular, special deals encouraged credit to connected firms and contributed to a real estate boom. On the limits of special deals to generate long-term growth, Acemoglu pointed out that China's approach constitutes a unique experiment. Industrial policies that ultimately generated sustained innovation have been typically accompanied by political and institutional changes, he noted. The future of the Chinese economy will tell whether industrial policies can foster innovation without broader transformations, he suggested. The authors seconded the opinion of Acemoglu on the role of state capacity in China. They were also in agreement with the importance of export orientation but put forth another mechanism. Exports offer an escape valve for companies facing local protections, they argued.

The rest of the discussion focused on the nature of incentives for local officials, echoing a point raised by one of the discussants, Antoinette Schoar. Erik Hurst inquired about the role of growth targets imposed by the central government and the potential political tournaments they induce across regions or municipalities. The authors emphasized the role of financial incentives over career concerns. They identified three potential drivers that could explain the officials' actions and performance. First, they could be intrinsically motivated and benevolent. Second, they could act in their self-interest and seek power and influence. Or, third, they could respond to implicit equity stakes. Financial incentives are the most plausible explanation in the case of special deals, according to the authors. Rents can only be extracted after wealth has been created, which disciplines the local officials' decisions, they argued.

The authors concluded the discussion by providing further details about the institutional context in which local officials operate. A common misconception is that the Chinese government is a homogeneous, unified entity, they argued. In reality, decisions are decentralized and uncoordinated at times. Regulations at the central and local levels might even conflict. Local officials sometimes have to violate regulations issued by the central authority to proceed with local projects, which entails career risks, the authors suggested.

7

Climate Change, Climate Policy, and Economic Growth

James H. Stock, *Harvard University and NBER*

The topics of climate change and climate change policy encompass a complex mixture of the natural sciences, economics, and a mass of institutional, legal, and technical details. This complexity and multidisciplinary nature make it difficult for thoughtful citizens to reach their own conclusions on the topic and for potentially interested economists to know where to start.

This essay aims to provide a point of entry for macroeconomists interested in climate change and climate change policy but with no special knowledge of the field. I therefore start at the beginning, with some basic background on climate change, presented through the eyes of an econometrician. I then turn to climate policy in the United States. That discussion points to a large number of researchable open questions that macroeconomists are particularly well suited to tackle.[1]

Let me summarize my four main points. First, although a healthy dose of skepticism is always in order (as academics it is in our DNA), simple and transparent time series regression models familiar to macroeconomists provide independent verification of some key conclusions from climate science models and in particular confirm that essentially all the warming over the past 140 years is because of human activity, that is, is anthropogenic. Figure 1 shows time series data on annual global mean temperature since 1860, when reliable instrumental records start. As seen in the figure, the global mean temperature has increased by approximately 1 degree Celsius, compared with its 1870–90 average value. This increase in temperatures drives a wide range of changes in climate, including droughts, more hot days, and more intense rainfalls and storms, all of which vary regionally. Because climate science uses large, opaque calibrated models of the climate system, there is room for confusion among legitimately skeptical outsiders about just how much of the global warming observed since the industrial revolution results from human

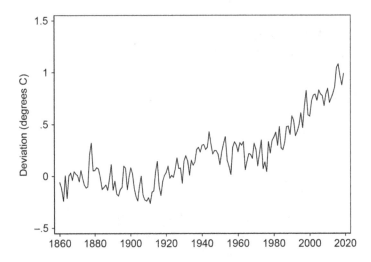

Fig. 1. Global mean temperature deviated from its 1870–90 mean (Hadley Earth Observatory, HadCRUT4 series at https://crudata.uea.ac.uk/cru/data/temperature).

activity, that is, is anthropogenic. Standard time series regressions provide a simple, transparent, and (I argue) reliable alternative, at least for modeling the relation between emissions and temperature. According to a regression decomposition I present later, anthropogenic sources account for essentially all of the warming in figure 1. The main driver of that warming is anthropogenic emissions of carbon dioxide (CO_2) from burning fossil fuels. The simple regression on which these estimates are based lacks nuance but the results accord with and, therefore, provide support for the more complex models used by climate scientists.

Second, policy will play a crucial role in decarbonizing the economy. As shown in figure 2, in the United States, energy-related CO_2 emissions peaked in 2007 and then fell 12% by 2018. This fact has led some on the environmental left to argue that we have turned a corner and are on an inevitable path to decarbonization and some on the right to argue that the free market will lead to decarbonization so policy interventions are costly and superfluous. But this narrative, however appealing, is false. Instead, the decline in emissions since 2007 is mainly the consequence of the financial crisis recession and the fracking revolution, which made natural gas cheap enough that it has partially replaced a higher-carbon fossil fuel, coal, for generating electricity. In contrast to the rosy narrative, the most recent projections by the US Energy Information Administration (EIA) indicate that, under current policy, the United States will not be close to hitting its pledged 2025 emissions-reductions target under the now abandoned Paris climate accord.

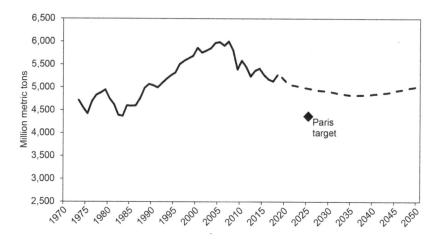

Fig. 2. US CO_2 emissions from energy consumption, 1973–2018, with US Energy Information Administration projections (dashed), 2019–50 (US Energy Information Administration, *Monthly Energy Review* [June 2019] and 2019 *Annual Energy Outlook*, reference case).

Third, looking beyond the short-term Paris target, the multitude of climate policies currently in place in the United States, from federal to state to local, fall far short of what is needed to achieve decarbonization on a timescale consistent with avoiding very severe damages from climate change. With some exceptions, existing policies interact in complex ways that lead to inefficiencies, are subject to industry capture, tend to be expensive as measured by cost per ton of CO_2 avoided, and are small bore in the sense that their scope for emissions reductions is small. The large-scale, more efficient policies typically favored by economists, such as a carbon tax or its cousin, cap and trade, have dim prospects because they either have already been rejected politically (e.g., cap and trade), create significant political liabilities (e.g., a carbon tax), or have been weakened or reversed through the regulatory process (e.g., the Clean Power Plan [CPP], the Obama administration's plan for a cap-and-trade system within the power sector). Moreover, the absence of a price on carbon is but one of the externalities plaguing climate policy, and carbon pricing alone at politically plausible levels is unlikely to be particularly effective in reducing emissions from the oil and gas used in the transportation, commercial, and residential sectors.

Fourth, the political constraints on and intrinsic limitations of Pigouvian carbon pricing mean that economists need to look elsewhere for efficient climate policies. I believe that the most important place that economists can add value to the climate policy discussion now is by focusing on policies that drive low-carbon technical innovation. This view is informed by positive political economy—what politicians seem willing to do, by empirical evidence and some key success stories about technology-pushing policies, and by a small but insightful literature on carbon prices, research and development (R&D) subsidies, and induced technical change. Ultimately, decarbonization will occur not by forcing consumers and businesses to choose expensive low-carbon technologies over inexpensive fossil fuels but by ensuring that those green alternatives are sufficiently low cost that they are largely chosen voluntarily. Consumers and firms will need to choose low-carbon energy not because it is the right thing to do, but because it is the economical thing to do, even if there is not a meaningful price on carbon. The transition to a low-carbon economy will require a low-cost alternative to fossil fuels. The key policy question is, How can we most efficiently promote the development of advanced low-carbon technologies? This difficult question is one that economists are well equipped to tackle.

I. Some Climate Change Econometrics

The increase in global mean temperature in figure 1 happened in stages, initially rising starting around World War I, followed by a plateau in the 1950s through 1970s, then taking off in earnest around 1980. A natural question is, How much of this increase is anthropogenic? An oft-cited response is that 97% of climate scientists agree that global warming is mainly because of human activities (Cook et al. 2013). As part of the scientific community, we should trust in the peer review process and thus in the science underlying that consensus. That said, the models on which those conclusions are based are large, complex, and difficult for outsiders to evaluate. This complexity has opened the door to debate about the scientific consensus, which in turn raises the question of whether there are ways to estimate the extent to which this warming is anthropogenic that are simpler, transparent, and stay close to the data. Fortunately, the tools of time series econometrics provide such estimates.

The starting point is the principle that Earth's temperature is proportional to the thermal energy flux hitting its surface. This includes energy from the sun and energy radiated from Earth that is absorbed by atmospheric gasses and reradiated back to Earth. This latter source is the greenhouse effect. These energy fluxes, called radiative forcings, are shown in figure 3: CO_2, methane, trace gasses like hydrofluorocarbons, solar radiative forcing (the wiggles are sunspot cycles), and sulfur oxides, which have negative radiative forcings because they reflect sunlight back into space. All the gasses have natural components, but the changes in these

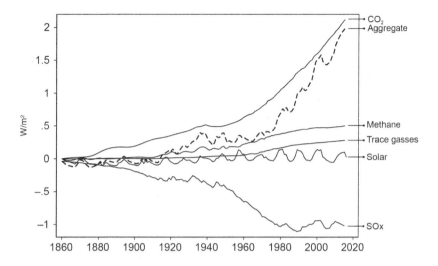

Fig. 3.   Radiative forcings (see Montamat and Stock 2019 for original data sources).

radiative forcings over this period are almost entirely anthropogenic (sulfur oxides are also emitted from volcanic eruptions in addition to burning high-sulfur fossil fuels; however, their presence in the atmosphere is transitory). The dashed line is the sum of these radiative forcings.

A very simple model of Earth's temperature is that it is proportional to the sum of the radiative forcings. With the additional assumption that total radiative forcings are an integrated process, this simple model implies that global mean temperature and radiative forcing are cointegrated (Kaufmann, Kauppi, and Stock 2006; Kaufmann et al. 2013); that is, there is a cointegrating relationship of the form $T_t = \alpha + \theta RF_t + u_t$, where RF_t is the sum of the radiative forcings in figure 3 and u_t is integrated of a lower order than RF_t and θ is the cointegrating coefficient.[2]

Figure 4 overlays the global temperature series in figure 1 with the predicted value of temperature, $\hat{\theta}RF_t$. The estimate of θ used in figure 4 (0.489, standard error [SE] = 0.041) is the benchmark estimate from Kaufmann et al. (2006, table 2, col. 2), which was estimated using data from 1860–1994, the full data set available at the time. The in-sample fit of the dynamic ordinary least square estimate (through the vertical line in 1994) captures the overall pre-1994 trend, although there are short-run fluctuations in temperature around this trend that are not captured by this long-run relationship.

Because this model was fit using data through 1994, there is a clean out-of-sample test of this very simple model. The test is nontrivial: temperatures increased since 1994, but irregularly, with a famous decade-long "hiatus" starting in 1998. How did this simple model do?

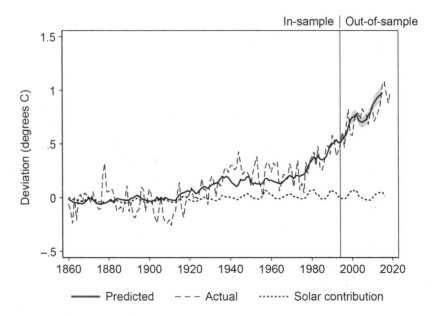

Fig. 4. Temperature and fitted values based on radiative forcings. Estimation 1860–1994. Shading is 67% confidence interval conditional on radiative forcing. Predicted value uses dynamic ordinary least square cointegrating vector from Kaufmann et al. (2006, table II[2]). Temperature (dashed line) is deviated from its 1870–90 mean. The solid line is the predicted value from the benchmark cointegrating regression in Kaufmann et al. (2006) ($\hat{T}_t = \text{const} + 0.489\text{RF}_t$), which they estimated using data from 1860 to 1994. The vertical line demarks the in- and out-of-sample time periods for that estimate. The shading around the predicted value post-1994 is a one SE band for the predicted value using their reported SE of $\hat{\theta}$. The dotted line is the contribution of natural variation in solar radiation to temperature, estimated using the Kaufmann et al. (2006) regression.

It turns out that it did quite well. As discussed in more detail in Kaufmann et al. (2011), the model provides a parsimonious explanation of the hiatus as due in part to a lull in solar activity and to new dirty coal-fired power plants coming online in China, which produced sulfur oxides and a cooling effect.[3]

This simple model provides a standard regression decomposition of the post-1880 warming into a natural component, an anthropogenic component, and a residual. One way to do this is to consider the counterfactual in which all the gasses simply equaled their averages in the late nineteenth century. The dotted line in figure 4 is the predicted natural component arising from variation in solar flux. Initially, nearly all the variation in the predicted value of temperature was from variation in solar radiation. But starting around 1920, greenhouse warming started to kick in. During the 1950s through the 1970s, the warming effect of CO_2 and methane was largely offset by sulfur oxides emitted from coal power plants. As those emissions were cleaned up to mitigate local pollution and acid rain, CO_2 took over as the main driver and warming accelerated.

According to this very simple model, of the 0.81 degree Celsius of warming from the 1870–90 average through the 2006–15 average, 0.84 degree (SE = 0.07) is due to greenhouse gasses, 0.01 degree (SE = 0.004) is due to an increase in solar intensity, and –0.04 degree is an unexplained residual.[4] Thus, according to this decomposition, essentially all of the observed warming is anthropogenic in origin, up to a residual of approximately 5%.

The full decomposition based on this simple regression model is given in table 1. As this decomposition shows, the key driver is CO_2, and its impact on warming would have been greater had it not been for the additional, and unhealthy, increase in SO_x pollutants produced by burning high-sulfur fossil fuels, especially high-sulfur coal.

The virtue of this model is its transparency and its good performance in a 2-decade, true out-of-sample test. But the model is an extreme simplification of highly complex climate processes and is silent about the wide variation in climate change effects stemming from this temperature increase. Those effects are extensively documented in the climate science literature.[5] Many are also amenable to validation using econometrics.[6] To me, the numerical alignment of the estimates from this very simple model with the climate models justifies confidence in the climate science models.

Table 1

Decomposition of the Change in Global Mean Temperature from 1870–90 Average to 2006–15 Average

	Change or Predicted Change (°C)	Standard Error
Greenhouse gasses:		
CO_2	.96	.08
Methane	.24	.02
Trace gasses	.13	.01
SO_x	−.49	.04
Subtotal, gasses:	.84	.07
Solar	.01	.004
Subtotal, predicted:	.85	.07
Actual	.81	
Residual	−.04	

Note: Predicted values and standard errors are based on the cointegrating regression used for the predicted values in figure 3 and described in Section I.

II.   What Is the Progress to Date on Reducing Carbon Emissions?

As I mentioned, a popular narrative is that the downturn in US CO_2 emissions since 2007 demonstrates that we have turned a corner and are on a path toward decarbonization. According to this narrative, we are reducing emissions because of energy efficiency improvements, the expansion of wind and solar for electricity generation, and an increasing cultural awareness of the importance of conserving energy and going green. This narrative is popular among environmentalists, who say that decarbonization will be cheap; conservatives, who say that market forces are resulting in decarbonization already; and green investors, who proclaim a bright future for their low-carbon investments.

I wish that this rosy narrative were true, but it is not. Macroeconomists will not find it surprising that the big drop in emissions occurred in 2009, when energy demand plummeted as the economy tanked. Since then, the fracking revolution has resulted in low natural gas prices, which has led to replacing coal generation with natural gas generation.[7] Because burning coal emits more CO_2 than burning natural gas per kilowatt-hour of electricity generated, switching from coal to natural gas reduces CO_2 emissions.

Because the 2009 recession and the advent of fracking were one-time events, they do not constitute a change in the trend, just a shift in the level of emissions. Indeed, in 2018, US energy-related CO_2 emissions increased by 2.9%. The US EIA projects coal use for electricity to be roughly flat from 2020 to 2050.[8] As shown in figure 2, emissions are projected to plateau at current levels, as energy efficiency improvements and renewables just offset growing energy demand. Indeed, the silver lining of the substitution of natural gas for coal resulting from fracking hides a cloud, which is the substantial investment in natural gas pipelines and generating facilities that could lock in future emissions else risk the political and economic disruption of stranded natural gas assets.

This projection leads to the question: If CO_2 emissions remain at their current rate, what is their short-run effect on temperature? In recent work with Giselle Montamat, we use a natural experiment instrumental variables approach to estimate the short-run temperature effect of emission without adopting any particular model of long-run persistence. We estimate that 10 years of emissions at the current rate would increase temperature over those 10 years by 0.13 degree Celsius (Montamat and Stock 2019). This might not seem to be by much, but it is more than one-eighth the total warming to date and amounts to 1 degree Fahrenheit over

3 decades. Moreover, this is just the impact effect, and the cumulative effect would be even larger as the pulse works through Earth's system.

In short, climate change is anthropogenic and it is happening now on a human timescale. The planet is already experiencing temperature records and increasingly damaging hurricanes and typhoons, wildfires, droughts, and heat waves. Additionally, sea levels have been and will be rising because of thermal expansion of water and melting of glaciers and ice sheets. Under a business-as-usual scenario, the mean sea level is projected to rise by between 55 and 95 centimeters by the end of this century.[9] These consequences of human emissions of greenhouse gasses are not a "new normal." Rather, they will become more severe as temperatures rise.

The future consequences of climate change remain uncertain. For example, the amount by which sea levels rise depends in part on the extent to which glaciers and ice sheets melt. In climate science, events such as the melting of the West Antarctic Ice Sheet or, much worse, the melting of the Greenland Ice Sheet, are referred to as abrupt irreversible events. Those events are not expected to happen in this century, although they could be triggered irreversibly in the first half of this century. They could add multiple meters to sea level rise. Similarly, there is considerable uncertainty about the pace of extinctions that are being and will be induced by climate change. The severity of these and other aspects of climate change depends on whether cumulative emissions get high enough to trigger such transformations.[10] That, in turn, depends on climate policy decisions made by our generation, arguably within the next decade or two.

III. US Climate Policies: Historical Evidence on Efficiency and Effectiveness

This brings us to a discussion of climate policies, where I focus on the United States. First, however, I digress briefly on the externalities these policies aim to address and on current estimates of the value of one of these, the carbon externality.

A. Digression on Externalities

There are two main market failures that climate policy aims to address: the carbon price externality and the R&D externality. In some instances, network externalities are also important, such as the chicken-and-egg problem of electric vehicles and charging stations.

The climate externality that has received the most attention by economists is the carbon price externality. The starting point estimate for assigning a value to this externality is the social cost of carbon (SCC), which is the monetized net present value of the damages from emitting a marginal ton of CO_2. The final estimate of the SCC released under the Obama administration is approximately $50 per ton for emissions in 2020 (US Government Interagency Working Group on the Social Cost of Greenhouse Gasses 2016). (To get a sense of orders of magnitudes, a short ton of subbituminous coal from a federal mining lease in the Powder River Basin currently sells for approximately $12; when burned, it emits 1.7 metric tons of CO_2, which has approximately $84 of climate damages evaluated at an SCC of $50. The climate damages from burning a gallon of gasoline are approximately $0.45, also evaluated at an SCC of $50.) There is widespread recognition that the scientific basis for this $50 estimate of the SCC needs to be solidified. To this end, Resources for the Future is coordinating a major research project involving energy-climate labs at Chicago and Berkeley, along with academics from other universities, which (among other things) is implementing suggestions made by the National Academy of Sciences (2017) for improving the estimate of the SCC. Because this work is still in progress, for this paper I use the provisional $50 per ton estimate for the SCC.

I now return to the discussion of US climate policies.[11] These policies fall into four categories: regulation, narrowly targeted policies, carbon pricing, and technology-pushing policies.

B.   *Sectoral Regulation Based on the Clean Air Act*

The Clean Air Act is the legal authority used for the two most ambitious regulatory attempts to date to reduce greenhouse gas emissions, the CPP that applied to the power sector and the Corporate Average Fuel Economy (CAFE) standards that applied to automobile emissions (and thus mileage). With careful attention to detail, regulations under the Clean Air Act can be efficient and effective. For example, the CPP developed by the Obama administration used Clean Air Act authority to construct a mass-based cap-and-trade system for the power sector that is broadly considered to be workable and cost-effective. Estimates are that the CPP would have achieved substantial emissions reductions with an average cost around $11 per ton CO_2, which is well below the SCC benchmark.[12] Initial estimates suggest that the CPP would have led to significant emissions reductions and would have been a meaningful step toward decarbonizing the power sector. The CPP was, however, stayed by the Supreme

Court and subsequently was replaced by the Trump administration with an alternative, the Affordable Clean Energy plan. Under that plan, there are strict limits on the measures that states can require, and states have the ability to waive or reduce the emissions reduction measures specified in the federal plan. As a result, the Affordable Clean Energy plan is projected to have negligible effects on emissions.[13]

Regulatory approaches, whether under the Clean Air Act or more generally, have multiple drawbacks. Although some regulations can be efficient (the CPP being a prime example), many are not, in the sense that they result in emissions reductions that are costly per ton compared with the SCC. For example, there are many papers in environmental economics highlighting inefficiencies in the CAFE standards on automobile emissions.[14] Estimates of emission reduction costs from that program range from $50 to more than $300 per ton. In addition, under existing legislative authority, regulatory approaches are limited in scope and are at best a partial solution to the climate problem. Moreover, regulations can be changed, and indeed the climate policy of the Trump administration largely consists of reversing Obama-era climate regulations. Finally, recent changes at the Supreme Court increase the odds that expansive interpretations of Clean Air Act authority to regulate greenhouse gasses will not be upheld. It is important to study the history of these regulatory approaches to inform policy design, and there are circumstances in which narrowly proscribed regulation might be the most efficient way to regulate emissions (e.g., command-and-control regulation of methane emissions in oil and gas drilling). That said, because of its limitations, I expect that regulation under the Clean Air Act is unlikely to play a major role in reducing emissions going forward.

C. Narrowly Targeted Policies

The second category of climate policies is what I will call narrowly targeted. Examples include home weatherization programs, mandates to use biodiesel and corn ethanol in our fuel supply, and state-level renewable portfolio standards (RPSs). The costs of these policies vary widely. In a few cases, such as blending corn ethanol to comprise 10% of retail gasoline (the dominant blend in the United States), costs per ton are low or even negative. In many cases, however, the costs are high. For example, replacing petroleum diesel with biodiesel has a cost per ton of between $150 and $420, depending on the feedstock and how the incidence of the biodiesel tax credit is treated. Moreover, many of these policies interact in ways that increase costs but do not materially reduce emissions.

For example, some states both have a RPS and participate in a regional cap-and-trade program for the power sector, such as the Regional Greenhouse Gas Initiative in the Northeast. Because electricity is provided on a multistate grid and cap-and-trade allowances are tradable across states, mandating clean energy in one state increases the number of allowances, reducing their cost and allowing more carbon emissions in other states in the regional program, a phenomenon that environmental economists refer to as "leakage."

Within this catch-all group, one set of policies—namely, RPSs—does have the possibility of being impactful and cost-effective. Concerning impact, 29 states have renewable energy standards and some states, including California and New York, have announced midcentury goals of generating electricity that emits no greenhouse gasses. In theory, RPSs could become much more effective and efficient if all or nearly all states were to adopt them and if interstate trading of RPS allowances were introduced. With the important caveat that RPSs do not cover nuclear or other nonrenewable zero-carbon sources, a nationally tradable RPS system would approximate a national clean energy standard. This system would be less efficient than having a uniform price on carbon for the power sector, but it could come close (Goulder and Hafstead 2016, 2018), at least for the initial tranche of reductions. A noteworthy political economy feature of a nationally tradable RPS allowance market is that it would facilitate decarbonization in participating states with low RPS targets, more than achieving their targets with the cost underwritten by states with ambitious targets.

With the exception of RPSs, this family of narrowly targeted policies tends to be small bore and in this sense is at best complementary in a broader package of solutions.

D.   Pricing Carbon

The third set of policies are carbon pricing policies. Although efforts to adopt a cap-and-trade program in the United States with the Waxman-Markey bill of 2009 failed, other countries and some states have adopted cap-and-trade systems or a carbon tax or fee on at least some sectors.

The cost of a carbon tax depends on how the revenue is recycled. Here, I focus on the case in which it is returned by lump-sum rebates, as proposed by the Climate Leadership Council. In a recent book, Goulder and Hafstead (2018) use a multisector computable general equilibrium model to estimate the effect of carbon taxes with this and other revenue recycling schemes, along with other economy-wide climate policies. For a $20 per ton tax that increases by 4% per year and lump-sum recycling, they estimate that the level of gross domestic product (GDP) would be reduced by 1% over 30 years, amounting to an average reduction of GDP growth of just three basis points per year.

It is also possible to look at actual macro outcomes for countries that have adopted a carbon tax. Preliminary empirical results for European countries, some of which have adopted carbon taxes, suggest small and statistically insignificant macroeconomic effects of a carbon price on growth (Metcalf and Stock, forthcoming; Metcalf 2019). These preliminary findings are consistent with the small GDP effect predicted by Goulder and Hafstead (2018).

Goulder and Hafstead (2018) estimate that US emissions would be reduced by about one-third by 2050 if a $20 per ton tax were implemented. This finding aligns with estimates by the US EIA (2014, side case GHG25) and others (e.g., Larsen et al. 2018). These estimates underscore a key point: a carbon tax alone, at least at levels that are potentially politically viable, is insufficient to decarbonize the economy. An economist might retort that this statement is a non sequitur: if the carbon tax is set at the Pigouvian amount to equal the externality, then marginal cost equals marginal benefit and that is the optimal path and we should not adopt decarbonization as a goal or standard. But that reaction assumes that we can estimate the marginal benefit with some precision, it ignores the fact that other externalities are involved, and it fails to grapple with the deep uncertainty and potentially very negative outcomes arising from climate change.[15]

It is important to understand that the emissions reduction from a carbon tax is nonlinear in the tax rate. A relatively small tax, say $20 to $30, essentially decarbonizes the power sector. But a tax of $20 per ton corresponds to $0.18 per gallon of gasoline. The demand reduction effects of this increase in driving costs are negligible: using the gasoline demand elasticity of −0.37 from Coglianese et al. (2017) and $3.50 per gallon gasoline, a $20 per ton carbon tax would decrease gasoline demand by only 2%. As inexpensive electric vehicles become increasingly available, the gasoline price elasticity could increase as buyers switch from gasoline to electric vehicles. Still, it is hard to imagine that many consumers will decide to purchase an electric vehicle simply because gasoline prices go up by $0.20, or even by $0.50. Thus, increasing the tax has a declining marginal effect on emissions reduction. A similar argument applies to other large sectors that are technologically difficult to decarbonize, such as aviation and building heating. Said differently, marginal abatement costs are sharply increasing so with current technology initial emissions reductions are relatively inexpensive, but deeper emissions reductions are not.

Clearly, a carbon tax gets the vote of economists: a petition spearheaded by Janet Yellen supporting a carbon tax with per-capita lump-sum rebates was signed by more than 3,500 economists (including all living former chairs of the Federal Reserve, 27 Nobel Laureates, and 15 former chairs of the Council of Economic Advisers). But support for a carbon tax outside this core voting group is less clear. In 2014, Australia terminated its experiment with a carbon tax, which had been passed just 2 years earlier. Indeed, one of the virtues of a carbon tax is that its price certainty stimulates investment—price certainty, that is, unless the tax is repealed. In the United States, climate has become a partisan issue and it is hard to see how a carbon tax will be passed anytime soon. And these political considerations aside, it is important to remember that a carbon tax by its nature plucks only the currently low-hanging fruit and addresses but one of the externalities that vex climate policy.

E.   Technology-Pushing Policies

This brings me to the fourth set of policies, technology-pushing policies. Energy R&D subsidies directed by the federal government have a decidedly mixed record (think fusion energy). But if one interprets technology-pushing policies more broadly, there are policies that arguably have been quite effective as well as some that have not. Here, I provide three examples of the former and one of the latter. My evidence is hardly rigorous by the profession's standards for identification of causal effects, but (as I return to it later) it is sufficiently suggestive to be informative and to suggest directions for future policy research.

The basic story line of this family of policies is induced technological progress. This goes under a number of other names, such as learning by doing or moving down the cost curve. Even if there were a carbon price, there would be technical innovations that would not happen, or would be inefficiently slow to happen, because the benefits of that innovation are not fully appropriable. This situation is exacerbated by the absence of a carbon price.

The first example is the suite of policies that have mandated or subsidized purchases of photovoltaics. From 2010 to 2015, the price of solar panels fell by two-thirds.[16] This decline coincided with a 250% expansion in purchases. Of course, the fact that sales increased when the price went down does not prove anything and points to the key identification problem when studying learning by doing. There is strong anecdotal evidence, however, that these purchases were in part exogenous, driven by political dynamics. Three key mass-purchase programs were the German feed-in tariffs of the mid-2000s, the California Solar Initiative starting in 2006, and the US federal residential solar tax credit starting in 2008. A small number of well-identified studies support this narrative, notably Gerarden (2018), but more work is needed.

The second example is battery electric vehicles. The biggest driver of electric vehicle costs is battery costs. As figure 5 shows, one can think of a price-mileage frontier that has shifted to the right and flattened over the 9 model years from 2011 to 2019. The regression line estimates a linear frontier, in which the slope represents the marginal cost of additional range (additional battery capacity) and the intercept represents all the other features of electric vehicles, most of which are common to gasoline vehicles. (This line is illustrative only because it does not control for other vehicle attributes, which could be correlated with range especially for luxury vehicles.) With the introduction of the Chevrolet Bolt in 2017, prices of battery electric vehicles with ranges that are useful for most urban driving are now approaching mass-market pricing, especially when

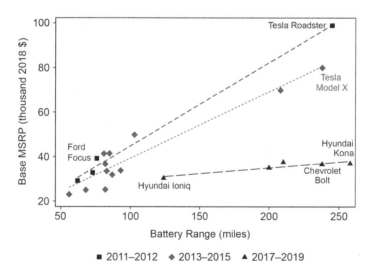

Fig. 5. Improvements in price-range trade-off in battery electric vehicles. The vertical axis is the base manufacturer's suggested retail price (MSRP) in thousands of 2018 dollars, and the horizontal axis is the driving range on a single battery charge. This figure updates figure 3 in Gillingham and Stock (2018; which uses data provided by Jing Li) to include vehicles introduced in model year 2019.

one considers that the marginal cost of driving is substantially less for an electric vehicle than a gasoline vehicle. Although these prices are manufacturer's suggested retail prices, which are before the federal income tax subsidy and any state incentives, these prices do not necessarily reflect marginal cost of production because there are hidden subsidies in this market through the CAFE standards and California low-carbon fuel standard credits. Moreover, there is anecdotal evidence that pricing is below marginal cost as automakers compete for shares in this emerging market. In any event, this shift of the frontier to the right and its flattening are consistent with demand pull policies reducing costs of producing electric vehicles, regardless of range, and of reducing battery prices through learning by doing and economies of scale.

The third example is offshore wind, where too prices have come down by more than 60% in 10 years (US Department of Energy 2018, 50). These systems remain noncompetitive with fossil fuels so essentially none of this production would have occurred without policy-induced demand. Here too, anecdotal evidence suggests that the price reductions stem in large part from learning by doing in construction, design, and installation of offshore wind turbines.

The fourth example is low greenhouse gas, second-generation biofuels stimulated through the Renewable Fuel Standard. Unlike the other three examples, this program has failed to induce meaningful cost declines or production increases. As argued in Stock (2015, 2018), in my view the key reason for this failure is not the technology but rather fundamental design flaws in the Renewable Fuel Standard program that led to a high degree of uncertainty in the value of the subsidy and even in whether the program would be in existence for the productive lifetime of a second-generation plant. The result was an initial flurry of investment as the program started, which turned into plant closings and canceled plans as investors avoided investment in the face of unexpectedly high uncertainty. The story of investment collapsing in the face of uncertainty is familiar to macroeconomists (Bernanke 1983; McDonald and Siegel 1986), and the failure of the Renewable Fuel Standard to promote second-generation biofuels provides a cautionary example in the energy area.

IV. Looking Ahead

For decarbonization to happen in the time frame that avoids large climate changes, its cost must be contained. The technologies of today—namely, wind and solar generation and, perhaps in the near future, electric vehicles—are cheap enough that they provide a meaningful first step. But deep decarbonization hinges on the development of low-cost clean technologies, including negative-emission technologies.[17] Although a carbon tax is likely to be effective and efficient, were it to be adopted, it seems that its core support base is the membership of the American Economic Association; moreover, it is but a partial solution. Technology-pushing programs comprise climate policies that we have seen both to be politically acceptable and to be effective, at least based on the limited research to date. Normally we worry that such programs can be captured, and certainly the biodiesel mandate is one such example. But there is ample evidence of capture of energy policy by fossil fuel interests, so maybe some capture by, for example, the solar installation industry or the offshore wind industry provides some balance; at least, this seems like a defensible and researchable proposition.

These observations suggest that the path forward, at least among efficient and effective policies, is likely to involve technology-pushing policies and, perhaps, infrastructure investment to address specific network externalities. A carbon price, however meritorious, can wait. To some economists, this view might sound like apostasy, but in fact it has some support in the theoretical literature.[18] For example, Acemoglu et al. (2016) show that in an endogenous growth model, research subsidies early on can substantially reduce the size of a carbon tax needed for a given carbon reduction. Their result has been generalized by Lemoine (2018), who underscores that innovation is critical to climate change policy.

The view that the key to avoiding the worst outcomes of climate change is developing efficient technology-pushing policies leads to many researchable problems. To name but a few: What is the evidence on induced technical change in the energy industry? What is the optimal design of technology-pushing policies? How does this relate to dynamics and uncertainty? What is the right trade-off between credibility and flexibility in policy making that spans decades? There is a base of high-quality recent work to start from, including Acemoglu et al. (2016), Aghion et al. (2016, 2018, 2019), and Akcigit, Hanley, and Stantcheva (2017). That said, the remaining researchable questions abound. Macroeconomists have much to contribute to this research. The research questions are interesting, policy is evolving rapidly, and the stakes are high.

Endnotes

Author email address: Stock (James_Stock@harvard.edu). This essay was originally presented as a dinner speech at the NBER Macroeconomics Annual conference, April 11, 2019. I thank Ken Gillingham and Derek Lemoine for helpful comments. For acknowledgments, sources of research support, and disclosure of the author's material financial relationships, if any, please see https://www.nber.org/chapters/c14264.ack.

1. Not coincidentally, the organization of this talk tracks my own interest and involvement in the topic, which started in the 1990s with some latent skepticism regarding large climate science models. From 2012 to 2014, I had the energy-economics portfolio at the Council of Economic Advisers, a period in which the Clean Power Plan and other federal climate initiatives were being developed and proposed. Since returning to academics, I have continued to conduct research in climate economics and policy.

2. This relationship can be derived from a single-equation energy balance model. In discrete time, the energy balance model is $\Delta T_t = -\lambda T_{t-1} + bRF_t$, where T_t is temperature, RF_t is radiative forcing, t is measured in years, and b adjusts for units. This solves for $T_t = b(1 - (1 - \lambda)L)^{-1}RF_t = (b/\lambda)RF_t + c^*(L)\Delta RF_t$, where $c^*(L)$ is the summable residual lag polynomial from the Beveridge-Nelson decomposition. If RF_t is well approximated as integrated of order 1, then this mass balance equation implies that T_t and RF_t are cointegrated of order (1,1) with cointegrating coefficient b/λ. If RF_t is persistent but not necessarily integrated of order 1, then T_t will inherit the persistence properties of RF_t and will share a common long-run trend with RF_t. Here, we follow Kaufmann et al. (2006) and adopt the cointegrated of order 1 model. For more on the energy balance model derivation sketched here, see Kaufmann et al. (2013) and Pretis (2020).

3. The story of the hiatus is interesting and more nuanced than the curtailed account here. Other proposed explanations (not mutually exclusive) include possible temperature mismeasurement (Karl et al. 2015; but see Hausfather et al. 2017), reductions in radiative forcing due to volcanic activity (Gregory et al. 2016), and natural fluctuations in ocean circulation cycles that increased heat uptake in the deep oceans (Balmaseda, Trenberth, and Källén 2013; Liu, Xie, and Lu 2016).

4. As of this writing, 2015 is the final year for which all radiative forcings are available.

5. See, for example, IPCC (2014) and US Global Change Research Program (2018).

6. See, for example, the research associated with the Oxford Climate Econometrics program at http://www.climateeconometrics.org/.

7. From 2008 to 2016, total US coal production (including metallurgical coal) fell by 433 million tons. Coglianese, Gerarden, and Stock (2018) estimate that 92% of this decline was because of the large drop in the price of natural gas, with an additional 6% due to environmental regulations that came into effect during that period. Fell and Kaffine (2018) focus on daily shifts in generation and find that wind prices also play a role in the decline.

8. US EIA, *2019 Annual Energy Outlook*, reference case projection table 15.

9. IPCC (2014), AR5 chapter 13, figure 13.11. The local incidence of sea level rise is affected by ocean currents and other factors. It turns out that Boston is on the high end of these effects, so that local sea level rise is projected to be 20% to 70% greater than the global mean rise. To visualize what 1.5 meters of sea level rise means for Cambridge (where the NBER Macro Annual conference is held), launch the National Oceanographic and Atmospheric Administration's Sea Level Rise Viewer at https://coast.noaa.gov/slr/.

10. For an in-depth introduction to the science of abrupt irreversible events, see National Academy of Sciences (2013).

11. This discussion focuses on public policies. There has been increasing interest in voluntary personal actions that can result in a greener lifestyle and reduce the carbon footprint of an individual or an organization. Such actions range from investing in green bonds, to purchasing carbon offsets for air travel, to purchasing a hybrid or electric vehicle, to eating less beef. Some of these voluntary actions can have meaningful impacts; for example, in 2018 Xcel Energy, a large, coal-heavy electric utility based in Minnesota, announced a target of 100% carbon-free electricity by 2050 and is retiring coal plants early as it works toward that goal. But as long as it is it is cheaper or more convenient to emit carbon than not, voluntary programs can go only so far.

12. Unless explicit references are provided, costs per ton for climate policies are taken from and documented in Gillingham and Stock (2018).

13. The US EPA estimates that the Affordable Clean Energy plan will reduce power sector CO_2 emissions by 0.5% in 2035, relative to the no-regulation alternative (US EPA 2019).

14. See, for example, Jacobsen (2013), Sarica and Tyner (2013), and Ito and Salee (2018).

15. In a seminal contribution, Weitzman (2009) lays out a model in which the possibility of so-called climate catastrophes provides reasons for action to decarbonize now, even if the probabilities of those events are unknown. Also see Pindyck (2012).

16. See Gillingham and Stock (2018) for sources, discussion, and references.

17. A negative-emissions technology removes CO_2 from the atmosphere, on net. Examples include some biofuels (through sequestration in the root system), air capture and sequestration of CO_2, and electricity generated by burning biomass with carbon capture and sequestration. Broadly speaking, sequestering carbon is more expensive than not doing so; thus, regardless of technology developments, the deployment of negative-emissions technologies requires a price on carbon.

18. Although a carbon tax has the votes of economists generally, views on it are somewhat mixed among environmental economists. At one extreme, a senior environmental economist recently said to me in complete seriousness, "If we can't have the first best [a carbon tax] then we should all just burn in Hell." At the other extreme, Wagner and Weitzman (2015, 26–27) write, "So instead of shouting 'Carbon tax' or 'Carbon cap,' economists ought to work constructively with what we have—second, third, and fourth-best solutions and worse—that create all sorts of inefficiencies, unintended consequences, and other problems, but that roll with the punches of a highly imperfect policy world and may even remove some existing imperfect policy barriers at the same time." I fall much closer to the latter than the former end of this spectrum.

References

Acemoglu, Daron, Ufuk Akcigit, Douglas Hanley, and William Kerr. 2016. "Transition to Clean Technology." *Journal of Political Economy* 124 (1): 52–104.

Aghion, Philippe, Antonin Bergeaud, Timothee Gigout, Mathieu Lequien, and Marc Melitz. 2019. "Spreading Knowledge across the World: Innovation Spillover through Trade Expansion." Manuscript, Harvard University.

Aghion, Philippe, Antonin Bergeaud, Mathieu Lequien, and Marc Melitz. 2018. "The Impact of Exports on Innovation: Theory and Evidence." Manuscript, Harvard University.

Aghion, Philippe, Antoine Dechezleprêtre, David Hémous, Ralf Martin, and John Van Reenen. 2016. "Carbon Taxes, Path Dependency, and Directed Technical Change: Evidence from the Auto Industry." *Journal of Political Economy* 124 (1): 1–51.

Akcigit, Ufuk, Douglas Hanley, and Stefanie Stantcheva. 2017. "Optimal Taxation and R&D Policies." Working Paper no. 22908, NBER, Cambridge, MA.

Balmaseda, Magdalena A., Kevin E. Trenberth, and Erland Källén. 2013. "Distinctive Climate Signals in Reanalysis of Global Ocean Heat Content." *Geophysical Research Letters* 40:1–6.

Bernanke, Ben S. 1983. "Irreversibility, Uncertainty, and Cyclical Investment." *Quarterly Journal of Economics* 98 (1): 85–106.

Coglianese, John, Lucas Davis, Lutz Kilian, and James H. Stock. 2017. "Anticipation, Tax Avoidance, and the Elasticity of Gasoline Demand." *Journal of Applied Econometrics* 32 (1): 1–15.

Coglianese, John, Todd Gerarden, and James H. Stock. 2018. "The Effects of Fuel Prices, Environmental Regulations, and Other Factors on U.S. Coal Production, 2008–2016." Manuscript, Harvard University.

Cook, John, Dana Nuccitelli, Sarah A. Green, Mark Richardson, Bärbel Winkler, Rob Painting, Robert Way, Peter Jacobs, and Andrew Skuce. 2013. "Quantifying the Consensus on Anthropogenic Global Warming in the Scientific Literature." *Environmental Research Letters* 8 (2): 24024–7.

Fell, Harrison, and Daniel T. Kaffine. 2018. "The Fall of Coal: Joint Impacts of Fuel Prices and Renewables on Generation and Emissions." *American Economic Journal: Economic Policy* 10 (2): 90–116.

Gerarden, Todd. 2018. "Demanding Innovation: The Impact of Consumer Subsidies on Solar Panel Production Costs." Manuscript, Dyson School of Applied Economics and Management, Cornell University.

Gillingham, Kenneth, and James H. Stock. 2018. "The Cost of Reducing Greenhouse Gas Emissions." *Journal of Economic Perspectives* 32 (Fall): 53–72.

Goulder, Lawrence H., and Marc A. C. Hafstead. 2016. "General Equilibrium
Impacts of a Federal Clean Energy Standard." *American Economic Journal: Economic Policy* 8 (2): 186–218.

———. 2018. *Confronting the Climate Challenge: U.S. Climate Policy Options.* New
York: Columbia University Press.

Gregory, J. M., T. Andrews, P. Good, T. Mauiritsen, and P. M. Firster. 2016.
"Small Global-Mean Cooling Due to Volcanic Radiative Forcing." *Climate Dynamics* 47:3979–91.

Hausfather, Zeke, Kevin Cowtan, David C. Clarke, Peter Jacobs, Mark Richardson, and Robert Rohde. 2017. "Assessing Recent Warming Using Instru-
mentally Homogeneous Sea Surface Temperature Records." *Science Advances*
3:e1601207.

IPCC (International Panel on Climate Change). 2014. "AR5 Synthesis Report:
Climate Change 2014." https://www.ipcc.ch/report/ar5/syr.

Ito, Koichiro, and James M. Sallee. 2018. "The Economics of Attribute-Based
Regulation: Theory and Evidence from Fuel Economy Standards." *Review of Economics and Statistics* 100 (2): 319–36.

Jacobsen, Mark R. 2013. "Evaluating US Fuel Economy Standards in a Model
with Producer and Household Heterogeneity." *American Economic Journal:
Economic Policy* 5 (2): 148.

Karl, Thomas R., Anthony Arguez, Boyin Huang, Jay H. Lawrimore, James R.
McMahon, Matthew J. Menne, Thomas C. Peterson, Russell S. Vose, and
Huai-Min Zhang. 2015. "Possible Artifacts of Data Biases in the Recent Global
Surface Warming Hiatus." *Science* 348 (6242): 1469–72.

Kaufmann, Robert, Heikki Kauppi, Michael L. Mann, and James H. Stock. 2011.
"Reconciling Anthropogenic Climate Change with Observed Temperature
1998–2008." *Proceedings of the National Academy of Sciences* 108 (29): 11790–93.

———. 2013. "Does Temperature Contain a Stochastic Trend: Linking Statistical
Results to Physical Mechanisms." *Climatic Change* 118 (3–4): 729–43.

Kaufmann, Robert, Heikki Kauppi, and James H. Stock. 2006. "Emissions, Con-
centrations and Temperature: A Time Series Analysis." *Climatic Change* 77 (3–4):
249–78.

Larsen, John, Shashank Mohjan, Peter Marsters, and Whitney Herndon. 2018.
"Energy and Environmental Implications of a Carbon Tax in the United States."
Columbia University Center for Global Energy Policy. https://energypolicy
.columbia.edu/research/report/energy-economic-and-emissions-impacts
-federal-us-carbon-tax.

Lemoine, Derek. 2018. "Innovation-led Transitions in Energy Supply." Working
Paper no. 23420, NBER, Cambridge, MA.

Liu, Wei, Shang-Ping Xie, and Jian Lu. 2016. "Tracking Ocean Heat Uptake during the Surface Warming Hiatus." *Nature Communications* 7:10926.

McDonald, Robert, and Daniel Siegel. 1986. "The Value of Waiting to Invest."
Quarterly Journal of Economics 101 (4): 707–27.

Metcalf, Gilbert E. 2019. "On the Economics of a Carbon Tax for the United
States." *Brookings Papers on Economic Activity* 2019 (Spring): 405–58.

Metcalf, Gilbert E., and James H. Stock. Forthcoming. "Measuring the Macroeconomic Impact of Carbon Taxes." *American Economic Review.*

Montamat, Giselle, and James H. Stock. 2019. "Quasi-Experimental Estimates of the Transient Climate Response Using Observational Data." Manuscript, Harvard University.

National Academy of Sciences. 2013. "Abrupt Impacts of Climate Change: Anticipating Surprises." https://www.nap.edu/catalog/18373/abrupt-impacts-of-climate-change-anticipating-surprises.

———. 2017. "Valuing Climate Damages: Updating Estimation of the Social Cost of Carbon Dioxide." https://www.nap.edu/catalog/24651/valuing-climate-damages-updating-estimation-of-the-social-cost-of.

Pindyck, Robert S. 2012. "Uncertain Outcomes and Climate Change Policy." *Journal of Environmental Economics and Management* 63 (3): 289–303.

Pretis, Felix. 2020. "Econometric Modelling of Climate Systems: The Equivalence of Energy Balance Models and Cointegrated Vector Autoregressions." *Journal of Econometrics* 214 (1): 256–73.

Sarica, Kemal, and Wallace E. Tyner. 2013. "Alternative Policy Impacts on US GHG Emissions and Energy Security: A Hybrid Modeling Approach." *Energy Economics* 40 (suppl C): 40–50.

Stock, James H. 2015. "The Renewable Fuel Standard: A Path Forward." Report, Columbia Center on Global Energy Policy. https://energypolicy.columbia.edu/research/report/renewable-fuel-standard-path-forward.

———. 2018. "Reforming the Renewable Fuel Standard." Report, Columbia-SIPA Center on Global Energy Policy (February). https://energypolicy.columbia.edu/research/report/reforming-renewable-fuel-standard.

US Department of Energy. 2018. "2017 Offshore Wind Technologies Market Update." https://www.energy.gov/eere/wind/downloads/2017-offshore-wind-technologies-market-update.

US EIA (Energy Information Administration). 2014. "Annual Energy Outlook 2014." https://www.eia.gov/outlooks/archive/aeo14/.

US EPA (Environmental Protection Agency). 2019. "Regulatory Impact Analysis for the Repeal of the Clean Power Plan, and the Emission Guidelines for Greenhouse Gas Emissions from Existing Electric Utility Generating Units." https://www.epa.gov/stationary-sources-air-pollution/regulatory-impact-analysis-repeal-clean-power-plan-and-emission.

US Global Change Research Program. 2018. "Fourth National Climate Assessment." https://www.globalchange.gov.

US Government Interagency Working Group on the Social Cost of Greenhouse Gasses. 2016. "Technical Support Document: Technical Update of the Social Cost of Carbon for Regulatory Impact Analysis Under Executive Order 12866." August. https://www.epa.gov/sites/production/files/2016-12/documents/sc_co2_tsd_august_2016.pdf.

Wagner, Gernot, and Martin L. Weitzman. 2015. *Climate Shock*. Princeton, NJ: Princeton University Press.

Weitzman, Martin L. 2009. "On Modeling and Interpreting the Economics of Catastrophic Climate Change." *Review of Economics and Statistics* 91 (1): 1–19.